THE LOST PEACE

Also by Robert Dallek

Harry S. Truman

Nixon and Kissinger: Partners in Power

An Unfinished Life: John F. Kennedy, 1917–1963

Flawed Giant: Lyndon B. Johnson and His Times, 1961–1973

Hail to the Chief: The Making and Unmaking of American Presidents

Lone Star Rising: Lyndon Johnson and His Times, 1908–1960

Ronald Reagan: The Politics of Symbolism

The American Style of Foreign Policy: Cultural Politics and Foreign Affairs

Franklin D. Roosevelt and American Foreign Policy, 1932–1945

Democrat and Diplomat: The Life of William E. Dodd

ROBERT DALLEK

THE LOST PEACE

LEADERSHIP IN A TIME OF HORROR AND HOPE, 1945–1953

HARPER

An Imprint of HarperCollins*Publishers*
www.harpercollins.com

HarperCollins books may be purchased for educational, business, or sales promotional use. For information, please write: Special Markets Department, HarperCollins Publishers, 10 East 53rd Street, New York, NY 10022.

Grateful acknowledgment for permission to reproduce illustrations is made to the following: *Courtesy of Harry S. Truman Library*: insert page 4, top; page 5, top; page 6, top; page 6, bottom; page 7, bottom; page 8, bottom; page 9, top; page 10, top; page 10, bottom; page 11, bottom; page 15, top; page 15, bottom. *Courtesy of the National Archives*: insert page 1, top; page 1, bottom; page 8, top; page 11, top; page 14, bottom. *Department of State, Courtesy of Harry S. Truman Library*: insert page 13, bottom. *Economic Cooperation Administration, Courtesy of Harry S. Truman Library*: insert page 13, top. *National Park Service, Abbe Rowe, Courtesy of Harry S. Truman Library*: insert page 7, top; page 12, top; page 14, top. *Office of the U.S. Chief of Counsel, Courtesy of the Harry S. Truman Library*: insert page 2, top; page 3, top. *Terry Savage, Courtesy of Harry S. Truman Library*: insert page 9, bottom. *U.S. Army, Courtesy of Dwight D. Eisenhower Presidential Library and Museum*: insert page 16, bottom. *U.S. Army Signal Corps, Courtesy of Harry S. Truman Library*: insert page 2, bottom; page 3, bottom; page 4, bottom; page 12, bottom. *U.S. Army Air Corps, Courtesy of Harry S. Truman Library*: insert page 5, bottom. *U.S. Navy, Courtesy of Harry S. Truman Library*: insert page 16, top.

FIRST EDITION

Designed by Eric Butler

Library of Congress Cataloging-in-Publication Data

Dallek, Robert.
    The lost peace: leadership in a time of horror and hope, 1945–1953 /
Robert Dallek.—1st ed.
        p. cm.
    Includes bibliographical references and index.
    ISBN 978-0-06-162866-5
    1. World politics—1945–1955. 2. World War, 1939–1945—
Peace. 3. Cold War. I. Title.
    D843.D21 2010
    909.82'4—dc22   2010005727

10   11   12   13   14   OV/RRD   10   9   8   7   6   5   4   3   2   1

To John W. Wright
For his wise counsel and friendship

An assembly of great men is the greatest fool upon earth.

—Benjamin Franklin

There are in every age, new errors to be rectified
and new prejudices to be opposed.

—Samuel Johnson

CONTENTS

PREFACE

This is a book about the generation of leaders in the years of upheaval between the close of World War II and the early Cold War. It is not a comprehensive history about why and how the Cold War began. Rather, it is an attempt to underscore the misjudgments and unwise actions that caused so much continuing strife and suffering, and suggest alternatives that might have made for greater international harmony.

While I highlight the failings of the notable men who dominated the scene during this time, I am not intent on denying them their due, or in the case of the greatest villains of the day, revising their reputations for wrongdoing. My greatest interest is in revisiting the decision making and events of the period as a cautionary tale—a reprise of what went wrong as a call for future improvement in world affairs, or an educator's lesson of what might have been done to avoid the difficulties that beset strong and weak nations around the globe.

Such an exercise in finger-pointing and advice-giving is bound to provoke debate. The what-ifs of history are always risky propositions, more the product of speculation than persuasive evidence. I would be the first to grant that my suggested remedies for the missteps of the period reflect the historian's advantage over leaders who could not know how things would turn out. During his presidency, John F. Kennedy told the historian David Herbert Donald, "No one has a right to grade a President—not even poor James Buchanan—who has not sat in his chair, examined the mail and information that came across his desk, and learned why he made decisions." Yet it is the historian's job not only to examine the record as fully as possible but also to render judgments on how past officeholders performed. Otherwise, we are no more than chroniclers telling a story without meaning.

I hope my retrospective suggestions on how world leaders might have done better for the millions of people they governed are seen as a constructive exercise that encourages reflection on their limitations. The fact that men and women gain governing power—whether by democratic elections or extraconstitutional means—is no guarantee of wise leadership.

The success of this book depends less on whether I stimulate a chorus of approving nods on the alternatives I see to some of their actions than on renewed discussion of how the most powerful men of the 1940s and early '50s performed, and—more importantly—what their mistakes tell us about crafting more considered actions in the future. That most of the book's focus is on leaders' shortcomings is not meant as a lament about the limits of governments to act more wisely. The post-1945 era had its share of sensible actions between nations. I hope my discussion of wrong turns, then, is seen not as a cry of despair but as a reminder that we can do better in resolving conflicts and promoting international cooperation.

R.D.
Washington, D.C.
September 2009

INTRODUCTION

I have no high opinion of human beings: they are always
going to fight and do nasty things to each other.
—George F. Kennan, 1976

At the start of 1945, total war had absorbed the world's energies for almost ten of the century's first forty-four years. Winston Churchill thought of the period between 1914 and 1945 as "another Thirty Years' War." And in 1948 he lamented "the fact that after all the exertions and sacrifices of hundreds of millions of people and of the victories of the Righteous Cause, we have still not found Peace or Security." It was, in his words, "the human tragedy."

So much of what happened throughout the twentieth century, Churchill believed, was preventable. World War II, he told Franklin Roosevelt, should have been called "The Unnecessary War," as many said of the century's first great war. And could also be said of much of the post-1945 international strife.

It may well be that a human affinity for struggle and conflict make war—whether among tribes, religions, or nations—inevitable. But heads of state have always had the power to influence events, especially at the end of World War II, when the defeat of Nazism, Fascism, and Japanese militarism presented an uncommon opportunity for more rational, humane governance.

The rise of new international conflicts or the failure to secure a stable, more durable peace can be blamed on a blundering generation of leaders around the world. If this had been a period when American, European, and Asian rulers were notable for their limitations, the lost opportunity might be more understandable. But the sitting and emerging chiefs of state were as able and effective a group of executives as we have seen in any one generation in modern times. This is not to suggest that they were so superior in understanding and judgment to most other preceding and subsequent heads of government that they could do no wrong; they were as vulnerable to human miscalculation as all of us. Still, they were impressively talented politicians blessed by circumstances favorable to changing international relations for the better. But they didn't, or at least fell well short of what they might have accomplished. Why and how the world's leaders blundered is the focus of this book.

At the start of the twentieth century, some European thinkers saw the state of war as essential to a nation's survival. Not only did external threats from other countries that coveted territory and resources beyond their borders encourage national militancy between states, but the discipline of a command system also seemed likely to make citizens more productive and the nation more prosperous. And even more than any material benefits generated by a country at war were the intangibles—national pride in disciplined forces performing heroic deeds has had enduring universal appeal. Being "too proud to fight" has never been a match for courageous warriors ready to give their lives for some larger good.

Yet while national leaders have always justified war by invoking the nobility of patriotic sacrifice, they have also made the case for war as a prerequisite for lasting peace. How many in the aggressor nations in 1914 or 1939, however, especially the mass of Germans who rallied to Adolf Hitler's marching orders, would have chosen war if they knew what costs in suffering these conflicts would produce without the promised respite from bloodshed? The horrors of the years between 1914 and 1945 undermined the belief of even the most confident advocates of military action that they could turn the world toward long-term peace. The brutal trench warfare and strains on civilian populations of 1914–18 that destroyed 18 million lives convinced some observers in the 1920s and '30s that total war between advanced industrial societies was too destructive to victors and vanquished alike to let countries ever fight again. As French premier Georges Clemenceau said after 1918, "War is a series of catastrophes that results in a victory."

Although a formidable pacifist movement sprang up in Europe and America after 1918, millions of people, especially in the defeated nations, turned the war into a holy crusade. They prided themselves on having fought for a larger good, believing the sacrifice of so much blood and treasure a noble enterprise. This pride, combined with the losers' passion for revenge and the economic collapse of the 1930s, renewed millions of people's faith in the regenerative powers of violence: it allowed Hitler to launch Germany, and ultimately all Europe and the world, into the second great war in a generation. The savagery of the conflict, however, makes it difficult to understand how anyone in Germany, Italy, Japan, and Russia, the aggressor nations, could have justified it as worthy of moral support. The image of the Soviet Union as a victim of aggression should be balanced against its attacks on Finland and Poland.

World War II consumed as many as 50 million lives, giving warfare an unprecedented claim on merciless brutality. War had always produced terrible acts of inhumane violence, but never on a scale like that of 1939–45.

The war may be recalled not just as an all-out conflict between belligerents but also as the collapse of civilized behavior. The combined German-Italian air attacks on Republican-controlled cities in the Spanish Civil War of 1936–39, most notably the assault on the Basque town of Guernica, which Pablo Picasso memorialized in his universally recognized painting; the Japanese "Rape of Nanking" in 1937, in which as many as 300,000 Chinese were brutally killed; and

the Nazi air raids on London that launched the round of devastating
bombardments against innocent civilians, which eventually led to
the Allied firebombings of Dresden and Tokyo and the slaughter of
over 100,000 Japanese in the atomic decimations of Hiroshima and
Nagasaki—all were calculated acts of destruction in the service of
what the belligerents justified as self-defense and deserved punishment of ruthless enemies.

The Nazi scorched-earth devastation of Russia, which took over
25 million military and civilian lives, aimed to destroy Stalin's Communist regime and subjugate what the Nazis considered Russia's subhuman Slavs. An orgy of rape and killing by invading Soviet troops
in Germany in 1945 was accepted by most people in the West as
understandable, if not justifiable, acts of revenge. By contrast, the
massacre of over 20,000 Polish officers by the NKVD (Soviet secret
police) on orders from Stalin and the Politburo was seen in the West
as an act of Soviet ruthlessness to eliminate competitors for the future
control of Poland. For the sake of wartime unity, however, London
and Washington accepted Soviet assertions of German culpability.

The Bataan Death March in the Japanese-American conflict was
one of the most infamous episodes in the Pacific War. More than
70,000 already undernourished U.S. and Filipino troops were forced
to walk without food and water some eighty miles to prison camps,
while being beaten and bayoneted along the way. The Japanese cruelty
to surrendering forces, which they viewed as unworthy of honorable
treatment, stirred passions for revenge against an enemy seen as un-
deserving of regard as fellow human beings. Images of Japanese as
bloodthirsty fanatics committing atrocities—and metaphors about
exterminating vermin, usually yellow rats—abounded in the United
States during the war.

Japanese troops, who died by the tens of thousands rather than
surrender to the Americans in their Pacific Island campaigns, saw
capture as too frightening and death as more honorable than giving
up. Indoctrinated with propaganda that U.S. Marines had gained

admission to the corps by killing their parents, the Japanese believed that American captors would reciprocate the ferocity that they themselves used against their prisoners. And there was some basis for their fear: inflamed by stories of Japanese brutality toward captives, eagerness to die for their emperor, and booby traps on surrendering troops, American soldiers killed combatants trying to surrender, mutilated their bodies, and turned body parts into souvenirs.

Although Germany's Nazis were regarded with deep animus in the United States during the war, the Germans were not seen as barbaric as the Japanese. Ernie Pyle, America's most famous wartime correspondent, said that "in Europe we felt that our enemies, horrible and deadly as they were, were still people. But out here [in the Pacific] I soon gathered that the Japanese were looked upon as something subhuman and repulsive; the way some people feel about cockroaches or mice." Though Germany was "a heretic" or lapsed sinner from universal standards, these were standards "the Japanese never knew."

The perception about the Nazis and Germany changed, however, in 1945 with revelations about the Holocaust, the greatest organized slaughter of the entire war: Hitler's campaign of extermination against the Jews. The Nazi obsession with the Final Solution, *Judenrein*, ridding Europe of all of its 8.8 million Jews, came close to realization. The destruction of 90 percent of the Jewish populations of Germany, Austria, Poland, and the Baltic countries as well as 75 percent of Holland's, 60 percent of Belgium's, and 26 percent of France's Jews largely achieved Hitler's design.

Allied victory in 1945 against so malign a force as Nazism and Japanese militarism was an extraordinary moment—not simply because the most destructive war in history, which had left many of the world's major cities in rubble, had ended, but also because the mood of cynicism about human behavior made it difficult for even the most optimistic among the victors to imagine a future without war. U.S. general George C. Marshall, Franklin Roosevelt's chief of staff, declared, "If man does find the solution for world peace, it will

be the most extraordinary reversal of his record we have ever known."
While 81 percent of Americans in 1945 believed that the United
States should "join a world organization with power to maintain
world peace," only 15 percent was confident that a United Nations
could prevent future wars.

And yet leaders among the victors, buoyed by their success in such
a deadly struggle, believed that their triumph was bound to bring
more tranquil times, if not permanently, at least for a while. War and
defense preparations would not disappear entirely, but the appetite
for anything resembling the global conflicts of the first half of the
century had been sated. The world's leaders saw peace or an aversion
to large-scale combat as a reflection of what their masses insisted on.
"There go the people. I must follow them, for I am their leader,"
one nineteenth-century French politician declared. Woodrow Wilson
similarly remarked that "statesmen have to bend to the collective will
of their people or be broken."

Alexis de Tocqueville made the same point about the world's emerging democracies in the first half of the nineteenth century when he
wrote, "No man can struggle with advantage against the spirit of his
age and country, and however powerful a man may be, it is hard for
him to make his contemporaries share feelings and ideas which run
counter to the general run of their hopes and desires."

Winston Churchill was never willing to be so self-effacing about
his or anyone else's leadership of a democratic nation. He decried the
"part that humbug plays in the social life of great peoples dwelling in
a state of democratic freedom." (He might have had in mind a February 1945 survey in America asking whether Washington or Lincoln
was the greater president: some of those choosing Lincoln thought
he was the author of the Declaration of Independence, the discoverer
of America, or the first one to say the world was round. One man
chose Washington, because his picture was on the one-dollar bill.)
Churchill belittled those who were so ready to take the nation's pulse
and temperature and "keep their ears to the ground. All I can say

is that the British nation will find it very hard to look up to leaders who are detected in that ungainly posture," he declared. The leader's work, he believed, was to goad the mass public into a greater realism about the issues and possible solutions before it.

Churchill understood that however beholden a head of government might be to the people, he could not deny responsibility for the actions of his administration, especially in a tyrannical system where a dictator, relying on terror tactics, encouraged murderous passions. To be sure, Hitler's crimes against humanity could not have occurred without the help of German and foreign collaborators. Still, at the heart of Germany's malign deeds were Hitler and his Nazi chiefs—Joseph Goebbels, Heinrich Himmler, and Hermann Göring, to mention the most prominent members of the Nazi inner circle, and the Wehrmacht generals who enthusiastically implemented their war plans.

The failure by the most powerful and influential leaders of the twentieth century to attain the elusive goal of world peace at a time when their citizens were thirsting for tranquillity, deepens the puzzle about the failed search for international concord, especially when it was so transparent that modern weaponry made militarism and war a prescription for economic and social disintegration that did more to destroy nations than to save them. After the development of the hydrogen bomb in the 1950s, the atomic bombings of Japan were seen as a small instance of how advanced societies could be devastated in a total nuclear war. "I know not with what weapons World War III will be fought, but World War IV will be fought with sticks and stones," Albert Einstein said.

How then to evaluate the leadership of the period between the closing months of World War II and the first years of the Cold War, the time frame of this book, which shaped international relations for years to come? It was a moment when the most talented and memorable government chiefs in modern history ruled or vied for power in their respective countries—America, Britain, China, France, Germany,

India, Japan, the two Koreas, Russia, and Vietnam—and were making indelible marks on their nations and the world.

It was also a time when the leaders and their nations in America, Europe, and Asia considered how to change foreign affairs after the most destructive war in history had discredited Nazism, Fascism, and Japanese militarism. The years between 1945 and 1953 seemed ripe for a calculated revolution in world politics, or at least some more rational approach to international differences that, if squandered, would cast a shadow over the leaders responsible for what some hoped could be long-term peace.

There was no reluctance by the victorious Allies and the new generation of political leaders in the defeated countries to compel the Germans, Italians, and Japanese to abandon their systems of failed governance, which had inflicted so much suffering on so many around the globe. A larger problem for the victors, however, was whether their politicians and peoples could curb the suspicions and rivalries that could jettison the cooperation that had brought them successfully through the war.

In the last year of the fighting, every major Allied figure began discussing the preservation of the alliance for the sake of future peace. Roosevelt spoke to this concern in January 1945, when he used his annual State of the Union message to call for a "peoples' peace" that would prove "durable and secure." He did not see a time when power politics would entirely disappear, he said, but he hoped it could be subordinated to men's better angels.

General Douglas MacArthur, commander in chief of ground forces in the Pacific, echoed Churchill and Roosevelt in September 1945 during the surrender ceremony on the deck of the battleship *Missouri* in Tokyo Bay. Remembering Abraham Lincoln's appeal for malice toward none at the close of the Civil War, MacArthur declared that the two countries do not meet "in a spirit of distrust, malice or hatred." He invoked "a higher dignity" than the celebration of the victor over the vanquished and "the hope of all mankind" for "a better world." In a speech broadcast to the American people at the conclusion of the ceremony, MacArthur described the war as man's "last chance. If we do not now devise some greater and more equitable system, Armageddon will be at our door. The problem is basically theological," he said, "and involves a spiritual recrudescence and improvement of human character. . . . It must be of the spirit if we are to save the flesh."

To Toshikazu Kase, the Japanese translator at the surrender ceremony, who anticipated the occasion as "the worst humiliation," MacArthur's words left him "spellbound and thunderstruck" at the general's generosity. The quarterdeck of the battleship had become not a place of unbearable embarrassment but "an altar of peace."

The horrors of the twentieth century's two unlimited wars provoke unanswered and possibly unanswerable questions. How could supposedly effective leaders, with the skills to gain the headship of such large advanced industrial nations, have been so blind to the miseries they would inflict upon their own peoples as well as those they saw as enemies? When someone asked Stalin at the end of the war if Hitler was "a lunatic or an adventurer," he responded: "I agree that he was an adventurer. But I can't agree he was mad. Hitler was a gifted man. Only a gifted man could unite the German people."

Stalin could have been speaking of himself in explaining how so many Europeans and Asians could have followed the dictates of men whose decisions produced such catastrophes for them.

But how could anyone, after witnessing the repression and slaughter of the war years, have believed, as Stalin did, that might alone made right or guaranteed a nation's security? To be sure, one lesson of World War II was that a poorly armed nation was an inviting target to an aggressor. Yet another transparent lesson was that might alone was no guarantee of a nation's defense against conflict and loss.

I do not pretend to have any simple explanation for why so many millions of people were drawn to mass murderers like Hitler, Stalin, and Japan's military chiefs. It is easy to understand why, after witnessing the horrors these men perpetrated on the world, defeated peoples would yearn for an alternative to militarism and war as a defense against external dangers.

Despite the attraction of a more benign way of assuring future peace than military might, it is not so difficult to understand why the success of the victors' armed forces created a compelling appeal to sustained reliance on strength of arms as a guard against foreign threats. And yet, as the German and Japanese experiences might have suggested to the Allies, a buildup of military power is no assurance of national safety. Still, in a world in which trust is in such short supply, reliance on other nations' goodwill seems less wise than strength of arms.

This is not a book condemning national defense arrangements, though there is much to be questioned. Rather, it is an attempt to revisit the end-of-war and immediate postwar events by asking why, in spite of the uncivilized acts of violence that had dominated international affairs, men and women all over the globe could still imagine that traditional power politics could assure their national safety and a wider peace. In short, what drove the postwar leaders of the most powerful and populous nations around the globe to act as they did?

In 2005, I had a conversation with a French attorney visiting the United States. We talked about his children, who were in their twenties, and how different their outlook was toward their country and the world than what he—a man in his fifties—had heard from his parents, who were part of the World War II generation. His children, he told me, certainly identified themselves as French, but unlike his parents they also viewed themselves as Europeans, or as citizens of a larger community. I asked him if he thought his children could imagine another war between France and Germany or any of the Western European states. "Certainly not," he replied.

It was a reflection of the sea change that had taken place in Europe.

The pain and suffering of the century's two continent-wide wars had brought the Western Europeans, in spite of themselves, the wisdom to replace armed conflicts with cooperative assemblies and institutions. The United States, which through the first hundred and fifty years of its history had largely isolated itself from foreign wars, succumbed to the curse of every emerging modern power, a military-industrial complex that President Dwight Eisenhower described in 1953 as the bane of America's existence. Eisenhower was not decrying the need for arms or denying that the country justifiably felt embattled, but, as his successor in the presidency, John F. Kennedy, would say in his inaugural address, "Now the trumpet summons us again—not as a call to bear arms, though arms we need—not as a call to battle, though embattled we are—but a call to bear the burden of a long twilight struggle . . . against the common enemies of man: tyranny, poverty, disease and war itself."

I hope my exploration of timeless questions about the search for long-term postwar peace sheds some light on the roots of the individual and mass conduct that dominated national behavior in the years between 1945 and 1953. Since neither unwise acts of war nor mass illusions are about to disappear, it seems important to make every effort to come to a greater understanding of the acts of history that in some form or other are all too likely to reoccur. To be sure, the wars of the post-1945 era have been on a different scale and in different places and circumstances, but there have been indisputable similarities to earlier moments of violence and hope, as well as similarly poor judgments on the part of both the public and their chiefs.

On balance, the postwar generation did well enough in averting greater catastrophes than the world might have experienced. Nevertheless, it made its share of missteps, which are better considered than ignored. I take limited account of most of the achievements of the end of war and postwar leaders not out of any desire to diminish their accomplishments, but in the belief that their errors in judgment are more usable lessons of the past. As McGeorge Bundy, John Kennedy's and then Lyndon Johnson's national security adviser, noted later about his role in expanding U.S. involvement in Vietnam, "I had a part in a great failure. I made mistakes of perception, recommendation and execution. If I have learned anything I should share it." He added, "Because it matters what lessons are learned . . . there are lots of errors in the path of understanding."

PART I

A WILDERNESS
CALLED PEACE

London, Moscow, and Washington: Friends in Need

The only thing worse than having allies is not having them.
—Winston Churchill

I n the second half of 1944, as Winston Churchill, Franklin Roosevelt, and Joseph Stalin laid plans to confer in the coming year about postwar arrangements, they tried to mute long-standing suspicions of each other's intentions. Without continuing cooperation that had brought them to the edge of victory against powerful German resistance across Russia, the Middle East, Italy, and now Western Europe, Churchill and Roosevelt foresaw another period of international tension that could provoke a new global conflict in the not too distant future. Stalin was deeply cynical about his allies and even less confident about avoiding another war unless he could arrange Soviet territorial and strategic advantages that would inhibit the reemergence of Western anticommunism.

Yet however much Churchill and Roosevelt hoped they might find means to blunt differences with Moscow, they were also doubtful that the national and ideological competition between East and West would disappear and sharply reduce their reliance on traditional military, economic, and political instruments of defense against an aggressive adversary.

Between January 31 and February 11, 1945, the Big Three, as the leaders of Britain, Russia, and the United States were described in the last year of the war, met at Malta and Yalta to plan the postwar organization of Europe and Asia. Outwardly, Churchill, Roosevelt, Stalin, and their staffs were pledged to sustained cooperation. And the conversations among them gave little indication that their unspoken assumptions about each other jeopardized the future peace. Yet their personal and national histories made them doubtful about their allies' intentions and prospects for postwar harmony.

Churchill's life experience inclined him to see future strife with Moscow. Churchill "lived for crisis," the historian A. J. P. Taylor said. "He profited from crisis. And when crisis did not exist, he strove to invent it. . . . He did not share the contemporary belief in universal improvement nor did he await the coming of some secular Heaven on Earth. He strove to ameliorate hardships without ever expecting that they would be finally removed."

From his earliest days, Churchill had been ambitious for power and dominance, ambitions that were reflected in a combative personal nature. Combined with his long-standing fear of the Soviet Communist threat to Great Britain's world position, this character made Churchill as much an adversary as a compliant friend to Stalin and Russia.

Churchill was born in November 1874 into a British noble family. His father, Lord Randolph Churchill, the son of the seventh duke of Marlborough, was a distant figure, who had little involvement in his son's rearing. To Winston, his absent father was more an idealized representative of the family's values than a flesh-and-blood character with whom his son directly engaged. As a boy, Winston imbibed the heroic attitudes of his class and times. He dreamed of "military glory," of the chance to join the ranks of Britain's greatest heroes who had rescued the nation from defeat and humiliation and received the Victoria Cross from the sovereign. His ambitions resembled those of earlier generations of English noblemen. The principal difference between Winston and most of his privileged contemporaries is that they outgrew their boyhood fantasies, and he never relinquished them.

After a time at Harrow School, where he exhibited behavior problems and performed poorly, Winston sought admission to the Royal Military Academy at Sandhurst, which he won on his third try, demonstrating his keen determination to become an army officer. At Sandhurst, he seemed to find his calling, earning high marks and graduating eighth in a class of 150 in 1894. Eager for action and adventure that would test his courage, satisfy a yearning to serve queen and country, and expose him to dramatic events that he could record for a larger public in articles and books that could make him famous, Churchill won postings to the British Empire's outlying regions of Pakistan, Egypt, and the Sudan. He was not disappointed: exhilarating combat against seemingly primitive tribesmen gave him the chance to feel heroic and write newspaper stories that put him before potential British voters.

In 1899, Churchill unsuccessfully stood for a seat in Parliament. Although intent on trying again in the following year, he used the time between elections to serve as a correspondent in South Africa, where the British were fighting the Boer War. Captured by the Boers and held as a POW in Pretoria, he had the satisfaction of escaping after a month and then rejoining the army to participate in successful campaigns in South Africa and the Sudan.

In 1900, after returning to Britain, Churchill won election to Parliament as a Conservative, but soon found himself in opposition to his party's support of the protective tariff. Shifting his allegiance to the Liberal Party, he established himself as a national figure, his reputation as an independent maverick feeding his self-image as a courageous battler who put principle above slavish party loyalty.

Between 1908 and 1919, Churchill held a succession of cabinet posts, including First Lord of the Admiralty during World War I, where he shouldered responsibility for a failed invasion of the Ottoman

Empire at Gallipoli that compelled his resignation and threw him into one of the periodic depressions he called his Black Dogs. Unlike so many other contemporaries, who saw the failure at Gallipoli and the larger cost of the war in blood and wealth as reasons to turn away from force in response to international conflicts, Churchill found relief in action. His down moods induced aggressive deeds more than passivity. In November 1915, he rejoined the army to command a battalion in France.

During subsequent service in the War Office, Churchill was an architect of the Allied intervention in Russia after the revolution of 1917 had turned into a conflict between Communists and defenders of the czarist regime. Churchill was no admirer of the Russian monarchy, but he thought that "Bolshevism should have been strangled in its cradle." In the 1920s, he praised Italy's Benito Mussolini for fighting communism. In his war memoirs, after Il Duce had become Adolf Hitler's ally, suffered defeat, and been lynched in Milan by anti-Fascist partisans, Churchill described him as an "adventurer," but justified his assumption of dictatorial powers as a response to communism.

In the 1920s and '30s, Churchill opposed the pacifism that had developed as a reaction to wartime losses and postwar European tensions threatening another war. In the 1930s, he was also critical of Spain's Republican government, which was supported by the Communists in a civil war with Francisco Franco's Fascists. In response to Italo-German intervention in the fighting that helped Franco defeat the Republic, Churchill favored a policy of strict Anglo-French neutrality.

Although he would later be on record as regretting the Fascist victory, Churchill continued to see Spain's Marxists as a dreadful alternative. With the goal of "absolute power," they had inflicted a reign of terror on Spain characterized by "wholesale cold-blooded massacres of their political opponents and of the well-to-do." If he had been a Spaniard, he later wrote, the Communists "would have murdered me and my family and friends." He continued to believe that Britain's best course had been "to keep out of Spain."

Churchill was as vocal about Prime Minister Neville Chamberlain's appeasement policy, which he described after the Munich concessions to Hitler on Czechoslovakia as a "defeat without a war." He said of Chamberlain, "You were given the choice between war and dishonour. You chose dishonour and you will have war."

Churchill wisely advocated rearmament against the Nazi menace, and favored an alliance with Soviet Russia to deter Hitler from an attack on Poland. The defense of Britain's national security trumped his anticommunism. He condemned the Nazi-Soviet nonaggression pact of August 1939 as "an unnatural act" that only totalitarian despots could have signed and then survived the repressed public condemnation in their respective countries. "The fact that such an agreement could be made," Churchill asserted, "marks the culminating failure of British and French foreign policy and diplomacy over several years."

Churchill also saw the pact as a demonstration of how "crafty men and statesmen" can be "misled by all their elaborate calculations." It would take only twenty-two months for Hitler's attack on the Soviet Union to reveal the hollowness of the Hitler-Stalin pact. Governments with "no moral scruples," Churchill added, gain only temporary advantages from betraying their true interests. "The Russian nation in its scores of millions were to pay a frightful forfeit."

For Churchill, the 1930s have been described as the wilderness years, a time when his views were largely out of sync with the national mood that favored appeasement and avoidance of war at almost any cost. His determination to persevere through this difficult period rested on convictions that he was right and that his public positions would eventually be vindicated. His affinity for what he could see as heroic opposition to wrongheaded popular sentiment helped sustain him through a phase of personal depression over the public's blindness and his political isolation.

The outbreak of World War II in September 1939 restored Churchill's public influence. The war brought him back into the government as First Lord of the Admiralty. Germany's conquest of Poland, followed by Hitler's successful spring offensive in the West, toppled Chamberlain's government and elevated Churchill to the post of prime minister, where he famously offered nothing but "blood, toil, tears and sweat."

Churchill's inspirational rhetoric at the time of Britain's peril, especially after the fall of France in June 1940, when Britain stood alone against Hitler's triumphant military, was partly a function of the inner struggle against despair that had plagued him throughout his life. In the aftermath of Hitler's 1939–40 victories, when so many of his countrymen feared for Britain's future, Churchill's personal history made him the nation's perfect leader. Having struggled through periods of defeat and renewed success, Churchill could impart a message of hope during a time of loss. He rallied Britain with words that he could have told himself in past moments of hopelessness. It was a marvelous example of how one man's life experience could serve a whole nation in its struggle to chase away gloom and turn retreat into a sustained fight for victory.

In rallying the nation, Churchill drew once again not only on his personal experience with overcoming setbacks but also on his affinity for the hero's role—the fulfillment of long-standing fantasies of power in the service of valiant deeds. "In my long political experience," Churchill wrote later, "I had held most of the great offices of State, but I readily admit that the post which had now fallen to me [of prime minister] was the one I liked the best. . . . Power in a national crisis, when a man believes he knows what orders should be given, is a blessing." Fighting Hitler perfectly suited Churchill's attraction to a contest with someone he identified as pure evil. It gave him "enormous vitality." He found the energy to work almost nonstop in his drive to destroy Hitler and the Nazis. They were ideal enemies for someone who craved a contest with wickedness that could give him the wherewithal to resist his affinity for depression and immobility.

In June 1941, after Hitler attacked the Soviet Union, Churchill unhesitatingly identified Britain as Stalin's ally. "The Nazi regime is indistinguishable from the worst features of Communism," Churchill declared in a radio address the night of Hitler's attack on Russia. "No one has been a more consistent opponent of Communism than I have for the last twenty-five years. I will unsay no word that I have spoken about it." But the realities of defeating Hitler required a different approach to the Soviet Union. The primary goal was "to destroy Hitler and every vestige of the Nazi regime." Churchill promised to fight him by land, sea, and air until "we have rid the earth of his shadow and liberated his peoples from its yoke."

When Churchill's private secretary asked if his reputation as an arch anti-Communist was not being compromised by aid to Moscow, he replied, "Not at all. I have only one purpose, the destruction of Hitler. . . . If Hitler invaded Hell I would make at least a favourable reference to the Devil in the House of Commons." His implicit reference to Stalin as the devil was a telling expression of how he viewed the Soviet dictator: a useful ally in the struggle against Hitler and Nazism, but a ruthless tyrant nonetheless who after the war would likely revert to a reach for world power through the eclipse of Britain and the extension of communism around the globe.

In December 1941, when Stalin pressed British foreign secretary Anthony Eden, who had come to Moscow for conversations, to agree to postwar Soviet control of the Baltic states and eastern Poland, Churchill refused, telling Eden that the Soviets had acquired this territory "by acts of aggression in shameful collusion with Hitler. The transfer of the peoples of the Baltic states to Soviet Russia against their will would be contrary to all the principles for which we are fighting this war and would dishonour our cause."

Yet in October 1944, with Soviet armies moving decisively into southeastern Europe, Churchill met with Stalin in Moscow to discuss the fate of the Balkans. The sixty-seven-year-old Churchill and the sixty-five-year-old Stalin showed the effects of age and the burdens of their wartime responsibilities. Churchill was short, fat, and stoop-shouldered, his ruddy complexion betraying his years of heavy alcohol consumption. A damaged left arm from a childhood accident, facial scars from a smallpox attack at the age of seven, a yellowish complexion, and tobacco-stained teeth made the diminutive Stalin a match for the imperfect Churchill.

Together, hunched over a table in the Kremlin, they cynically divided up responsibility for the postwar Balkans: the Soviets were to have 90 percent control in Rumania, 75 percent in Bulgaria, and 50 percent in Hungary and Yugoslavia, with an equal share of power for Britain, which would have 90 percent dominance in Greece along with the United States. Churchill suggested burning the paper on which they recorded what they called the percentages agreement. He feared the reaction to their disposal "of these issues, so fateful to millions of people, in such an offhand manner." But Stalin, who had no qualms about eventual public knowledge of how great power arrangements were made, urged Churchill to keep the paper. In the same meetings, Churchill emphasized to Stalin how essential their friendship was to a future without war. "Perhaps it is the only thing that can save the peace for our children and grandchildren," he said. "Hopes are high for the permanent results of victory," he added.

The percentages agreement with Stalin speaks volumes about Churchill's belief that unless he reined in Soviet ambitions in the Balkans by acknowledging their respective spheres of control, Moscow would impose itself on all the countries in the region. It was also Churchill's way of buying big power peace at the cost of small nations' autonomy. The division of power was the kind of language Churchill and Stalin understood. While Stalin agreed to Churchill's proposal, it was only a temporary arrangement that served the war effort. Who controlled what in the Balkans, Stalin believed, would be decided not by a paper pledge but by who had troops on the ground. "How many divisions does the pope have?" Stalin famously asked an adviser who warned him against open verbal clashes with the Vatican.

Roosevelt was no less mindful of power considerations. In August 1943, almost two years after an Anglo-American agreement for joint research on atomic energy, and a year after development and manufacture of a bomb had begun, the president and prime minister signed an agreement promising not to use an atomic weapon against each other or against a third party without mutual consent. They also agreed not to share information about atomic development with another country unless both saw it as acceptable. It was an unspoken commitment to exclude the Soviet Union from knowledge that could help it build a bomb, or to give Britain a military advantage in a postwar Europe over which London and Moscow would presumably exercise greatest control.

A year later, after a second Anglo-American conference in Quebec to discuss postwar arrangements, Churchill and Roosevelt traveled to the president's home at Hyde Park, New York, where they made their exclusion of Soviet access to their knowledge of atomic development more specific. In an aide-mémoire of a September 19, 1944, conversation, they agreed that the Russians were not to share in the control and use of atomic power. Because the Danish physicist Niels Bohr had urged both Churchill and Roosevelt to reach an agreement with Moscow on international control of atomic energy, they included a proviso that said, "Enquiries should be made regarding the activities of Professor Bohr and steps should be taken to ensure that he is responsible for no leakage of information, particularly to the Russians."

After discussing this agreement with the president, Vannevar Bush, the chairman of the president's Military Policy Committee on Atomic Energy, wrote a coworker on the atomic project: "The President evidently thought he could join with Churchill in bringing about a US-UK postwar agreement on this subject by which it would be held closely and presumably to control the peace of the world." Bush knew that atomic research had not been and could not remain the exclusive province of one or two nations. While Britain and the United States might win the race, currently against Germany, to build an atomic bomb, eventually scientists in other nations, who were part of an international community of atomic researchers, would duplicate what the British and Americans had achieved. Trying to exclude the Soviets from knowledge that London and Washington were forging ahead on atomic research would do little else than arouse old suspicions that the West intended to prepare itself for the defeat of communism.

Roosevelt's suspicions of Stalin and Soviet intentions were never as strong as Churchill's. Like Churchill, Roosevelt was part of a native aristocracy. It was a nobility of wealth, however, rather than bloodlines, even though Franklin's mother, Sara Delano Roosevelt, prided herself on being able to trace her ancestry back to European aristocrats and *Mayflower* émigrés. Unlike Churchill, who had spent his childhood largely in the care of hired help, Roosevelt's boyhood was marked by close ties to his parents. His father, James Roosevelt, "showered him with attention . . . affectionately teaching him to sled, skate, toboggan, ride, fish, sail, and farm. Sara also doted on the boy, keeping diaries with almost daily records of his achievements," as if she were anticipating his fame.

Like Churchill, Franklin also burned with ambition, although it seems to have been less the product of neediness or a compulsion to satisfy a yearning for attention, regard, and unqualified love. Franklin's drive for distinction seems to have originated more in a sense of entitlement—a gentleman's right to govern and see to the well-being of those less endowed than he was. Franklin Roosevelt's idea of the presidency, some said, was Franklin Roosevelt in the presidency.

Nevertheless, Roosevelt's reach for power and fame was not simply the birthright and altruism of a privileged man. Few of his classmates, who were also indulged by attentive parents and learned the obligations of Christian gentlemen at Groton and Harvard, devoted themselves to public life as Franklin did. He found special pleasure in outdoing competitors for high office and using power to bestow gifts on those in need.

An attack of poliomyelitis in 1921 at the age of thirty-nine that left him paralyzed from the waist down may have heightened Roosevelt's desire for public distinction, but his desire for high station preceded his paralysis. His distant cousin Theodore Roosevelt was a model he aspired to imitate as early as the 1890s, when TR was police commissioner in New York City, a state assemblyman, assistant secretary of the navy, a hero in the Spanish-American War, governor of New York, and vice president. TR's almost eight years in the White House between 1901 and 1909 encouraged Franklin to have thoughts of ascending to the presidency as well. When he won a New York State Senate seat in 1910, appointment as Woodrow Wilson's assistant secretary of the navy in 1913, and nomination to the vice presidency in 1920, Franklin saw himself as fulfilling his greatest hopes. James Cox's defeat by Warren G. Harding in 1920, which denied Franklin the vice presidency, and the onset of polio in 1921, which limited his political activities, would be only temporary setbacks.

During the next seven years, despite his disability, Roosevelt remained active in Democratic Party politics, winning the national spotlight in 1924 with a brilliant nominating speech for New York Governor Al Smith—"the Happy Warrior"—at the national convention. Although Smith lost the presidential nomination that year, he succeeded in 1928, once again with Roosevelt's help. Backed by Smith and a unified party, Roosevelt won the New York governorship in 1928 and again in 1930. During his two terms, he established himself as a leading progressive combating suffering in the Great Depression. His nomination and election to the White House in 1932 opened the way to bold leadership in response to the country's worst economic downturn in history.

The similarity to Churchill's rise to power is striking. Like Churchill, Roosevelt weathered a personal crisis that prepared him to deal with public distress much the way he countered his polio and loss of mobility. A beleaguered Britain could take hope from a man who had surmounted career setbacks or defeats that jeopardized his prospects for holding any high office. Likewise, Roosevelt's physical disability made him an unlikely candidate for president, but his doggedness had not only returned him to the public arena, it also recommended him to Americans in a time of crisis as someone who understood how to cope with and overcome disabling problems.

In a time of isolationism, Franklin, like Theodore, thought of himself as a foreign policy leader. He was warmly disposed to American involvement in World War I and supported Wilson's postwar plan for a world organization that could prevent future conflicts through collective security. Disillusionment over the postwar reversion to power politics and the onset of the Depression eclipsed internationalism in the 1920s and '30s and dissuaded Roosevelt from his eagerness to involve the United States in overseas affairs.

Although he devoted himself to a domestic New Deal between 1933 and 1938, Roosevelt believed it essential for his administration to exert some influence against acts of aggression in Europe and Asia. By contrast with Churchill, he saw Soviet Russia less as a menace to the Western democracies than as a potential ally against Fascist gains. In 1919–20, when the first Red scare, a reaction against anarchists and Bolsheviks, swept the United States, Roosevelt refused to join the hysteria.

Six months after becoming president in 1933, Roosevelt reversed the Republican policy of refusing to recognize the Communist government of Soviet Russia. He expected a return to normal relations to foster trade and boost the U.S. economy. He also hoped that Japan, which had seized Manchuria in 1931–32, might see Washington and Moscow as coming together to restrain Japanese aggression in Asia. Unlike Churchill, with his fears of a Bolshevik contagion spreading across Europe, Roosevelt did not see Russia as a direct threat to the United States, despite a small but activist Communist Party in America with ties to the Soviet Comintern promoting Communist control in other countries. Eager for access to Russian markets, American business chiefs favored a restoration of relations. Conservative newspaper publisher Roy Howard said that "the menace of Bolshevism in the United States is about as great as the menace of sunstroke in Greenland or chilblains in the Sahara."

Roosevelt saw the Soviet Union as more of a domestic political problem than a threat to America and other democracies. To convince Americans, especially Catholics who were offended by Soviet anticlerical propaganda, that normalization of relations was a way to temper Communist ideology, Roosevelt concocted a story about Maxim Litvinov, commissar for foreign affairs and the chief Soviet negotiator. Assuming an anecdote he told his cabinet would be leaked to the press, Roosevelt described how he had pressured Litvinov into agreeing to freedom of religious worship for Americans in the USSR. He had embarrassed the commissar by telling him, "Now you may think you're an atheist . . . but I tell you, Max, . . . before you die, you will believe in God." Roosevelt thought that "the expression of his face" meant that "he knew I was right." Secretary of Labor Frances Perkins said that "Roosevelt would only tell the Cabinet what he wanted them to hear." And it may be assumed that only the details he wanted revealed ever reached the press.

Although Roosevelt's hopes for productive relations with Moscow were disappointed in the 1930s and by the Nazi-Soviet nonaggression pact in August 1939, he did not think an alternative anti-Nazi Soviet agreement with Britain and France would have helped the Allies much in a war with Hitler. Moreover, when the Soviets seized parts of eastern Poland, Roosevelt did not designate Moscow a belligerent and invoke America's neutrality law against her. He hoped to keep a line open to Stalin that would deter him from joining Hitler in fighting Britain and France.

Nor did he publicly protest Moscow's seizure of the Baltic states in September and October 1939 or exert much pressure on the Soviets not to invade Finland in November. He feared that such actions would agitate U.S. isolationists into believing that he was about to involve the United States in the war. More important, it might jeopardize a revision of American neutrality laws to allow the sale of war goods to Britain and France on a cash-and-carry basis.

Roosevelt was not without anger toward Moscow for what he saw as its unprincipled opportunism. At a White House gathering in February 1940 of the left-wing American Youth Congress, he described the Soviet Union as "a dictatorship as absolute as any other dictatorship in the world." He decried its alliance with Hitler and its invasion of "infinitesimally small" Finland. Privately, he described the Soviet attack as "this dreadful rape of Finland," and wondered "why one should have anything to do with the present Soviet leaders because their idea of civilization and human happiness is so totally different from ours." Nevertheless, beyond sending a cable to Soviet president Mikhail Kalinin asking restraint in dealings with the Finns and facilitating a $10 million loan to Helsinki, which fell far short of the $80 million they had asked for, he took no overt steps to punish Soviet actions. On the contrary, Soviet purchases of U.S. goods during the Finnish war more than doubled from the previous year.

When Hitler invaded the Soviet Union in June 1941, Roosevelt quickly concluded that Russia's survival could "mean the liberation of Europe from Nazi domination—and at the same time I do not think we need worry about any possibility of Russian domination," he said privately. He saw Soviet ineffectiveness in its management of its economy and its war with Finland as evidence of a weak nation. His eagerness to supply Russia ran counter to the judgment of his military chiefs, who did not think the Soviets could hold out for more than three months or could possibly defeat Hitler's armies. Like Churchill, Roosevelt believed that it was vital to supply the Soviet military as fast as possible so that they could maintain resistance until at least October, when the weather would rescue Russia by bogging down Germany's war machine in freezing winter rain and snow.

To get supplies to Russia in the summer of 1941, Roosevelt had to overcome doubts in his administration about Soviet capacity to offer effective military resistance and convince subordinates that ruthless Soviet indifference to anything but their own interests was essential if they were going to survive the Nazi invasion. Roosevelt's army chief of staff, General George C. Marshall, complained that Soviet ambassador Constantine Oumansky "will take everything we own if we submit to his criticisms." Secretary of War Henry Stimson described Oumansky as "nothing but a crook" and "a slick, clever little beast." Nevertheless, under the president's prodding and their own conviction that the "maintenance of an active front in Russia" was America's and Britain's best strategy for ultimate victory, they worked to speed the delivery of munitions and fuel.

In the spring and summer of 1942, after Japan's Pearl Harbor attack had brought the United States into the war and the Soviets found themselves hard pressed to hold the line against a Nazi offensive in the Caucasus, where thousands of Soviet troops were being killed or captured each day, Stalin sent Foreign Secretary Vyacheslav Molotov to London and Washington to press Churchill and Roosevelt to relieve Soviet forces by drawing off German divisions to a second front in Western Europe.

The fifty-one-year-old Molotov was a dour workaholic, who Lenin had nicknamed "Iron-Arse" because of his indefatigable work habits. "Small, stocky with a bulging forehead, chilling hazel eyes blinking behind round spectacles, and a stammer when angry," he was "Stalin's closest ally." They had met in 1911 when they worked as editors for *Pravda*, the underground Bolshevik newspaper. A devoted Communist who was exiled twice by the czar's government for revolutionary activity, Molotov came across to some as a "colorless bureaucrat . . . who always wore a suit and tie." Leon Trotsky called him "mediocrity personified," a man of inflexible discipline who was famous for taking thirteen-minute naps. He won favor through his dedication to Stalin and commitment to destroying any and all opponents of their power.

Although Roosevelt understood the near impossibility of launching a successful cross-Channel assault on occupied France in the summer or fall of 1942, he promised Molotov that the Allies would mount such an attack before the end of the year. In a subsequent meeting with Churchill in Washington, he and Roosevelt agreed that the best chance for a campaign that could divert German forces from Russia would be in North Africa, where the British were fighting to maintain the Mediterranean lifeline to their Middle Eastern and Asian colonies.

The conversations involving American and British military chiefs and the president's and prime minister's principal advisers reflected the tension everyone was under at the time, as they desperately tried to find a formula to keep Russia in the war until they could strike the Germans in France. In a meeting between Churchill and Harry Hopkins, Roosevelt's principal envoy to London and Moscow, the prime minister exploded at Hopkins's failure to consult him before seeing his staff officers, tearing pages out of a book of army regulations and throwing them on the floor as he shouted at Hopkins.

Hopkins took it in stride. Prima donnas didn't bother him. He was a tough-minded administrator who took on some of the hardest jobs Roosevelt needed done, from domestic welfare reform to wartime dealings with Stalin and Churchill. A son of the Middle Border, where he attended Grinnell College in Iowa, and then learned his craft as a social worker in the New York City slums, he was, in one description, "a lean, loose-limbed, disheveled man, with sharp features and sardonic eyes. . . . His manner was brusque and studiously irreverent; his language, concise, pungent, and often profane. . . . He was at his best under pressure," notable for a "you-can't-put-that-over-on-me expression" and a talent for getting things done. Churchill valued Hopkins's direct line to the president (in 1940, FDR had moved him into the White House) and self-confidence about finding solutions to even the most daunting problems, calling him "Lord Root of the Matter."

Churchill's agitation partly came from a commitment to carry a message to Stalin that his allies could not open a second front in Europe in 1942. Traveling to Moscow in August, Churchill "pondered on my mission to this sullen, sinister Bolshevik state I had once tried so hard to strangle at its birth and which, until Hitler appeared, I had regarded as the mortal foe of civilized freedom." On his flight to Russia to deliver the bad news about holding off a European invasion until 1943, Churchill felt as if he were "carrying a lump of ice to the North Pole." A British general said, "We were going into the lion's den and we weren't going to feed him."

The Soviet leader Churchill met for the first time in 1942 had a reputation as a brutal dictator who had ruled the Soviet Union since Lenin's death in 1924. His policies of forced collectivization of agriculture and rapid industrialization had modernized the Soviet Union at the cost of millions of lives. In August 1942, when Churchill asked him, "Have the stresses of this war been as difficult for you personally as carrying through the policy of collective farms?" "Oh, no," Stalin replied. "That was especially difficult." "What did you do with all the rich peasants—the kulaks?" Churchill asked. "We killed them," Stalin coolly responded. Churchill said later, "With the World War going on all round us it seemed vain to moralise aloud."

Purges of dissidents in the 1930s had added to Stalin's image as a ruthless leader who had sent thousands to perish in the gulags of Siberia and forced the relocation of ethnic groups threatening Soviet unity by asking for greater autonomy.

As Stalin himself understood, by World War II, he had become something of a mythological or larger-than-life figure. When one of his sons tried to use the family name to his advantage, Stalin berated him, shouting, "You're not Stalin and I'm not Stalin. Stalin is Soviet power. Stalin is what he is in the newspapers and the portraits, not you, no not even me!" He and the Bolshevik Party had become one and the same. Stalin embodied the party's affinity for conspiracies against alleged domestic enemies and the murderous rooting out of anyone suspected of the slightest doubts about Communist goals and power.

Born in 1878 in Gori, Georgia, Stalin was the son of a cobbler and a peasant mother. He had a tumultuous childhood, marred by an abusive alcoholic father who eventually abandoned the family, an attack of smallpox at the age of seven that left him with facial pock-marks that disfigured his appearance, a carriage accident at the age of ten that permanently injured his left arm and exempted him from military service in World War I, and a community in which Stalin participated in gang warfare. An exceptionally bright child who stood first in his class, he was awarded a scholarship to attend an orthodox seminary in Tbilisi. Although spending five years at the seminary, he rebelled against its teachings, becoming a revolutionary and labor organizer and supporting himself by criminal activities that led to three convictions and imprisonments.

In 1913, he published the treatise *Marxism and the National Question* under the name Stalin, "man of steel," abandoning his family name of Dzhugashvili. In 1917, after four years in penal exile, he settled in Saint Petersburg, where he joined Lenin, Trotsky, Mikhail Kalinin, and Molotov in working to oust Alexander Ke-rensky's provisional government, which had just overturned czarist rule. During the subsequent civil war between the Bolsheviks and the anti-Communist White Russians for control of Russia, Stalin was a political commissar in the Red Army. In 1924, in a power struggle after Lenin died, Stalin defeated the party's Trotskyites, who favored international revolution over Stalin's "Socialism in one country." By the time Churchill arrived in Moscow for their discussions, Stalin had controlled the party's apparatus for eighteen years and had trans-formed himself into the nation's indispensable leader.

The man Churchill met was a brusque, self-absorbed character with limited empathy for the suffering of his countrymen, but also an extraordinary talent for reading the public mood. One of the most ruthless and effective tyrants in history, he understood that he was driven by inner demons but took solace in the thought that most other successful political leaders were also troubled by personal conflicts that made them different from people who did not reach for control over their country's masses. In 1949, after hearing that James Forrestal, the former American secretary of defense, had committed suicide, Stalin described him as one of many "abnormal people" in public life.

There are, however, degrees and degrees of abnormality, and Stalin's pathology put him at the far end of the scale, alongside Hitler and other ruthless murderers with extraordinary power to act out their worst instincts. Stalin was a Marxist evangelist with a paranoid personality in a paranoid world. Intrigue, brutal repression, plots, and counterplots punctuated his years in power. The purges of the 1930s did little to relieve his suspicions and his drive to destroy his perceived enemies or anyone who failed him. This is not to suggest that Stalin couldn't be cunning and calculating, with a firm grip on reality, but these attributes are not consistently at odds with an untrusting mind. Stalin's distrust of almost everyone did not prevent him from taking forceful actions that gave him an enduring grip on power at home and in dealings abroad.

During a wartime visit to Moscow of France's Charles de Gaulle, Stalin, in a drunken scene that offended and horrified de Gaulle, toasted his comrades with banter that must have sent chills down their spines, singling out civil and military officials he promised to shoot or hang if they fell short in meeting their responsibilities. "That's the custom in our country!" he shouted. "Noticing the distaste on de Gaulle's face, Stalin chuckled: 'People call me a monster, but as you see, I make a joke of it. Maybe I'm not so horrible after all.' " De Gaulle knew it was no joke. It was common knowledge that it took more courage for Soviet forces to retreat and face extermination by "interceptor battalions" positioned behind Soviet lines than to advance against the Germans.

The three men who led the Allies through the fighting were at times as much competitors as collaborators. At their first meeting in Tehran in November 1943, Churchill passed a silver cigar case to his two colleagues with the inscription "To Winston: From his fellow conservatives, 1925." Not to be outdone, Roosevelt sent a silver cigarette case around the room inscribed, "To Franklin from his Harvard classmates, 1904." Refusing to be one-upped by the two "capitalists," Stalin offered them cigarettes from a case that had found its way from Budapest into his possession with the inscription "To Count Karoli: From his friends at the Jockey Club, 1910." Was this Stalin's way of telling his capitalist colleagues that he remained a good Communist, an advocate of redistributing wealth?

In his initial conversation with Stalin, in which Churchill explained the difficulties of crossing the English Channel in 1942, Stalin sat scowling and impatiently fidgeting as Churchill spoke; he came across as an angry scold. He doubted that he could take anything Churchill said at face value. Earlier in private, he had said, "I dislike and distrust the English. They are skillful and stubborn opponents. . . . If England is still ruling the world, it is due to the stupidity of other countries, which let themselves be bluffed."

Stalin chided Churchill by declaring that "a man who was not prepared to take risks could not win a war." But when Churchill described the air campaign they expected to mount against German cities in the coming months, Stalin brightened. And when the prime minister outlined the planned invasion of North Africa, as a prelude to a European attack in 1943, Stalin, the atheist, exclaimed, "May God prosper this undertaking."

By the next day, however, with news of continuing losses in the desperate fighting to save Stalingrad pouring in, Stalin had turned unpleasant again, upbraiding Churchill with an attack that described the British navy as having "turned tail and fled from the battle. The British are afraid of fighting," Stalin said, and urged Churchill not to see the Germans as "supermen." Churchill responded with a passionate defense of British courage, reminding Stalin that Britain had fought alone for over a year before Russia or America entered the war. Churchill also complained to Stalin that "there was no ring of comradeship" in Stalin's attitude, and predicted that "victory was certain provided we did not fall apart."

Stalin softened at Churchill's spirited defense of Anglo-American commitment to destroy Hitler. But to test Churchill's goodwill, he promised to share information with Churchill's military chiefs about Soviet military inventions and asked, "Should there not be something in return . . . an agreement to exchange information of inventions." Churchill promised to "give them everything without any bargaining," but offered no specifics.

Stalin was undoubtedly probing to see if Churchill would tell him anything about Anglo-American efforts to develop an atomic bomb. Soviet sympathizers in the Manhattan Project had already informed Stalin of the work going forward on the weapon. A truly farsighted understanding that such a weapon would principally be used to terrorize an enemy by decimating his population centers rather than on a battlefield, where it could equally destroy opposing forces, should have persuaded the president and prime minister to assure Stalin that they intended to eliminate such weapons after the war, as poison gas had been banned after World War I.

Churchill's failure to say anything deepened existing suspicions between the Allies. It is unlikely that even if Churchill and Roosevelt had taken Stalin into their confidence on the Manhattan Project, it would have disarmed his doubts about their future intentions toward Communist regimes. He would have suspected some trick on his allies' part. It was not just Stalin's personal and, more generally, Soviet paranoia that dominated their thinking. For Stalin and his collaborators, struggle and distrust were constants in their dealings with each other and the outside world. Still, a general word about Anglo-American hopes of developing a super bomb might have slightly eased some of the hidden tensions between them. It would not have required any commitment to share anything, since the A-bomb was nothing more than a hope at that point, but it could have softened some of the suspicions that the Western Allies were not as committed to destroying Hitler's Germany as Moscow was.

Churchill ended the meeting hopeful that he had convinced Stalin of the wisdom of a second front in North Africa. "It is my considered opinion," he cabled Roosevelt, "that in his heart so far as he has one Stalin knows that we are right." They "parted on most cordial and friendly terms," he also advised the president, and described himself as "definitely encouraged by my visit to Moscow. . . . Having made their protest," the Russians "are entirely friendly." He had every hope that there would be no "serious drifting apart."

In fact, he and Roosevelt were less than certain. Throughout the fall they were filled with anxiety that the convulsive struggle for Stalingrad in southern Russia might inflict a decisive defeat on the Soviets. Roosevelt promised to speed desperately needed supplies to the Soviet front as fast as possible and assured Stalin that America's highest priority was not an all-out assault against Japan but Hitler's defeat as a prelude to beating the Japanese. They also urged Stalin to meet them somewhere in Africa in January to reach "vital strategic decisions" or "to determine a common line of military strategy." Because they believed that a second front in Europe in 1943 was unlikely, or at best could be mounted in the fall on a limited scale, they wanted a face-to-face discussion in which they could ease Stalin's disappointment by promising other offensive action that might draw off German divisions from the Russian front.

But Stalin, who explained that the urgency of the current fighting compelled him to stay home, declined the suggestion. While he certainly had his hands full with the current all-out struggle for Stalingrad, he wanted no part of a meeting in which his two allies might try to talk him out of a cross-Channel attack in 1943. In two messages to Churchill on November 28 and December 6, and another to Roosevelt on December 14, he pressed for assurances that a large offensive in the West remained on board for the coming spring.

Russian doubts at the time about their allies expressed themselves in a widely circulated Soviet cartoon depicting "six fat British generals with names like 'Don't hurry' and 'General what if we get beaten.' " Churchill sat opposite them next to two bottles of whisky. Sir Archibald Clark Kerr, the British ambassador to Moscow, who was in London for conversations in mid-December, warned that a failure to open a second front in Europe in 1943 would sit very badly with Stalin and might join with other circumstances to lead him to make a separate peace with Hitler.

Churchill and Roosevelt decided to go ahead with a meeting without Stalin in Casablanca, Morocco's largest city, in North Africa. When the president told Churchill that he and Hopkins would travel under the code names Don Quixote and Sancho Panza, the prime minister teased, "How ever did you think of such an impenetrable disguise?" Churchill "traveled to the meeting in a blue R.A.F. uniform under the alias Air Commodore Frankland. 'Any fool can see that is an air commodore disguised as the Prime Minister,' " one of his companions joked. Roosevelt's journey by train to Miami and plane to Brazil, across the south Atlantic to British Gambia, and on to Casablanca took five days.

Despite his absence, Stalin cast a long shadow over the meeting, which went on for ten days between January 14 and 24, 1943. A decision to postpone a limited cross-Channel attack until fall, when sufficient U.S. troops and a larger complement of landing craft had become available, meant convincing the Soviets that an attack on Sicily and then Italy aimed at the collapse of Mussolini's Fascist government and a diversion of German forces to defend the Italian peninsula would be an appropriate strategy for the coming year. To make up for anticipated Soviet complaints, Churchill and Roosevelt agreed to give a high priority to doing "everything short of prohibitive cost" to supply Stalin's forces. With American military chiefs, however, warning that losses to convoys supplying Russia threatened to impede Anglo-American attacks on Sicily and across the Channel, Churchill declared his intention to tell Stalin "the facts" if the losses became "too great."

To soften the blow that a limited assault on Western Europe would not come until autumn, Roosevelt prodded Churchill into announcing their intention to aim at unconditional surrender by the three Axis powers. It was a way to assure Stalin that there would be no compromise peace with Hitler, Mussolini, or Japan's military rulers that would leave the Soviet Union vulnerable to future Axis aggression. Roosevelt was also concerned to blunt criticism in the United States and abroad over a decision to collaborate with Admiral Jean Darlan, the commander in chief of all Vichy forces, to head off French resistance to the U.S invasion of North Africa. In short, an arrangement with Darlan was a temporary expedient; potential arrangements with enemy leaders were out of the question.

A Churchill-Roosevelt message to Stalin summarizing the results of their deliberations put the best possible face on their plans for action in 1943. They emphasized the advantages they saw in additional Mediterranean operations, expanded bombing of Germany, and all-out efforts to meet Soviet needs for supplies that would bolster their struggle against the Nazis. As for crossing the Channel, they promised only to "prepare themselves to re-enter the Continent of Europe as soon as practicable."

Churchill had no doubt that the news would disappoint and enrage Stalin. He thought that nothing would satisfy Stalin short of placing fifty or sixty divisions in France before the summer of 1943. Churchill was right: In February and March, Stalin pressed for more substantive details on the extent and timing of an invasion. When Roosevelt explained that they were trying as hard as possible to prepare themselves for a cross-Channel assault in August, Stalin insisted that conditions on his front demanded an attack considerably before the summer. When Roosevelt would only promise to mount an invasion "at the earliest practicable date," Stalin gave stronger expression to his displeasure: He warned that Hitler was rehabilitating and reinforcing his armies for a spring and summer offensive in Russia; it is "essential for us that the blow from the West be no longer delayed. . . . I must give a most emphatic warning . . . in the interest of our common cause, of the grave danger with which further delay in opening a second front in France is fraught."

During April, with no new German offensive under way and Stalin thrown on the defensive by charges that his military had executed thousands of Polish officers captured during the Soviet occupation of eastern Poland in 1939, complaints about Allied hesitancy in saying when an invasion would occur temporarily disappeared. Public assertions that the Nazis had killed the Polish officers allowed Churchill and Roosevelt to mute the issue, but both had their doubts about the Soviet denials. Churchill said privately, "There is no use prowling round the three-year-old graves of Smolensk."

Roosevelt now tried to arrange what he described to Stalin as an "informal" meeting between the two of them without military staffs and just a few aides. He suggested that they meet on either the Russian or American side of the Bering Straits, which would make it easier to exclude Churchill and avoid a formal conference with "official agreements or declarations." He hoped that they could achieve an agreement on their military actions and the broad outlines of what their next step would be if there was "a crack-up in Germany next winter."

Roosevelt hoped to achieve a number of things by an informal meeting. He believed he could disarm Stalin's concerns about a second front by making clear that only tactical considerations stood in the way, and that these would be solved by the spring of the next year. Second, he wished to win Stalin's private commitment to join the war against Japan shortly after Germany's surrender. He saw this as vital in forcing a Japanese collapse before American troops might have to invade their home islands and risk large numbers of casualties.

Third, he hoped that Stalin and he could speak candidly about Russia's "postwar hopes and ambitions" in relation to the Balkan states, Finland, and Poland.

In addition to military strategy and postwar arrangements, Roosevelt believed that he could use a meeting to influence America's domestic outlook on postwar international affairs. He was understandably worried that the intense isolationist sentiments of the post-1918 years not govern national thinking after the current fighting ended. Nor did he believe that Wilsonian collective security was a realistic alternative. By the spring of 1943, however, Americans were already thinking about a brave new world that might emerge from the fighting. The popularity of *One World*, an April 1943 book by Wendell Willkie, FDR's Republican opponent in 1940, put Roosevelt on notice that internationalism in the United States was viewed as the fulfillment of Woodrow Wilson's dream of international peace through a new world organization.

The bedrock of this cooperation was harmonious relations among the United States, Russia, Britain, and China. Moreover, it envisioned a world in which other nations yearned to become just like the United States. As *Time* publisher Henry Luce announced, the coming decades would become an "American Century." For Roosevelt, who felt compelled to cater to public illusions if he were to prevent a return to isolationism, a meeting with Stalin could be advertised as a first step along the road to the sort of international harmony that Americans wanted to believe was the natural state of affairs between nations rather than the kind of power politics that had brought on the two world wars.

Despite initial receptivity to Roosevelt's proposal for a meeting, Stalin rejected the suggestion in May when Churchill and FDR informed him that they were now committed to a cross-Channel attack in the spring of 1944. Stalin threw back at them their repeated unfulfilled promises to attack in 1943. He said that the Soviet government could not reconcile itself to the Anglo-American indifference to Russia's needs in the war against their enemy. He ominously warned them that "this is not simply a matter of disappointment of the Soviet Government, but a matter of preservation of its confidence in the Allies." Rather than drawing the United States and Britain closer to the Soviets, the tribulations of the fighting were deepening the suspicions between them and making it less certain that friendship rather than prewar antagonisms would follow the common struggle against the Axis.

Although less important to Roosevelt and the American public in the war years, relations with France were also a source of concern. France's shocking capitulation to Germany after only two months of fighting in the spring of 1940 had soured Roosevelt on France's place in the pantheon of great powers. Although he had recognized France's Vichy government, which owed its existence to collaboration with Nazi Germany, Roosevelt considered that a policy of strict expediency. He hoped to use the connection to Marshal Henri Philippe Pétain's government as a way to keep the French fleet and its North African colonies out of German hands.

Roosevelt saw no significant place for a French representative in the postwar peace arrangements, even for General Charles de Gaulle, who had made himself the head of Free French forces in London by refusing to concede defeat. In spite of his status as an exiled general in a foreign capital with no army to command, de Gaulle exerted influence by his manner and determination. At six foot four, he towered over Churchill and Roosevelt, whose disability confined him to a sitting position.

A haughty aristocrat with a dismissive manner, whose personal style and unyielding defense of what he considered French interests offended the president, de Gaulle reciprocated what he saw as Roosevelt's small regard for France's future autonomy. "Behind his patrician mask of courtesy," de Gaulle wrote later, "Roosevelt regarded me without benevolence. [He] meant the peace to be an American peace, convinced that he must be the one to dictate its structure, that the states that had been overrun should be subject to his judgment, and that France in particular should recognize him as its savior and its arbiter." When they clashed at Casablanca over wartime arrangements for control of France's colonial territories and postwar leadership, Roosevelt saw de Gaulle as an unelected spokesman whose pretensions to power gave him an inflated sense of importance; in private, the president unflatteringly described de Gaulle as believing he was a cross between Joan of Arc and Clemenceau.

Like the problems with Stalin, however, all this was to be kept hidden for the sake of the war effort. Pressing de Gaulle to shake hands publicly with General Henri Giraud, a rival for French leadership, and issue a joint declaration, Roosevelt told de Gaulle, "In human affairs, the public needs a drama." De Gaulle did not dispute the president's observation: "We took care not to meet head on, realizing that the clash would lead to nothing and that for the sake of the future, we each had much to gain by getting along together." Yet however much Roosevelt wanted a show of unity, he had no intention of supporting de Gaulle's reach for power. On his return to Washington, Roosevelt told the American Society of Newspaper Editors that he had tricked de Gaulle into shaking hands with Giraud. "Look at the expression on de Gaulle's face!" he snidely told the editors about photos of the incident. France, the president asserted, would decide its postwar fate not by de Gaulle's dictates but by democratic means.

Churchill's dealings with de Gaulle were more cordial, but essentially reflected their respective national interests. He had no illusions about de Gaulle, as he told a secret session of the House of Commons in December 1942. He admired de Gaulle "because he stood up against the Men of Bordeaux [Vichy] and their base surrender at a time when all resisting will-power had quitted France." At the same time, however, Churchill complained that de Gaulle's actions during his visits to French colonial territories "left a trail of Anglophobia behind him." Churchill had no interest in facilitating de Gaulle's postwar control of France; like FDR, he wanted this left to the desires of the French people.

But Churchill admired de Gaulle's extraordinary independence and devotion to French interests. When Churchill threatened to cut him loose from British support if he did not reach an accommodation with Giraud, de Gaulle seemed unresponsive. He would not let on that he needed Churchill's support. He acted as if he were "Stalin, with 200 divisions behind his words. . . . England's grievous offence in de Gaulle's eyes," Churchill said, "is that she helped France. He cannot bear to think that she needed help. He will not relax his vigilance in guarding her honour for a single instant."

Churchill and Roosevelt were at odds, not over assuring a representative government for France after the war, but over the restoration of France's place in Europe and the world. Churchill envisioned a strong France as a bulwark against a resurgent Germany and an aggressive Soviet Union on the continent, and as a stabilizing international force in its renewed governance of its African and Asian colonies. Churchill believed that the dissolution of the French empire would represent a threat to Britain's imperial rule as well. And in November 1942, he famously declared, "I have not become the King's First Minister in order to preside over the liquidation of the British Empire."

Roosevelt, by contrast, hoped that the occupation and transformation of Germany and accommodations with Russia could reduce the need for French influence in Europe. Moreover, he favored a system of trusteeships for former French colonies that could head off anticolonial postwar struggles fueled by aspirations for national self-determination. His anticolonialism also masked an interest in temporarily projecting American sea and air power into former French territories such as Dakar in West Africa and Indochina as a way to assure U.S. national security and international stability.

Despite their differences over France's future, Churchill and Roosevelt agreed that managing relations with Russia formed their greatest wartime and potential postwar challenges. In the summer of 1943, after the defeat of Nazi forces at Stalingrad earlier in the year, the Soviets began a series of successful offensives against the Germans. Coupled with the conquest of Sicily and the collapse of Mussolini's government in July, which compelled the deployment of German divisions to Italy, this success eased Stalin's demands for an immediate second front. When he believed that Churchill and Roosevelt were excluding him from a say in armistice arrangements with Italy, however, he complained about being treated as "a passive third observer. I have to tell you," he wrote, "that it is impossible to tolerate such a situation." Although a full explanation of how they were demanding Italy's unconditional surrender satisfied Stalin, Churchill said privately, "Stalin is an unnatural man. There will be grave troubles."

Churchill particularly worried that a Soviet advance into the Balkans would doom those countries to Russian domination. Roosevelt was concerned as well about Soviet ambitions, and despite a determination to give highest priority to a cross-Channel attack, which he and Churchill now set for May 1944, he did not exclude the possibility of seizing upon German weakness in the Balkans to fill the vacuum with British and U.S. forces. The key Roosevelt saw to disarming Stalin's suspicions of his allies and his plans for Soviet control of occupied countries to his west was face-to-face meetings. These became presidential priorities in the last months of the European fighting.

FROM TEHRAN TO
ROOSEVELT'S DEATH

Wars teach us not to love our enemies, but to hate our allies.
—W. L. George, English novelist

By September 1943, Roosevelt was more eager than ever to meet with Stalin. He hoped to convince Stalin not to annex the Baltic states of Estonia, Latvia, and Lithuania or to arbitrarily seize territory that could undermine postwar relations with the West. With a promise now from his allies that the European invasion was only eight or nine months off and Soviet forces moving toward defeat of German armies in Russia and eventual control of Eastern Europe, Stalin agreed to meet in Iran in November or December.

The meeting from November 28 to December 1 in Tehran was notable both for agreements on immediate military plans and for conflicts over postwar arrangements for Poland and the Baltic states and a new world league muted by wartime exigencies.

During four days of discussion, Stalin's unremitting pressure for confirmation of a second front in Europe won Roosevelt's enthusiastic and Churchill's grudging approval. The prime minister wanted to keep open the possibility that Anglo-American forces in the Mediterranean might seize upon Nazi weakness in the Balkans to help Yugoslav partisans led by Josip Broz Tito holding down twenty-one German divisions. But Stalin saw it as a potential diversion from the invasion of France, which he continued to see as vital to his fighting front, where Soviet forces had still not driven German armies out of Russia. Churchill suspected that Stalin's motives were as much political as military: Stalin did not want Allied armies in southeastern Europe, where they could interfere with his plans for expanded Soviet influence.

Stalin also elicited tacit agreement to new Polish borders that expanded Russia's western frontier and compensated Poland with additions of East German territory. Out of deference to FDR, who had to face Polish American voters in 1944, the details of such a settlement were left for a later date. Stalin promised to enter the fighting against Japan within three months after Germany surrendered and deferred to Roosevelt's insistence on establishing a world organization rather than regional committees policing their spheres, as Churchill and Stalin preferred.

Churchill, who had the weakest hand to play at the conference, fretted over the potential conflicts he saw emerging between the Allies. At the end of the first day's discussions, he candidly told Roosevelt and Stalin "that, although we were all great friends, it would be idle for us to delude ourselves that we saw eye to eye on all matters." When Churchill said, "I believe that God is on our side," Stalin countered, "And the devil is on my side. Because, of course, everyone knows that the devil is a Communist—and God, no doubt, is a good Conservative."

The conversations left Churchill morose: there might "be a more bloody war in the future," he told Lord Moran, his physician. "I shall not be there. I want to sleep for billions of years." He saw "impending catastrophe. . . . I believe that man might destroy man and wipe out civilization. Europe would be desolate and I may be held responsible."

Churchill was wisely skeptical of Stalin's long-term goodwill. Stalin had come to the conference full of suspicions about his allies. To refute Nazi propaganda that he planned to bolshevize all of Europe and ease Allied doubts about his postwar intentions, he had dissolved the

Communist International, or Comintern, in May 1943. Moreover, in September he had ended his government's antireligion policy, allowing churches and seminaries to reopen, citizens to attend religious services, and the Russian Orthodox Church to publish a journal.

Stalin flew to the conference filled with apprehension about potential rivals for power in the Soviet Union. Never hesitant to exile or eliminate anyone he saw as a threat to his control, Stalin understandably saw every Soviet power broker as harboring secret plans to replace him. Never having flown before, he feared a plot to sabotage his plane. At the last minute, he insisted on switching from his aircraft to one assigned to several of his associates.

At the start of the conference, Stalin urged Roosevelt to stay at the Soviet embassy in Tehran, where he was housed, claiming that Nazi assassins hoped to ambush the president as he traveled back and forth between the U.S. and Soviet compounds. When Roosevelt, who hoped to disarm Stalin's suspicions, accepted the invitation, Stalin arranged to put listening devices in his rooms. Each morning Stalin would get a briefing from his spies, and he marveled at Roosevelt's naive "private" discussions. Stalin wondered if Roosevelt knew he was being bugged and was putting on a show for Stalin's benefit. There is no evidence that Roosevelt had such suspicions, but it's entirely possible that he purposely spoke glowingly of Stalin in the belief that his Soviet host was monitoring his conversations.

No detail was too small for Stalin in his quest for an advantage over his allies: he rehearsed his conversations with associates, even planning where and with whom he would sit during the formal discussions and social gatherings.

Stalin worked hard to hide his true feelings about his allies. He had "a very captivating manner" when he chose to use it, Churchill said. To ingratiate himself, Stalin verbally abused some of his associates, suggesting that they were the architects of unsuccessful policies: "Come here, Molotov," he shouted at his foreign secretary before the president and prime minister, "and tell us about your pact with Hitler."

During a Soviet banquet, Stalin proposed that fifty thousand German officers be executed. Churchill strongly objected, saying that such an action would offend the British sense of justice. "The British Parliament and public will never tolerate mass executions. . . . The Soviets must be under no delusion on this point." To lighten the moment, Roosevelt joked that perhaps they could compromise on forty-nine thousand. When Roosevelt's son Elliott, who had accompanied his father to the conference, declared, "Wouldn't the fifty thousand fall in battle anyway?" and clinked glasses with Stalin, Churchill exploded, exclaiming, "How dare you," and, jumping to his feet, headed out of the room. Stalin and Molotov followed him and, clapping hands on his shoulders from behind, stood "grinning broadly, and eagerly explaining that they were only playing, and that nothing of a serious character had entered their heads."

Although Churchill was not "fully convinced that . . . there was no serious intent lurking behind," he returned to the dinner. He undoubtedly could not forget the thousands of Polish officers who had been executed in the Katyn Forest, or Stalin's revelation to him that he had ordered the shooting of captured working-class German soldiers who, when asked why they had fought for Hitler, said "they were executing orders." It was later that evening that Churchill conveyed his anguished picture of the future to Lord Moran.

Roosevelt left the meetings with a greater sense of hope, though less than confident that the future would see continuing good relations with Moscow. Eager to tamp down Stalin's doubts about his allies' ultimate goodwill, Roosevelt refused to hold private conversations with Churchill that might arouse Stalin's suspicions of Anglo-American cooperation aimed against him. At every chance, he teased Churchill in front of Stalin as a way to suggest some distance between them. At a minimum, out of a concern to convince Americans that the future promised postwar Soviet-American harmony and a world receptive to an international role for the United States, Roosevelt told his secretary of labor, Frances Perkins, in the expectation that their discussion would leak to the press, that he and Stalin got along so well he called him "Uncle Joe." Stalin "came over and shook my hand. From that time on our relations were personal. . . . The ice was broken and we talked like men and brothers."

Roosevelt urged Stalin, for the sake of American public opinion, to give the Baltic states of Latvia, Lithuania, and Estonia a say in their postwar governance. He "jokingly" assured Stalin that he had no intention of going to war with the Soviet Union over Baltic self-determination, but explained that it would be a significant issue in the United States and that it would help him "personally" if Stalin at least made some reference to future elections expressing the will of the Baltic peoples.

In a radio talk to the nation after returning from Tehran, the president expressed confidence that a Wilsonian world of self-determination and peaceful cooperation would emerge from the war. As for Stalin, he "got along fine with Marshal Stalin. . . . I believe that we are going to get along very well with him and the Russian people—very well indeed."

At a press conference, when a reporter asked for the president's personal impressions of Stalin, he replied, "We had many excellent talks," and predicted "excellent relations in the future." When another journalist asked what type of man Stalin was, Roosevelt answered, "I would call him something like me . . . a realist."

Privately, Roosevelt was more skeptical. After they left Tehran, the president expressed doubts to Churchill about Stalin's promise to declare war on Japan, and said it was a "ticklish" business keeping the "Russians cozy with us." He called Soviet entrance into the fighting against Japan a matter of "nip and tuck." As for Stalin's commitment to a postwar world organization, Roosevelt told a senator that the Soviets shared Churchill's affinity for a regional system of collective security. "I'll have to work on both of them," he said. Excessive American idealism or overdrawn ideas about a perfect world free of power politics worried FDR. The issue, he told his undersecretary of state, was "not whether the United States could make the world safe for democracy, but whether democracy could make the world safe from another war."

For Roosevelt, an essential requirement of postwar peace was America's readiness to replace outdated isolationism with sustained involvements abroad. Achieving this goal was his highest priority. He believed that an economic safety net would be the country's greatest concern, and he spoke to this fear in his January 1944 State of the Union message. He proposed an economic bill of rights that would guarantee everyone an education, a decent paying job, good housing, and adequate medical care. He saw U.S. internationalism and domestic economic security as the fulfillment of his foreign policy and domestic agendas. And this would mean running for yet another term. He was reluctant to do it. But having already broken the two-term tradition, he rationalized seeking another four years as less of a break with the past.

A greater deterrent was his health. Although he was only 62 at the end of January, he was feeling the strains of eleven years as a crisis president and the consequences of twenty years of physical immobility caused by his paralysis. Continually tired by 1944, he also gave those closest to him pause by his gray appearance, hand and head tremors, and occasional periods of lost concentration. An examination at the Bethesda Naval Hospital showed disturbing evidence of the president's physical deterioration—high blood pressure, an enlarged heart and indications of cardiac failure. The president's obvious reluctance to be told anything about his condition persuaded his doctors to keep their concerns to themselves. Moreover, they believed that a regimen of less work, more exercise in a swimming pool, fewer cigarettes than his habitual pack a day, a low-salt, reduced calorie diet, and regular doses of digitalis could slow his deterioration and keep him in sufficiently good shape for another presidential term.

Roosevelt dropped hints to people close to him that he was aware of his medical problems, and closely followed his doctors' orders. He shared the belief with Democratic Party leaders that if he did not run, the Republicans were likely to take back the White House and reverse at least part of his New Deal and possibly return the country to isolationism. Although the eventual Republican nominee, Governor Thomas E. Dewey of New York, avowed a commitment to internationalism, he was a recent convert from isolationism; and Roosevelt did not trust that as president he would lead the United States into the United Nations. FDR told one of his sons that he was determined "to maintain a continuity of command in a time of crisis"—not only to assure the unconditional surrender of Germany and Japan, but also to guarantee that the United States would take a place in the new world organization to preserve the peace.

Despite his health problems, Roosevelt managed to stay on top of events during 1944, including the D-day invasion in June, conferences with Churchill at Quebec and Hyde Park in September, and his fourth election to the White House in November. The demands of these developments took an additional toll on his health, as did his worries over worsening relations with Moscow. As Soviet armies advanced into Eastern Europe and victory over Germany became more likely, Stalin grew less cooperative. In August, he refused to allow British or American air forces hoping to drop supplies to the Polish underground fighting German forces in Warsaw to land on Soviet airfields. It was clear to Churchill and Roosevelt that Stalin, who denounced the Polish fighters as "a group of criminals," wanted no part in helping a Polish force that might resist Soviet control of their country. As Stalin's armies waited on the Vistula, Hitler's troops decimated the Polish underground fighting them in Warsaw.

In September, warnings from U.S. ambassador Averell Harriman in Moscow that the Soviets "have held up our requests with complete indifference to our interests and have shown an unwillingness even to discuss pressing problems" troubled Roosevelt. He shared Harriman's belief that the Soviets were inclined to act as "a world bully wherever their interests are involved." Stalin's insistence on making all sixteen

Soviet republics members of the United Nations and giving each of the six members of a security council an all-inclusive veto particularly upset Roosevelt. It was small wonder that he and Churchill reaffirmed their decision to withhold information about the atomic bomb from Stalin. Although doubts about permanently preventing Soviet acquisition of a bomb may have given them some pause, it seemed most prudent to keep at least some temporary advantage over Moscow that might help inhibit their postwar imperial ambitions. Still, for the sake of domestic opinion and out of hope that he might yet advance cooperation with the Soviets, Roosevelt looked forward to sitting down again with Stalin at another conference early in 1945.

After Tehran, Churchill also worried about future relations with Moscow. As he traveled back to England, he put the best possible face on Russian occupation of the Baltic countries and Eastern Europe as their armies drove back the Germans. He told Eden that Moscow's "tremendous victories . . . deep-seated changes . . . in the Russian State and Government [and] the new confidence which has grown in our hearts toward Stalin" made him more receptive to accommodation with Soviet territorial ambitions. But "most of all is the fact that the Russians may very soon be in physical possession of these territories, and it is absolutely certain that we should never attempt to turn them out." While the Soviet victories had "very largely settled" the fate of the Baltic states, Churchill saw room to negotiate an honorable settlement for Poland.

At the same time, however, he wanted no public acknowledgment of Soviet control of Estonia, Latvia, or Lithuania or discussions about Poland: it "might have disastrous effects in the United States in the election year, and there is no doubt that we should ourselves be subject to embarrassing attacks in the House of Commons if we decided the fate of the countries." Churchill's public line was that Stalin had abandoned the Comintern or Soviet encouragement of communism abroad and now was to be treated as a trusted ally.

In conversations with Polish exile leaders in London, Churchill and Eden quoted Stalin as promising Poland freedom from Soviet interference in a choice of government. Yet Churchill reflected his real view of Soviet intentions toward Poland when he privately urged increased matériel for Polish forces: "Now that the Russians were advancing into Poland," he said on February 3, 1944, "it was in our interest that Poland should be strong and well-supported. Were she weak and overrun by the advancing Soviet armies, the result might hold great dangers in the future for the English speaking peoples." In March, when he found it impossible to work out an accommodation between the Polish exile government in London and Stalin, Churchill privately said that he would like to tell the Russians that "I fight tyranny whatever uniform it wears or slogan it utters." In a glum mood, he told his intimates, "We live in a world of wolves—and bears."

During the rest of 1944, he remained on edge about Soviet intentions in eastern and southeastern Europe, where their armies were taking control. His trip to Moscow in October principally aimed to work out accommodations over the Balkan countries and Poland. He was greatly concerned that civil wars might break out in the Balkans, and he wrote Roosevelt, "Probably you and I would be in sympathy with one side and U J with the other." Despite the percentages agreement for the Balkans, much back-and-forth with Stalin and the London Poles over Poland's future boundaries, and a "most friendly" atmosphere during the Moscow conversations, Churchill still saw "many vexatious points to settle" and felt "powerless in the face of Russia."

For Stalin, 1944 was much less troublesome than for Roosevelt or Churchill. The year was notable for battlefield victories that lifted a siege around Leningrad, cleared the Crimea of German forces, recaptured most of the Baltic states, put Soviet armies on the outskirts of Warsaw, ousted Germany from Bulgaria and Rumania, and opened the way to the conquest of Hungary, Czechoslovakia, and east Prussia.

The victories increased Stalin's absolute control of the Soviet Union and made him less concerned about offending his allies. At home, he ruthlessly approved the relocation of 1.5 million ethnic minorities— the national aspirations of the Armenians, the Balkars, the Bulgarians, the Chechens, the Crimeans, the Ingush, the Kalmucks, and the Tatars, which had been encouraged during the earlier fighting to compete with German promises of independence, were now ruthlessly repressed as a danger to Soviet unity. About half a million of the ethnics sent to the east died in transport or the prison camps, where they lived in misery. Lavrenty Beria, the head of Stalin's secret police and a principal facilitator of the ethnic cleansing, was known to have said, "When you stop murdering people by the millions, they start to get notions." The killing and repression of these minorities stifled any hope they had for self-determination.

Whatever the appearance of agreement with Churchill and Roosevelt on the Balkans and Poland, Stalin had no intention of conceding anything that might jeopardize Soviet interests. He wouldn't, for example, give in to Allied pressure for his armies to battle their way into Warsaw and save Polish resistance fighters, who, Stalin believed, could become the leaders of an anti-Soviet government. The Poles perished in the streets and sewers of the city, where they were overwhelmed by superior Nazi arms.

Reluctance, however, to do anything that might jeopardize the D-day invasion in June set limits on Soviet differences with their allies. Nor did Moscow wish to clash openly with London and Washington about Eastern Europe and discourage hopes that Stalin would be deferential to British and American pressure for self-determination. Stalin also worried that open tensions might jeopardize a multibillion-dollar reconstruction loan he hoped to receive from the United States. During the Moscow talks in October 1944 with Churchill and Eden, Stalin had gone out of his way to create a cooperative atmosphere that left Churchill believing that they might achieve realistic accommodations and a future without conflict between the Allies.

All three leaders agreed at the end of 1944 on the need for another personal meeting that could address immediate designs for ending the war against Japan and postwar questions: issues about an international peacekeeping organization, the occupation of Germany, and the governance of southeastern and Eastern European countries, especially Poland, remained unsettled.

Churchill confronted the closing months of the fighting with mixed feelings. He saw Stalin as gratifyingly restrained about a Communist uprising in Greece and as reluctant to become a party to any quarrel over Yugoslavia. Stalin's agreement to a mid-January 1945 offensive in the East to help relieve pressure on Allied armies fighting the Battle of the Bulge in Belgium also pleased Churchill. He told the House of Commons on November 29, 1944, "The 'united powers of the Grand Alliance' were never more closely and intimately and comprehensively united than they are at this time."

To accommodate Stalin, who said his health would not allow him to leave his country, the seventy-year-old Churchill and the increasingly ill Roosevelt agreed to meet in Yalta on the Black Sea in the Crimea, a more-than-six-thousand-mile journey by sea and air for the frail president. Their agreement to the arduous journey was a demonstration of their regard for the sacrifices the Soviets had made in the fighting and of their eagerness to disarm Stalin's suspicions that if he traveled outside the Soviet Union, he would be at some kind of disadvantage in conference discussions. What this would be, no one could say, but it would certainly make it more difficult to ensure his personal safety, which he believed was constantly in jeopardy. Yet whatever Stalin's motives, it was a measure of the Churchill-Roosevelt determination in the closing months of the fighting to sustain good relations with Stalin that they were willing to suffer the inconvenience of so long a trip.

Churchill told Hopkins that ten years of research could not have unearthed a worse place to meet. Retreating German troops had turned Yalta, Sevastopol, and the whole of the Crimea into a wasteland. Sarah Churchill, Winston's daughter, who accompanied him to Yalta, wrote her mother that Sevastopol had "not a house in view standing or unbroken." When Roosevelt saw the devastation wrought by the Germans, he told Stalin that he hoped he would propose another toast to the execution of fifty thousand German army officers. Churchill hoped to ward off the lice and typhus infecting the Crimea by bringing "an adequate supply of whiskey" with him. He described Yalta as "The Riviera of Hades."

Fears of postwar problems shadowed Churchill's optimism. He cautioned Roosevelt against removing U.S. troops from Europe too rapidly after the fighting: with no French army to fill the vacuum, he wondered, "How will it be possible to hold down Western Germany beyond the present Russian occupation line?" He foresaw a rapid disintegration, as after 1919. He fretted over likely parliamentary resistance to the financial burdens of a postwar army that could contain Russian ambitions in Europe. He was cast down by Soviet obstinacy on Poland and the prospect of a powerful Soviet military presence in Central Europe.

In January 1945, he privately despaired of this "new, disgusting year." He told Roosevelt that the upcoming Yalta meeting "may well be a fateful Conference, coming at a moment when the Great Allies are so divided and the shadow of the war lengthens out before us. At the present time," he wrote on January 8, "I think the end of this war may well prove to be more disappointing than was the last."

Roosevelt shared Churchill's concerns. He also doubted that Stalin would relinquish his control over Eastern Europe. His stubborn insistence on meeting at Yalta impressed the president as an indication of how unbending Stalin would be in the talks. In a conversation with his secretary of war, Henry Stimson, in December, Roosevelt said that "Stalin had taken Britain's desire to have a cordon sanitaire of friendly nations around it in past years as an excuse now . . . to have Czechoslovakia, Poland, and other nations whom it could control around it." Stimson agreed and doubted the wisdom of sharing information about the atomic bomb with Stalin. He considered it "essential not to take them [the Soviets] into our confidence until we were sure to get a real quid pro quo from our frankness." Roosevelt "thought he agreed."

When he discussed postwar Europe with a bipartisan group of U.S. senators before departing for Yalta, Roosevelt said that spheres of influence were a reality that he had no current hope of abolishing. The "idea kept coming up," he explained, "because the occupying forces had the power in the areas where their arms were present and each knew that the other could not force things to an issue. He stated that the Russians had the power in Eastern Europe, that it was obviously impossible to have a break with them and that, therefore, the only practicable course was to use what influence we had to ameliorate the situation."

At the same time, Roosevelt told Harriman, who was on home leave from Moscow, that "he wanted to have a lot to say about the settlement in the Pacific, but that he considered the European questions were so impossible that he wanted to stay out of them as far as practicable except for problems involving Germany." When Arthur Bliss Lane, former U.S. ambassador to Warsaw, pressed him to insist on Polish independence in talks with Stalin, Roosevelt flared, "Do you want me to go to war with Russia?"

Harriman wrote, after another discussion with Roosevelt, that the president "consistently shows very little interest in Eastern European matters except as they affect sentiment in America." With U.S. public opinion turning negative toward Britain over interventions in Greek and Italian affairs that registered as blatant demonstrations of traditional sphere-of-influence diplomacy, and toward Russia for its unyielding determination to impose a Communist regime on Poland, Roosevelt was fearful of reviving isolationist sentiment. The *New York Times*, apparently relying on a leak from the White House, reported that the president had sent Churchill a message in January saying that "the American people are in a mood where the actions of their allies can precipitate them into wholehearted cooperation for the maintenance of the peace of Europe or bring about a wave of dis-illusionment which will make the isolation of the nineteen-twenties pale by comparison." The country was unhappy with its allies for practicing power politics.

The Big Three convened at Yalta on February 4. Two days earlier, however, Churchill and Roosevelt met on Malta in the Mediterranean. The president no longer resisted meeting Churchill without Stalin, hoping no doubt to send the Soviets a signal that Britain and America might gang up on them if they proved too unyielding in the upcoming talks. With U.S. forces just recovering from setbacks in the Battle of the Bulge in Belgium, and Soviet troops approaching Berlin, the Russians had an advantage that the president and prime minister thought they might counter with a meeting that could arouse Stalin's concerns about their intentions.

Roosevelt and Churchill had three discussions during their day on Malta—a social get-together over lunch, a conference with their military chiefs in the evening, and a dinner meeting about future political problems. Although Roosevelt's appearance shocked the British—it seemed to one observer that the president was so frail that "he is hardly in this world at all"—he nevertheless was fully in command of himself and alert to the proceedings.

Churchill set the tone when he said at the evening meeting that "it was essential that we should occupy as much of Austria as possible, as it was undesirable that more of western Europe than necessary should be occupied by the Russians." Roosevelt had no objection. Churchill wrote his wife, "The misery of the world appalls me and I fear increasingly that new struggles may arise out of those we are successfully ending." At the same time, however, the president did not wish to make political commitments that might create unnecessary tensions with the Russians. Consequently, nothing of political importance was discussed over lunch or dinner. It frustrated Eden, who complained to a diary that "we were going into a decisive conference and had so far neither agreed what we would discuss nor how to handle matters with a Bear who would certainly know his mind."

The Yalta conference, which lasted a week—February 4 to 11—is the most overrated event of World War II. While every major issue—from Germany's occupation, to Soviet entrance into the Pacific War, to Poland's autonomy, to the organization of a United Nations—was considered, the impact of these discussions was much less than the participants believed or perhaps hoped at the time. "We really believed in our hearts that this was the dawn of the new day we had all been praying for," Harry Hopkins said later. Roosevelt had some hope that accommodations with Stalin would lead him to grant the East European countries his armies were occupying a substantial measure of domestic autonomy if they adopted a pro-Soviet foreign policy. Similarly, Churchill recalled that at the first plenary session of the conference at 5:00 p.m. on February 4, "We had the world at our feet. Twenty-five million men marching at our orders by land and sea. We seemed to be friends."

In an appearance before a joint congressional session on March 1, Roosevelt declared the meeting to have been a great success. But its final result, he said in a plea for an end to isolationism, would depend on the Congress and the American people: "lasting results" would require "active support" from both for "the general conclusions reached at Yalta." The conference, he declared, "ought to spell the end of the system of unilateral action, the exclusive alliances, the spheres of influence, the balance of power, and all the other expedients that have been tried for centuries—and have always failed. We propose to substitute for all these, a universal organization in which all peace-loving Nations will finally have a chance to join." The results of the conference represented "the beginnings of a permanent structure of peace."

Roosevelt's optimism might be attributed to his debilitated condition, which made him unrealistic about what the conference had achieved. There is no doubt that he was not at his best during the discussions, and that he was dying by the time he returned to the United States. He had a limited attention span during the talks and, according to one British observer, "does not know what he is talking about and clings to one idea."

During an address to a joint congressional session, his appearance and spoken delivery shocked members of Congress, who had not seen him for a while: he uncharacteristically delivered his speech sitting down, making a unique reference to his disability and his weariness from a journey of fourteen thousand miles. "He spoke haltingly, slurring some of his words and stumbling over part of his text; his right hand trembled, and he awkwardly turned the pages of his speech with his left hand."

Yet however much his weakened condition limited his conference interactions, Roosevelt's preoccupation during the conference and his public pronouncements afterward were calculated to encourage American internationalism he believed essential to the future peace. He was not very confident that the Yalta agreements represented the potential shift in world affairs he described. When he saw Assistant Secretary of State Adolf Berle Jr., who had great doubts about Stalin's intentions, the president threw his arms up and declared, "I didn't say the result was good. I said it was the best I could do." He explained that because the Soviets had their armies in Eastern Europe, the Allies had no recourse but to rely on Stalin's promise to hold free elections in the liberated countries. As he worked on his congressional address, he told Sam Rosenman, his speechwriter, that he doubted whether Stalin would follow through on this commitment. His continuing silence at the conference about the development of an atomic bomb was another indication of the limits of Roosevelt's trust in future Soviet actions.

For Churchill, the conference was a series of high and low notes. He and his staff were amazed and impressed with the degree to which the Soviets managed to provide for all their creature comforts in so devastated an area. On arrival, they were greeted with a "most magnificent luncheon . . . champagne, caviar, every luxury." Churchill's daughter, Sarah, wrote her mother, "Whatever material difficulties of this place our paws are well buttered here. Wow." Churchill said of the palaces in which he and Roosevelt were housed, "We squat on furniture carried with extraordinary effort from Moscow and with plumbing and road-making done regardless of cost in a few days by our hosts, whose prodigality excels belief."

Churchill was certainly gratified by Stalin's agreement to a Polish coalition government and free elections for liberated East European countries, British and American demands for a French occupation zone, and a seat on the Allied Control Council for Germany, and to a less dominant Soviet role in a United Nations organization. On the seventh and last day of the conference at a dinner at his residence, Churchill offered a toast that one of his associates described as "insincere, slimy sort of slush." He referred to "a time when the Marshal was not so kindly to us, and I . . . said a few rude things about him, but our common dangers and common loyalties have wiped all that out. We feel we have a friend whom we can trust, and I hope he will continue to feel the same about us."

At the same time, however, like Roosevelt, Churchill was less than confident that alliance arrangements would endure. Midway through the conference, at a dinner hosted by Stalin, Churchill prophetically urged his two allies not to "under-estimate the difficulties. Nations, comrades in arms, have in the past drifted apart within five or ten years of war. Thus toiling millions have followed a vicious circle, falling into the pit, and then raising themselves up again. We now have a chance of avoiding the errors of previous generations and of making a sure peace." Yet, at the end of the day, he believed that "the only bond of the victors is their common hate," which he feared would disappear once Germany was defeated.

For Stalin, the conference was an opportunity to lull his allies into believing that he shared their concern with establishing an ideal structure of peace as opposed to securing Russia from foreign and domestic dangers by his own devices. Because he had so much credit with the Allies for having borne the principal burdens of the fighting against Germany and because the Americans were so eager for him to enter the war against Japan, he could assert Soviet demands up to a point over Poland and Eastern Europe without overtaxing the support of his allies. Stalin's need, however, for a postwar U.S. loan and his understanding that Washington and London would have atomic bombs before Moscow did made him cautious about antagonizing them.

Neither Stalin's interest in a loan nor his concerns about the A-bomb were great enough to make him trust his country's future security to a world organization, or to the goodwill of any other country. He liked Roosevelt and appreciated his apparent regard for him and the sacrifices of the Soviet nation. But he could not imagine giving the United States or Britain a determining say in how the Soviet Union would protect its future safety from another devastating attack on its homeland.

However much the United States and Britain had contributed to Soviet military success against the Nazis with supply shipments, day and night bombing of Germany, and what Stalin saw as the peripheral offensives in North Africa and Italy and the "belated" cross-Channel attack, he believed—and with some substantial justification—that the Red Army and Soviet citizens, at a cost of some 25 million lives, were the ones that had "torn the guts out of Hitler's war machine." In short, Soviet Russia could only survive if it looked to its own interests rather than depending on the generosity of any outside forces.

There was a substantial measure of rational calculation here for the leader of a nation that had suffered so terribly in the war. But Stalin's resistance to an enduring accommodation with the West also rested in significant part on fears bred by the history of Soviet Russia under his rule. His life experience and understanding of political power made him distrustful of anyone he did not control. For Stalin, power rested in intimidation and dominance. As demonstrated by his brutal repression of anyone representing the slightest challenge to his authority, he could not live with anything resembling political pluralism. Democracy, a word he used frequently in his discussions with foreign visitors, meant not representative government but the well-being of the masses as determined by him and him alone.

The Soviet prisoners of war, for example, who had glimpsed the higher living standards of their captors, were potential critics of the Communist system; they represented a threat to the Soviet state, or so Stalin believed. True, some of them had collaborated and fought with the Nazis, but many had committed no greater crime than having been captured. This was enough, however, to send them into exile or confinement in a prison camp, where many of them perished.

It was de Gaulle who had the most clear-eyed view of Stalin. Not burdened with the responsibilities shouldered by Churchill and Roosevelt for postwar accommodations that could maintain world peace, de Gaulle had the detachment to take a more realistic measure of the Red Czar.

His meeting with Stalin in December 1944 left de Gaulle with "the impression of confronting the astute and implacable champion of a Russia exhausted by suffering and tyranny but afire with national ambition. Stalin was possessed by the will to power. Accustomed by a life of machination to disguise his features as well as his inmost soul, to dispense with illusions, pity, sincerity, to see in each man an obstacle or a threat, he was all strategy, suspicion and stubbornness. . . . As a communist disguised as a Marshal, a dictator preferring the tactics of guile, a conqueror with an affable smile, he was a past master of deception. But so fierce was his passion that it often gleamed through this armor, not without a kind of sinister charm." But beneath Stalin's "good-natured appearances, the fighter engaged in a merciless struggle was apparent." In the Soviet world, de Gaulle found an "abyss separating words from deeds."

In the two months following Yalta, the extent to which Stalin was set upon a course of external control in Eastern and Central Europe without regard for local self-determination became evident to Roosevelt and Churchill. Stalin's eagerness for safety from Germany in his reach for external dominance did not trouble them as much as his resolve to impose his will on Soviet-occupied areas, despite promises to the contrary. More troubling, it suggested a vision of greater Soviet ambition to control countries farther to the West by helping to elevate allied Communist parties. The hope that their shared sacrifices in defeating Germany would convince Stalin that they had no hostile intentions toward his government and that he would see pro-Soviet foreign policies by East European neighbors as sufficient to assure their domestic self-determination was a mirage.

By the end of March, Roosevelt bluntly told Stalin, "I cannot conceal from you the concern with which I view the development of events of mutual interest since our fruitful meeting at Yalta. The decisions we reached there were good ones. . . . We have no right to let them be disappointed." He complained of "a discouraging lack of progress made in carrying them out . . . particularly those relating to the Polish question." Stalin's decision not to send Foreign Secretary Molotov to a United Nations organizing conference in San Francisco scheduled for April also frustrated Roosevelt. He warned that if the agreements on Poland and a world organization were not implemented, "all the difficulties and dangers to Allied unity which we had so much in mind in reaching our decision at the Crimea will face us in an even more acute form."

At the same time, a Soviet-American clash over negotiations between German and U.S. representatives in Switzerland about the surrender of German forces in Italy intensified differences. Believing that the Germans hoped to free Allied armies in the west to limit Soviet advances in the east, Stalin upbraided Roosevelt for hiding the conversations from him, questioned the motives for holding them, and warned that they jeopardized "trust among the Allies." An astonished president angrily replied that there were no political designs in the Swiss discussions aimed at inhibiting Soviet advances in Germany. "Frankly," Roosevelt concluded, "I cannot avoid a feeling of bitter resentment toward your informers, whoever they are, for such vile misrepresentations of my actions or those of my trusted subordinates."

Churchill's distress at the rising tensions registered in a prediction to Roosevelt that "the brutality of the Russian messages" might "foreshadow some deep change of policy for which they are preparing." He believed it "of the highest importance that a firm and blunt stand should be made at this juncture by our two countries in order that the air may be cleared and they realize that there is a point beyond which we will not tolerate insult. . . . If they are ever convinced that we are afraid of them and can be bullied into submission, then indeed I should despair of our future relations with them and much else."

Roosevelt was in "general agreement" with Churchill's conclusion: "We must not permit anybody to entertain a false impression that we are afraid," he cabled on April 6. "Our Armies will in a very few days be in a position that will permit us to become 'tougher' than has heretofore appeared advantageous to the war effort." Five days later, after the tensions over the Swiss "negotiations" had faded away, Roosevelt struck a more optimistic note with Churchill. Ever hopeful that Stalin would liberate himself from his suspicions and accept his allies' sincere good intentions, Roosevelt urged patience: "I would minimize the general Soviet problem as much as possible because these problems, in one form or another, seem to arise every day and most of them straighten out as in the case of the Bern meeting. We must be firm, however, and our course thus far is correct."

Stalin would not reward Roosevelt's decent intentions with reduced suspicions of his allies or, as a consequence, any modification of his reach for Soviet control of adjacent or even distant countries. Nothing, apparently, could convince Stalin that the outside world was anything but a cauldron of current and potential enemies. It is probably impossible for someone as wedded to repressive brutality as he was to see anything but similar motives in others—whether at home or abroad.

While Churchill ultimately proved to be more realistic about what America and Britain faced in their future dealings with Moscow, Roosevelt's eagerness to give change a chance is not to be decried. After so vivid a demonstration of the human capacity for brutality, it was not unreasonable to hope that a leader and nation so victimized by wartime horrors would at least want to try, however tentatively, dealing more humanely with other nations and peoples. It was conceivable that most Germans and Japanese would see the end of the war and their failed experiments in ruthlessness as a chance for something new. Nor could Stalin have believed that Roosevelt and Churchill were ready to let either German or Japanese leaders off without retribution.

Stalin, however, couldn't accept that his allies meant what they said about postwar goodwill. He could not imagine a world without conflict: he believed that Hitler's anticommunism would outlive Germany's defeat and that his allies, who would soon revert to their prewar anti-Bolshevism, would find a new generation of German anti-Communists to strike against socialism. The coming era would not be a time for continued collaboration with the West but a new chapter in the struggle between capitalism and communism, which Stalin was preparing to meet by seizing all the advantages he could. Surely there is some basis to Stalin's expectations—neither Churchill nor Roosevelt nor many of their principal advisers took a strictly benign view of Stalin and the Soviets; they were all too ready to share Stalin's convictions about the inevitable incompatibility of their respective systems. Nevertheless, by refusing to entertain the possibility that more accommodating actions toward the West might result in long-term good relations, Stalin helped plunge the world back into a new round of tensions and conflict that risked even greater devastation than suffered during World War II.

On April 12, the day after his last message to Churchill, Roosevelt died suddenly at his retreat in Warm Springs, Georgia. The president's death stunned and pained both Churchill and Stalin. "I am much weakened in every way by his loss," Churchill told an aide. He wrote Eleanor Roosevelt that he had "lost a dear and cherished friendship which was forged in the fire of war." To Harry Hopkins, he said, "We have lost one of our greatest friends and one of our most valiant champions of the causes for which we fight. I feel a very painful personal loss quite apart from the ties of public action which bound us so closely together. I had a true affection for Franklin."

"Stalin's fondness for Roosevelt was as genuine a diplomatic friendship as he ever managed with any imperialist," Stalin's biographer writes. When Stalin paid his respects to Harriman, he was "deeply distressed" and held Harriman's hand for thirty seconds. He later described Roosevelt in private as "a great statesman, a clever, educated, far-sighted and liberal leader who prolonged the life of capitalism."

In the larger scheme of things, Stalin's regard for the president was of small consequence. Neither Roosevelt's nor Churchill's continuing presence on the scene was a deterrent to Stalin's determination to assure Russia's security and international power. Roosevelt's passing and the presence of a new president in whom Stalin had no trust only stiffened his resolve to advance Russia's might. A wartime need for each other gave the alliance a limited life. Once the Nazi danger disappeared, the innate differences between the Soviets and the West became a force that no political leader in Britain or the United States could overcome.

Stalin's suspicions of the ill will he believed foreign leaders harbored toward him, joined with nationalistic strivings for security from attack and ideological convictions about inevitable conflicts between capitalists and Communists, led him to reject Allied initiatives to promote long-term cooperation. Whatever the blunders of his Western partners in inflaming his distrust, it was Stalin, above all, who assured that the postwar world would continue its traditional rivalry among the great powers in what came to be called the Cold War.

COLLAPSE AND RENEWAL

I renounce war for its consequences, for the lies it lives on and propagates, for the undying hatred it arouses, for the dictatorships it puts in place of democracy, for the starvation that stalks after it.
— Harry Emerson Fosdick, liberal Baptist
minister of New York's Riverside Church

Roosevelt's death left Churchill and Stalin worried about dealing with Harry S. Truman, the new president they had never met and couldn't imagine being the equal of his predecessor.

Churchill thought it extraordinary that "Roosevelt had not made his deputy and potential successor thoroughly acquainted with the whole story and brought him into the decisions that were being taken. This proved of grave disadvantage to our affairs." Truman had to step "at a bound from a position where he has little information and less power into supreme authority. How could Mr. Truman know and weigh the issues at stake at this climax of the war?"

It was a telling point: Roosevelt met with Truman only twice during the eighty-two days of his fourth term, and their discussions were brief and perfunctory. Roosevelt apparently believed that his health problems would not cut short his life, or at least would not affect him before the war ended. Moreover, he didn't seem to think that Truman needed to know about the atomic bomb or postwar plans. This may have had less to do with Roosevelt's limited regard for his vice president than his own uncertainty about whether the bomb would be available or would even need to be used. Always the "chameleon on plaid," as Herbert Hoover called him in 1932, Roosevelt disliked planning too far ahead. Like Lincoln, who freely acknowledged that events shaped him more than he shaped them, Roosevelt may have said nothing about postwar plans because he had them on hold until time and circumstance dictated what they would be.

It may also have been that Roosevelt could not imagine dying and having Truman as his replacement. He should have remembered what he said in a speech on the eve of the 1932 presidential election: "There is no indispensable man." Telling Truman about the bomb and confiding his hopes for the postwar world would have cost Roosevelt little time or energy. But it ran counter to his typical dealings with political associates; taking others into his confidence was simply not what he did. When Secretary of the Interior Harold Ickes told FDR that he was the most difficult man he had ever worked with, Roosevelt asked, "Because I get too hard at times?" Ickes replied, "No"; it was because "you won't talk frankly even with people who are loyal to you. You keep your cards close up against your belly. You never put them on the table." And although this technique had served Roosevelt well throughout his career, it was a mistake to ignore the possibility that he might die and leave his vice president unprepared to deal with inevitable end-of-war problems.

Like Churchill, Stalin had great doubts about Roosevelt's successor and his preparation to deal with postwar challenges. Unlike Churchill, however, familiarity bred not regard but disdain. Stalin simply could not believe that Truman could measure up to his predecessor. After meeting the new president at Potsdam in July, Stalin said, "They couldn't be compared. Truman's neither educated nor clever."

It was easy to underestimate "the little man from Missouri," as critics described him. At five feet eight inches and 150 pounds, he was not an imposing figure. Poor eyesight—uncorrected vision of 20/50 in his right eye and 20/400 in his left eye, which made him close to blind without thick glasses—gave him an owl-like appearance and added to impressions of someone who had to grope his way through life. A double-breasted gray or blue suit with a neatly folded handkerchief in his breast pocket and a bow tie suggested, as his daughter Margaret said, a fellow who "had just stepped from a bandbox." He was an undeniably conventional midwestern sort: his dress, manner of speaking—the Missouri twang—Masonic ring, and outlook on the world were familiar to anyone who had grown up in any of the country's heartland towns or small cities.

The trajectory of Truman's life and political career deepened impressions of his ordinariness. His early years in Independence, Missouri, a suburb of Kansas City, where after high school, he worked as a bank clerk and then with his father on a family farm, gave no hint of his exceptional future. Service in World War I as a captain of artillery with a Missouri National Guard regiment added to views of him as a fine young man whose patriotism and conformity fit comfortably into the local elected offices he held in the ten years after 1924, including presiding judge of Jackson County, which made him the chief executive officer or mayor of Kansas City. His election to the U.S. Senate in 1934 seemed explicable not by any special personal attributes but by his ties to the corrupt Pendergast machine and by Roosevelt's popularity, which tipped numerous races to unimpressive Democratic candidates.

Truman's six years in the Senate and narrow reelection in 1940 seemed to confirm his standing as a relatively minor senator who would never rise higher. His amiability and loyalty to the party and the president made him one of the Senate's workhorses rather than one of its show horses like Louisiana's flamboyant Huey Long, whose ambition for higher office was an open secret.

In his second term, Truman's chairmanship of a subcommittee investigating waste and profiteering in the country's defense buildup projected him onto the national consciousness, including his appearance on the cover of *Time* on March 8, 1943, making him a potential vice presidential nominee in 1944. A division in the Democratic Party between liberal supporters of sitting vice president Henry Wallace, a man known for his eccentricities and hopes for world harmony, and southern conservatives favorable to South Carolina's Jimmy Byrnes, a former senator, Supreme Court associate justice, and war mobilization director, known as "Assistant President," opened the way to Truman's candidacy. Although he had no close ties to Roosevelt and was dismissively described as "the Second Missouri Compromise," Truman's uncontroversial party standing made him the ideal middle-ground alternative as FDR's running mate.

Truman's sudden elevation to the presidency left Americans at home and their allies abroad demoralized about the country's leadership at a time when so many crucial postwar issues faced the nation and the world. Because he was mindful of the universal doubts about his capacity to replace Franklin Roosevelt, Truman made every effort to indicate that he would be fulfilling FDR's designs.

Within hours after Roosevelt's death, Truman cabled Churchill that he intended to preserve the "solid relations which you and the late President had forged between our countries." He declared himself ready to address the "urgent problems requiring our immediate and joint consideration" and added: "I am, of course, familiar with the exchanges which you and President Roosevelt have had between yourselves and with Marshal Stalin. I also know what President Roosevelt had in mind as the next step." Of course he didn't know, or even know about the atomic bomb; nor did Secretary of State Edward Stettinius, who helped draft the cable, know any more than Truman. Truman's message was small comfort to Churchill.

Truman's assumption of power was even more disturbing to Stalin and the Soviets. They knew that two days after Hitler had attacked them in 1941, Truman had said publicly, "If we see that Germany is winning, we ought to help Russia, and if Russia is winning, we ought to help Germany, and that way let them kill as many as possible, although I don't want to see Hitler victorious under any circumstances. Neither of them think anything of their pledged word."

* * *

The only ones buoyed by the news of Roosevelt's death were Adolf Hitler and the Nazi leaders around him. When Joseph Goebbels, his propaganda minister, called to give him the news, Hitler excitedly told Albert Speer, his armaments minister, "Here, read this! Here . . . we have the great miracle that I always foretold. Who's right now? The war is not lost. Read it. Roosevelt is dead!" Hitler seemed to think that "the hand of Providence" had rescued him and Germany from defeat.

It was a characteristic expression of Hitler's distorted, grandiose thinking. Journalists, biographers, historians, and social psychologists have struggled to understand how so ruthless and ultimately destructive a man could have won and sustained a hold on as advanced a nation as Germany, with a history of artistic, scientific, and technological achievements the envy of any society. One would like to think that the events that brought Hitler to power and allowed him to drive his country and the world into such a disastrous war and led so many Germans to join him in the annihilation campaign against world Jewry were unique and could not reoccur. But given the conflicts and bloodletting that have followed World War II, the irrational passions that gave someone like Hitler so much power remain a cautionary tale the world does well to recall. His ruthlessness and ability to put this ruthlessness into action may be more of an object lesson than anyone would care to think.

Hitler's troubled childhood and early adult years, notable for a father who beat him, his failing grades in high school, which he quit at age sixteen, his rejection by Vienna's Academy of Fine Arts, his frustrated artistic ambitions, and his homelessness and residence in a poor workingmen's shelter in 1909–10 after his parents had died may partly explain his grandiosity, paranoia, and messianic obsessions—a thousand-year Reich, a world without Jews.

Hitler's exposure to anti-Semitic writings, including Martin Luther's *On the Jews and Their Lies*, his abrasive clashes with Jewish school cohorts in Linz, Austria, where he spent part of his adolescence, and the culture of Vienna, a hotbed of anti-Semitism where he moved in 1905, may have shaped his hatred of "international Jewry." But his rage passed the bounds of accepted anti-Semitic ideas. For Hitler, the fight against Jews represented an apocalyptic struggle to overcome a menace that he saw as a threat to not only Germany but the entire world.

None of the preludes in Hitler's formative years can fully explain his life story. Like Hitler, other young Germans suffered physical and psychological abuse and were also exposed to anti-Semitic or other ethnic and religious bigotry, but they did not become tyrants who single-mindedly devoted themselves to the destruction of Jewry and millions of others in a war to conquer Europe and become a memorable world figure. No one can confidently reconstruct the internal forces that made Hitler, Hitler. The search for the sources of his megalomania and a description of his personality seem useful primarily as a warning against future infatuations with leaders promising national salvation through emotionally appealing but rationally simplistic nostrums.

Nevertheless, it is difficult to imagine the seminal events of the 1930s and '40s without Hitler. He played a central role in the world in those two decades. But it is also essential to recall the national and international circumstances that opened the way to Hitler's extraordinary career in inflicting unprecedented suffering on Europe and much of the world. Germany's defeat in World War I made Hitler's nationalistic appeals and attacks on foreigners, including Jews, as the architects of the country's postwar disarray especially appealing. The economic collapse of the 1930s that deepened the anguish of millions of Germans provided Hitler with an additional opportunity to exploit public discontent with promises of national salvation through National Socialism.

The outbreak of World War I in 1914 gave Hitler a chance to experience the exhilaration of surviving combat and winning medals for heroism. It gave him credentials as well to enter German politics as a devoted patriot determined to restore Germany's power and honor after the humiliating surrender in 1918 that had reduced Germany's territorial holdings and required her to pay huge reparations to the victors for damages caused by the war. Although born in Austria and not receiving German citizenship until 1932, Hitler was the convert who was more German than the Germans.

After leaving the army in 1920, Hitler joined the German Workers' Party in Munich and became a leading figure in its ranks, changing the party's name to the National Socialist German Workers' Party and calling attention to himself and the party's platform with speeches denouncing the "November criminals," the republican politicians who "stabbed the army in the back" by agreeing to a degrading peace treaty, the Jews, Communists, Social Democrats, and anyone else supporting the Weimar Republic. In 1923, after a runaway inflation triggered by the printing of millions of reichsmarks to meet reparation payments imposed by the Versailles Treaty, Hitler led a failed coup against the Bavarian and Berlin governments that landed him in prison for eight months.

His brief imprisonment was a small price to pay for an action that won him a national reputation as a forceful nationalist. The appearance of his two-volume political testament *Mein Kampf,* written in 1924 when he was in prison and 1925 when he was barred from public speaking after his release, gave him a further hold on the public's imagination. His depiction of an apocalyptic conflict between Jews and Aryans and the need for an all-out war against the Marxists, who he depicted as nothing more than agents of Jewish ambition for national and international control, provided a simple formula for the rebirth and dominance of Germany that resonated with Germans across all social lines. However distorted, Hitler's description of a Jewish conspiracy to destroy Aryan peoples in the service of their ambition for world control was the shared view of many other Germans.

The onset and spread of the Great Depression in 1930–31 greatly strengthened Hitler's appeal. In September 1928, the Nazis won only 810,000 votes, or 2.6 percent of the national vote, and twelve seats in the Reichstag. Two years later, this leaped to 6.4 million votes, or 18.3 percent of the national total, giving the Nazis 107 elected deputies. By January 1933, Hitler had used the economic crisis and immobility of a divided government to become chancellor. After a crisis in February provoked by a Reichstag fire blamed on the Communists, Hitler won passage of his Enabling Act to suppress competing political parties. The death in August 1934 of President Paul von Hindenburg, a national war hero and a major remaining restraint on Nazi consolidation of power, allowed the cabinet to abolish the presidency and declare Hitler Germany's führer, or supreme commander of the state, the military, and the Nazi Party. A national plebiscite confirmed Hitler's assumption of total control with 84 percent popular approval.

Between 1934 and 1940 an expansion of the economy, partly engineered by massive defense spending to rebuild the German army and develop an air force, combined with a series of foreign policy successes to make Hitler almost universally popular at home and feared abroad. The occupation of the Rhineland in 1935, the triumph at Munich in September 1938, when the British and French governments acquiesced in Hitler's demands for return of the Sudetenland from Czechoslovakia, the lightning victory over Poland in 1939, and the conquest of Western Europe, with the stunning defeat and occupation of France in 1940, moved Germans to celebrate Hitler as a godly figure, a rescuer who was restoring Germany to its role as a great nation. A seventeen-year-old girl declared him "a great man, a genius, a person sent to us from heaven."

His success spurred auto-intoxication not only among the masses, but also in himself. He now believed that he was certain to be remembered as a twentieth-century Napoleon or a German leader on a par with Bismarck. No one inside or outside the government could successfully oppose him or deter him from expanding the war he described as fulfilling Germany's destiny. His power was now so complete that his control gave new meaning to the term totalitarianism.

Hitler's manipulation of the masses through nationalist appeals was a case study in the power of modern propaganda techniques. But beyond the use of radio, film, and mass rallies with flags and pageantry that evoked excitement bordering on hysteria was Hitler himself—the Führer, the national hero who provided, as many at the time saw it, "order, authority, greatness and salvation." The military victories of 1939–40 convinced millions of Germans that Hitler was a modern-day prophet who could do no wrong. The great majority of Germans were ready to follow him wherever he might lead.

Although blind faith in Hitler's power to rescue Germany from domestic and foreign threats remained for some throughout the war, his hold on a majority of Germans could not outlive the downturn in Nazi battlefield fortunes. The Soviet victory at Stalingrad in early 1943 broke the string of uninterrupted successes and began a downward spiral of defeats that punctured Hitler's image as invincible. It also marked the onset of a physical and emotional collapse. When one of his generals, who had not seen him for fourteen months, met with Hitler in February 1943, he was shocked by the change in his appearance and demeanor: "His left hand trembled, his back was bent, his gaze was fixed, his eyes protruded but lacked their former luster. . . . He was more excitable, easily lost his composure and was prone to angry outbursts."

A failed attempt on Hitler's life in July 1944 that killed some of his associates but inflicted only relatively minor wounds on him renewed convictions that Providence had spared the Führer to lead Germany to victory. Hitler himself believed that he had been shielded from harm in order to save Europe from Bolshevism. He comforted himself with thoughts that even the Western powers would one day come to see that they had fought on the wrong side in the war and that he had rescued them as well.

Nevertheless, the willingness of high military officials to plan a coup for which they paid with their lives raised doubts about Hitler's absolute control of the army and his government. The brutal executions of some of the conspirators—killed in the most agonizing way possible, hung on meat hooks—suggested that Hitler and his loyalists were venting their rage at all the opponents who were bringing them down. Round-the-clock bombing of German military targets and cities, the successful Allied invasion of France, and the steady advance of Soviet forces across Eastern Europe and into East Prussia and Silesia deepened fears among diehard Nazis and the more general public that Germany was doomed.

In November 1944, one resident of the Stuttgart region may have spoken for many others discouraged by the mounting defeats and largely unopposed air raids when he said, "The Führer was sent to us from God, though not in order to save Germany, but to ruin it. Providence has determined the destruction of the German people, and Hitler is the executor of this will."

It was not Providence that was punishing Germany; rather, it was the results of the nation's reckless two-front war against not only Britain and Russia but also the United States, which had been drawn into the fighting by Japan's attack on Pearl Harbor in December 1941. Although it seems certain that the United States and Germany would eventually have fought each other, it was Hitler, convinced of his invincibility, who declared war on the Americans four days after the Japanese surprise attack.

The last four months of the war in Europe, between February and May, brought home to millions of people everywhere the monstrous price of the conflict. The Allies dropped nearly half a million tons of bombs on Germany, double the amount of 1943, including an incendiary February 14 raid on Dresden, a communications and railway center, that killed as many as 35,000 civilians in a firestorm consuming the city and blanketing it in a haze that made aerial estimates of the damage impossible two days after the attack. Soviet abuse of

German civilians, who were now among the millions of refugees fleeing before the Soviet advance, was widespread: notably, rape, plundering, and indiscriminate killing of men, women, and children. No civilized standard can justify the atrocities committed by the Soviets. The Germans were reaping the whirlwind of their crimes in the Soviet Union, which Soviet troops witnessed as they recaptured the devastated cities and towns of their homeland.

On the battlefields, the loss of life and wounded among Allied and German forces in the closing months of the fighting numbered in the hundreds of thousands. The annihilation of Jews in Nazi concentration camps and on death marches to prevent them from being rescued by advancing Allied troops, particularly in the east, where so many of the camps were located, continued at a frenzied pace.

When Dwight Eisenhower, U.S. commander of Allied forces in Europe, visited one of the captured camps, he told his wife, "I never dreamed that such cruelty, bestiality, and savagery could really exist in this world! It was horrible." He wrote chief of staff General George C. Marshall, "The things I saw beggar description." A room piled high with naked corpses of inmates who had starved to death was one piece of evidence of the Nazi crimes against humanity. Eisenhower tried to ensure that as many journalists and British and American officials visited the camps as possible to guard against future complaints that the destruction of nearly 6 million Jews was seen as an exaggeration or "propaganda."

Eisenhower had reason for concern about public acceptance of Nazi crimes. In July 1944, Soviet troops captured Majdanek, the Nazi death camp on the outskirts of Lublin, Poland. In August Alexander Werth, a Russian-born British journalist, sent the BBC an account of the camp's "industrial undertaking in which thousands of 'ordinary' Germans had made it a full-time job to murder millions of other people in a sort of mass orgy of professional sadism, or, worse still, with the business-like conviction that *this was a job like any other*." The BBC, Werth noted, "refused to use it; they thought it was a

Russian propaganda stunt, and it was not until the discovery in the West of Buchenwald, Dachau and Belsen that they were convinced that Majdanek and Auschwitz were also genuine." In the 1990s the historian Deborah Lipstadt demonstrated in public and legal battles with David Irving, a Holocaust denier, that Eisenhower's concern was prophetic.

Well after it was clear that Germany was defeated and nothing could be gained by additional fighting, Hitler insisted on last-ditch efforts based on fantasies of some miracle reversal of fortunes. In December 1944, he pressed the case for the Ardennes offensive in Belgium in hopes of recapturing Antwerp, the principal seaport under Allied control, and cutting off the flow of supplies to their front lines. He hoped such a victory might convince the British and Americans to make peace and join with him in preventing Soviet occupation of Germany and the spread of communism across Europe.

In January 1945, after the German offensive in the west failed and the Soviets began a winter campaign in which they massively outnumbered German forces in troops and matériel, Hitler was largely resigned to defeat. But since he planned to kill himself rather than be captured by Soviet troops fighting their way into Berlin, he cared nothing for the fate of his countrymen, who would have to suffer additional losses before he was dead and they could surrender. A debilitated physical and mental condition during the closing months of the war may partly explain Hitler's irrational determination to fight to the bitter end: exhausted and sickly, he seemed to have aged overnight; his unsteady walk, trembling hands, sickly pallor, and inability to speak coherently for long stretches of time impressed visitors to his bunker that they were witnessing someone suffering from a nervous collapse.

But Hitler's long-term outlook eclipsed his medical and emotional breakdown in explaining his refusal to concede defeat: he was incapable of acknowledging failure, especially as a consequence of his decisions. He blamed Germany's defeat on traitors in the army, who caused the reverses in Russia, poor leadership by some of his generals, Hermann Göring's false promises about the Luftwaffe's capacity to combat the Allied air war and defeat their ground forces, and, above all, the weakness of the German people. If he carried on until the last moment, he imagined, he would be remembered not as a deluded dictator who brought incomparable suffering on his people but "as a German hero brought down by weakness and betrayal." He said the war would be celebrated as "the most glorious and valiant manifestation of a nation's will to exist."

Determined not "to fall into the hands of enemies who, for the amusement of their whipped up masses, will need a spectacle arranged by Jews," Hitler put a bullet in his brain on April 30, two days before Soviet troops captured his bunker in the heart of Berlin. Slavishly following the Führer's instructions to the last, aides burned his body in the garden of the Reich Chancellery. When the remnants of the Nazi government announced the Führer's death on May 1, it described him as having fallen in combat rather than as a suicide. The fiction was meant to prolong troop morale lest they see Hitler as having abandoned them and given up the fight against Bolshevism. The war finally ended on May 8 after, their attempts to surrender only to British and U.S. forces having failed, the Germans agreed to unconditional surrender on all fronts.

The truth about Hitler's death could not be hidden, just as his hope of some grand historical redemption could not eclipse the horrors he and his regime had perpetrated. He is justifiably remembered as the embodiment of evil, a tyrant whose absolute power allowed him to act upon his maniacal fantasies of conquering all Europe and purifying it by eliminating Jews and "subhuman" Slavs. He had imagined the triumph of a master race—Aryan Germans breeding superior human beings, who would rule the continent for a thousand years. Instead, of course, he caused untold misery across Europe and around the world. The most amazing fact is not the existence of someone with such distorted, madcap ambitions, but his ability to mobilize so many millions of supposedly civilized countrymen to act upon his grandiose imaginings.

In the end, Hitler accurately glimpsed only a bit of the future, which was of no consequence in salvaging his reputation. As he assumed, the Soviet-Western alliance could not outlast the war. There was no chance that he could have exploited Allied tensions to serve his ends. His abuse of civilized standards assured that neither Stalin nor Churchill nor Roosevelt nor Truman would seize any German olive branch to settle for anything but unconditional surrender and the total destruction of the Nazis. The awful destruction Hitler perpetrated in Russia and in bombing raids against Britain's cities and his reputation in the United States as a ruthless dictator ruled out compromises with him.

Nevertheless, tensions persisted, particularly in the exchanges between Stalin and Roosevelt over the negotiations in Switzerland, which revealed Stalin's enduring distrust of his Western allies. Despite Roosevelt's counsel of patience to Churchill about difficulties with Moscow, the prime minister remained skeptical of Stalin's good intentions. In April, as the Anglo-American and Soviet armies moved toward the destruction of Nazi forces in their respective parts of Germany, Churchill was eager to have Allied armies from the west reach Berlin and Prague before the Soviets did. And British general Bernard Montgomery and American general George Patton were only too ready to contemplate a confrontation with the Soviets, limiting their occupation of Central and Eastern Europe.

Dwight Eisenhower, however, wanted no part of it. Although he would offer a different version of events later, when the Cold War had begun and he had entered politics, in the spring of 1945 he tried to allay Soviet suspicions about collaboration with Germany to inhibit their advance and to give full recognition to their principal part in destroying Hitler's armies.

By this point, Eisenhower shared Roosevelt's hope and that of most Americans that collaboration with Soviet Russia remained not only possible but essential to postwar peace. Having seen the horrors perpetrated by industrial societies fighting a total war, Eisenhower shared the widespread American hope that the murderous consequences of the fighting would result in sober rejection of any future arms race or great power rivalry threatening the outbreak of yet another, even more destructive war. While he could rationalize leaving the conquests of Berlin and Prague to Soviet armies so that U.S. forces could occupy southern Germany, where he feared a rump Nazi government might try to relocate from Berlin, his principal reasons were to satisfy Soviet wishes to capture Germany's capital and not to inflame Soviet suspicions of their allies as eager to limit their presence in Central Europe.

In the first months of 1945, a majority of Americans shared Roosevelt's and Eisenhower's hopes for a benign Soviet Union and a world without war. Fifty-five percent of surveyed Americans said that Russia could be trusted to cooperate with the United States after the fighting. American political leaders—former vice president Henry Wallace and former ambassador to Moscow Joseph E. Davies on the left, and former president Herbert Hoover and *Time* publisher Henry Luce on the right—forecast the likelihood of lasting friendship with the USSR. In March 1943, *Life* magazine, another Luce publication, had described the Russians as "one hell of a people . . . [who] to a remarkable degree . . . look like Americans, dress like Americans and think like Americans." The NKVD was "a national police similar to the FBI." That summer, conservative congressman John Rankin of Mississippi declared communism a dead letter in Russia, where it was being run out of the country.

But it wasn't only Americans who were so optimistic about postwar developments; great numbers of Soviet citizens dreamed of postwar harmony as well. They imagined that the demise of Russia's principal European enemy and continuing good relations with the United States and Britain would amount to a more relaxed future in world affairs and higher standards of living at home. Former foreign secretary Maxim Litvinov believed that after the fighting, Russia would be able to "cash in on the goodwill she had accumulated in Britain and the United States" to maintain enduring cooperation, resulting in the rebuilding of Russia's economy. Relying on numerous conversations in different parts of Russia, where he served as a wartime correspondent, Alexander Werth recalled that "the Russian people in 1944 liked to think that life would soon be easier, and that Russia could 'relax' after the war. The 'lasting alliance' with Britain and the USA had much to do with it."

That summer, a Soviet official declared before the Society for Cultural Relations with Foreign Countries, "When the war is over, life in Russia will become very pleasant. . . . There will be much coming and going, with a lot of contacts with the West. Everybody will be allowed to read anything he likes. There will be exchanges of students, and foreign travel will be made easy." Even if the Communist Party was trying to lull the public and westerners with so rosy a picture to keep up wartime morale, it suggests that the government's highest officials, whatever they really believed, saw a yearning on the part of many Russians for such an outcome and felt compelled to have a Soviet representative give assurances of such better days ahead.

In the spring of 1945, no one could imagine the brave new world coming into existence until Japan joined Germany in unconditional surrender. The Pacific War to that point had been a costly struggle against well-prepared and determined Japanese forces. Despite the American desire to concentrate on Europe first, the Pacific fighting demanded an almost equal share of U.S. men and matériel to contain Japanese advances across the Pacific. In 1942, in the first months of the conflict, the Japanese drove British forces out of Burma, captured Hong Kong, Malaya, and Singapore, where a British garrison of 85,000 men surrendered in what Churchill later described as "the worst disaster and largest capitulation of British history," sunk the battleship *Prince of Wales* and the cruiser *Repulse*, demonstrating that air forces could sink the most powerful warships afloat, and threatened India. At the same time, the Japanese overwhelmed U.S. forces in Guam and Wake Island, conquered the Philippines, and occupied parts of New Guinea and the Solomon Islands in the southwest Pacific, from which they threatened Australia.

The only satisfactions Americans found among these early defeats were the actions of General Douglas MacArthur and Colonel Jimmy Doolittle. In March, Roosevelt ordered MacArthur to leave the Philippines for Australia, where he was to become commander in chief of the Southwest Pacific area. At sixty-two years of age, MacArthur was already something of a national legend. He had graduated at the top of his class from West Point in 1903, served with great bravery and distinction in World War I, and been army chief of staff in the 1930s.

MacArthur was one of the country's best known generals, a military leader on a par with the nation's most respected battlefield officers in the Civil War and World War I. He had a reputation as a man of exceptional intelligence and courage; Chief of Staff George Marshall named him "our most brilliant general." Having won twenty-two medals in his almost forty-year army career, he was also considered one of the country's bravest officers. He was celebrated as a soldier who had defied death in combat, deliberately exposing himself to every sort of peril.

MacArthur's ego was a match for his talents. Clare Boothe Luce, *Time* publisher Henry Luce's wife, said that his egotism "demanded obedience not only to his orders, but to his ideas and his person as well. He plainly relished idolatry," and surrounded himself with sycophants. He consciously aimed to build an image of himself as apart from America's other World War II commanders. Just as General George C. Patton impressed himself on the nation as the country's leading tank officer, who distinguished himself by his fierce determination to take the offensive and a pearl-handled revolver strapped to his hip, so MacArthur was notable for his sunglasses, corncob pipe, and staged performances before photo journalists, like his wading through the surf in the invasion of the Philippines in 1944. Although he never hesitated to expose himself to danger on the front lines, his men disliked his posturing and described him as "Dugout Doug" for staying bunkered in Corregidor and visiting besieged troops on the Bataan Peninsula only once during the Japanese siege in 1942.

Franklin Roosevelt understood MacArthur's importance as a national icon and his talents as a general, but he didn't trust him. In 1933, when FDR wanted to cut the army's budget to divert badly needed federal funds to domestic relief, MacArthur had a fit: "When we lost the next war," he told the president, "and an American boy, lying in the mud with an enemy bayonet through his belly and an enemy foot on his dying throat spat out his last curse, I wanted the name not to be MacArthur but Roosevelt." MacArthur's comment infuriated Roosevelt: "You must not talk that way to the president," he snapped. Refusing MacArthur's offer to resign, Roosevelt persuaded him to stay. But he considered MacArthur, next to Louisiana senator Huey Long, the most dangerous man to democracy in the country.

For his defense of the Philippines against superior Japanese forces, MacArthur became "a symbol of national defiance." When he arrived in Australia after a hazardous crossing of 560 miles in PT boats and a nine-hour plane trip from the southern Philippine island of Mindanao, MacArthur uttered the famous remark—"I came through and I will return"—that inspired hope and made him America's most prominent war hero.

The following month, when Doolittle led an air raid on Tokyo with sixteen B-25 bombers flying from an aircraft carrier some 650 miles from Japan, it gave Americans the feeling that the country was fighting back and would eventually carry the full weight of the war to Japan. The incarceration of some 110,000 Japanese Americans in what Roosevelt called "concentration camps" away from the West Coast, where they were feared as potential saboteurs, also gave Americans a sense of striking at the enemy. It was, however, less an act of national defense than an assault on loyal citizens, which the U.S. Supreme Court later called the greatest breach of American civil liberties in history. The action spoke more to the low state of American morale in early 1942 and the nation's irrational fear of and racism toward Japanese Americans than to any wise measure of national security.

Symbolic slaps at Japan, however, could not substitute for substantive victories. Consequently, in May and June, when U.S. naval forces repulsed Japanese efforts to seize Port Moresby in New Guinea in the Battle of the Coral Sea and, more decisively, Midway Island, 1,100 miles northwest of Hawaii's main island of Oahu, it generated realistic hopes that the war was turning in America's direction. At a minimum, the victories eased fears of Japanese troop landings in Australia and Hawaii.

The victory would take almost four years of savage and costly fighting. Throughout 1943, Japanese resistance in battles for the Solomon Islands, New Guinea, and New Britain convinced U.S. military planners that it might take until 1948 or 1949 to end the war. But at the Quebec conference in August 1943, General Marshall warned that if Germany were defeated in 1944 or 1945, public demoralization would set in if it took an additional three or four years to win in the Pacific.

During 1944, revised plans to end the Far East war within twelve months of Germany's collapse were made uncertain by fierce opposition to American campaigns in the Central Pacific's Gilbert, Marshall, and Caroline Islands. The battle for Tarawa, for instance, a narrow strip of land in the Gilberts that became a valuable airfield for future operations, was a particularly bloody fight against three thousand well-entrenched Japanese troops. It was a prelude to the fighting in the Palaus in the western Carolines and, more famously, Iwo Jima, a five-mile-long island halfway between the Marianas and the Japanese home islands. In one of the most costly battles of the Pacific War, more than 6,800 marines lost their lives in overcoming 21,000 Japanese troops, only about 1,100 of whom were taken prisoner. The rest perished in combat or committed suicide. The victory gave U.S. air forces a valuable base from which to raid Japan and a memorable, even if staged, flag-raising on Mount Suribachi that boosted morale among U.S. forces and Americans at home.

The closer American troops got to Japan, the fiercer the combat. In Okinawa between April and June 1945 the Japanese lost more than 107,000 men and what remained of its principal naval vessels; but it was at the cost of some 12,000 U.S. seamen and ground troops, with almost 32,000 wounded, 30 U.S. ships sunk, and another 368 damaged.

Japanese determination to fight to the last man, and to sacrifice their lives for their emperor rather than face defeat, convinced Americans that total victory was the only reasonable way to deal with so fanatical an enemy. Suicidal banzai charges in several of the early island battles and, beginning in 1944, kamikaze pilots flying their planes into U.S. ships, coupled with stories of Japanese atrocities against captured troops and subject populations, made Americans all too ready to see the Japanese as subhuman. By contrast, the Japanese thought of themselves as representing a "pure spirit" turning back a "demonic onslaught."

The Japanese government encouraged all 73 million citizens of the home islands to think of themselves as part of the kamikazes, or Japan's "Special Attack Force," as they described units on suicide missions. Japanese civilians were encouraged to believe that they had no choice: government propaganda described Anglo-American intentions dating from the nineteenth century as hegemony in Asia. Japan's war was a "counteroffensive of the Oriental races against Occidental aggression" or a conflict to prevent the West from turning Japan into a "slave state." One Japanese writer later described this appeal as "the mesmerizing grandeur of massive destruction."

To Americans, the quintessential "Jap" was Hideki Tojo, the country's prime minister. In a *Life* magazine photo article titled "How to Tell Japs from Chinese," Tojo was described as "a 'typical' Japanese, whose squat long-torsoed build, massively boned head, flat pug nose, and yellow ocher skin 'betrays aboriginal antecedents.' "

It was not Tojo's physical appearance, however, that made him an object of contempt or put him at the center of public animus in the United States. He was considered a principal war criminal: as a commanding general in China between 1935 and 1938, the architect of Japan's aggression; as minister of war in 1940–41, a proponent of the Axis alliance with Germany and Italy; and as prime minister beginning in October 1941, the man most responsible for Pearl Harbor. For almost three years he had directed Japan's war efforts, the official most responsible for Japanese aggression and atrocities. Despite his resignation after Japan's defeat in Saipan in the Marianas in June 1944, which convinced many Japanese that the war effort was doomed, Americans continued to see Tojo as the leading villain in the Pacific War. In September 1945, he was identified as one of forty Japanese war criminals. A failed suicide attempt seemed to confirm his guilt; he was convicted of "conspiracy, waging an aggressive war, and ordering, authorizing, and permitting atrocities," and was executed in December 1948.

The vicious Pacific fighting and the conviction that the Japanese would rather die than surrender gave license to American military chiefs to adopt extreme measures of destruction against Japanese combatants and civilians alike. In 1944 the B-29 Superfortress, the largest World War II bomber, which could carry a four-ton bomb load and travel 3,500 miles on a round trip, became available, and devastating incendiary raids on Japanese cities began. In March 1945, 334 B-29s hit Tokyo in a raid that killed more than 83,000 residents by incineration, injured another 40,000, and destroyed about a quarter of the city. The heat from the firebombing boiled the water in canals, and people who ran into the water to escape the flames were boiled alive or asphyxiated by the veil of smoke that surrounded them. The fire consumed everything it touched; wooden structures fueled the flames, and the metal in buildings and bridges melted.

By June, Japan's six leading industrial centers lay in ruins. By the end of the fighting, sixty-six major cities had suffered immobilizing damage. Forty percent of Japan's urban areas had been destroyed, with 30 percent of their populations homeless; in Tokyo, 65 percent of all homes were reduced to rubble. Of the nearly 400,000 Japanese civilians killed in air raids, a majority of them lost their lives in the incendiary raids.

Although U.S. military planners had made plans to burn up Japan's combustible cities even before Pearl Harbor, the implementation of such a strategy awaited the development of the B-29 and the leadership of Major General Curtis LeMay, who saw the Superfortresses and firebombings as a formula for a quicker end to the war without a costly invasion of Japan.

LeMay pioneered the tactic of low-level nighttime attacks, more effective than daytime high-altitude precision bombing, which could not pinpoint war-making factories scattered in civilian districts of the cities as well as in remote parts of the country. To ease consciences over attacking civilians, American planes dropped leaflets prior to raids, warning civilians to leave the cities that were designated targets. Nevertheless, the Japanese saw air raids on defenseless civilians as inexcusable, and so had no qualms about summarily executing captured B-29 crews. Nor would they have hesitated to execute LeMay as a war criminal had they won the war. LeMay himself acknowledged this likelihood and justified the raids by describing them as a necessity that seemed likely to shorten the war and save both American and Japanese lives.

Among the many frustrations in the prolonged war against Japan was the unreliability of China. For both military and domestic political purposes, Roosevelt felt compelled to identify China as one of the Big Four, giving Chiang Kai-shek's Nationalist government standing on a par with Britain, Russia, and the United States. China's history as a victim of Japanese aggression and earlier imperialism gave China a special appeal to Americans as their favorite wartime ally. American missionaries, aided by Henry Luce, the publisher of *Life* and *Time* magazines and the son of missionaries in China, where he was born, promoted an idealized picture of China's government under Chiang Kai-shek, a Christian who gave validation to the century-long work of America's missionaries. The missionary propaganda and the view of China as a victim of Fascist aggression convinced Americans that China should play a major role in the postwar world equal to that of Great Britain and the Soviet Union.

Yet the reality of a poor country divided by civil strife between Chiang Kai-shek's ruling Nationalists and Mao Tse-tung's opposition Communists limited China's contribution to the war effort and potential postwar influence. Moreover, Chiang's determination to rely on the United States to fight Japan and preserve his government's military capacity against the day when he expected to fight Communist insurgents made China a secondary battleground against Japan.

When Churchill visited Washington in January 1942, he marveled at what he saw as American naiveté about China. He later complained that he "found the extraordinary significance of China in American minds, even at the top, strangely out of proportion." Americans seemed to consider China's armies the equal of British and Soviet fighting forces. "If I can epitomize in one word the lesson I learned in the United States," he told his commanding general in the Far East, "it was 'China.' "

Nevertheless, Roosevelt believed that so large a country with such untapped resources and a population of a half billion people could not be consigned to a minor role in world affairs. His objective was to encourage perceptions, whatever the reality, of a great nation contributing to the defeat of Japan and the shape of postwar Asia. In February 1942 he appointed General Joseph W. Stilwell commander of U.S. Army forces in China, Burma, and India (CBI) and as chief of staff to Chiang Kai-shek, who was named supreme commander of all forces in the CBI area. The title reflected not expectations of China's direct military contribution to the war but a desire to raise Chiang's public standing, encourage the Chinese to keep fighting, and compel Japan to maintain a large force in China.

In February 1942, after Stilwell met with Roosevelt to discuss his assignment, he expressed in a characteristically blunt diary entry what he thought of the president and his mission in China. He described Roosevelt during a twenty-minute meeting as "very pleasant and very unimpressive. As if I were a constituent in to see him. [The president] rambled on about his idea of the war." It was "just a lot of wind. After I had enough, I broke in and asked him if he had a message for Chiang Kai-shek. He very obviously had not and talked for five minutes and hunted around for something world-shaking to say." Finally, he asked Stilwell to tell the generalissimo that "we are in this thing for keeps, and we intended to keep at it until China gets back all her lost territory." He wanted Stilwell to discourage Mme Chiang Kai-shek from making a planned visit to the United States.

Roosevelt's unstated message was: I'm sending you on something of a fool's errand. Yes, we want China to keep fighting, but we have no intention of making CBI a principal war theater alongside Europe. So, let's jolly Chiang along with just enough matériel to keep his armies fighting, and let's keep his wife away from Washington, where she could generate political pressure for greater help than a wise strategy dictates. In June 1942, Roosevelt told his ambassador in London that he hoped to keep the Chinese happy and fighting by "telling stories and doing most of the talking." Chiang was willing to accommodate Roosevelt and the Americans as long as they met his self-serving approach to the war: "Americans are expected to go on carrying the load in the air, bringing in supplies, and building up a force that will make China safe for the Kuomintawo [Chiang's Nationalists]," Stilwell observed.

If Roosevelt had any doubts about the accuracy of Stilwell's analysis, a visit to Washington by Mme Chiang in the winter of 1943 dispelled them. A Wellesley graduate with an excellent command of

English and an understanding of American sympathy for her country, which she exploited to the fullest, Mme Chiang irritated Roosevelt to no end during a stay at the White House. During a press conference with the president, when he told reporters that the United States would send supplies to China just as fast as the good Lord would allow, she embarrassed him by responding, "Mr. President, I understand that you have a saying in your country that the Lord helps those who help themselves." In a speech before a joint congressional session, she made such a strong impression that the military chiefs worried that her appeal for greater help to China might undermine their Europe-first strategy. Roosevelt confided to Secretary of the Treasury Henry Morgenthau that he was "just crazy to get her out of the country."

The president told Eleanor Roosevelt that despite impressions of a delicate sophisticated lady who wore stylish black silk dresses with a slit up the side and smoked British cigarettes, Mme Chiang was "as hard as steel." He did not think that she was the sort of leader "who was guiding her country toward a democratic future."

Stilwell deepened the president's impressions of a corrupt, repressive, but ineffective Chinese government. "Anything that is done in China," he told the war department, "will be done in spite of, and not because of, the Peanut [Stilwell's derogatory name for Chiang] and his military clique." Stilwell advised Marshall that the Chinese army "is generally in desperate condition, underfed, unpaid, untrained, neglected, and rotten with corruption. We can pull them out of this cesspool, but continued concessions have made the Generalissimo believe he has only to insist and we will yield."

Despite his understanding that Chiang's regime was anything but democratic and receptive to reform, either in his government or his army, Roosevelt refused to come down hard on him. He believed that Chiang's problems in trying to control a country that was so poor and divided were beyond anything American pressure could change. He told Marshall that Stillwell's gruff approach to Chiang was the wrong way to go about dealing with him: "One cannot speak sternly to a man like that or exact commitments from him the way we might do from the Sultan of Morocco."

Roosevelt feared that excessive demands on Chiang might lead to a collapse of his government and its war effort, however limited. Tokyo's need to keep a large force in China limited its capacity to fight U.S. troops in the Pacific Island campaigns. Roosevelt hoped that China would eventually become a prime base of operations against Japan: airfields from which American planes could readily reach Japan in 1942–43 could be invaluable in forcing an early Japanese surrender, but only if Chinese armies protected the bases from Japanese attacks. Roosevelt also believed that China's collapse would play havoc with his postwar vision of a cooperative China helping police East Asia and the Pacific. A stable China might also become a counterweight to Russia in the Far East, where Roosevelt saw the possibility of postwar great power tensions.

By 1944–45, however, Roosevelt understood that Japan's defeat would have to be the result of island conquests in the Pacific leading to a possible direct invasion of her home islands. But he continued to fear a Chinese collapse that could burden American forces with having to overcome Japanese armies in China. His eagerness to assure Soviet entry into the war against Japan rested on the hope that Soviet troops could tie down Japanese forces in Manchuria and help compel a Japanese surrender in China after a successful invasion of Japan. Roosevelt also feared that a Chinese collapse would discourage American participation in postwar international affairs.

Because he found it increasingly unlikely that he could force Chiang into military or political actions that served U.S. purposes, Roosevelt tried to solve his China problems by working out an accommodation with Stalin. At Yalta, Stalin made clear that he wanted the transfer of southern Sakhalin and the Kuril Islands from Japan to Russia, access to a warm-water port—Darien on the Kwantung Peninsula—and use of Manchurian railways. Roosevelt said he favored the Soviet demands but could not speak for Chiang. In return,

Stalin promised to enter the war against Japan within three months of Germany's collapse and to support a Nationalist-Communist coalition government.

Although Churchill, Roosevelt, and Stalin signed an agreement at Yalta saying that Soviet claims "shall be unquestionably fulfilled after Japan has been defeated," they also included a provision that the understanding "will require concurrence of Generalissimo Chiang Kai-shek." Roosevelt had no doubt that Chiang would see the Soviet demands as a small price to pay for the preservation of his regime. Stalin, too, assumed that Chiang and Communist leader Mao Tse-tung would sign on to the arrangement. Roosevelt and Stalin had high hopes that the agreement would prevent a conflict in China that could seriously strain U.S.–Soviet relations.

But both of them were thinking more in terms of their respective interests than what either Chiang or Mao preferred. For Roosevelt, the agreement impressed him "as the last best hope for preserving a weak but stable China as a cooperative ally on the world scene." For Stalin, it meant averting a Chinese civil war that could lead to China's exclusive control by the Nationalists or the Communists, either of whom might see fit to refuse Soviet demands after victory in a civil conflict. Moreover, Stalin was not eager for a Chinese Communist regime that might challenge Soviet leadership of international communism. Neither Roosevelt nor Stalin foresaw their inability to control events in China, or if they did, were willing to acknowledge it.

By the time of Roosevelt's death in April 1945, the worldwide destruction in the fighting had produced unimaginable losses. No one, then or later, could possibly assess the full extent of the physical and psychological damage. Somewhere between 50 and 60 million people perished between 1939 and 1945—perhaps 60 percent of them noncombatants killed by air raids, disease, executions, and famine. The war uprooted an additional 16 million people in Europe, who struggled to survive the turmoil.

A staggering amount of property damage compounded the sense of loss: in the Soviet Union, hundreds of cities and towns and thousands of villages were largely razed or left as burned-over shells of what they once were. Nearly three-quarters of all Soviet industrial plants and some 60 percent of the country's transportation facilities were destroyed. City after city in Germany had been reduced to rubble, with millions of civilians displaced. France and the Low Countries did not escape the damage: bridges and rail lines as well as rivers and harbors were rendered inoperable by the combat. The Continent's industrial and agricultural production were down to half of prewar levels, with creature comforts like good housing and modern plumbing a luxury beyond the reach of millions. It was apparent that the reconstruction of Europe would cost billions of dollars, and that it would be years before its residents could resume anything resembling a normal prewar life.

Only the United States emerged from the war with its population largely intact and an expansive economy that dramatically raised the country's standard of living from where it had been in the 1930s. True, some 12 million Americans served in the armed forces, and 419,000 died in combat, but the loss of life was relatively small alongside the 325,000 British military and civilian deaths in a population roughly one-fourth that of the United States, and much smaller than the millions who perished in China, Germany, Japan, and the Soviet Union. Russia's casualties were at least fifty times that of America's.

Although Americans mourned their losses as much as any other combatant, they did not have to anguish over civilian deaths from air attacks on their cities, and they lived with a sense of mounting exhilaration over battlefield victories and a belief that America's resurgent prosperity would make her the most powerful nation in the world after the war. The GNP more than doubled in the four years between 1940 and 1944, from $101 billion to $214 billion; unemployment dropped from 14.6 percent to 1.2 percent; and the share of income made by the wealthiest 5 percent fell from 25.4 percent to 15.8 percent, demonstrating a greater equality of economic well-being than at any time to that point in the country's history. Americans entered the postwar era confirmed in a long-standing conviction that their system of governance and economic exchange made them a fit model for the rest of the world.

It was not just optimism that distinguished the American outlook, but also high hopes that the postwar world would, as Roosevelt predicted after returning from Yalta, replace traditional national security arrangements with Woodrow Wilson's vision of collective security through a more effective international organization than the League of Nations. This time, Americans looked forward not to a league of nations but a union of nations, suggesting a commitment to larger idealistic goals by the world's governments than was implied in a less cohesive league.

Nothing better signaled the renewed American affinity for world cooperation than the rise in public regard for Woodrow Wilson. During the 1920s and '30s, Wilson was a sort of national pariah. The Senate's rejection of the League of Nations in 1919 and again in 1920, as well as the resurgent isolationism of the two decades, put Wilson in bad odor as a utopian dreamer whose hopes for international peace through a world league were thoroughly discredited. The 1934 Nye Senate Committee hearings about international arms traffic suggested that bankers and munitions makers, who were described as the driving force behind U.S. involvement in World War I, had made Wilson a tool of their self-serving interests. Although Wilson continued to have his faithful followers, no one on the national scene in the 1930s could imagine majority support for anything associated with Wilson's idealism. Roosevelt, who had been assistant secretary of the navy in Wilson's administration and a warm supporter of the league until his run for the presidency, made sure to keep his distance from Wilson's memory during his election campaigns in 1932 and 1936.

The shift in mood came with the onset of the war in 1939, and especially after Pearl Harbor. Opinion surveys in 1942 revealed a revived sympathy in the country for participation in a postwar league.

Americans now felt guilty for having rejected Wilson's assertions about the League of Nations and the need for participation in international affairs; in 1942, a sympathetic Broadway play about the betrayal of Wilson's vision was an initial indication of the shifting mood. During 1944, as postwar peace plans became a national focus, Wilson emerged as a heroic leader who had been ahead of his time. Wilson now morphed into "The Unforgettable Figure Who Has Returned to Haunt Us. . . . The word 'Wilson' now has a new definition," the editors of *Look* declared. "It means peace."

The Wilson revival reached a high point with the release of a 1944 Twentieth-Century Fox feature film biography. In this early Technicolor production, Wilson all but deserved sainthood, and Senator Henry Cabot Lodge, his principal rival in the fight over the Versailles Treaty and the League of Nations, became the familiar Hollywood villain whose appearance on the screen provoked boos and catcalls. The film reached millions of Americans and rivaled the other great spectacle of five years before, the Civil War epic *Gone With the Wind*. As a celebration of internationalism, the movie made the public eager for a postwar organization that could save the world from another great war.

Ever attentive to the shifting national mood, Roosevelt became an outspoken advocate in deliberations with London and Moscow of the prime need for a new peacekeeping body in postwar international relations. Roosevelt had his doubts about the effectiveness of collective security by the world's nations and quietly emphasized his preference for the "four policemen," Britain, China, the United States, and the USSR, assuming responsibility for regional and world peace. But mindful of how vital the American people considered a world organization, Roosevelt proposed at Yalta that the organizing conference meet in San Francisco. The venue would underscore America's backing for the league and put the focus on the Pacific, rather than Europe, which was more of a red flag to isolationists.

Churchill and Stalin were only too happy to have the UN founding conference in the United States. Like Roosevelt, Churchill doubted that collective security was a realistic possibility in a world of self-interested nation-states. The Soviets had even greater doubts about the utility of a world organization, where they believed clashing national interests, rather than international harmony, would be on full display. Moreover, they were even more doubtful than American skeptics about the likely effectiveness of giving the world community a say in the survival of individual nations.

Soviet fears of being outvoted in an international organization that could threaten their perceived security needs made them resistant to Roosevelt's proposal for a United Nations. If they agreed to such a plan, they wanted a veto power over all UN actions, above all, anything involving their own interests. They also asked that all sixteen Soviet Socialist Republics become members of the organization, assuring Moscow of a reliable number of votes against anything they opposed and appeasing nationalistic aspirations among the many ethnic groups comprising the Soviet Union.

Roosevelt saw agreement to the Soviet proposals as calculated to destroy American public support for a new world body. He insisted that nothing be leaked to the press about the Soviet demands. The State Department labeled the sixteen Soviet republics idea the "X Matter" and kept all references to it in a department safe. Roosevelt warned the Soviets that their proposals violated American ideas about fair play and would discourage smaller countries from joining the new organization and cause the Senate, as in 1919–20, to reject American membership.

At Yalta, however, as a trade-off for tacit Anglo-American assent to Soviet control of Poland, Stalin reduced his demand for sixteen Soviet republics in the UN to two or three and agreed that states involved in a dispute should not have veto power or a vote on the issue as long as the collective action did not threaten either military intervention or economic sanctions. It was a non-concession: the UN would not be able effectively to punish Moscow for any violations of the organization's rules. Stalin hoped that giving the Ukraine, Belarus (White Russia), and Lithuania UN Assembly seats would quiet the most intense independence sentiments among his countries' minorities.

Churchill, who wanted to extend membership to some British Commonwealth countries, supported Stalin's request for additional seats. Churchill also insisted that the UN have no say in the affairs of Britain's colonies. Assurances that UN trusteeships would apply only to colonies of the Axis powers eased Churchill's fears. Roosevelt now also saw to American interests: worried that Stalin's demands for two or three additional UN votes would ignite public resentment, Roosevelt asked and received British-Soviet approval for U.S. parity in assembly seats.

In 1945, if Americans had learned about the self-serving decisions of the Allies in planning the United Nations organization, it would have shattered some, if not most, of their idealistic hopes for the new world league. But Roosevelt took pains to assure that the public did not learn the full substance of plans for the UN before it became a reality. Stalin, by contrast, tried to downplay the importance of the emerging organization by telling the president that Soviet foreign secretary Molotov would not be able to attend the organizing conference in San Francisco beginning on April 25 and that the Soviet ambassador to Washington, Andrei Gromyko, would come instead. Roosevelt bluntly told Stalin that "Molotov's absence would be construed all over the world as a lack of comparable interest on the part of the Soviet Government in the great objectives of this conference." In reply, Stalin gave rhetorical support to the importance of the emerging UN but insisted that Molotov had to be present when the Supreme Soviet of the USSR met at the same time.

Stalin's explanation was transparently false: he could have postponed the Moscow meeting if he wanted. He may have hoped to extract some concession from Roosevelt for Molotov's attendance in San Francisco. But he gave no indication that this was his intention. He made clear, however, that neither world nor American opinion would sway him about Poland or the UN or anything else; Soviet interests were his only concern. "As regards various interpretations, you understand," Stalin told the president, "this cannot determine the decisions which are to be made."

After Roosevelt died, Averell Harriman, American ambassador to Moscow, seemed to convince Stalin to send Molotov to San Francisco as a show of regard for the president's memory and as "the most effective way to assure the American public and the world at large of the desire of the Soviet Government to continue collaboration with us and the other United Nations." It would also help Truman "in solidifying him with the American people," Harriman advised Stalin. Stalin must have been amused that Harriman was so ready to grant him a say in U.S. domestic affairs. Seizing on the chance to bank some credit with the new president, Stalin, declaring that "President Roosevelt has died but his cause must live on," agreed to Harriman's request.

While some small sentiment about the late president may have entered into Stalin's reversal, it seems more likely that he wanted the more formidable Molotov in San Francisco to fend off possible pressures from the new Truman administration, which he believed would be more resistant to Soviet demands than Roosevelt had been. Through listening devices in the U.S. embassy and diplomatic apartments, Stalin apparently had a good idea of the influence that Harriman, who had been taking a tough line toward Moscow in private, would exert on Truman, someone with no foreign policy experience and a need to depend on his Soviet experts.

Truman immediately lived up to Stalin's and Molotov's expectations. Before the meeting, Truman privately remarked that relations with Moscow had been too much of "a one-way street . . . it was now or never" to correct course. He also said that plans for a UN would go forward no matter what the Soviets did. If they chose not to join, "they could go to hell."

On April 23, when Molotov came to the White House before

proceeding to San Francisco, Truman, following Harriman's advice and that of other members of the State, War, and Navy departments, gave him a blunt talking-to. Truman was incensed over the fact that Molotov's arrival in the United States coincided with Moscow's recognition of a pro-Communist Polish government it had put in place. When discussions at the State Department and then with Truman at the White House produced no glimmer of Soviet accommodation on Poland, Truman gave Molotov what he later described as "a straight one-two to the jaw." He instructed him to tell Stalin that the United States expected him to live up to his agreements. Truman threatened to cut off economic aid if they couldn't find common ground. When Molotov tried to turn the discussion to the war against Japan, Truman abruptly cut him off. The seemingly unflappable Molotov, a survivor of the bloodiest of Kremlin purges, turned "a little ashy." "I have never been talked to like that in my life," he said angrily. "Carry out your agreements and you won't get talked to like that," Truman replied coldly.

Truman's tough response persuaded Stalin to adopt a more cautious approach to the new administration. Aware of American progress on an atomic bomb, he may have believed that Truman's hard line reflected a conviction that he would not need Soviet help in defeating Japan and might be intent on threatening Moscow with the new weapon if Stalin proved too obstinate on postwar arrangements. Moreover, Stalin remained eager not to squander a continuing sense of obligation to Russia for its defeat of the Nazis and its claim on a reconstruction loan.

At the very least, Stalin saw it as wise to be more accommodating in San Francisco, where the Americans hoped to launch a more peaceful world. In a radio address to the representatives of forty-six nations attending the opening session of the conference, Truman declared it vital for the meeting to create "the essential organization to keep the peace. . . . If we do not want to die together in war, we must learn to live together in peace." The new organization would be "a permanent monument to those who gave their lives that this moment might come."

American secretary of state Edward Stettinius followed Truman's call to grand purposes with another of his own. As chairman of the opening session, Stettinius urged the delegates to believe in the manageability of their task. It was not only possible to achieve the ambitious goal of establishing an effective world peace organization—it was essential. Despite fears of renewed conflicts that would defeat the purposes of the conference, Americans in San Francisco and commentators across the country on the emerging UN continued to invest high hope in a new world peacekeeping organization.

American optimism is not difficult to understand: the country had come through the war largely unscathed, or with far less damage than any of the other belligerents and far better prospects for the resumption of a prosperous national life. The president and secretary of state also had personal biographies that made them upbeat about what they and the United States and a world following America's lead could achieve.

Truman never saw himself as anything but an ordinary American who had been given the opportunity to accomplish extraordinary things. His elevation to the presidency was nothing he ever imagined but came to him by dint of circumstance: he had risen from Missouri farmer to World War I army captain to local officeholder to U.S. senator to vice president and president. And while he was entirely willing to acknowledge how much of a part luck or accident had played in his good fortune, he also believed that his personal attributes had something to do with landing him in the White House. Now he hoped that a combination of favorable developments and his commitment to a new world league would make the UN a reality.

Truman saw establishing the international organization as not only wise policy but also good domestic politics. A public conviction that FDR had made a special connection to Stalin, which had overcome difficulties between them, convinced Truman that for the sake of both international progress and national harmony, he would need to do the same. Because the Stalin-Roosevelt connection had been forged in face-to-face meetings, Truman hoped that future conversations with Stalin would persuade him to continue taking "a reasonable attitude," as he apparently had in discussions with FDR.

Stettinius's vision of a new era in international relations also partly rested on a record of personal success. He had been a highly successful businessman, and chairman of the board of U.S. Steel. Roosevelt had brought him into government to help manage the country's wartime industrial production and lend-lease. His effectiveness had persuaded Roosevelt to make him undersecretary of state in 1943, where he had reorganized the department. His effectiveness in preliminary talks on the founding of the UN had persuaded the president to appoint him secretary of state when Cordell Hull resigned for health reasons in November 1944.

Although associates at the State Department and in the press saw Stettinius as handsome, affable, charming, and adept at muting personal tensions, they considered him something of a lightweight, a man with limited knowledge and understanding of the world. Nevertheless, they appreciated that he brought an enthusiasm and optimism to his leadership of the San Francisco meeting that might, in conjunction with the president's genuine commitment to U.S. support for a new world league, bring the deliberations to a successful conclusion.

It was a daunting task that took two months of tense bargaining and left many doubtful that the result would make the world any safer from future conflicts. Soviet-American clashes over the admission of two Soviet Republics, Ukraine and Belarus, of Argentina with a pro-Fascist history, and a suspect Poland under Soviet control, as well as a renewed struggle over the veto power or Russia's ability to block action against potential acts of aggression repeatedly brought the conference to the edge of collapse.

These events occurred against a backdrop of Soviet-American

tensions: a Truman decision to cut off lend-lease shipments to Russia in mid-May seemed to signal an end to wartime cooperation. But the law governing lend-lease mandated an end-of-war stoppage and a mission to Moscow at the end of the month by Harry Hopkins, who had been Roosevelt's personal conduit to Stalin, temporarily eased difficulties and facilitated compromises that gave birth to the United Nations. The conversations with Stalin, Harriman advised the president, were "a great help. If it were possible to see him more frequently, many of our difficulties could be overcome." The report increased Truman's eagerness for a personal meeting.

The new organization, however, seemed unlikely to have the power to prevent future wars. Like its League of Nations predecessor, decisions over war and peace would remain invested not in the world organization but with the great powers or coalitions of states jousting with each other for national security and international control.

John F. Kennedy, the son of prominent wealthy businessman and former ambassador to Britain Joseph Kennedy, correctly pronounced on the results of the San Francisco meeting. A navy veteran with credentials as a war hero and the author of a popular 1940 book on foreign affairs, *Why England Slept*, Kennedy covered the conference for two Hearst newspapers. He thought the new world body would "reflect the fact that there are deep disagreements among its members. . . . It is unfortunate that unity for war against a common aggressor is far easier to obtain than unity for peace." He did not think that people all over the world were "horrified by war to a sufficient extent" that they were ready to relinquish national sovereignty to a world government. "War will exist until that distant day when the conscientious objector enjoys the same reputation and prestige that the warrior does today."

New Yorker editor E. B. White shared Kennedy's pessimism. He came away from San Francisco with the feeling that nation-states were incapable of "applying law and justice to each other. . . . Justice and law do not now operate and will never operate until there is international government." He complained that "under all is the steady throbbing of the engines: sovereignty, sovereignty, sovereignty."

Kennedy and White were less cynical than realistic. While President Truman's injunction to the new organization "not [to] fail to grasp this supreme chance to establish a world-wide rule of reason—to create an enduring peace under the guidance of God" was an appropriate expression of hope at the close of the conference, his words could not overcome the limitations of the UN in its reach for international peace. It lacked the wherewithal to prevent the numerous wars and civil upheavals that would plague the world through the rest of the century and beyond.

Yet in spite of its shortcomings, the UN would have its share of unanticipated accomplishments: aid to displaced persons and victims of natural disasters such as famines, tsunamis, cyclones, and floods, support for environmental protections and nuclear nonproliferation, peacekeeping troops holding off explosions of ethnic cleansing and cross-border violence, and monitors trying to assure honest elections in countries struggling to establish representative governments.

Moreover, Kennedy and White were too pessimistic about the capacity of national states to curb their militarism or affinity for organized violence. The reluctance of either Germany or Japan to rebuild armies and navies that consumed so much of their country's resources in the 1930s and '40s suggests that defeat, unlike after World War I, was not a lost memory or a spur to overcome past humiliations by acts of revenge. Only in response to Cold War tensions would Germany re-create an army in 1954.

The same was not true of the United States and Soviet Russia, the greatest victors in World War II. The devastation suffered by the Soviet Union became not an inducement to passivity but a reason to build as powerful a military machine as possible—one that could ensure the safety of the country from a rerun of the horrors suffered between 1941 and 1945. Similarly, the United States saw the war as a cautionary tale: isolationism and unpreparedness had been prescriptions for war, not peace. However much war seemed a monstrous alternative to peace, Soviet and American leaders made their differences not a rationale for heroic efforts at accommodation—although initiatives in that direction were not lacking, especially from the American side—but a basis for distrust and fear, the twin sources of preparations for war.

Ultimately, one of the great tragedies of World War II after the death of so many millions was that it became not an object lesson in how devastating modern weaponry had made wars of any kind—not just total war—but the foundation for military buildups by America and Russia, the two greatest victors in the conflict. Soviet defense investments deprived the consumer economy of resources that could have improved Russia's low living standards. Ironically, Soviet military outlays ultimately contributed more to the collapse of Soviet communism than to its preservation.

In the United States, President Dwight Eisenhower's 1961 warning against the dangers of the military-industrial complex came too late to forestall the destructive influence of the national security state. The permanent defense establishment—especially civilian national security officials bolstered by widespread, overwrought fears of communism—not only undermined democratic processes and liberties at home but also produced unwise actions abroad: witch hunts and the suppression of dissenting domestic opinion, the subversion of foreign governments in Latin America, Asia, and the Middle East, unnecessary wars in Vietnam and Iraq. The die was cast in the war years after Pearl Harbor and by the evolving tensions between East and West in the months between the closing days of World War II and the ossification of the Cold War in 1947.

4

HOPE AND DESPAIR

There, then, he sat, the sign and symbol of a man without faith,
hopelessly holding up hope in the midst of despair.
— Herman Melville, *Moby-Dick*

Now I am become death, the destroyer of worlds.
— J. Robert Oppenheimer, 1965, recalled quoting the
Bhagavad Gita, the Hindu scripture, as his reaction to
the atomic bomb test in New Mexico on July 12, 1945

With the war over in Europe, costly fighting still ahead against Japan, and a United Nations organization given life in June, Truman wanted to believe that Stalin and the Soviets would be eager to find enough common ground with the United States to ensure the peace for as far into the future as either of them could see. And yet the recent divisions over Poland and Eastern Europe raised serious doubts about the durability of the East-West alliance.

A meeting between Churchill, Stalin, and Truman, which all three agreed was needed to settle postwar arrangements for Germany, was scheduled for mid-July in Potsdam, a suburb of Berlin. The discussions seemed likely to be a major test of what to expect from the Big Three powers in postwar Europe.

The end of the war had freed Stalin to consult his worst angels. He had never entirely trusted his allies: knowing how quick he would be to exploit any irresoluteness they showed toward his reach for Soviet national security advantages, he assumed they were as ruthlessly self-serving as he was. In 1944 he confided his suspicions of the British and Americans to Milovan Djilas, Marshal Tito's Yugoslav representative: his alliance with the English did not mean "that we have forgotten who they are and who Churchill is." Stalin recalled the British and American interventions in the post–World War I civil war between Red and White Russians in support of the conservatives. "And Churchill?" he asked rhetorically. "Churchill is the kind who, if you don't watch him, will slip a kopeck out of your pocket! And Roosevelt? Roosevelt is not like that. He dips in his hand for bigger coins. But Churchill? Churchill—even for a kopeck."

The establishment of pro-Soviet regimes in Eastern Europe in the closing months of the war had convinced Churchill that nothing but the firmest response to Moscow would secure Polish independence and impede Communist domination of eastern Central Europe, the Balkans, and parts of Western Europe, where he expected Stalin to encourage Communist parties to reach for control or at least a share of power. Three days after Roosevelt's death, Churchill cabled Truman, "I am much concerned at the likelihood of Russian armies occupying large parts of Austria before any decisions are agreed for allied action in that country. I fear that this may have incalculable effects if we do not at once make clear to the Russians our very real interest in what happens in Austria." Truman entirely agreed, and his response convinced Churchill that the new president "is not to be bullied by the Soviets."

Churchill also made his concerns clear to Stalin. At the end of April, he bluntly cabled him that "there is not much comfort in looking into a future where you and the countries you dominate, plus the Communist parties in many other States, are all drawn up on one side, and those who rally to the English-speaking nations and their associates . . . are on the other. It is quite obvious that their quarrel would tear the world to pieces and that all of us leading men on either side who had anything to do with that would be shamed before history."

By May, Churchill was convinced that "nothing can save us from a great catastrophe but a meeting and a showdown as early as possible at some point in Germany." He told Truman that "correspondence" could not settle current differences and "that, as soon as possible, there should be a meeting of the three heads of Government."

Churchill was so distrustful of Stalin's intentions and so determined to resist them that he asked British military chiefs to develop a plan of attack against the Soviet Union. Titled "Russia: A Menace to World Civilization" and code-named "Operation Unthinkable," it was seen by Sir Alan Brooke, the chief of the General Staff, as "fantastic and the chance of success quite impossible." The very existence of such a plan, however, spoke volumes about the extent to which East-West relations had deteriorated rapidly in the days after victory in Europe.

Truman saw the need for a meeting, but resisted a suggestion that he travel first to London, where Churchill promised him "a great reception from the British nation." Churchill wanted them to send a message to "U. J.," as he and FDR had privately referred to Stalin, by flying together to the conference in Germany. Truman vetoed this proposal as well: "In order to avoid any suspicion of our 'ganging up' it would be advantageous for us to proceed to the meeting place separately."

Truman disliked traveling to Europe for a confrontational conference. "I am getting ready to go see Stalin and Churchill," he wrote his mother, "and it is a chore. I have to take my tuxedo, tails, Negro preacher coat, high hat, low hat and hard hat. . . . I have a brief case filled up with information on past conferences and suggestions on what I'm to do and say. Wish I didn't have to go but I do." He confided to a diary as a navy cruiser carried him across the Atlantic, "How I hate this trip!" The thought that he might not measure up to his two counterparts—"Mr. Russia and Mr. Great Britain," he called them—worried him. He viewed himself as something of an interloper, a replacement for the irreplaceable Roosevelt, who he believed had made an indelible mark on Churchill and Stalin.

His anxiety about replacing Roosevelt is entirely understandable. Roosevelt's presence—as the longest-serving president in American history, the architect of the country's economic recovery and its victory in the greatest war ever fought—seemed essential to closing out the Pacific fighting and meeting postwar challenges: demobilization and economic stability at home and reconstruction abroad. As worrisome for Truman, would either Churchill or Stalin show him the regard they had for FDR? Even though he was president, with all the power that implied, would he be able to exert the sort of influence on the British and Soviet representatives that his predecessor surely could have commanded?

To ease his fears, Truman asked Eleanor Roosevelt for advice about dealing with Churchill. She responded: "If you talk to him about books and let him quote to you from his marvelous memory, everything on earth from Barbara Frietchie to the Nonsense Rhymes and Greek Tragedy, you will find him easier to deal with on political subjects. He is a gentleman to whom the personal element means a great deal."

Truman took some comfort from knowing that he had a way with people—that he had managed to get as far as he had by winning the Missouri public and tough-minded Washington politicians to his side. Moreover, the presence of colleagues he trusted, especially men who had had direct contact with Stalin and Churchill, also eased his concerns: the new secretary of state, James Byrnes; Roosevelt's principal chief of staff, Admiral William D. Leahy; General George C. Marshall; Ambassador Averell Harriman; and Soviet expert Charles Bohlen, who was to be his translator.

Truman had been particularly eager to replace Stettinius with Byrnes—not only because he barely knew Stettinius and had a warm relationship with Byrnes dating from their days in the Senate, but also because Byrnes, as secretary, with no constitutional provision for a vice president to replace Truman, would be next in line for the presidency should Truman die. Since Roosevelt had seen Byrnes as a potential successor, Truman believed it would reassure the public that two men FDR considered suited to be president would be representing the country at Potsdam and in other end-of-war and postwar dealings.

The presence of his close friends and poker-playing cronies from Kansas City days—Charlie Ross, now his press secretary; General Harry Vaughan, White House military aide; and Fred Canfil, the U.S. marshal of Kansas City, now Truman's special bodyguard—lightened the president's daily burdens during the crossing when they played poker and, after, at the conference, when they gave him occasional moments of relaxed conversation. Truman took special amusement from introducing Canfil to the Russians as "Marshal Canfil," suggesting to them that he was a high-ranking military man they had never heard of.

After Truman met Churchill on the morning of July 16 in Potsdam, he came away with renewed confidence in himself. With Stalin not arriving until the next day, Churchill had convinced Truman to see him as a prelude to formal conference sessions. Although they had spoken by telephone several times in the three months since Truman had become president, it was a chance to establish the personal rapport Mrs. Roosevelt had recommended. Because Truman still worried that Stalin would see their preliminary meeting as teaming up against him, he resisted discussing conference issues.

Their meeting took place at Truman's residence three miles outside of Potsdam, a three-story villa, which Truman described as having a "nightmare" interior with heavy dark furnishings that seemed to reflect the gloom that had settled over postwar Berlin. Despite a meeting notable for its absence of substantive discussion about postwar problems, Truman made a positive impression on the prime minister. Churchill saw him as someone with a "gay, precise, sparkling manner and obvious power of decision."

Truman was less impressed with Churchill. "We had a most pleasant conversation," he confided to a diary. "He is a most charming and a very clever person—meaning clever in the English not the

Kentucky [horse] sense. He gave me a lot of hooey about how great my country is and how he loved Roosevelt and how he intended to love me etc. etc. . . . I am sure we can get along if he doesn't try to give me too much soft soap. . . . Soft soap is made of ashhopple lye and it burns to beat hell when it gets into the eyes."

Truman also found Churchill's pleasure in the sound of his own voice disconcerting. He later complained that "Churchill was a man who didn't listen very often. . . . He was more of a talker than a listener. He liked to talk, and he was one of the best." After Stalin and Churchill proposed that Truman act as chairman at the Potsdam conference, Truman found it as "hard as presiding over the Senate. Churchill talks all the time and Stalin just grunts but you know what he means."

After their morning meeting, Churchill and Truman separately visited Berlin's inner city, which Churchill said "was nothing but a chaos of ruins." The people, notable for their "haggard looks and threadbare clothes," had been the victims of Hitler's fight to the "bitter end." Truman thought "that a more depressing sight than that of the ruined buildings was the long, never-ending procession of old men, women, children wandering aimlessly along the autobahn and the country roads carrying, pushing, or pulling what was left of their belongings. . . . I saw evidence of that great world tragedy, and I was thankful that the United States had been spared the unbelievable devastation of this war."

The scenes of destruction made Truman melancholy about prospects for civilized behavior. "What a pity that the human animal is not able to put his moral thinking into practice!" he told his diary. "I fear that machines are ahead of morals by some centuries. We are only termites on a planet and maybe when we bore too deeply into the planet there'll be a reckoning—who knows?"

As Truman and Churchill saw, the key to future peace would be dependent on Stalin's accommodation with the West. However much the president admired Churchill for his courageous leadership in the face of overwhelming odds at the start of the war, Truman saw him as too belligerent or ready for confrontation with the Soviets. He had greater hope than Churchill that they could sustain good relations with Stalin. Moreover, he was confident that Britain's dependence on the United States for reconstruction of its shattered economy would force Churchill to follow his lead on working out differences with Moscow and setting them on a long-term path toward peace.

Truman was much less certain about taming Stalin. He was the riddle, the mystery, the enigma, as Churchill had said of Russia, in the yearning for an era of quiet in international affairs. Stalin understood that his country's defeat of the Nazis had now made it the dominant power on the Continent. When he came a day late to the conference, he justified it as the result of a slight heart attack. But he was in fact making a statement about relative might: his allies—Britain and America—had to wait on him to discuss Europe's future. While he was eager for U.S. financial help in rebuilding Russia's shattered infrastructure, his armies were now in a position to shape the life of the eastern part of the Continent and possibly part of Western Europe and East Asia as well. U.S. eagerness for help in ending the Pacific War had allowed Stalin to make several successful demands on FDR for Soviet advantages in Japan and China.

Soviet power was on full display at Potsdam. Some twenty thousand Soviet troops—seven NKVD or secret police regiments, including sixteen companies of NKVD soldiers to guard Stalin's phone lines, and nine hundred personal bodyguards—oversaw the generalissimo's safety.

Churchill and Truman were sympathetic to Stalin's determination to secure his country's future safety. But his refusal to give ground on Anglo-American demands about Poland and Eastern Europe generally frustrated them and made them believe he was interested less in good relations with his allies or democratic outcomes for countries they liberated from the Nazis than establishing Soviet dominance on the Continent as the best way to assure Soviet security. They were, however, reluctant to believe that after all the suffering in the war Stalin would be so reckless as to risk renewed conflict for the sake of Russian Communist ambitions.

And Stalin, who assumed he could achieve his foreign policy goals without provoking Britain or the United States into retaliatory actions, presented enough of a friendly face at the conference to keep Anglo-American hopes alive for mutually acceptable dealings. In his social exchanges with Churchill, Stalin displayed "an easy friendliness," which Churchill found "most agreeable." As Stalin puffed on a cigar at the conference's opening session in the Cecilienhof Palace, a Tudor-style structure built for Germany's crown prince in 1917, Churchill told Stalin that a photo of him smoking "a Churchillian cigar" would "create an immense sensation. . . . Everyone will say it is my influence." Stalin predicted that the result of a current British Parliamentary election would favor Churchill and his conservative party. "It seemed plain," Churchill concluded, "that he hoped that his contacts with me and [Foreign Secretary Anthony] Eden would not be broken."

Truman also saw Stalin's beneficent side, or at least the reasonable, accommodating character he pretended to be. When he came to call on July 17, before the first formal session of the conference convened, Truman was struck by how short in stature Stalin was, at five foot six. It must have given Truman some feeling of strength to learn that at five foot eight he was taller than both Churchill and Stalin. The fact of their relative height, which he made note of in a diary and repeated over ten years later in his memoirs, registered strongly on him.

Truman tried to establish a rapport with the formidable Stalin by declaring at once that he was someone who did not beat around the bush or use diplomatic language. After hearing both sides of an argument, he would simply say yes or no. Stalin seemed to like the president's forthrightness. Truman remembered being "impressed by him. . . . He looked me in the eye when he spoke, and I felt hopeful that we could reach an agreement that would be satisfactory to the world and to ourselves." Truman's remarks seemed to put Stalin in "a good humor. He was extremely polite, and when he was ready to leave he told me that he had enjoyed the visit."

Truman was especially pleased that in this first conversation, Stalin repeated the promise he had made at Yalta, that he would join the war against Japan three months after the German defeat. Truman considered this a primary objective of the meeting, and thus recorded in a diary after Stalin left, "I can deal with Stalin. He is honest—but smart as hell." Searching for comparisons to other powerful figures he had known in his life, Truman thought of him as a Russian Tom Pendergast, the Democratic Party boss in Kansas City, who Truman saw as tough and even ruthless but likable and loyal to his friends.

Truman's inclination to trust Stalin, or at least hope that they could get along, reflected the American affinity for friendly dealings in a peaceful world. Like most of his countrymen, Truman wanted to believe that the horrors of the war had sobered leaders and peoples everywhere into extending themselves as far as possible in reaching agreements that promised a more benign future. As Americans had believed since the founding of the Republic, the path to such an outcome would be through not traditional power politics supported by armies and navies, but respect for an international rule of law against aggression and self-determination for all nationalities.

Charles Bohlen, an American diplomat in Moscow whose close-up observations of events under Stalin gave him a greater hold on Soviet realities, was not taken in by the Russian leader's posturing. "There was little in Stalin's demeanor in the presence of foreigners that gave any clue of the real nature and character of the man. . . . He was exemplary in his behavior. He was patient, a good listener, always quiet in his manner and expression. There were no signs of the harsh and brutal nature behind this mask." Like his fellow Soviet expert George F. Kennan, Bohlen believed that Americans had to curb their traditional aversion to power politics and see the world in general and Stalin and the Soviets more specifically for what they were.

On July 17, the second day of the conference, in another private meeting at Stalin's residence during a return courtesy call, Truman found the generalissimo even more cordial than the day before. Stalin reciprocated the president's hospitality with a sumptuous lunch. He declared his eagerness to continue Soviet-American cooperation, but complained that it was made difficult by misperceptions in their respective countries. Truman promised to try to correct this impression in the United States, and Stalin with "a most cordial smile . . . said he would do as much in Russia."

It was not misperceptions, however, that divided the two countries; it was the realities of distrust generated by clashing interests and ideologies. As soon as conference discussions focused on Germany, Italy, Poland, Rumania, Bulgaria, Hungary, Finland, and a Truman proposal for freedom of movement on all of the world's inland waterways, Allied differences became evident. Soviet ideas about the occupation of Germany, reparations for war damages, revised eastern borders, and what constituted democratic governments in Poland and other liberated countries sparked renewed antagonism.

The Allies quarreled over the admission of Italy, Romania, Bulgaria, and Hungary to the United Nations. Churchill and Truman supported Italy's inclusion, and the exclusion of the Balkan countries until the Soviets allowed democratic elections. But Stalin objected that Italy had an unelected government imposed by its occupiers, and since the Balkan states did not have Fascist governments, they should be considered democratic. Churchill angrily replied that Italy had a free press and freedom of movement for both its citizens and foreigners, but none of this was so in the Balkans, where Western diplomats lived as if under house arrest. "An iron fence had come down around them," Churchill protested.

"Fairy tales!" Stalin replied.

Eight days into the conference, British election results that toppled Churchill's government and made Labor Party chief Clement Attlee prime minister and Ernest Bevin foreign secretary opened an additional divide between Stalin and the West. Although British voters, having suffered through the depression and the war, had demonstrated their eagerness for a cradle-to-grave welfare state by electing Attlee by a landslide, Stalin saw Attlee as a stuffed shirt, a typically formal Englishman who lacked Churchill's talent and effectiveness. Stalin also preferred Foreign Secretary Anthony Eden to Bevin, an outspoken anti-Communist trade unionist. Churchill and Eden were the devils Stalin knew, as opposed to devils who had no motivation to accommodate him without a common enemy. With both wartime partners gone, Stalin could not imagine a future without a reversion to the natural antagonisms between evangelical capitalism and messianic communism.

Truman was also disappointed by Churchill's defeat. He wrote his daughter that "Attlee is not so keen as old fat Winston," and while he thought Churchill was too "windy," he was reliable. He didn't feel comfortable with either Attlee or Bevin, who he called a couple of "sourpusses." Attlee, "an Oxford graduate," whose "deep throated swallowing enunciation" made him at times difficult to understand, and Bevin, "a John L. Lewis" or "tough guy" type, reminded Truman of the American labor bosses he had been dealing with all his life and didn't like.

Churchill's defeat should have alerted Truman to the shifting mood in the victorious nations. Success in the war meant not just an end to the fighting but an opportunity to shift from wartime sacrifices to a focus on domestic benefits—the chance to use wartime savings to buy homes and cars and all the household electronic gadgets the war had taken out of production. The premium now was on not sacrifice but indulgence, a sort of reward for the hardships of the war years. Moreover, in Britain and America, people wanted not conservative rhetoric about self-reliance, free enterprise, and competition but assurances of well-paying jobs, affordable health care, and old-age pensions. Churchill's loss marked a dramatic turn from war to peace in Britain. Until Japan was finished off, however, Americans would have to hold their yearnings for peace and material consumption in check.

The continuing talks at Potsdam kept end-of-war issues very much before the Allied leaders. Although Stalin, Truman, and Attlee, who had replaced Churchill at the conference, managed to reach agreements on the occupation of Germany and distribution of reparations from its industrial plant as well as on a Soviet part in the war against Japan beginning in August, Truman, by the end of the talks, was not fooled by Stalin's false camaraderie. Eager not to jeopardize Stalin's promise to enter the Pacific War or to provoke domestic recriminations by showing any daylight between his and Roosevelt's policies toward Moscow, Truman publicly put a positive face on Soviet-American dealings at this final Big Three wartime meeting.

In private, however, Truman was scathing about what his discussions with Stalin and the Soviets taught him. He considered them impossibly self-serving and unyielding in their determination to squeeze every possible advantage from an adversary. "You never saw such pig-headed people as are the Russians," he wrote his mother. "I hope I never have to hold another conference with them—but, of course, I will." Worse, they were a ruthless crowd. He still thought Stalin likable enough, but the Soviet leader presided over a regime that was "police government pure and simple. A few top hands just take clubs, pistols and concentration camps and rule the people on the lower levels."

During the conference, the Pacific War preoccupied Truman. Because the savagery of the fighting had increased as U.S. forces had advanced across the Pacific (over half of America's military casualties in the Pacific fighting occurred in the last year of the war), he feared that an invasion of Japan could cost tens of thousands of American lives. Stalin's promise to enter the fighting held out hope that Japan might surrender before U.S. air and land forces wreaked destruction on its home islands. At a minimum, Truman believed that a Soviet offensive could prevent possibly a million Japanese troops in China from returning to defend against an invasion.

The other possibility was that atomic bombs would be ready before the end of the summer, and their use on Japan could bring a quick end to the war. Because Truman came to Potsdam uncertain about both Soviet intentions and the bomb's availability, he worried that the Pacific War could last well into 1946 or longer and test the American public beyond its patience for unconditional surrender. It could also undermine his presidency and his power to manage a smooth transition to postwar life. Consequently, Stalin's promise to join the fighting in August buoyed him greatly.

News of a successful atomic test at Alamogordo in the New Mexico desert boosted Truman even more. On the evening of July 16, Truman received first word of a successful test explosion earlier that day. On the morning of the eighteenth, additional word came of the successful test results. But it wasn't until July 21 that he had a detailed report on the power of the new weapon.

General Leslie R. Groves of the Army Corps of Engineers, the officer in charge of the Manhattan Project, as the bomb's development organization was code-named, described the extraordinary power of the explosion. "The test was successful beyond the most optimistic expectations of anyone," equivalent to fifteen to twenty thousand tons of TNT, at a conservative estimate, he wrote, with "tremendous blast effects . . . a lighting effect . . . equal to several suns in midday . . . a blind woman saw the light . . . a huge ball of fire . . . mushroomed and rose to a height of over ten thousand feet . . . light from the explosion was seen . . . to about 180 miles away"; a window was broken 125 miles from the blast; a seventy-foot steel tower, the equivalent of a six-story building, half a mile away, which "none of us expected to be damaged," was pulverized.

Groves also sent Truman and Secretary of War Henry L. Stimson the eyewitness account of General Thomas F. Farrell, who was at a control shelter ten thousand yards from the point of explosion. The test results produced shouts of glee from the scientists, who had worked so hard to achieve what at times appeared impossible: "All seemed to sense immediately that the explosion had far exceeded the most optimistic expectations and wildest hopes of the scientists. All seemed to feel that they had been present at the birth of a new age—The Age of Atomic Energy. As for the present war, there was the feeling that no matter what else might happen we now had the means to insure its speedy conclusion and save thousands of American lives. As to the future . . . the effects could well be called unprecedented, magnificent, beautiful, stupendous and terrifying."

Truman was "immensely pleased. The President was tremendously pepped up by it and spoke to me of it again and again when I saw him," Stimson recorded. "He said it gave him an entirely new feeling of confidence and he thanked me for coming to the Conference and being present to help him in this way." Churchill and Harriman saw a striking change in Truman's demeanor and behavior after he read Groves's report. "He stood up to the Russians in a most emphatic and decisive manner," Churchill noted. "He told the Russians just where they got on and off and generally bossed the whole meeting."

Some of the scientists greeted the successful A-bomb test with as much anguish as elation. Robert Oppenheimer, the lead physicist on the project, was exhilarated at the culmination of the work, but he told one of his colleagues, "Now we're all sons-of-bitches." Within days of the test, Oppenheimer rued the forthcoming use of the bomb on Japan: "Those poor little people, those poor little people," Oppenheimer said, "referring to the Japanese." Three months later, Oppenheimer wrote, "If atomic bombs are to be added as new weapons to the arsenals of a warring world, or to the arsenals of nations preparing for war, then the time will come when mankind will curse the names of Los Alamos and Hiroshima."

Truman was not unmindful of the future dangers posed by the weapon. "We have discovered the most terrible bomb in the history of the world," he recorded in a diary on July 25. Remembering his Bible, he said the bomb could be "the Second Coming in Wrath. It may be the fire destruction prophesied in the Euphrates Valley Era after Noah and the fabulous Ark." Yet he saw an upside to the discovery: "It is certainly a good thing for the world Hitler's crowd or Stalin's did not discover this atomic bomb. It seems to be the most terrible thing ever discovered but it can be made useful."

But how? He hoped that telling Stalin might pressure the Soviets into more accommodating dealings with his allies. Truman knew that Roosevelt and Churchill had tried to keep Moscow in the dark about the development of the bomb. Truman had no quarrel with that act of distrust. He consulted Churchill at once on how to tell Stalin so that it would do more to limit than increase tensions with Moscow. They agreed that he should not be given "any particulars," meaning that they would continue holding back information that could help the Soviets develop the bomb. They also considered whether a formal or informal discussion would be best.

Truman preferred a casual approach. A formal conversation might produce pressure to tell more than they wanted to say and could lead to demands that tripartite scientific and military committees be set up to bring Moscow into discussions of the bomb's development and use against Japan. They thought that they could avoid such demands by mentioning the weapon to Stalin almost as an afterthought at the conclusion of a conference session.

At the close of the July 24 meeting, Truman stood up from the conference table and walked alone over to Stalin, who was standing next to his translator. "I casually mentioned to Stalin that we had a new weapon of unusual destructive force," Truman remembered saying. "All he said was that he was glad to hear it and hoped we would make 'good use of it against the Japanese.'" Churchill, who was standing fifteen feet from them and knew what Truman was doing, watched with the keenest interest. The expression on Stalin's face never changed. Churchill was "sure that he had no idea of the significance of what he was being told. . . . If he had the slightest idea of the revolution in world affairs which was in progress his reactions would have been obvious. . . . [Instead] his face remained gay and genial and the talk between these two potentates soon came to an end."

Churchill and others watching the exchange, who reached similar conclusions, couldn't have been more wrong. Kept up to date on the Manhattan Project by the British physicist and naturalized citizen Klaus Fuchs, Stalin understood that Truman's report was the culmination of what the Americans had been working toward. In fact, Soviet scientists were also trying to build a bomb. But a lack of uranium oxide had limited their progress on Operation Borodino, the code name for their program. To speed production, Stalin had been determined to capture Berlin before the Americans or British—not only as a symbolic demonstration of Soviet military victory but also as a way to assure long-term Soviet presence in the German capital and the capture of the Kaiser Wilhelm Institute for Physics, in a suburb of Berlin, where German uranium was supposed to be stored.

When Stalin reported his exchange with Truman about the "new weapon" to Molotov, Gromyko, and Marshal Georgy Zhukov that evening, Molotov, who was in charge of the Soviet bomb project, said, "They're raising their price." Stalin replied, "Let them. We'll have to talk it over with [the lead Soviet research scientist, physicist Igor] Kurchatov and get him to speed things up." Stalin told Molotov and Gromyko that the Allies "are hoping that we won't be able to develop the Bomb ourselves for some time" and "want to force us to accept their plans. Well that's not going to happen." Stalin then "cursed them in what Gromyko called 'ripe language.' " He now replaced Molotov with Beria as the official responsible for accelerating Soviet progress.

The Anglo-American-Soviet discussions about the A-bomb were a mutual exercise in bad judgment; they may be described as the beginning of the Cold War. Churchill and Truman knew that Stalin had discussed sharing information on weapons development in 1942. And while the atom bomb was anything but a conventional armament, they surely understood, as Roosevelt had, that if and when Stalin learned of secret U.S.-British nuclear research, it would inflame his suspicions of them and make it more difficult to cooperate in a postwar world. Given how eager they were to deter him from considering a separate peace with their unconditional surrender declaration and their repeated assurances of a second front, how could they not understand how secretiveness about such a revolutionary weapon would revive prewar tensions? Moreover, they knew that physicists everywhere had been discussing atomic research for a number of years, and that all of the belligerents were aware of its potential use in a superweapon. Rather than believing that Stalin's bland reaction signaled his ignorance of Anglo-American nuclear research, they should have been convinced that he knew of their work on a bomb and was posturing for political reasons.

How much better it might have been if Truman and Churchill had invited Stalin to a confidential meeting with only translators present and told him not only about the bomb but also of their eagerness to prevent a future nuclear arms race by strictly limiting scientific and technical information about the bomb.

Stalin might have then acted like a spurned suitor, who despite all his country's sacrifices in the war was being treated more like a potential enemy than an ally. But if he had been capable of greater openness and stated his fears of Germany's military revival, insisted on assurances against such a development, and promised self-determination for East European countries in return for a commitment to Germany's permanent demilitarization, the march toward East-West conflict might have been averted. It's even conceivable that Stalin's candid insistence on pro-Soviet governments west of Russia's immediate borders and expressions of support for representative governments in Greece, Turkey, and all of Western Europe, which he had no intention to make Soviet satellites, might have brought a vastly different result after 1945.

Of course, Stalin's paranoia and his ideological conviction that conflicts with capitalist states were inevitable made accommodation unlikely. Moreover, any inclination he had to be more cooperative in dealings with the West were countered by his understanding that neither the United States nor Britain were about to start a war with him in 1945. Nonetheless, the A-bomb gave America a military advantage that he could imagine Washington using against the USSR, especially because it was the sort of action he himself might have taken if he had such an edge. Greater openness about the bomb would at least have given Washington and London a moral high ground, which they could have used in the developing battle for hearts and minds in the Third World. Such openness might have been dismissed by emerging nations as moral posturing, but nothing would have been lost by telling Moscow about the bomb—no one was suggesting helping Stalin build his own weapon—and it could have countered later recriminations in the United States about America's part in causing the Cold War.

All this is to suggest that both sides might have been prepared to make commitments to words and deeds that could have altered traditional power politics. Not surprisingly, after so devastating a war, both sides were making rhetorical pronouncements, as they had after World War I, on their determination to move the world in a new direction toward lasting peace. But it was rhetoric devoid of firm conviction: the terrible losses in a global conflict had made the great powers more determined than ever to make their highest priority not world peace but the security of their respective nations. That is certainly understandable, but greater regard for each other's safety from future attacks would not necessarily have translated into diminished national security.

It is not difficult to understand the different outlooks between East and West. Stalin and his Soviet cohorts genuinely saw capitalist countries as their devout enemies—no matter the collaboration in the war or their rhetoric about future joint efforts for peace. The desire to survive had propelled the wartime cooperation, but Western evangelism about economic and political freedom had made conflict with communism inevitable, or so Stalin firmly believed. Similarly, London and Washington found it difficult to imagine a benign Soviet Russia, which did not see itself as the center of world revolution against open societies across Europe and around the globe. Nor could they forget the appeasement of the dictators in the 1930s; the lesson learned was to stand firm when a totalitarian regime showed any signs of aggression. It was a prescription for the same old nationalistic rivalries under a different name, which was all too likely to lead to future wars.

"A sense of reality," Canadian Liberal Party leader and former Harvard scholar Michael Ignatieff writes, "is not just a sense of the world as it is, but as it might be. Like great artists, great politicians see possibilities others cannot and then seek to turn them into realities. To bring the new into being, a politician needs a sense of timing, of when to leap and when to remain still. Bismarck famously remarked that political judgment was the ability to hear, before anyone else, the distant hoof beats of the horse of history."

The experience of the recent past, rather than the long-term future or "distant hoof beats," also shaped decisions about ending the Pacific War. Forcing Japan's unconditional surrender as quickly and inexpensively in the cost of American lives was Truman's foremost priority.

Stalin told the president at Potsdam that Japanese officials had approached Moscow about mediating peace talks, but Truman had no interest. He assumed that Tokyo would insist on concessions to end the fighting, and this would have meant abandoning FDR's unconditional surrender doctrine. Considerations of postwar peace in Asia and domestic politics deterred him from letting Tokyo make demands of any sort, especially now that atomic bombs seemed likely to compel Japanese capitulation without concessions. When Stalin indicated that he would give no encouragement to Japanese interest in talks, Truman agreed.

The Japanese in fact wanted a commitment to leave Emperor Hirohito on the throne. But in July 1945, the White House viewed this as unacceptable. The emperor was as much a symbol of Tokyo's aggression and brutal war policies as any single Japanese, and the suggestion that he be left in power was seen as letting a leading war criminal escape punishment and remain in a position to stimulate future acts of national aggression. After all, everything the Japanese did in the war was supposedly in the service of their emperor. To fail to punish him, or at a minimum, dethrone him, which even without the war appealed to Americans with their antimonarchist tradition, was to abandon a commitment to making those responsible for all the suffering pay a price.

In a pronouncement from Potsdam on July 26, Britain, China, and the United States stated their intention "to prosecute the war against Japan until she ceases to resist." The alternative to surrender was the "complete destruction of the Japanese armed forces and . . . the utter destruction of the Japanese homeland." The declaration demanded the total elimination from power of those who had misled Japan in its quest for world conquest. "We do not intend that the Japanese shall be enslaved as a race or destroyed as a nation, but stern justice shall be meted out to all war criminals. We call upon the government of Japan to proclaim now the unconditional surrender of all Japanese armed forces. . . . The alternative for Japan is prompt and utter destruction."

Tokyo's response was "silent contempt" for what it feared would lead to the overthrow of an emperor they considered a God who bound them together as a people; his demise was tantamount to a loss of national identity. The declaration "appalled" MacArthur, who believed that the Japanese "would never submit to allied occupation unless he [the emperor] ordered it."

Unless the Japanese surrendered at once, Truman felt compelled to go forward with plans to use atomic bombs against their homeland. As a consequence, on August 6, a single U.S. B-29 aircraft, the *Enola Gay*, bombed Hiroshima with devastating results. The city of

300,000 was turned into "a burning pyre." Perhaps as many as eighty thousand people died instantly. They were the lucky ones: within days and weeks after the bombing another fifty to sixty thousand suffered agonizing deaths from radiation poisoning. On August 9, when Japan still had not surrendered, a second bomb was dropped on Nagasaki, where seventy thousand Japanese lost their lives. Although both cities were described as military targets, it was mainly civilians who died.

Were the atomic bombings necessary? Would Japan have surrendered without them before an invasion that was planned for November 1? A debate has raged in recent years over the answer to this question. In 1946 journalist John Hersey's description of the horrors caused by the Hiroshima bombing provoked national and international discussions of the need for such a devastating attack. The development of hydrogen bombs in the next decade added to the feeling that such weapons of mass destruction should be barred from use, as poison gas had been after World War I. In 1995, the fiftieth-anniversary remembrance of the Hiroshima attack, a planned *Enola Gay* exhibit at the Smithsonian Institution in Washington, D.C., touched off a fierce argument over how to describe the necessity for the only use of nuclear weapons in history. The exhibit went forward with a sanitized commentary that avoided editorial content and simply described the dropping of the bomb.

Defenders of the decision to drop the bomb argued that because an invasion of Japan would have cost so many thousands of American and Japanese lives, it was right to have forced Tokyo's surrender, which occurred on August 14 after the Hiroshima and Nagasaki attacks. Moreover, at the time, most on the Allied side saw the atomic bombings as essentially a more efficient way to strike at enemy cities than the earlier large-scale air raids that caused such massive damage to Berlin, Tokyo, and numerous other German and Japanese population centers.

Churchill recalled that there was never an actual decision to use the bomb. It was simply a given. With $2 billion invested in developing the weapon, and under the assumption that Roosevelt would have used it, Truman and his advisers could not imagine holding back on something that they assumed would spare the loss of American lives in what they believed would be a fiercely resisted invasion. "There never was a moment's discussion of whether the atomic bomb should be used or not," Churchill wrote later. "To avert a vast, indefinite butchery, to bring the war to an end, to give peace to the world, to lay healing hands on its tortured peoples by a manifestation of overwhelming power at the cost of a few explosions seemed, after all our toils and perils, a miracle of deliverance." Churchill never heard "the slightest suggestion that we should do otherwise."

Critics of the decisions to bomb Hiroshima and Nagasaki believe that Japan was on its last legs and that a blockade of its home islands, along with a demonstration of the bomb's power, could have persuaded Tokyo to surrender. In October 1945 a special Truman envoy, sent to survey conditions in Japan, reported that some of the American officers he spoke to concluded that Japan's disarray was so great prior to the Hiroshima and Nagasaki attacks that the atomic bombs speeded Japanese surrender by only a few days. The postwar U.S. Strategic Bombing Survey of the Pacific fighting asserted that even without the atomic bombs or an invasion, Japan would have been compelled to surrender before the end of 1945 and "in all probability" before November 1. Since this was guesswork by the analysts, their conclusions are and will remain open to dispute.

Critics also argued that Truman missed a chance to bring the war to a prompt end by failing to seize upon Japanese peace feelers to the Russians earlier in the summer; this would have meant accepting a demand to drop unconditional surrender, and specifically the removal of Hirohito from power and the elimination of the monarchy. Given that Truman in fact made this concession in August, when he agreed that Hirohito could remain as head of state on the understanding that supreme command in Japan would rest with the occupation authorities, critics of the atomic bombings were convinced that Truman unnecessarily resorted to the sort of savagery that the Allies had been fighting.

On August 15, when the emperor spoke directly on the radio for the first time to the Japanese people, he tried to find words that could make capitulation and humiliation palatable. Without mentioning either surrender or defeat, he urged his subjects to "endure the un-endurable," and to view his decision to stop fighting as leading the world into a new era of peace. Making implicit reference to the devas-tation caused by the atomic bombings, he warned that a continuation of the fighting could mean "the extermination of our race," which he then equated with "the destruction of all human civilization." He put the best possible face on surrender by predicting that it would now "open the way for a great peace for thousands of generations to come." The symbolic architect of Japan's aggression, which had inflicted such terrible suffering across so much of Asia, paradoxically presented himself as an agent of world peace.

However absurd, Hirohito's pronouncement foretold the great transformation that would now occur in response to Japan's defeat and the American occupation. Unlike the Americans, British, and Russians, who saw their victories as an affirmation of their respective agendas, the thoroughly defeated Japanese felt compelled to move in a new direction. The worshipful attitude toward the armed forces that had dominated Japanese thinking throughout the war gave way to contempt for veterans at all ranks. Antagonism was especially re-served for returning soldiers and sailors from China and the Pacific Islands, as reminders of national defeat and embarrassment.

The defeat and total repudiation of the civilian and military chiefs who had been such false prophets served as a critical starting point for a sea change in Japan's national outlook. Without such regrets, it would have been nearly impossible to chart a fundamental change of course in international affairs.

Churchill, Roosevelt, Stalin, and now Truman and their respective countries, who had sacrificed so much in the fighting, saw every reason to believe that a continued assertion of national interest or of what each believed essential to their well-being served not only themselves but also the world. None of them—leaders or peoples—had the imagination to hear those "distant hoof beats of history" that could have persuaded them to make the compromises needed to avert the international tensions and nuclear arms race that have come to threaten the survival of all humanity.

It was not as if a benign course of action on atomic power, which might have helped reduce future tensions, hadn't occurred to responsible Americans. In the spring of 1945, even before the Alamogordo test, a group of University of Chicago scientists who were part of the Manhattan Project unsuccessfully tried to make the case to Truman against using the bomb on Japan. Once the United States dropped the bomb, they asserted, "it would be very difficult to persuade the world" that America was "to be trusted in its proclaimed desire of having such weapons abolished by international agreement." Seventy-two percent of 150 scientists in the Manhattan Project favored a demonstration of the bomb to force Japan's surrender rather than an attack without a warning of what was coming.

Secretary of War Henry Stimson and Chief of Staff George Marshall were not indifferent to such concerns. They told a group of atomic scientists that they were sympathetic to their worries. Stimson described the bomb as a potential "Frankenstein which would eat us up." He favored a postwar "international control body" with power over atomic energy. Marshall supported the possibility of bringing two Russian scientists to New Mexico to witness the initial test.

Oppenheimer and some other scientists, who accepted the military's decision to use the bombs against Japan, took solace in hoping that the demonstration of the atom's destructiveness might shock the world into ending war. Future conflicts with atomic attacks would likely be seen as acts of mutual destruction or mutual national suicide. Even Stalin saw the use of the bomb as an act of "superbarbarity" in a barbaric war. "There was no need to use it," he said privately. "Japan was already doomed." But instead of convincing him to abandon plans to build a Soviet bomb, it persuaded him that he had no choice: "A-bomb blackmail is American policy," he declared.

Stalin now believed that a nuclear-armed United States, which previously seemed to lack the wherewithal to challenge Russia in Europe, where the Soviets would have superior land armies and the Americans would be eager to bring their troops home, could threaten the USSR with A-bombs delivered by air forces. In Stalin's view, Washington's acquisition of atom bombs changed the power balance in Europe and intensified his determination to match America's new-found power by pressing the case for the Soviet nuclear program.

In September, after Japan's surrender, Stimson made the case to Truman for shared international control that would include the Soviets and aim to outlaw proliferation of atomic bombs. He argued that the United States and Britain would not be able to maintain a monopoly on the weapon and that any attempt to do so would provoke an arms race with Moscow that would eventually threaten nuclear war. Stimson believed that a prompt, direct approach to the Soviets about the bomb would provide the best opportunity "to proscribe atomic weapons and to encourage scientific collaboration" for peaceful uses.

But memories of Germany's appeasement, Japanese perfidy, and postwar Soviet aggressiveness in Eastern Europe persuaded Truman that Russia was not to be trusted and that a likely arms race would allow the United States, with its superiority in resources and know-how, to maintain its advantage over any competitor. The key to peace was not in idealistic cooperation but in unsentimental assertiveness of American strength. At the beginning of October, when Truman made it clear that he would not share America's bomb-building capacity with other nations, newspapers around the country endorsed his announcement as a wise defense of the nation's future security.

When a friend privately asked the president if the "armaments race is on," he said yes, and predicted that "we would stay ahead." He described "America's control of atomic power as a 'sacred trust.' "

Truman's statement is understandable in the context of 1945: having defeated the most terrible regimes in history, the president and the great majority of Americans saw themselves as trustees of the good, of a set of civilized values that any rational person would prefer to the ruthless convictions that had driven America's enemies. But the assumption that the United States would always represent the best in human behavior was less than convincing. As George Kennan would point out thirty years later, exaggerated fears might drive even the most well intentioned leaders into the use of nuclear weapons that would produce "utter disaster for all of us," as was the case during the Cuban missile crisis of 1962, when Moscow and Washington came close to an unwanted nuclear conflict.

Kennan came to believe that "the nuclear bomb is the most useless weapon ever invented. It can be employed to no rational purpose." He acknowledged the appeal of "deterrence," the belief that the bomb was a guard against its use by others against us and the fact that there had been no war between great powers since 1945. But Truman's idea that America's continued possession and control of these weapons of mass destruction would likely make the world safer from war was an illusion. The possession of these armaments by one nation was bound to lead to an arms race, as Truman acknowledged already had begun in 1945. And once begun, it took on a life of its own, as arms races always have throughout history.

Because humans, Kennan said, "are always going to be part animal, governed by their emotions and subconscious drives rather than by reason," it was essential "to see that the weapons they have are not too terrible. . . . This is why I feel that the great weapons of mass destruction . . . should never be in human hands." No one, no one, he emphasized, was to be trusted with them, especially because their availability could trigger their use not because of a conscious decision to start a war but as a weapon to preempt an anticipated attack—whether real or imagined.

Truman understood that one nation's possession of the bomb would provoke others to develop it. So he simultaneously approved a long-term plan to work toward international control of atomic power through a United Nations–designated agency. But it was already too late to head off the arms race. Molotov announced in a Kremlin speech in November 1945 that the Soviet Union had every expectation of developing atomic power "soon," and criticized the United States for thinking it could sustain a monopoly. It is unlikely that the Soviets would have genuinely cooperated on any U.S. proposal that held back Moscow's reach for nuclear weapons. While U.S. officials at least gave consideration to proposals that might avert an arms race, Moscow refused to believe that it could be the equal of the United States if it agreed to any sort of international control over atomic power. Advocates of cooperation now feared that the world was headed for a nuclear holocaust.

Because such a prospect shadowed both Moscow and Washington, U.S. and Soviet leaders continued to hope that they could find grounds for agreement that would assure each of them a secure future. But it was a forlorn hope. Four months after the war in Europe and less than a month after fighting ended in the Pacific, suspicions that each was determined to do in the other's social system—communism versus capitalism—dominated Soviet and American thinking rather than faith in appeals to accommodation.

At a meeting in London in September, the Council of Foreign Ministers, a tripartite forum set up at Potsdam to negotiate postwar peace treaties for Germany, Italy, Eastern European countries, and Japan, quickly reached an impasse. Secretary Byrnes expressed amazement that Molotov doubted America's good intentions toward other nations, while Molotov could not understand why Byrnes saw the Soviet Union as aiming not at national security in its dealings with its East European neighbors, but world conquest.

Both sides made their distrust of one another apparent. "I do not understand your Secretary of State," a Russian official said to a member of the U.S. delegation. "We have been told that he is a practical man, but he acts like a professor," who lectures us without regard for our point of view. "When is he going to start trading?" Molotov made his irritation clear to Byrnes: at a reception, he asked Byrnes if he had an atomic bomb in his pocket. Byrnes, who had preceded his trip to London with private comments about carrying a bomb with him to the conference to intimidate the Russians, replied, half jokingly, that indeed he did and would threaten Molotov with it if he didn't come to an understanding with him. At a banquet, Molotov defiantly toasted Byrnes by declaring, "Of course, we all have to pay great attention to what Mr. Byrnes says, because the United States are the only people who are making atomic bombs."

Byrnes was not unmindful of the need to bend: worried that an open break with the Russians would remind Americans of the failed peace plans after World War I and spark renewed isolationism, he told John Foster Dulles, an international lawyer who had been Governor Thomas Dewey's principal foreign policy adviser in his 1944 presidential campaign and was the Republican Party's token member of the delegation in London, "I think we pushed these babies about as far as they will go and I think that we better start thinking about a compromise." But Dulles would not hear of it, and threatened to tell the press that Byrnes was appeasing the Russians. Nothing in 1945, or for years after, could be worse for a foreign policy official than to be described as an "appeaser." The same went for Soviet officials. Neither side, then, felt free to give ground, and so the conference ended in an unproductive deadlock. The Soviets saw no point in issuing a closing communiqué that falsely described meaningful steps toward agreement on any major issue.

Soviet-American tensions extended to postwar arrangements in Asia. After Tokyo surrendered, Molotov told Harriman that the Soviet entrance into the Pacific War on August 8 entitled it to share in Japan's postwar governance. Specifically, Molotov asked that two Soviet generals be included at the surrender ceremony on the *Missouri*, with veto rights over Japan's terms of capitulation. Harriman indignantly refused, and Truman followed up by rejecting Stalin's request that Soviet troops be allowed to occupy northern Hokkaido. He agreed to fulfill the Yalta commitment to Soviet control of the Kuril Islands, but made it clear that the administration of postwar Japan was entirely an American affair, with MacArthur as the governing authority.

The decision to have an exclusive U.S. occupation rested on not only the conviction that American forces had almost single-handedly defeated Japan but also the desire to demonstrate that, unlike after 1918, it was possible to re-create a totalitarian enemy in America's image. This was clearly out of reach for all Germany, where the country was divided into American, British, French, and Soviet zones and was already a subject of contention between East and West. With Japan under exclusive U.S. administration, however, Washington could hope to fulfill the cherished Wilsonian dream of refashioning a totalitarian, militaristic society by imposing a "democratic revolution from above" or "reform from on high" in Japan. True, an Allied Control Council for Japan would be established, but Washington and MacArthur never allowed it any substantive power over occupation policy.

Initially, American commanders entering Japan feared that they might have to deal with enduring resistance punctuated by suicide attacks. Bands of roving youths refusing to acknowledge defeat posed a challenge to the Japanese, who were eager to comply with the emperor's command, and U.S. troops landing at a Tokyo airfield. They anticipated violent opposition that could result in additional deaths and American acts of repression.

But in fact the Japanese response to their defeat was surprisingly cooperative. "They acted as if we were partners in a common cause. Japs saluted us. We saluted them," an American correspondent reported. Indeed, most Japanese seemed almost "euphoric" that the war was over and that they could try to transform themselves into a more peaceful and prosperous nation.

As he understood and indeed relished, MacArthur, as Supreme Commander for the Allied Powers (SCAP), was at the center of Japan's planned transformation. Ironically, the occupation imposed changes on the Japanese not by popular demand but by fiat. The democratic institutions were mandated by MacArthur, an American proconsul, and his legion of well-intentioned imperialists, rather than chosen by voters at the polls. Some Japanese feared that the anticipated "revolution" would prove to be no revolution at all but an acceptance by passive Japanese of the dictates of a new emperor or colonial master.

MacArthur was exceptionally shrewd and effective in playing the proconsul. He understood the Japanese affinity for a benign new emperor. On his arrival in Tokyo, when over thirty thousand Japanese troops with fixed bayonets lined his fifteen-mile route from an airfield to his downtown hotel residence, MacArthur's aides feared an attack that could launch the occupation on a violent note. But MacArthur, who had insisted that his staff not be armed as a demonstration of their confidence in Japan's acceptance of its defeat, viewed the Japanese troops standing at attention with their backs turned to the road as "a sign of submission and respect." In his first orders to American occupation forces and Japanese authorities, he counseled "generosity and compassion" by expressing concern to alleviate a widespread food shortage.

MacArthur's famous grandiosity was a perfect fit for the start of the occupation. He declared himself intent on carrying "to the land of our vanquished foe the solace and hope and faith of Christian morals." The pompous rhetoric reminded some Americans of the general's imperiousness, and they worried that he was simply not the right man for the job of transforming Japan into a democratic society. But it was his assertion of control, indeed his insistence on obedience, that greatly appealed to a people used to submissiveness, making MacArthur such a good fit for his assignment. His "Jovian image of decisiveness and absolute authority," his "'imperious aloofness and lordly graciousness,'" one Japanese commentator said, "established the prestige of the occupation."

While never allowing the Japanese to forget that they were defeated and beholden to American generosity in both day-to-day and long-term arrangements, MacArthur ensured that the occupation be not a draconian demonstration of wrath and vengeance imposed on a hated enemy but a respectful expression of regard for an honorable adversary. The disarming of Japanese troops, for example, was not to be done by U.S. forces but by their own commanders, as a way to insulate them from humiliation that could make them more difficult to deal with in the future. As a member of MacArthur's staff said, "We must restore security, dignity, and self-respect to . . . a warrior nation which has suffered an annihilating defeat."

MacArthur's points of reference in governing Japan "were Washington, Lincoln, and Jesus Christ," one critic said. Yet however much his administration was the product of his biases, it was an effective prescription for demilitarizing and democratizing Japan. Truman and the State, War, and Navy departments were not uniformly happy with the degree of authority that MacArthur had assumed, but the need for a controlling power that could fulfill the dream of uplifting a fallen enemy and transforming it into an extension of the United States—the forty-ninth American state, as one Japanese later proposed—was too compelling to dispute.

The occupation of Japan was one of those unpredictable developments that surprised even the most prescient experts about what to expect at war's end. That so violent a conflict, in which both sides had descended into acts of such horrendous destruction, should have evolved into a relatively benign occupation with genuine displays of regard for each other's humanity is a reassuring testament to human decency. The Japanese and Americans who had showed themselves ready to inflict every sort of cruelty on each other suddenly collaborated in the arduous task of reconstructing a broken society. None of this is to suggest that Japan was restored to a decent living standard overnight. Hunger and misery would plague the Japanese for months after the fighting ended. But from the first, the watchword was not enduring mutual hatred and revenge, but finding ways to rebuild and reconcile differences.

The Japanese, so thoroughly defeated in the war, were receptive to a fresh start, even if a foreign conqueror dictated it. The fact that America had won the war was a compelling reason for the Japanese to embrace the victor's values. At the same time, MacArthur's position of control encouraged him to be generous in applying U.S. standards to a conquered society. He wisely saw that a draconian occupation was less likely to bring needed change to Japan than one marked by a spirit of reconciliation.

As the war ended, the need for a successful occupation of Japan—that is, one promising a peaceful transition and a shift to American political and social values—took on heightened importance when set alongside developments in Europe and the rest of Asia. The establishment of the United Nations under U.S. leadership generated hope that the post-1945 era would not be like the twenty years after World War I. But political differences with Moscow over postwar Europe, as well as developments in Korea, Indochina, and China as Japan collapsed, raised doubts about peace anywhere in the world.

In the summer of 1945, only 15 percent of Americans were confident that the United Nations would be able to prevent future wars. Only half the country trusted Russia to cooperate with the United States in the future, and 60 percent of Americans opposed loaning either Britain or Russia billions of dollars for postwar reconstruction. The negative feelings about the wartime allies raised fears of renewed isolationism among Americans familiar with the disillusionment after 1919 that had made the country so reluctant to play a major role in overseas affairs.

Korea was a minor concern or a nonissue for the great majority of Americans. But those who attended to events there could not have much hope that it would be a model of political tranquillity in northeast Asia. Initially Koreans, who had suffered under Japanese control since early in the century, were happy that Japan's defeat would liberate them from colonial rule. But no one in the United States or among the troops who were rushed to Korea from Okinawa to occupy the southern part of the country knew how to manage the transition to self-rule. Lieutenant General John Hodge, who led U.S. forces into Korea, was so worried that Soviet occupation north of the thirty-eighth parallel and Communists in the south would turn all of Korea into a Soviet satellite that he initially relied on Korean collaborators with the Japanese to administer the U.S. sector. This enraged Korean nationalists, who hated their Japanese oppressors and were furious at Hodge's insensitivity to their feelings.

Hodge, who knew next to nothing about Korea, operated on a day-to-day understanding of what needed to be done. End-of-the-war chaos, including economic disarray and political turmoil threatening a Communist takeover, dictated Hodge's actions. He feared an extension of Soviet power comparable to Moscow's control of Eastern Europe. As Hodge's political adviser put it, South Korea was "a powder keg ready to explode at the application of a spark."

It was all enough to make Americans doubt the wisdom of continuing U.S. involvement in such remote parts of the globe, where ideological and local antagonisms unresponsive to outside pressures, even from a country with atomic bombs, trumped America's grandiose hopes of representative government and peaceful social interactions under a rule of law.

Indochina—Cambodia, Laos, and Vietnam—was another secondary or obscure issue to most Americans; here again, though, no one could take hope that the world was entering a postcolonial era with reduced tensions that eased great-power competition and dangers of civil wars.

Roosevelt had viewed French Indochina as a prime example of exploitive European colonialism, and an area where a joint Sino-American trusteeship would prepare Cambodians, Laotians, and Vietnamese for independence. By the beginning of 1945, however, reluctant to use U.S. troops to liberate the area from the Japanese, he was willing to let France assume the burden if it promised to establish a trusteeship that led to independence for the native peoples. He believed it would be "dangerous" to world peace to alienate 1.1 billion Asians by trying to reestablish colonial rule.

In March and April of 1945, Roosevelt backed away from his support of independence when de Gaulle warned that U.S. policy threatened France with falling "under the Russian aegis. . . . When Germany falls they will be upon us," de Gaulle told the U.S. ambassador in Paris. "If the public here [in France] comes to realize that you are against us in Indochina there will be terrific disappointment and nobody knows to what that will lead. We do not want to become Communist; we do not want to fall into the Russian orbit, but I hope that you do not push us into it."

De Gaulle's determination to reestablish French rule in Southeast Asia was a monumental blunder. It is understandable that he saw the re-creation of France's colonial empire as essential to the country's amour propre, but he was blind to the terrible price France and ultimately the United States would pay in blood, treasure, and prestige. De Gaulle's fixation on reestablishing France's colonial rule is a testimony to how shortsighted even the most astute of political leaders can be. His ability to restore a measure of French power after defeat in World War II was a testimony to his political effectiveness. His determination to re-create France's colonial empire was a study in imperial overreach.

Within days after Roosevelt's death, Truman's State Department assured the French that they had no intention of interfering with their sovereignty in Indochina. Focused on mustering U.S. forces for an invasion of Japan's home islands rather than diverting them to Southeast Asia and eager to shore up France in Western Europe against any Soviet reach for control, Truman was ready to support France's wish to reestablish its colonial rule in Indochina. At Potsdam, he and Churchill had agreed to Indochina's occupation by Chinese troops north of the sixteenth parallel and British troops south of the dividing line. De Gaulle and the French assumed that this was a temporary arrangement that would precede the reestablishment of French control. Truman assumed the same, and the replacement of the British and Chinese forces in Indochina by French troops was welcomed in Washington.

It was, however, a bitter disappointment to Ho Chi Minh, the Vietnamese Communist leader who had been collaborating with America's Office of Strategic Services (OSS) against the Japanese and was pressing Washington to support Vietnam's self-determination. A symbol or bellwether of the emerging anticolonial struggles in Asia, Africa, and the Middle East, Ho's campaign for independence dated back to 1919, when he had presented a petition to the American delegation in Paris that echoed America's 1776 Declaration of Independence.

Ignored by the Americans (not until the 1960s would the gaunt, slight Vietnamese with a goatee become a familiar figure in the United States), Ho spent the 1920s and '30s schooling himself in Western and Soviet politics and culture. Beginning in 1911, at the age of twenty-one, and already an avowed nationalist, he had moved to Paris and spent the next thirty years living in France, the United States, and Britain, where he worked in various hotel restaurant jobs, and in Soviet Russia and southern China, where he held positions with the Russian and Chinese Communist Parties.

In 1941, following the Japanese takeover of Indochina, Ho established a Vietnamese independence movement and organized guerrilla opposition to Vietnam's Vichy French and Japanese rulers. On September 2, 1945, after Japan's surrender, he announced the establishment of a Democratic Republic of Vietnam (DRV) in Hanoi. Washington was too distracted by European and other Asian concerns and too worried about antagonizing the French to fulfill U.S. anticolonial promises, specifically for Indo-Chinese independence under an avowed Marxist. Neither Ho nor Americans in general, who had hoped for a revolutionary turn against empires at the close of the war, nor those in particular who sympathized with Vietnamese hopes for self-determination were pleased with Washington's indifference to Vietnamese nationalist aspirations. But compared with European, Japanese, and Chinese affairs, Indochina was barely a blip on American consciousness in the summer of 1945.

China was another matter entirely. It was central to American hopes for postwar peace and democracy in Asia. To preserve a semblance of America's grand vision about a China that could be allied with the United States in advancing Asia toward a stable postwar future, Roosevelt had agreed to Soviet demands for economic and territorial concessions in China. In return, Moscow was to pressure Mao's Communists into a coalition government with the Nationalists and recognize Chiang as the country's principal ruling authority.

Truman had no quarrel with Roosevelt's hopes for a peaceful Asia led by a stable China. But, as FDR would have, Truman found himself trapped by uncontrollable conflicts between American, Soviet, Nationalist, and Communist goals. Truman wished to fulfill the Yalta plan for Soviet concessions in China in return for support of a Chiang government including Communist Party representatives.

As the war ended in August and September, however, impediments to Washington's aims in China became evident. In August, Stalin signed a pact with Chiang's government, and Mao, under prodding from Moscow, traveled to Chungking for talks with the Nationalists. But the discussions were largely shadow boxing: neither the fifty-nine-year-old "indomitable and uninstructable" Chiang nor

Mao, who "claimed the Mandate of History, if not of Heaven," could imagine working together. They entered into a competition for control of territories occupied by Japanese troops. It was a reflection of their basic differences.

Chiang's government was notorious for its corruption and unpopularity among China's vast peasant population, which saw a bleak future for itself under Nationalist rule. The journalist Theodore White, reporting from China, described the Kuomintang as a "corrupt political clique that combines some of the worst features of Tammany Hall and the Spanish Inquisition." By contrast, Mao's Communists had built a substantial appeal to the peasant masses with promises of reform that would end political corruption and raise the country's standard of living. A long history of antagonistic ideologies and mutual distrust made a coalition all but impossible.

A State Department economist whom Truman had made an adviser to the Nationalist government warned the president that China was heading for a civil war that would be a disaster for U.S. policy. It would further undermine a weak economy plagued by periodic famines, compel the Soviets to back the Communists, and force the U.S. to support the undemocratic and unpopular Nationalists, whose unreliable military forces would be defeated. Truman was urged to send a prominent presidential envoy to pressure both sides into a political compromise.

The difficulty in taking up such a suggestion was America's transparent partiality toward the Nationalists, as evidenced by U.S. help in transporting Chiang's troops to areas under Japanese control before Mao's forces filled the vacuum. The conviction that Mao was a stalking horse for Soviet control in China was on the rise not only among Chiang's conservative American backers but also at Truman's White House. Like FDR, who had ignored a proposal from Mao in January 1945 to visit him in Washington, Truman could not countenance conversations with the Communists that might undermine Chiang. He saw them as revolutionaries tied to a worldwide

Communist movement committed to ousting the Nationalists and expanding Soviet influence in East Asia. Besides, Chiang had influential American backers ready to assault the president for betraying a wartime ally, who promised to be a more reliable postwar partner than a radical tied to Kremlin Communists.

Nevertheless, by the summer of 1944, the American press and Foreign Service officers in China were "beginning to doubt whether China will be a friendly democracy, protecting American interests in the Pacific." The British ambassador in Washington told the Foreign Office in August, "An ironical attitude to the claims of China to be a first-class power is only too observable. . . . The slump in general Chinese stock is an accomplished fact and appears to be increasing." Despite this recognition that Chiang was no democrat but a self-serving dictator who put personal power ahead of his people's well-being, his supporters saw him as a useful foil to Communist ambitions. *Time* publisher Henry Luce, their leading spokesman in 1945, featured Chiang on the cover of his magazine.

Chiang's principal advocate in the administration was U.S. ambassador to China Patrick Hurley. An Oklahoma oil man who had been Herbert Hoover's secretary of war, the conservative Republican Hurley was made ambassador in 1944 as cover for FDR's White House if Chiang's government collapsed under pressure from Hurley acting on Washington's instructions to form a coalition with the Communists.

Hurley had little knowledge of China, or of how to communicate with his hosts: he initially addressed the Chiangs as Mr. and Mrs. "Shek," and during a visit to Yenan, Mao's headquarters, treated bewildered Communist leaders to imitations of Indian war cries. He privately belittled Mao Tse-tung and Chou En-lai, calling them "Moose Dung and Joe N. Lie." He initially believed that a coalition was Chiang's best hope for survival, but after Chiang convinced him otherwise, he became a forceful advocate of preserving Chiang's rule on Chiang's terms. In 1945, when Hurley's embassy subordinates urged the need for a coalition if the Communists were not to take over China after a civil war, Hurley denounced them as "disloyal to him and to the U.S." The majority of America's conservative China watchers could accept only a China governed by Nationalists friendly to the United States.

After Potsdam, a few Americans maintained hope for a reformed world led by America, China, and Russia. Nations so sobered by two world wars in thirty years, they thought, would turn away from domestic and foreign conflicts and toward democratic governance at home and abroad. The majority, however, despite insistent demands for the reduction of America's armed forces—"Bring the boys home" was a popular postwar cry—was skeptical about a universal shift toward friendly dealings, believing that individual nations, above all the Soviet Union, remained eager "to dominate or run the world."

To guard against foreign dangers, three-quarters of Americans wanted the United States to maintain exclusive control of the atomic bomb. Only between 14 and 17 percent of opinion surveys supported transferring this power to the United Nations. However much German and Japanese defeat and the advent of nuclear weapons had altered power relations in Europe and Asia, nations' reliance on military might to assure their survival and selfish interests had not changed in the least.

5

IRREPRESSIBLE CONFLICTS?

There are now two great nations in the world which,
starting from different points, seem to be advancing toward
the same goal: the Russians and the Anglo-Americans. . . .
Each seems called by some secret desire of Providence one
day to hold in its hands the destinies of half the world.
—Alexis de Tocqueville, 1835

In late August 1945, Charles de Gaulle visited Truman in Washington. To his satisfaction, he found that France was now "considered as a great ally, wounded but victorious, and above all, needed" in the emerging conflict with Moscow. De Gaulle perfectly described the mood in the United States, which, as in Britain, was turning from matters of war and peace to domestic affairs. "Once the war was over," he recalled, "public opinion and policy alike cast off the psychology of union, energy and sacrifice and turned once more to interest, prejudice and antagonism." Where only 7 percent of Americans saw making peace as the most important problem facing the country, and only 2 percent cited the atomic bomb, 74 percent named jobs and strikes.

Truman impressed de Gaulle as having "abandoned the plan of a world harmony and admitted that the rivalry between the free world and the Soviet bloc now dominated every other international consideration." The president shared de Gaulle's belief that "it was . . . essential to avoid dissension and revolutionary upheaval, so that states not yet Communist would not be led to become so," meaning that

America needed to mute differences with France and to support its reconstruction.

Yet de Gaulle concluded that Truman's turn toward realism and away from dreams of American-led universal agreement did not reflect majority sentiment: Americans clung to illusions of omnipotence and the power to shape world affairs unilaterally. Victory without homeland devastation had sparked "overpowering activity and an intense optimism," de Gaulle said. America's economy was booming: the pent-up desire for housing, cars, and everything from meat to electric appliances that had been in short supply during the war was fueling an economic boom and rising prices.

Armed with atomic bombs, its power unsurpassed, America had become a world colossus and a model for what every nation everywhere aspired to—or at least, so Americans assumed. De Gaulle described it as the new American evangelism: "For a nation to be happy, it need only institute a democracy like that of the New World. . . . Confronted with its present danger, the free world could do nothing better, and nothing else, than adopt the 'leadership' of Washington."

De Gaulle's observations partly reflected his wounded national pride: France, humiliated by defeat and relegation to the status of a second-class power, was beholden to American largesse, which de Gaulle resented but in fact needed.

De Gaulle took satisfaction, however, from the awareness that the realities of power politics were compelling the Americans to cultivate allies. De Gaulle noted the emerging contradiction between, on one hand, American eagerness to see its success as an irresistible model that would convert friends and foes alike and, on the other, forebodings about postwar tensions that were forcing the United States into a sustained preoccupation with national defense and a reliance on the cooperation of other countries for its safety. A widespread preference for either of two generals, MacArthur or Eisenhower, as the country's next president in 1948 reflected underlying or muted concerns with foreign dangers as opposed to domestic problems.

In the fall of 1945, however, addressing external threats was not yet the country's or the administration's highest priority; external dangers could not be ignored, but more immediate domestic troubles— inflation, strikes, and consumer shortages—pushed foreign affairs into the background. "The Congress is balking; labor has gone crazy; management is not far from insane in selfishness," Truman recorded in an October diary entry.

A reversion to isolationism, however appealing in the midst of domestic difficulties, was out of the question, but clarity about external policy was put out of reach by inclinations to deny its importance and uncertainty about what to do: the Army, Navy, and State Department conferred on what might be necessary to meet overseas economic, political, and military challenges, but no one was prepared to say just what these might be. When Truman rejected the suggestions of a presidential working group that would focus on national security, neither administration officials nor the press objected that he was being too casual about the country's future defense. After the all-consuming demands of the war, Americans wanted a respite from foreign troubles.

Moreover, foreign affairs became a central element in domestic political divisions. Foreign policy had never been entirely divorced from partisan political conflicts in the United States. Challenging popular sentiment on overseas involvements that could cost Americans lives and money had always been a part of the national debate. U.S. importance in world affairs after World War II made arguments about how to meet foreign challenges more central to national political discussions than ever before, but it did not make for greater rationality about foreign policy. To the contrary, allegations of missteps overseas became a major weapon in the political campaigns of the outs against the ins.

After Potsdam, reflecting the current national preoccupation with domestic concerns, Truman was content to let his secretary of state manage day-to-day decisions on foreign policy. Jimmy Byrnes, who had resented FDR's decision to choose Truman instead for the vice presidency, was pleased to take responsibility from the president for what he believed should have been his job anyway. He quickly made his mark on the country's external relations. Drawing on his background in politics, where he had a reputation as a "conciliator and mediator," he advocated compromise with the Soviets as the surest route to postwar peace. In June 1945 Byrnes asked Joseph E. Davies, the former ambassador to Moscow and an outspoken Russophile, to become ambassador to London as a signal that Washington would resist Churchill's efforts to have the United States join Britain in "ganging up" on the Soviet Union. At the close of the Potsdam conference, Stalin had praised Byrnes's efforts to overcome differences, jokingly describing him as "the most honest horse thief he had ever met."

By contrast, Truman was seen by journalists and members of his government as erratic and indecisive in managing foreign affairs. He expressed his uncertainty in a comment to Treasury Secretary Henry Morgenthau: "You don't know how difficult the thing has been for me. Everyone around here that should know something about foreign affairs is out." His doubts produced complaints that on matters of military and diplomatic planning, administration "disarray" was "glaring."

Truman tried to reassure critics that he was personally managing the most important national security issue, control of atomic power. On October 3, he informed Congress that he favored international discussions but would keep expertise on the bomb strictly in American hands. At the end of the month, he used the occasion of Navy Day to speak publicly on his determination to pursue a principled foreign policy favoring self-determination for all nations and reiterated that U.S. control of the new weapon was "a sacred trust."

Stalin was never as conflicted as Truman and his administration about his foreign policy intentions: at the close of the war, "what Stalin was really after," George Kennan advised Washington, "was the expulsion of American influence from the Eurasian land mass generally, and its replacement by that of his own regime." Yet, as in the West, unforeseen circumstances and Stalin's personal limitations obscured and frustrated his ambitions.

In October, after he returned from Potsdam, Stalin suffered a heart attack. The war years and his profligacy with food and alcohol at all-night bacchanals had taken a toll on his health. Sixty-seven in 1945, he was suffering from arteriosclerosis that made him more petulant, unpredictable, and explosive. "He was very jittery," Molotov said. "His last years were the most dangerous. He swung to extremes." After one of these all-night orgies of drinking and eating, Stalin released his subordinates at 5:00 a.m. "On the way home, [Nikita] Khrushchev and [Mikhail] Bulganin, lay back [in their chauffered car], relieved to have survived: 'One never knows,' whispered Bulganin, 'if one's going home or to prison.'"

In October, Stalin went to a Black Sea retreat for six weeks to rest and recover. During his absence, Politburo members Molotov, Beria, Georgy Malenkov, and Anastas Mikoyan administered day-to-day affairs, though Stalin still ruled on all larger matters. When Stalin read that rumors about his health problems were circulating in the Western press and that Molotov and Marshal Zhukov might replace him, he became incensed at his associates. Molotov, in particular, who was urging a softer line toward the West, became the object of Stalin's wrath. But he wormed his way back into Stalin's good graces with requests for forgiveness that demonstrated his obeisance to his master.

The conflict between the two partly grew out of substantive policy differences: Molotov understood that the USSR could not possibly control the United States and push it out of Europe or East Asia, but Stalin would not relent on his goal. It made for tensions with Molotov and other Stalin lieutenants, who he saw defying him. Above all, it challenged Stalin's "insatiable vanity and love of power" and agitated his "inordinate touchiness, an endless vindictiveness, an inability ever to forget an insult or a slight. . . . He is said once to have observed that there was nothing sweeter in life than to bide the proper moment for revenge, to insert the knife, to turn it around, and to go home for a good night's sleep."

Although his ruthless, vindictive side was never far from the surface, Stalin muted it with ingenious political calculation and maneuvering. In the presence of foreigners, he masked his basest instincts: "There was no striving for effect," Kennan said. "His words were few. They generally sounded reasonable and sensible; indeed, they often were. An unforewarned visitor would never have guessed what depths of calculation, ambition, love of power, jealousy, cruelty, and sly vindictiveness lurked behind this unpretentious façade."

During the all-night dinners attended by his inner circle, the men he kept closest to him, Stalin was more overtly dominating and made himself the object of deference and rivalry for his attention. In his dealings with these men and Soviets more generally, it was possible to see Stalin's "unconscionable ambition and ruthlessness. . . . This was a man of incredible criminality, of a criminality effectively without limits; a man . . . without pity or mercy; a man in whose entourage no one was ever safe." And the people who were closest to him and shared most directly in his crimes were in greatest danger, because he could never trust anyone with his most closely held secrets.

Although Stalin's dinners were ostensibly devoted to policy discussions or what an associate called a "political dining society," they were Stalin's way of consolidating his control over the Politburo, the Communist Party leaders who uncritically accepted Stalin's dictates while publicly pretending to be part of a democratic inner circle voicing independent viewpoints that represented the many different ethnic and interest groups making up the Soviet Union.

The courtiers survived by reading Stalin's moods and responding to them with words and gestures that avoided anything that might distress him and appealed to his desire to be admired, put on a pedestal as some great historical figure. Anyone who made him uneasy risked exposure to sarcasm or a tongue-lashing, though revenge would more often take the form of an icy silence. More drastic consequences would usually occur later—after the offender had left Stalin's presence.

It seems reasonable to conclude, without formal discussion of psychopathology, that Stalin was uniquely abnormal, which says next to nothing about the man's troubled mind. But to what possible category can psychologists ascribe one who killed so many people with seemingly little, if any, regret? Even if we could classify him, it would provide little clue as to how he managed to hold so much power for so long in so large a nation.

A more important question: Was it ever possible to reach reliable agreements with Stalin? Kennan, who was one of a handful of American experts on Soviet Russia and had spent more than twenty years monitoring the inner workings of its operations, thought not. A man of exceptional intelligence with a genuine regard for Russia's language, culture, and history, Kennan was no knee-jerk anti-Communist but a thoughtful analyst committed to explaining, as best he could, why and how Stalin behaved as he did. Joining the Foreign Service in 1925 after graduating from Princeton, Kennan used his posting to the Baltic countries to monitor developments in the Soviet Union. When the United States gave formal recognition to Russia's Communist government in 1933, Kennan's expertise on Soviet Russia and a command of the Russian language won him a posting to Moscow.

Having served in Russia throughout the war, Kennan could speak with considerable authority on Stalin. "Unlike Lenin, who could view objective reality as something apart from himself," Kennan concluded at the end of the 1950s, "Stalin was able to see the world only through the prism of his own ambitions and his own fears." Because Stalin's dominance and outlook blurred the actual antagonisms between Russia and its rivals, Kennan could see no way to find shared interests that could ameliorate tensions between East and West. Lenin was more approachable. It was possible to communicate with him, as was the case later with Nikita Khrushchev and Mikhail Gorbachev, and therefore to doubt "whether an enemy with whom one can communicate is really entirely an enemy, after all."

Yet Stalin was not simply the sum of his distorted thinking about opponents. After the Nazi attack on Russia in 1941, he went into a blue funk at his failure to anticipate Hitler's "betrayal" of the Nazi-Soviet nonaggression pact of 1939. As the Nazis overwhelmed the Soviet armies in the opening days of the fighting, Stalin declared himself a failure: "Everything's lost," he told Politburo comrades. "I give up. Lenin founded our state and we've fucked it up." Stalin did not show up at the Kremlin for two days while the fighting fronts were collapsing. While his withdrawal was a genuine sign of a breakdown in this worst crisis of his career, it was also contrived "for effect." It was Stalin's way of demanding a reaffirmation of his authority from the Politburo. And it worked. He was assured that he was the indispensable leader, and he seized upon this renewed vote of confidence to destroy military chiefs who became the scapegoats for the defeats.

My point here is that Stalin did not function solely through his distorted views of reality, of which there were plenty. He also could see his way clear to deal with unpalatable truths—the sacrifices that would have to be made to defeat Hitler's armies, and after the war, the limits of what he could do to assure Russia's national security. In sum, however small the likelihood of accommodations with the West in the post-1945 years, it was not impossible. Had Stalin lived into the 1970s, for example, it is imaginable that like Khrushchev and Brezhnev he might have accepted détente as a necessary accommodation with the United States.

Jimmy Byrnes did not share Kennan's view of Stalin as having no interest in international agreements. Byrnes's assumption, however, would prove to be out of sync with current affairs. He attributed the stalemate at the London conference in September 1945 to Molotov, who, Byrnes believed, was at odds with his ostensible master.

When the London talks reached an impasse over postwar treaties, Byrnes took it as a personal failure and decided that he needed to go to Moscow. A Byrnes associate recorded in a diary, "He [Byrnes] is blue over outlook. [He] has no confidence in building peace with M[olotov], sees only solution for next meeting to be held in M[oscow] where he can deal with Stalin."

Mindful that Byrnes was vulnerable to his manipulation, Stalin agreed to have a Big Three foreign ministers' conference in Moscow in December. Kennan, then counselor of embassy, considered the meeting to sign peace treaties with defeated foes a serious mistake. "The entire world of thought out of which these encounters [Yalta, Potsdam, and now Moscow] arose was foreign and distasteful to me," he recalled. He saw them as doing nothing more than preserving "some fig leafs of democratic procedure to hide the nakedness of Stalinist dictatorship in the respective Eastern European countries." Kennan "saw little to be gained by our having anything at all to do with the new regimes in these countries." The Moscow talks seemed likely to convey the false impression that the United States had some influence "in the Soviet-dominated area, or that the countries in question faced anything less than the full rigor of Stalinist totalitarianism."

Kennan, who sat in on the meetings, recorded the pointlessness of the proceedings. Molotov "sat leaning forward over the table, a Russian cigarette dangling from his mouth, his eyes flashing with satisfaction and confidence as he glanced . . . [at] the other foreign ministers, obviously keenly aware of their mutual differences and their common uncertainty in the face of the keen, ruthless, and incisive Russian diplomacy. He had the look of a passionate poker player who knows he has a royal flush and is about to call the last of his opponents. He was the only one who was clearly enjoying every minute of the proceedings."

Kennan was scathing about Byrnes's reckless lack of preparation and self-serving motives: Byrnes's "main purpose is to achieve some sort of an agreement, he doesn't much care what. The realities behind this agreement, since they concern only such people as Koreans, Rumanians, and Iranians, about whom he knows nothing, do not concern him. He wants an agreement for its political effect at home." As far as Kennan could tell, Byrnes was little more than a slick, parochial politician angling to carry home a diplomatic agreement that he could trumpet in a run for the presidency.

Kennan's observations, which he confided to only a handful of embassy associates and a few sympathetic members of the Moscow diplomatic corps, had no impact on Byrnes's discussions. He drove forward on a variety of subjects, including shared information on atomic energy, European peace treaties, Japan's occupation, a coalition government in China, and a provisional Korean government; differences over Iran and Turkey were notable by their absence from the conference's final communiqué.

Although Byrnes would hail the outcome of the talks in a December 30 address to the nation as a return to Big Three cooperation similar to wartime collaboration, the results were much less than they seemed. The agreements, such as they were, did nothing to change current power arrangements in Eastern Europe, Asia, or the emerging nuclear arms race. The conference was most notable for its negative impact on the Truman-Byrnes relationship.

Truman complained that Byrnes proceeded without full consultation with the president and arrived at agreements that he could not fully endorse. Specifically, Truman objected to the commitments Byrnes had made to recognize the Soviet-controlled Bulgarian and Rumanian governments and to share scientific information with Moscow about atomic energy. In a letter to Byrnes on January 5, 1946, the president stated his dissatisfaction with Byrnes's freelancing, complaining that he had not been kept sufficiently informed, and declared his determination to warn the Soviets against threatening either Iranian or Turkish sovereignty. He decried Byrnes's compromising, which was code for the ultimate diplomatic blunder of appeasement, and promised that American foreign policy would now follow a tougher line, declaring, "I'm tired [of] babying the Soviets."

Whether Truman was kept as "completely in the dark" as he alleged is open to question. His differences with Byrnes rested on muted personal tensions and more overt disputes about what was realistic in dealing with the Russians. Truman had cause for annoyance with Byrnes's almost dismissive attitude toward him. Byrnes could not disguise his ongoing resentment that Roosevelt had chosen Truman over him for the vice presidency and that Truman instead of Byrnes was president and commander in chief. Truman, who jealously guarded the prerogatives of office and resented anyone who exacerbated his own abundant personal doubts about his fitness for the presidency (he had confided to Mrs. Roosevelt that alongside FDR, he could not think of himself as president), was stung by Byrnes's show of independence and, by December 1945, determined to dismiss him at the first opportunity.

Truman's personal antagonism to the man he now described as "my conniving secretary of state" combined with political pressures and policy differences to force a break with Byrnes. Before Byrnes went to Moscow, he had confronted an explosion of conservative opposition over sharing atomic energy information with the Soviets. In November, after Byrnes had reached an agreement with Attlee and Canadian prime minister Mackenzie King on how to go about bringing Russia and the United Nations into conversations on future control of nuclear weapons, he belatedly invited Michigan Republican senator Arthur Vandenberg and Texas Democrat Tom Connally, the ranking members of the Foreign Relations Committee, to endorse the procedure. They resented being presented with a fait accompli.

Two days before he left for Moscow, Byrnes's plans for conciliatory talks on atomic energy with the Russians provoked the senators' sharp opposition. Moreover, when he returned from the conference with an agreement that Vandenberg saw as failing to safeguard U.S. atomic secrets, the Truman White House became vulnerable to charges of appeasing the Russians. Separating himself from Byrnes by suggesting that the secretary had reached an agreement without the president's full endorsement protected Truman from Republican attacks. Truman also kept his distance from his secretary of state by insisting on stronger protections against Soviet use of U.S. technology to build an atomic arsenal. Although they played only a small role in the president's dealings with the Soviets over atomic power, such personal and political considerations demonstrated how crucial foreign policy questions had become enmeshed with domestic politics.

By the time Byrnes went to Moscow, Truman was already highly skeptical of the Soviets, whom he saw as untrustworthy, all too ready to reach agreements they would never honor. Soviet behavior toward Iran had intensified Truman's doubts. The Soviets had promised to remove troops from Iran's northernmost provinces, where they had been stationed since 1941 as a defense against a German takeover of Iranian oil fields, six months after the close of the war. But after the war ended in Europe, Moscow used Iranian threats to Russian security as a reason to delay a troop withdrawal. Soviet suspicions of Anglo-American interest in controlling Middle East oil and a perceived threat to Russian oil fields bordering Iran gave some substance to their fears.

With each side now distrustful of the other's professions of good intentions, and seeing the other as pursuing aggressive rather than defensive policies, Iran became a case study in how differing perspectives divided the wartime allies. Preventing Soviet dominance of the Persian Gulf, a Western lifeline to essential Middle East energy supplies, was seen in London and Washington as vital to the defense of Western Europe against a Communist stranglehold on its economy. On the other hand, forestalling Western control of a border country that could pose a threat to its Baku oil fields was, in Moscow's view, a sensible act of self-defense rather than one of hostile aggression.

The differences over Iran joined with suspicions of Soviet intentions toward Turkey to further erode wartime ties. Historical Russian interest in the Dardanelles, the passageway through Turkish territory into the Sea of Marmara running east of Istanbul and into the Black Sea, had long been a security concern. In 1944 attacks on Crimean targets by eight German warships that had passed through the straits without Turkish resistance had convinced Stalin that Turkish control of the Dardanelles had given a small nation "a hand on Russia's throat." At Yalta and Potsdam, Stalin demanded shared control of the straits with Turkey, a Soviet base in the Dardanelles, and return of Russian—or more precisely, Armenian—territory ceded to the Turks in 1921. Truman proposed internationalization of the Straits as a way to defuse the issue. But when Stalin rejected his proposal at Potsdam, pointing out that neither the British nor the Americans would agree to internationalize the Suez or Panama canals, Truman saw it as a prelude to a Soviet attack on Turkey.

Stalin dismissed talk of Soviet aggression against its southern neighbor as "rubbish." Truman, however, persisted in his belief that Stalin intended to seize the straits at the first opportunity, and the presence of 200,000 Soviet troops in Bulgaria gave resonance to his fears. Their withdrawal in November 1945, however, did not reassure the president, who assumed that they could return at any time. In December he privately expressed the conviction that the Soviets only understood force and that he regretted the absence of any divisions he could send to the eastern Mediterranean to dampen Moscow's ambitions.

American sleight of hand on limiting a Soviet role in Japan's occupation convinced Stalin that Washington was as intent on checking Soviet power in East Asia as Moscow had been in limiting Anglo-American influence in Eastern Europe and Iran. Although Byrnes had agreed to an Allied Control Council for Japan that included the Soviet Union, MacArthur's chairmanship of the council, which gave him controlling authority, meant that Moscow had no more than a symbolic presence in postwar Japan.

While the United States was firmly in control of Japan, it was uncertain about whether it would be able to keep Korea, which was under divided occupation by U.S. and Soviet troops, out of the Communist orbit. Likewise, Indochina, where the French were re-establishing colonial rule, was threatened by a Communist insurgency. The competition for dominance in East Asia, however, revolved around China—the biggest postwar prize in the battle for hearts and minds in the emerging East-West conflict.

The object of Roosevelt's and then Truman's policies was to tie the Chinese to the United States by keeping peace in Asia and promoting self-determination for former colonies. Because Chiang Kai-shek's Nationalist government was so weak, the United States had tried to avert a civil war that could give Communist insurgents, ostensibly tied to Moscow, control of the country. A coalition government of Nationalists and Communists supported by both Washington and Moscow seemed to be the best solution. For self-serving reasons, Stalin, who feared the emergence of a Chinese Communist regime as a rival for world control of Communist parties and a threat to U.S. influence in East Asia that might drag Moscow into a confrontation with America in China, was ready to sign on to such an arrangement. But neither Chiang nor Mao Tse-tung, both of whom believed they could outlast the other in a military contest, yielded to U.S.-Soviet pressure.

By the beginning of November 1945, military clashes between Nationalist and Communist troops in northern China, where Chiang's armies were trying to displace Japanese troops who had surrendered to Mao's forces, made prospects for a coalition government "almost hopeless" and the likelihood of a civil war all but certain.

U.S. officials in China, Russia, and Washington were convinced that the emerging struggle could expand Soviet influence in China. Kennan warned from Moscow that Stalin was pursuing "a fluid resilient policy directed at the achievement of maximum power with minimum responsibility on portions of the Asiatic continent lying beyond the Soviet border." He saw the Soviets aiming at the reacquisition of "all the diplomatic and territorial assets previously possessed on the mainland of Asia by Russia under the Czars; domination of the provinces of China in central Asia contiguous to the Soviet frontier," Outer Mongolia, Manchuria, and Sinkiang, where they could create a buffer against threats to "the industrial core of the U.S.S.R."; and control in northern China, where they hoped "to prevent other foreign powers from repeating the Japanese incursion," especially Britain and the United States.

General Albert Wedemeyer, Stilwell's replacement in the China, India, and Burma theater, echoed Kennan's concerns. Wedemeyer thought that Stalin's show of support for Chiang was a charade: he did not believe that the Sino-Soviet Friendship Treaty of August 1945 would forestall Russian plans to establish Communist regimes in Asia. Wedemeyer wanted U.S. forces to intervene in northern China, warding off Communist control. Patrick Hurley predicted that a civil war could only occur if Moscow sanctioned and supported Mao's ambitions to control all of China, and he had every reason to believe that this was Stalin's plan.

The pressure for a more aggressive role for U.S. forces in China alarmed John Carter Vincent, an expert on China and chief of the Far Eastern division of the State Department, who worried about being drawn into a civil war as Chiang's protector. He asked "whether we are not moving toward the establishment of a relationship with China which has some characteristics of a de facto protectorate with a semi-colonial Chinese Army under our direction?" One Pentagon planner complained "that 'that Communist' Vincent was causing trouble in China."

At the end of November, Hurley abruptly resigned as ambassador to China without first informing the president. His letter of resignation to Truman attacked administration policy as favoring the Communists in China over the Nationalists and democracy. The fault lay with "the career men in the State Department. The professional Foreign Service men sided with the Chinese Communist armed party and the imperialist bloc of nations whose policy it was to keep China divided against herself. Our professional diplomats continuously advised the Communists that my efforts in preventing the collapse of the Nationalist Government did not represent the policy of the United States. These same professionals openly advised the Communist armed party to decline unification of the Chinese Communist Army with the National Army unless the Chinese Communists were given control." Hurley was convinced that "a considerable section of our State Department is endeavoring to support Communism generally as well as specifically in China."

The overt sympathy for Mao's revolution by Foreign Service officers in China was indisputable. But it was not the result of any ideological affinity for Communism or Communist parties in Asia and elsewhere. Rather, it was the offshoot of the conviction that Chiang's regime was doomed and that the United States would do well to establish a working relationship with the likely future governing power in China, and in addition to getting on the right side of the winning political movement, it could help reduce Soviet influence throughout China and East Asia.

Hurley's sudden resignation and attack on administration policy enraged Truman. Although Hurley blamed Foreign Service officers and State Department officials, depicting them as at odds with the administration's policy of coalition government in China, his criticism suggested that the White House had failed by allowing career diplomats to favor the Communists and undermine the Nationalists. Some pro-Chiang supporters in the United States, who felt that Washington was not doing enough to support the Nationalists, concluded that Truman secretly favored the Communists. "See what-a-son-of-a-bitch did to me," Truman privately told his cabinet when learning of Hurley's resignation and letter. He understood that Hurley's accusations, however unfounded, could now become a political club against him.

Eager for both domestic political and foreign policy reasons to salvage the peace in China, Truman now asked George Marshall, who had just retired from the army, to mediate Nationalist-Communist differences. Marshall's military service dated from 1901, when he graduated from the Virginia Military Institute and became a second lieutenant. During World War I he was a principal aide to John J. Pershing, the commanding general of U.S. forces in France. A brilliant planner and organizer, he rose through the ranks to become Army chief of staff in World War II. Choosing Marshall to go to China was a demonstration of how much importance the White House placed on preventing a civil war between the Nationalists and the Communists. Marshall was as iconic a figure in Washington as anyone could find. His leadership of the military in the war and his reputation for nonpartisan national service had elevated him to the stature of a national hero on a level with the most storied military leaders in American history.

FDR had considered Marshall so indispensable to the overall war effort in Washington—despite the correct, formal relationship Marshall maintained with the president to assure sufficient detachment in deciding vital strategic questions—that he decided against sending him to London to organize and command the D-day invasion of Europe. Truman thought him a most remarkable man and the principal architect of America's victory in the war. At his retirement, Truman called him "the greatest military man that this country ever produced—or any other country for that matter." The general's standing with Republicans as well as Democrats gave him, Truman believed, immunity from the political attacks that Hurley's criticism seemed likely to generate from right-wing anti-Communist ideologues toward almost anyone else the president might send to China.

Marshall's instructions were to draw the opposing sides into a coalition government; the inducement was a $500 million grant to support a unified country's economic and military institutions. Most U.S. representatives in China saw Marshall's assignment as an impossible task. Marshall himself was not unmindful of the heavy odds against him. And so he made it a precondition of his mediation that the White House commit to supporting Chiang should his mission fail. He was less concerned with the domestic political repercussions of a Nationalist collapse than with a Communist advance in Asia that could threaten Japan's stability and America's national security.

Although Truman was not convinced that the Nationalists would produce anything resembling a democratic solution for China, he saw the alternative as politically destructive to his administration and to U.S. power in Asia. A Communist regime in China seemed certain to create a firestorm of criticism in the United States. The House Un-American Activities Committee chaired by conservative Texas Democrat Martin Dies had been raising questions since its founding in 1938 about subversive Communists in the U.S. government, who were alleged to favor "progressive" Communist regimes abroad.

During the 1944 campaign, Republican presidential candidate Thomas E. Dewey charged that Roosevelt had allied himself with the Communist Party of the United States. "Now the Communists are seizing control of the New Deal, through which they aim to control the Government of the United States," Dewey declared in the closing days of the campaign. Some Democratic Party leaders were convinced that voters in 1944 were more afraid of Communism than of Nazism or Fascism, which seemed certain to be destroyed by the end of the war.

The tensions with the Soviets over Eastern Europe, Iran, Turkey, and Japan had put Americans on edge about Communist aggression. It was unimaginable to millions of Americans, as well as to thoughtful government officials like Harriman, Wedemeyer, Undersecretary of State Dean Acheson, and Marshall, that China's Communist Party could be an independent entity that would not do Stalin's bidding. Even if they doubted this supposition, in the fall of 1945, the thought of challenging American assumptions about Communists, Chinese or otherwise, by supporting them over Chiang, a well-regarded U.S. friend, seemed like political suicide.

Yet there were reasons to believe that Mao and Chou En-lai, his brilliant deputy, were less than fixedly tied to Moscow. Early in 1945, they proposed to visit Washington for a conversation with the president, suggesting an interest in a relationship with the United States that would make them less dependent on the Soviet Union. Kennan saw reason to believe that the Chinese Communist Party bore considerable animus toward Moscow, which had used it for its own purposes rather than as a way to assure a Communist government in China. Moscow's reluctance to provide expanded aid that might help speed a victory against the Nationalists, as well as its Treaty of Friendship with Chiang, which put pressure on Mao to reach an accommodation with him, did not endear Stalin and the Soviets to China's Communists.

Yet in spite of Moscow's intentions, Mao's party had survived and grown in power on its own. Increasingly, it looked to itself in deciding what best served its interests. Long-standing suspicions of Russian eagerness to control Manchuria and other parts of China added to Mao's determination to act as independently of Stalin's dictates as possible.

Kennan voiced the conviction that whatever dependence China's Communists might have on Moscow, it would not last long should Mao's party gain control of the country. For hundreds of years, outside powers had tried and failed to rule China, Kennan observed. In time, Russia would come to the same pass: once the Communists took over the country, they would act with scant regard for Moscow's wishes. In the climate of suspicion in the United States about communism, which had been muted by the war and had resurfaced forcefully in 1945, however, it was all but impossible for Kennan's doubts to be heard, let alone acted upon. Unlike his February 1946 "Long Telegram" on Soviet behavior, Kennan's prescience about Mao's tensions with Stalin had no resonance in Washington.

There has been a long-standing argument that because of its knee-jerk anticommunism, Washington missed a chance to establish a working relationship with China's Communists. Knowledgeable

China scholars have their doubts about this assertion. The terms of the Sino-Soviet relationship were set as much, if not more, by Mao: his devotion to revolutionary principles and need to identify his party with radical change associated with Soviet communism rather than American capitalism made all the difference in shaping initial interactions between Washington and China's Communists.

Still, had the U.S. government abandoned Chiang for Mao and his transparently more popular party in China in 1945–49, it might have made a large difference in U.S.-China relations in the 1940s and '50s. It is difficult to believe that a friendly America offering financial and technical aid would not have trumped the need for a U.S. ideological bogeyman. At the end of the day, as in Russia, popular sentiment always put the national interest above support for any political party. And Russia's Communists, whose country had been a traditional exploiter of China, would have been hard pressed to convince most of China's Communist leaders that the Soviet Union was to be trusted more than a traditionally anti-imperial America, whose opposition to European and Asian colonialism made her a more natural friend of a new China. Alas, neither America's nor China's better angels prevailed, and both would pay a heavy price in the future.

In going to China, Marshall believed that his mission was vital not only to China's well-being but also to the United States and the world. "If the world wants peace," he told a press conference, "China's effort [at internal reconciliation] must succeed." He noted "the vital importance to the United States of the success of the present Chinese efforts toward unity and economic stability if we are to have [the] continued peace we hope for in the Pacific."

After Marshall arrived in China in December 1945, he refused to hear that he had accepted an impossible mission. General Wedemeyer and Walter S. Robertson, counselor at the embassy in Nanking, tried to apprise him of the difficulties. Robertson saw "no basis to hope that you could bring about a coalition government. They [the Nationalists and Communists] had no common ground for coalition, no common objective for China." As a fellow military man, Wedemeyer tried to warn Marshall what he was up against. But Marshall dismissed his pessimism, saying, "I am going to accomplish my mission and you are going to help me."

Although Marshall and some of his American aides would have periods of optimism over the next twelve months, it became clear to them by the end of 1946 that neither Chiang nor Mao trusted each other enough to work together for China's larger good. When occasional upturns in the mediations occurred, even someone as cynical about their chances of achieving anything as Wedemeyer could see Marshall as a kind of miracle worker: "He is well on the way toward the successful implementation of a plan that will integrate military forces of the Central Government and the Communists," Wedemeyer concluded three months into the mission. "All of this has been accomplished in the background of intrigue, mistrust, selfish personalities, and oriental cunning. Really a stupendous accomplishment." Wedemeyer doubted that anyone else "in the world could have done as much in so short a time."

The temporary gains were the result of a cat-and-mouse game between Chiang and Mao, each trying to convince Marshall and the Americans that the other side was responsible for the unfixable breach. Chiang was a masterful manipulator. He had no intention of bending to pressure from Marshall, whom he considered naive. After Marshall had been in China for a month, Chiang privately wondered, "Can it be that he [Marshall] has not yet understood the deceptive nature of Communist maneuvers? . . . [M]ore and more he is being taken in by the Communists. The Americans tend to be naive and trusting. This is true even with so experienced a man as Marshall." When Marshall threatened to cut off desperately needed economic and military aid, Chiang bristled at the pressure "to appease the Communists. The fact is to appease the Communists at this time is to yield to the Soviet Union." But Chiang would give the appearance of eagerness for a reconciliation, hoping to convince the Americans to sustain the support for him that he knew had significant backing among anti-Communist ideologues in the United States.

The forty-seven-year-old Chou En-lai, who conducted the negotiations for the Communists, was every bit as sly. Intimately familiar with the Nationalists, as someone who had been a part of the party's inner circle in the 1920s, and with the society of Europe, where he had lived for four years from 1920 to 1924, Chou, in Henry Kissinger's words, had a command of world affairs that was "stunning." Kissinger described him as "urbane, infinitely patient, extraordinarily intelligent, [and] subtle."

Although Chou and Mao saw the Nationalists as ruthless and corrupt, interested only in holding on to power that could serve their special interests, Chou brought all his considerable skills to bear as a diplomat and defender of his party's goals. He and Mao saw China's freedom from foreign domination and progress toward internal development as tied to Communist control. A brilliant cosmopolite, who spoke several languages, including English, Chou was "plausible in his approach and often completely open in his conversation, he seemed capable of reaching a workable arrangement with the Nationalists." But Chiang and most conservative supporters thoroughly distrusted him, as someone who had broken with Chiang's party in the 1920s. As the architect of the Communist party's famous 1934 Long March to a haven in Yenan on the Yellow River in central China, Chou was seen by Chiang as an unyielding ideologue. Worse, he considered Chou and Mao essentially agents of Russian ambitions in China.

Chiang's refusal to reach any kind of accommodation with adversaries would eventually cost him and the Nationalists their control of China. A course of rigorous reform to weed out the corruption in his administration and a commitment to economic and political change that could have partly accommodated Mao's party and millions of suffering Chinese might have averted a civil war, sustained strong U.S. support for his government, and kept him in power.

Similarly, the Truman administration and, as much to the point, substantial public opinion in the United States could have spared itself considerable future problems if it had been more flexible about dealing with China's Communists. Their proposal for talks with Roosevelt and willingness to engage in negotiations with Chiang's government were in part an attempt to lull the Nationalists into delays while they gathered the military wherewithal to defeat Chiang's armies. But it was also an indication of their antagonism to the Soviets and interest in finding an alternative to dependence on their support. A greater receptivity to Mao's Communists in 1945 might have averted the later bloodshed between the United States and China in Korea and pressured Moscow into earlier interest in détente, including international control of nuclear weapons.

Even if such an outcome was out of reach with Moscow, it was apparently there for the taking with China's Communists. As later events would demonstrate, Moscow and Peking were incompatible allies. Each considered the other a threat to its national security and independence. U.S. accommodation with China in the late 1940s, whether with a coalition government or a victorious Communist regime, could have put pressure on the Soviet Union and changed the early direction of the Cold War.

But Americans on the ground in Moscow and at the White House could not believe that a weak China, however great her potential as an international power, would generate much pressure on Stalin to compete with a Chinese Communist government for U.S. favor. And the wider public in the United States was so intent on ideal arrangements abroad promising long-term universal peace, and so convinced that Communist ideology trumped national differences, that it rigidly opposed a Chinese Communist regime seen as wedded to Moscow. Few envisioned a Sino-American alliance that might, by contrast, be a counterbalance to Soviet power.

Although neither the United States nor the Soviet Union had a direct hand in the postwar fate of British-controlled South Asia, both watched developments there with concern for how India's certain independence would affect their interests.

As World War II ended, it was clear to all but diehard imperialists that British rule in India was on its last legs. For some, like Churchill, who hoped that victory in the war might extend Britain's hold on its empire, this was difficult to accept: after Lord Mountbatten, Britain's last viceroy of India, put the finishing touches on independence in 1947, Churchill refused to speak to him for six years, telling him at a public reception, "What you did in India was like running your riding crop across my face."

In the 1920s and '30s, as prospects for independence grew, India's Hindus and Muslims entered into open warfare over rights and power in a free country. Mahatma Gandhi, the leader of the independence movement and an advocate of passive resistance, warned that Hindu-Muslim divisions would tear the country apart and weaken its ability to achieve self-governance. A devoted advocate of nonviolence as the surest, most humane path to independence, Gandhi endeared himself to the Indian masses with his ascetic lifestyle, becoming a familiar world figure who commanded an army of followers eager to sacrifice themselves to a cause larger than any individual's.

After a short time out of politics in the 1920s in protest against ongoing violence between India's Hindus and Muslims, Gandhi returned in 1930 to insist on an end to British rule, temporarily unifying India's factions against oppressive British economic policies that Indians believed sacrificed their needs to British interests. Although British leaders tried to find a means of uniting the country under a constitution promising shared power and fair treatment for both religions, the divisions were too great to overcome.

Churchill's refusal to "quit India," as Gandhi demanded during World War II, made the country's Hindus a nominal ally of the Japanese during the Pacific conflict. Attlee's assumption of the premiership in August 1945 opened the final phase of British rule in India. A British plan for preserving India as a unified but federated state with

Hindus and Muslims enjoying considerable autonomy had acknowledged limitations, but the alternative was "violence, chaos, and even civil war," which would be "a terrible disaster for many millions of men, women and children. . . . We appeal to all who have the future good of India at heart to extend their vision beyond their own community or interest to the interests of the whole four hundred millions of the Indian people," the British proposal declared.

Gandhi embraced the plan as an excellent solution to India's sectarianism and "a discharge of an obligation . . . the British owed to India, namely, to get off India's back." He described the proposed federation as containing "the seeds to convert this land of sorrow into one without sorrow and suffering."

In July 1946 Jawaharlal Nehru, the head of the Hindus' Congress Party, rejected the British plan. A Gandhi protégé and brilliant charismatic leader from a wealthy family that gave him the connections and talent to become India's first prime minister, Nehru stubbornly refused to compromise with Muslim demands for equal representation and power in the emerging nation. The unbridgeable Hindu-Muslim divide touched off a year of civil war that took thousands of lives and ended in August 1947 with the division of the subcontinent into separate Indian Hindu and Pakistani Muslim nations.

Gandhi, however, refused to accept "the 'vivisection' of his 'sacred Mother.' " Gandhi declared himself anguished at living in an India submerged in violence, but he could not prevent the brutality that consumed India as it split into two nations; nor could he anticipate the irony of his own assassination in January 1948 at the hands of a fanatical Hindu furious at a Gandhi campaign in support of reconciliation with Muslims.

Although Nehru would later regret his rejection of the compromise solution of a federated India that shared power between Hindus and Muslims, calling it one of the worst mistakes of his public life, he never explained why he had dismissed the proposed settlement. Was it a hatred of Mohammad Ali Jinnah, India's Muslim leader and founder of Pakistan, that animated Nehru, as well as the irreducible intolerance of Hindus and Muslims for each other? As prime minister of an independent India, Nehru shaped a democratic state that worked toward expanding the nation's economy to raise living standards for its millions of impoverished citizens, while promoting anticolonialism and peaceful solutions to international crises. Nevertheless, his role in splitting India left a legacy of hatred and bloodshed that haunts South Asia and the world to this day.

Nehru's misstep was another instance of misguided leadership in a time of possibility. As with other leaders, governments, and populations in Europe and Asia, policy choices and popular passions in India fostered tensions and violence that would plague South Asia for decades to come. Even the desire to avoid bloodshed, misery, and the investment of resources in weapons of destruction was insufficient to calm religious or ethnic fervor and encourage compromises that might have changed the lives of millions of people.

In most instances, a larger, seemingly more powerful group— whether the Russians against the smaller countries of Eastern Europe, the Chinese Nationalists versus the opposition Communists, or the Hindus pitted against India's Muslims—believed it could overwhelm or control the minority. Ideological illusions also drove less populous nations to assume that their superior technology or culture could allow them to best more populous foes—as witnessed in Hitler's Germany defying Britain and France and then Britain, Russia, and the United States, or in Japan's attacks on China and the United States. In 1945, the Soviet conviction that Russia's revolutionary zeal in support of a superior system of social and political organization would enable it eventually to defeat the more militarily powerful and prosperous West joined with the conviction that the Americans and their allies were so intent on destroying communism that it had no choice but to opt for confrontation over compromise.

"The greatest menace to our civilization today," the British historian Herbert Butterfield wrote in 1953, "is the conflict between giant organized systems of self-righteousness—each system only too delighted to find that the other is wicked—each only too glad that the sins give it the pretext for still deeper hatred and animosity."

As the saying goes, pride often precedes the fall. But minorities spurred by national identity or convictions of cultural superiority have sometimes outlasted more powerful foes. The countries of Eastern Europe, overcoming more than four decades of Soviet domination, have been one example. Germany and Japan, for all their military dominance and belief in superior racial and governmental systems, were exceptions: their thorough defeat in the war convinced them that their enemies in fact had not only superior power but wiser economic, political, and social systems, which they felt compelled to embrace.

After World War II, the Middle East became another arena for tensions and conflict between majorities and minorities and the clash of civilizations—Jews and Arabs versus Britain, and Jews versus Arabs.

Tensions in the region between competing nationalities, religions, sects, and tribes were long-standing and fierce. The collapse of the Ottoman Empire at the end of World War I had drawn Britain into the vacuum, where its control of Palestine was confirmed by a League of Nations mandate in 1922. That London had enlisted international Jewish support for its war effort with the Balfour Declaration in November 1917, which promised a homeland in Palestine, incensed the Arabs, who having finally obtained freedom from Turkish rule now feared that they would face loss of territory and control over their fate at the hands of a European Jewish population. The result was a series of violent clashes between Arabs and Jews in the 1920s that produced British restrictions on Jewish migration to Palestine.

The Nazi persecution of Germany's Jews in the 1930s gave growing appeal to a Zionist movement for a Jewish sanctuary in Palestine, the ancestral homeland of the Jewish tribes that had been dispersed throughout the Middle East, Europe, and America. At a world Zionist convocation in 1903, a majority of the delegates rejected a British offer for a homeland in Uganda in East Africa, voting instead for a return to Palestine.

The leader of modern Zionism was the Russian-born Chaim Weizmann. Trained as a chemist in Germany and Switzerland in the 1890s, Weizmann migrated to Britain, where he became a professor at Manchester University and won notoriety as the inventor of a synthetic acetone that aided the British war effort. His standing as one of the most respected and influential Jews in Britain allowed him to help shape Foreign Secretary Arthur Balfour's Declaration on Palestine. In early discussions on the declaration, when Balfour suggested an alternative homeland for world Jewry, Weizmann asked, "Would you give up London to live in Saskatchewan?" Failing to see the comparison, Balfour replied that the British had always lived in London. "Yes," Weizmann said, "and we lived in Jerusalem when London was still a marsh."

Nazi persecution spurred increased migration to Palestine in the 1930s, which resulted in renewed outbreaks of violent opposition from Arabs threatened with displacement. The Holocaust, which left a million displaced European Jews in 1945, created moral and practical demands on London to open Palestine to expanded Jewish migration and to honor Balfour's Declaration by partitioning the country into Arab and Jewish states.

The inevitable violence spurred by increased Jewish migration to Palestine arguably should have raised questions about an alternate haven for displaced Jews. It was understandable that Zionists early in the century rejected a suggestion of Uganda as the future homeland. Jews had no connection to East Africa that might have made the territory an appealing homeland, even after the experience of the 1920s and '30s suggested that it might be a safer refuge than Palestine.

Surprisingly, no one seemed to think of annexing a part of Germany comparable in size to the small area of Palestine to make up the new state of Israel. It would certainly have been as compatible for the tens of thousands of displaced European Jews, who eventually made their way to Palestine. True, a refuge in Germany would not have had the same appeal as a return to sacred ground in the Holy Land, to which Jews traced their roots. But a Jewish state in Europe, where most of the settlers in the new homeland had been born, could have avoided the bloodshed that followed the displacement in the Middle East of Arabs who saw their claims on Palestine as at least equal to those of Europe's persecuted Jews. Whatever resentment a Jewish settlement on German territory would have generated among Germans, they were in no position to resist, as demonstrated in their loss of East German territory to the new Poland.

In the end, the movement of Europe's homeless Jews to Palestine became the prelude to an expanded series of clashes. For both older Jewish residents and newer migrants, the Holocaust hung over their every action; no one could escape the fear of a new catastrophe in another setting, dealt by another more populous race of anti-Semites. For the Arabs, who felt persecuted by outsiders eager to control their oil resources and deprive them of self-determination, the Jewish resolve to populate and annex all or even part of Palestine represented another chapter in the history of Ottoman and now Western domination. The expanding Jewish presence in Palestine was a call to Arab resistance that matched the Jewish conviction that only a militant response to Arab hostility would save them from another disaster.

In January 1919 Weizmann and the future King Faisal I of Iraq had signed an agreement committing them to peaceful shared development of Palestine. But the distrust between two persecuted peoples was too great to bridge. It is difficult to imagine that even the most skillful expert in conflict resolution could have overcome the tensions between Arabs and Jews in Palestine in 1945.

The United States, which had never played more than a peripheral part in the Middle East, now became a principal power broker in the region. It was an unwelcome but unavoidable burden. In the year and a half after he became president, Truman complained that "the Jewish and Arab situation in the Near East . . . has caused us more difficulty than any other problem in the European Theater." Although he was openly sympathetic to the migration of 100,000 displaced Jews to Palestine, he resented the constant pressure from Jewish Americans to make it happen. "Jesus Christ couldn't please them when he was here on earth," he rhetorically said at a cabinet meeting, "so how could anyone expect that I would have any luck?" Arab intransigence against what Truman saw as a historically justified and now moral claim on a homeland left him frustrated. He doubted that there was a solution to this conflict of wills, but he intended to seek one nevertheless.

Successive administrations over the next six and a half decades had much the same experience: though partial solutions, like President Jimmy Carter's Camp David peace accords between Egypt and Israel in 1978, have bolstered hopes of arranging a broader settlement in the region, Arab-Israeli differences have repeatedly frustrated all comprehensive peace proposals.

Domestic political considerations partly shaped Truman's support for Jewish aspirations in Palestine. The absence of a significant Arab population in the United States and the presence of an influential Jewish American community, especially in New York, was vital. Although a strong element in Roosevelt's New Deal coalition, New York's Jewish voters had no such clear-cut loyalty to Harry Truman and could be alienated by White House foot-dragging on a Jewish homeland in Palestine. The president and his principal political advisers saw delay as potentially disastrous for him and his party in the 1946 congressional and 1948 presidential elections.

Several considerations, however, discouraged aggressive support for Jewish settlement and statehood in a predominantly Arab territory. An America favoring Jewish ambitions risked angering the Arabs, who could retaliate by withholding oil supplies and cozying up to Soviet Russia. But Truman took some reassurance from the understanding that Arab oil producers and their Western customers had shared economic interests: the Arabs needed the European and American markets, and the Europeans and Americans relied on Arab energy supplies to fuel their economies. The White House also assumed that agreements with atheist Communists would have little appeal to Muslim societies.

Nevertheless, if the United States pressed the case for opening Palestine to Europe's Jews and Arab violence ensued, it would put pressure on the White House to send peacekeeping forces to inhibit the fighting. Truman, however, made clear that he had no intention of sending troops into so potentially volatile and possibly unmanageable a conflict. He rationalized the announcement by saying it would be the business of the new United Nations and the international community to assume management of the problem. Indeed, wasn't this just what the UN had been created to do?

For some in the United States, like Ohio Republican senator Robert Taft, a potential rival for the White House in 1948, Middle East difficulties were a reason for America to return to prewar isolationism. He and others warned that involvement in this conflict and European and Asian tensions in general would drag America into endless international struggles that would become a standing drain on limited national resources.

Truman and a majority of Americans, however, believed that the United States, with its unprecedented power and influence, joined to an effective United Nations, was the world's best hope for long-term peace. Moreover, Pearl Harbor had convinced most Americans that air force, with the capacity to strike anywhere, had deprived the United States of the earlier safety that geography had given it.

Reflecting majority sentiment, Truman did not believe it possible for the United States to shun responsibility for involvement in overseas problems, including the Middle East, where most Americans favored a Palestinian homeland for Hitler's Jewish victims. Besides, as Truman said later, the Middle East was "one part of the world that has always interested me. . . . The whole history of that area of the world is just about the most complicated and most interesting of any area anywhere, and I have always made a very careful study of it," including the fact that "there has always been trouble there." Unlike "a violently opposition Congress whose committees with few exceptions are living in 1890" and, Truman feared, could allow the world to fall into another war, he intended to do his "job," which "must be done—win, lose or draw," including keeping the Middle East from provoking a wider conflict. Nevertheless, in the summer of 1946, he declared, "I have about come to the conclusion that there is no solution, but we will keep trying."

Sadly, he was all too right. In the fall of 1946, against State Department advice that continuing openly to support Jewish aspirations for a homeland would undermine U.S. national interests in the Middle East, the president endorsed a plan to partition Palestine into Arab and Jewish states. He refused to be swayed by the risk of a threat to oil supplies from doing what he said was "right."

But the moral argument hid his conviction that no aspirant for the White House in 1948, which he already was, could afford to lose New York's electoral votes. Moreover, his likely opponent would be Tom Dewey, the state's governor, and a Dewey presidency would produce U.S. backing for partition and make his opposition irrelevant. Since he believed he would lose the White House if he opposed partition and that a new administration would not only use his opposition against him in a campaign but also would support partition beginning in 1949, he saw both moral and political reasons to act as he did. A UN resolution in November 1947 supporting partition, and a British announcement that they would leave Palestine after it occurred in May 1948, left responsibility for keeping the peace to the UN.

The partition and British withdrawal on schedule left the United Nations and Washington struggling to head off bloodshed. But neither had the wherewithal or the will to enforce a proposal for a trusteeship that aimed to delay partition and provide a temporary solution. In fact, neither the UN nor the Truman administration had the power to halt the movement toward a two-state solution and the fighting that it provoked. Neither could come up with a better alternative. Jews in Palestine and the United States rejected trusteeship as delaying the inevitable establishment of a Jewish state, while Arabs refused to agree to Israeli independence. Because the existence of Israel seemed to be a foregone conclusion, Truman saw no reason to delay recognition and lose the political and moral advantages it gave him.

The decision to recognize Israel did not endear Washington to the Arabs, but it did not result in an immediate Soviet gain among them. As anticipated, Arab economic ties to the West were too strong to give Moscow an immediate advantage in the Middle East. In time, however, East-West competition for influence in the region would become a critical part of the Cold War.

6

THE TRIUMPH OF FEAR

. . .

The world, which seems
To lie before us like a land of dreams,

Hath really neither joy, nor love, nor light,
Nor certitude, nor peace, nor help for pain;
And we are here as on a darkling plain;
Swept with confused alarms of struggle and flight,
Where ignorant armies clash by night.

—Matthew Arnold, "Dover Beach," 1867

A cross Europe, the Middle East, and Asia, the end of the war brought not confidence in the future but doubt and apprehension. Recovery from the devastation wrought by the most destructive weapons in history seemed as arduous a challenge as anything faced by modern societies. And would the reconstruction be the prelude to yet greater future destruction in a world addicted to war?

For a country as damaged as the Soviet Union, the problem of mobilizing the public for the Herculean effort seemed particularly daunting. Having extracted so much from his long-suffering countrymen in the war, Stalin wrestled with questions of how to instill new resolve in the survivors of the Nazi invasion and occupation, which left few families without physical losses and emotional despair. When one of Stalin's inner circle recommended that two high-ranking officials accused of incompetence should be shot, Stalin replied, "It's easy to shoot people. It's more difficult to make them work," although he was all too happy to imprison and murder anyone justly or unjustly suspected of opposing him.

Andrei Zhdanov, a member of the Communist Party's Central Committee and party chief in Leningrad, was Stalin's number-two man after the war. Eighteen years Stalin's junior, he shared a love of history and literature with Stalin and was known as Stalin's "fellow intellectual." The offspring of middle-class educators, Zhdanov acted as a kind of court jester, entertaining Stalin by singing, playing the piano, and telling jokes. But Stalin also saw him as a man of substance who could be charged with the oversight of Soviet cultural affairs to promote national unity. Zhdanov declared that "with millions dead and the economy destroyed," the key to national revival was through "a new concept of spiritual values . . . based on classical [Russian] culture."

Zhdanov was also given control of foreign policy, which largely meant eradicating "alien influences" on popular thinking. While Stalin and Zhdanov expected to keep Soviet forces in Eastern Europe for the foreseeable future and then maintain control of the occupied countries with Soviet loyalists, they also aimed to ensure that contacts with Eastern Europeans did not infect Russia with subversive ideas. Exposure to the outside world inevitably produced comparisons that could not possibly favor Stalin's governance and the Soviet standard of living, even in Eastern Europe, where Western influences were commonplace. Soviet prisoners of war and soldiers who had been exposed to the outside world as well as those who had shown any affinity for their German occupiers were sent to the gulag, where they could not tell the masses what they had seen and absorbed from foreigners.

While Stalin was determined to close off Russia from the outside world, he was less keen on raising public morale and commitment to the Kremlin through associations with the country's long-term past. His objective was to reestablish the total authority of Communist ideology and to regenerate the excitement and hope associated with the Bolshevik revolution.

To move the country forward, Stalin believed it essential to assert total personal and Communist Party control at home and in Russia's near western and eastern neighbors abroad. As the war was coming to an end, he predicted that "the soldiers [would be] forgotten and lapse into oblivion." The first order of business was to eliminate the sway of the military chiefs who had brought victory in the war. They were seen as competitors for power with Stalin and the party. It meant consigning Marshal Georgy Zhukov, the greatest hero of the fighting, who was credited with the defeat of German forces at Moscow, Stalingrad, and Berlin, to the shadows. His hold on the public's sympathies was seen by Stalin and the Politburo as a potential challenge to their authority. During 1946, Zhukov disappeared from the Soviet state media. History was rewritten to give other lesser military chiefs credit for victories in the Great Patriotic War. Soviet citizens cynical about the Kremlin's manipulation of the past joked that the present and the future were easy to imagine. Only the past was unpredictable.

For Stalin, the public's enthusiasm for his Communist regime could no longer rest principally on promises of a better life for the masses. The moral and spiritual excitement generated by the revolution had waned. "The fire of revolutionary Marxism has definitely died out," Kennan told Washington in May 1945. Stalin had under his command "a submissive but no longer an inspired mass of followers."

Moreover, the higher standard of living in every Western non-Communist society was a testament to the productivity of private enterprise and capitalism's superiority to state ownership of the means of production. The need for isolation from the West chiefly rested on the demoralization and opposition to the Soviet experiment that contact seemed certain to bring. True, Stalin could still promise that in the long run communism would outstrip capitalism, which the

Great Depression of the 1930s had demonstrated was no panacea for workers seeking security from impoverishment. But the emergence of the United States as the world's most powerful and prosperous nation at the close of the war represented a transparent refutation to Soviet assertions of superiority as an economic and social system.

On February 9, 1946, in a nationally broadcast speech from Moscow's Bolshoi Theater, Stalin used the occasion of elections to the Supreme Soviet to make the case to his people for Soviet rule. Because he could not send Zhukov into obscurity without paying homage to the Soviet military, his speech celebrated the courage and brilliance of Soviet fighting forces.

Yet victory in the war was principally depicted as the result of socialism's great leap forward in preparing and supplying the country's military. Gone from the discussion was any mention of Allied supplies, of the sacrifices of British and American convoys ferrying munitions to the Soviet Union through hazardous waters. There was no question but that the lion's share of Soviet fighting capacity was homegrown. But ignoring the contributions of American lend-lease to Soviet success was a sign of the distance Stalin now believed essential to put between East and West. Stalin also declared that Soviet science would be a favored child in the future, signaling that Moscow would not allow the United States to maintain its monopoly of atomic bombs: "I have no doubt that if we give our scientists proper assistance they will be able in the very near future not only to overtake but even outstrip the achievements of science beyond the borders of our country," he declared.

More disturbing were assertions that the two world wars were the inevitable result of the competition produced by "monopoly capitalism." The rivalry among the capitalist states for raw materials and markets split them into hostile camps that ended in armed conflict. "Perhaps catastrophic wars could be avoided if it were possible periodically to redistribute raw materials and markets among the respective countries . . . by means of concerted and peaceful decisions," Stalin asserted. "But this is impossible under the present capitalist conditions of world economic development," more than suggesting that Soviet Russia would need to prepare itself for the inevitable round of future wars that could once again threaten its existence.

In Stalin's rendering of events, World War II tested the Soviet economic and social systems. The war proved "the foreign press"—which decried Soviet Russia as "a 'dangerous experiment' that was doomed to failure," a "house of cards" certain to collapse under the weight of the Nazi invasion—dead wrong. The Soviet victory not only refuted these assertions but also demonstrated that "the Soviet social system has proved to be more viable and stable than the non-Soviet social system, that the Soviet social system is a better form of organization of society than any non-Soviet social system." One can only imagine the extent of the cynical response to Stalin's pronouncement in a country that was struggling to repair its collapsed infrastructure and achieve a minimal standard of living.

Yet in Stalin's rendition of history, past superiority was insufficient to insulate the country from future dangers. The challenge now was to build upon past achievements with five-year plans that would "rehabilitate the devastated regions of our country" and increase the national economy threefold from its prewar levels. "Only when we succeed in doing that," Stalin ominously declared, "can we be sure that our Motherland will be insured against all contingencies. This will need perhaps another three five-year plans, if not more. But it can be done, and we must do it."

Stalin's principal associates echoed and expanded upon his pronouncements. Kennan reported from Moscow on the "militant" character of other Politburo members' speeches. They warned that "forces of Fascist reaction are still alive in . . . bourgeois democracies and elsewhere." Although they had defeated Nazi Germany and imperialist Japan, the Soviet Union was still facing "capitalist encirclement" and could put no faith in international collaboration. Kennan described "an attitude of total suspicion toward motives of

[the] outside world. . . . 'All those who may think of organizing new war against [the] Soviet Union should remember that it is already a mighty power,' " he quoted one speaker as saying.

In 1979, I had a firsthand encounter with the Soviet determination to portray itself as a great power. In September 1979, to commemorate the fortieth anniversary of the outbreak of World War II, the Yugoslavs invited historians from all the belligerents in the conflict to participate in a five-hour television discussion of the war. During a social gathering the evening before, the Soviet representative, a retired general from a historical institute, began talking about "the three world wars." I interrupted to ask what was the third world war. He dismissively declared: "The Russo-Japanese War, World War I, and World War II, and if you don't know this, you must be a sociologist and not an historian." I could not resist deflating him a bit the next evening before the cameras by asking him about the Nazi-Soviet nonaggression pact.

Whether Stalin actually thought that the capitalist nations caused the two world wars and would now threaten the world with another conflict by their competition with each other seems open to question. Walter Bedell Smith, the U.S. ambassador to Moscow beginning in 1946, saw divisions in the Politburo over what Russia might expect from the West: a divided group of nations that would fight one another or a coalition of states intent on combating communism. Stalin apparently sided with those who saw a temporary unity of purpose in the Western democracies, which felt endangered by the Soviet Union and were committed to bringing her down. He anticipated the revival of German power in "twelve to fifteen years." As the war was ending, Stalin privately predicted: "We shall recover in fifteen or twenty years, and then we'll have another go at it."

He also saw the danger of outside attack from the West, whether directly by Anglo-American forces armed with atomic bombs or by a resurrected Germany doing the bidding of Russia's former allies, as a powerful motivator of national unity. With famine afflicting Soviet citizens in 1946, Stalin badly needed something more to sustain his control than happy talk about the virtues of the Soviet system. As in the past, suppression of dissent by execution or imprisonment in the gulags staved off any meaningful threat to Communist power. But rhetoric about the danger of "the other"—ruthless, self-serving capitalist countries—seemed like an even more effective means of stimulating a new surge of national solidarity under a Communist Party promising to advance the well-being of workers at home and abroad. Intimidation and paranoia were Stalin's most effective weapons for defending his rule from any internal desire for a new regime.

The response in the United States to the rhetoric from Moscow among public officials and attentive citizens was a mixture of disbelief, self-reproach, and appeals for reciprocated militancy. Was Stalin threatening or at least preparing for a war with the United States? Truman and Dean Acheson, the undersecretary of state, scoffed at the idea. The president dismissed the belief in a February 1946 speech at the Women's Press Club in Washington, saying that it reminded him of a senator who cynically declared, "Well, you know, we always have to demagogue a little before elections." Averell Harriman, the tough-minded wartime ambassador to Moscow, also described the speeches as principally directed at the Soviet public. When Paul Nitze, a State Department official who was alarmed by Stalin's pronouncements, described them as a "delayed declaration of war on the U.S.," Acheson chided him for "just seeing mirages. Paul, you see hobgoblins under the bed. They aren't there. Forget it."

That Truman and Acheson were more concerned than they let on, and purposely played down the Soviet threat to head off an overreaction in the United States, is possible, and even probable. By early February 1946, both of them were already leery of Soviet intentions. Yet they also shared former vice president and now secretary of commerce Henry Wallace's feeling that too much harsh talk about Russia was provoking Stalin into a defensive reaction. When former U.S. ambassador to Moscow William C. Bullitt warned Wallace that

Stalin's speech signaled Soviet preparation for war against the West, Wallace told him that Stalin's rhetoric "was accounted for in some measure by the fact that it was obvious to Stalin that our military was getting ready for war with Russia; that they were setting up bases all the way from Greenland, Iceland, northern Canada and Alaska to Okinawa with Russia in mind. I said that Stalin obviously knew what these bases meant and also knew the attitude of many of our people through our press. We were challenging him and his speech was taking up the challenge."

Others took the Soviet rhetoric at face value and urged the need for reciprocated toughness. Although *Time* magazine conceded that Stalin's speech might have been given "for purely Russian reasons," it described his language as "the most warlike pronouncement uttered by any top-rank statesman since V-J Day." Associate Supreme Court Justice William O. Douglas labeled Stalin's talk a "Declaration of World War III." And the widely syndicated columnist Walter Lippmann wrote, "Now that Stalin has [decided] to make military power his first objective, we are forced to make a corresponding decision." Lippmann described the need for a "new mighty upsurge of national economy to balance it [the Soviet threat] and withstand it." Truman, however, dismissed this talk as excessive: "Russia couldn't turn a wheel over the next ten years without our aid," he said. He seemed to share Kennan's belief that "the Russians are a nation of stage managers; and the deepest of their convictions is that things are not what they are, but only what they seem."

The uncertainty over Soviet intentions was certainly justified. There can be no doubt that Stalin saw the Western democracies as a long-term threat to Communism and Soviet power in particular. Given Communist rhetoric about world revolution and the pre-1941 Western reaction to the Soviet regime, it's no wonder that Stalin felt as he did. After the collaboration in World War II, he certainly could have imagined a different future for Russia's relations with the capitalist democracies, but his fear that exposure of Soviet citizens to the more affluent and unregimented West would be enough to under-mine Communist control was an inducement to describe the United States and Britain, whether ill-intentioned or not, as the "enemy."

Stalin saw anticapitalist talk as essential to internal Soviet stability; his uncertain hold on a country in such continuing dire need pro-voked rhetorical overkill toward the West. Truman was right about the immediate limits to Russia's capacity to start an aggressive war. But Moscow's inflammatory rhetoric stirred fears in the United States that the Soviets were intent on war and would take the first possible opportunity to strike out at the West. Although Truman and others skeptical of Soviet capacity to pose a serious threat were much closer to the truth, both about their strength and their plans, they neverthe-less underestimated how quickly the Russians could build an atomic bomb and create a formidable military for the defense of its homeland and satellites.

Soviet preoccupation with issues of housing, food supplies, and other consumer shortages echoed anxieties in the United States. While Americans were far better off than the great majority of Rus-sians, they also worried about their creature comforts. In a January 1946 Gallup poll, 62 percent cited inflation, housing, food, cloth-ing, fuel shortages, and finding work as their greatest concerns. Out of eight issues Americans named as likely to be the most important in the November 1946 congressional elections, all but one, military training, were focused on domestic needs.

The great majority of Americans had only limited concerns about foreign threats, particularly from Russia. True, 59 percent of the country thought that one nation or another would like to control the world; but only 26 percent of those who felt this way, or about 15 percent of Americans, thought that the Soviets were intent on pro-jecting their power around the globe.

This outlook existed despite the news on February 16, 1946, of a Canadian spy ring passing atomic secrets to Moscow. After American columnist Drew Pearson revealed that spies had been operating out of Russia's Ottawa embassy, Canadian authorities arrested twenty-two Canadians, including scientists at Canada's National Research Council, its atomic energy agency, implicated in the espionage. A few days later, the arrest in London of the British physicist Klaus Fuchs, who had worked on the atom bomb in Canada and the United States, increased fears that the Soviets would soon be able to match the West in building nuclear weapons.

The revelations out of Canada and Britain may have influenced the results of a Gallup survey in March: three-quarters of Americans expressed support for congressional appropriations "to maintain a large force of secret service agents who would operate throughout the world to keep us informed of what other nations are doing." When asked if they thought "Russia will cooperate with us in world affairs," a majority of Americans said, "No." Only 35 percent of the country now had any confidence that the Soviets wanted to work for international accord with the United States. Seventy-one percent disapproved of "the policy Russia is following in world affairs," and two-thirds of the country rejected suggestions that it would be possible to cooperate with Britain and Russia in doing away with armaments and military training. More disturbing, 69 percent of Americans expected the United States to "find itself in another war . . . within the next 25 years."

One can only imagine how much better off Russia and the world would have been if Stalin and the Politburo had adopted a softer line toward the West. Soviet credibility with its former allies for the defeat of Nazism remained high. A cooperative posture would have generated support in the United States for aid to help Russian reconstruction and would surely have sat well with a majority of Russians yearning to improve their living standards. But the unyielding ideologues in the Kremlin could not acknowledge any limits to their ideas about class struggle and the long-term advantages of socialism over capitalism. The shortcomings of free enterprise had been fully exposed in the Great Depression, but its advantages had been made abundantly clear in America's wartime industrial mobilization and production, which had helped supply the Soviet military. Having killed and imprisoned so many in the name of socialism, Stalin and his associates could not accept that they were committed to an economic and social system more deeply flawed than that of their competitors in the West.

Nor could they conceive of relinquishing power. It would have been a repudiation of their life's work. It is impossible to believe that Stalin or anyone close to him considered sacrificing his power for the sake of the national well-being. Like most politicians in most countries, they assumed that their hold on authority was essential for their nation's future peace and prosperity. Saying they are wrong is not part of many politicians' vocabulary.

As the war ended in May 1945, Kennan tried to imagine a Russia maintaining good relations with the West; but he was not optimistic. He cabled the State Department that "the foreign resident, weary of both Russia's wars and Russia's winters, finds himself wanly wishing that the approaching political season might not be like the Russian summer: faint and fleeting." But he saw it as all too likely: he expected the war's end to bring not demobilization but the continued "building up of military power . . . an indispensable feature of the police state." With the disintegration of traditional rival powers on her frontiers, he expected Russia to have an unprecedented position of control on the Eurasian landmass, its appetite for dominance having been fed by "the age-old sense of insecurity of a sedentary people reared on an exposed plain in the neighborhood of fierce nomadic peoples."

Kennan saw no reason to dwell on the extraordinary opportunity for a genuine revolution in outlook that Russia's newfound power afforded it—a chance to turn away from the militancy that seemed certain to provoke a corresponding aggressiveness in threatened rivals. His inability to imagine this rested on the conviction that "no one in Moscow believes that the Western world, once confronted with the life-size wolf of Soviet displeasure standing at the door and threatening to blow the house in, would be able to stand firm."

Kennan worried that Americans were failing to take the full measure of the Soviet threat. In his warning to the State Department in May 1945, he cautioned,

> The Kremlin is counting on certain psychological factors which it knows will work strongly in Russia's favor. It knows that the American public has been taught to believe:
>
> a. That collaboration with Russia, as we envisage it, is entirely possible;
>
> b. That it depends only on the establishment of the proper personal relationships of cordiality and confidence with Russian leaders; and
>
> c. That if the United States does not find means to assure this collaboration . . . then the past war has been fought in vain, another war is inevitable, and civilization is faced with complete catastrophe.

In mid-February, Kennan recalls, he was under a miserable siege from a "cold, fever, sinus, tooth trouble, and . . . the aftereffects of the sulfa drugs administered for the relief of these other miseries." When a telegram arrived from Washington expressing puzzlement at Soviet resistance to participation in international financial institutions like the World Bank and the International Monetary Fund, created to advance postwar reconstruction and international harmony, it triggered pent-up frustrations with past Washington indifference to his warnings of Soviet hostility to the West. Tired of "talking to a stone," as he later put it, he decided to lay it on the line: "They had asked for it. Now, by God they would have it," he recalled in his memoirs.

Determined to avoid oversimplification, Kennan violated conventional practice and composed an eight-thousand-word response that he later compared to "an eighteenth-century Protestant sermon," a historian's pronouncement on past and current Soviet behavior and its "implications . . . for American policy." Twenty years later, he "read it over . . . with a horrified amusement," saying, "much of it reads exactly like one of those primers put out by alarmed congressional committees or by the Daughters of the American Revolution, designed to arouse the citizenry to the dangers of the Communist conspiracy."

Kennan described an implacable clash of wills and wits with Moscow. The Soviets could not imagine "permanent peaceful co-existence" with the capitalist countries. Their objective was to seek out every advantage against Western adversaries by building military strength at home and promoting conflict between the democracies abroad and subverting their societies through all possible means. He saw no prospect of altering this "neurotic view of world affairs." Diplomatic conversations were a charade on the Soviet side that afforded no opportunity for reasoned discourse. "We have here," he asserted, "a political force committed fanatically to the belief that with US there can be no permanent modus vivendi, that it is desirable and necessary that the internal harmony of our society be disrupted, our traditional way of life be destroyed, the international authority of our state be broken, if Soviet power is to be secure."

To Kennan's credit, he also explained that the Soviets were not "adventuristic" like Nazi Germany and ready to launch a military conflict, but cautious and calculating in their pursuit of imperial ambitions. Moreover, a cohesive, firm, and vigorous American response to Russia's actions could inhibit their designs. He saw no need to go to war with them and cautioned against any loss of "courage and self-confidence . . . [in] our own methods and conceptions of human society. . . . The greatest danger that can befall us in coping with this problem of Soviet communism is that we shall allow ourselves to become like those with whom we are coping."

Sadly, as Kennan came to understand and later lamented, his message of restraint made much less of an impression than his sermonizing about the Soviet Communist danger. As he himself explained later, his telegram, or at least the most inflammatory parts of it, resonated powerfully in Washington and ultimately across the United States. "More important than the external nature of observable reality, when it comes to the determination of Washington's view of the world, is the subjective state of readiness on the part of Washington officialdom to recognize this or that feature of it." It raised the question for Kennan—one that was "to plague me increasingly over the course of the ensuing years—whether a government so constituted should deceive itself into believing that it is capable of conducting a mature, consistent, and discriminating foreign policy. Increasingly, with the years, my answer would tend to be in the negative."

The hysterical anticommunism of the 1950s sparked by Joseph McCarthy and other politically self-serving flag-wavers greatly distressed Kennan as undermining chances for détente with the Soviet Union after Stalin died in 1953. Even before that, as Washington and its West European allies in 1948–49 moved toward a military alliance— the North Atlantic Treaty Organization (NATO)—Kennan found himself at odds with "practically everyone else involved—either in our own government, in the Western European governments, or, for that matter, in the Benelux countries" (Belgium, the Netherlands, and Luxembourg) on what he saw as "a militarized view of the Cold War." He described attitudes in the United States especially "from the congressional side [as] harsh, boorish, shortsighted, and—for me— deeply discouraging."

As far as Kennan could tell, no military threat existed that required the creation of a multinational defense organization. To the contrary, a military buildup was certain to create "a general preoccupation with military affairs, to the detriment of economic recovery and of the necessity for seeking a peaceful solution to Europe's difficulties." Moreover, European assertions that only a military alliance could ease their anxieties about a U.S. commitment to defend them filled Kennan "with impatience. What in the world did they think we had been doing in Europe these last four or five years? Did they suppose we had labored to free Europe from the clutches of Hitler merely to abandon it to those of Stalin?"

Kennan had it right. The creation of NATO provoked the organization of the Warsaw Pact and added a military standoff to the ideological, political, and economic tensions generated by the Cold War. It was another instance of an overreaction that increased the future costs to both sides of treasure and blood in limited wars and delayed possibilities of reaching a détente until the 1970s, when a balance of nuclear weapons made some kind of stand-down a logical alternative to the East-West arms race.

Domestic dislocations—strikes, shortages, inflation—and international tensions, principally with Moscow but also over China and the Middle East, took a toll on Harry Truman's public standing. During the first six months of 1946, the president's approval ratings fell by 20 points, from 63 percent to 43 percent; disapproval of his performance jumped from 22 to 45 percent. In December 1945 Truman joked with reporters that Civil War general William Tecumseh Sherman was wrong about war being hell; it was peace. Unlike Stalin, who could not imagine relinquishing power, Truman lamented his fate at having become president. The job, he complained, was like riding on the back of a tiger. He described the White House as the big white jail.

Nevertheless, as Truman also said, he had the job and intended to do it to the best of his ability. Moreover, he was convinced that his Republican critics were less likely to preserve peace and prosperity than he was. He was particularly concerned about the dangers of another war in which nuclear weapons could outstrip the horrendous devastation of World War II.

Like the president, millions of Americans shared concerns about a future in the shadow of atomic bombs. Numerous scientists and others worried that the proliferation of such weapons was a certainty unless wise leaders decided at once to forestall the development. Others took solace from the belief that modern science would find ways to defend against nuclear attacks, or that people everywhere would understand how impermissible the use of such destructive power would be. In October 1945, American nuclear scientists underscored the dangers to civilization in a five-point pronouncement on the need for international control of atomic energy: other nations would acquire the bomb; no effective defense would be possible against attacks; no country could assure its national security with a large enough arsenal to deter an opponent from an assault; an atomic war "would destroy 'a large faction of civilization' "; human survival would depend on international control of atomic weapons.

By 1981, thirty-five years later, Kennan could only imagine the survival of civilization not by international control but by elimination of the monster bombs that had become commonplace in nuclear arsenals. Historical experience had taught that despite past restraint, the existence of such weapons had repeatedly raised the possibility of their use. In 1953 Dwight Eisenhower, who had implicitly pledged during the 1952 presidential campaign to end the Korean War, gave public hints of atomic attacks on China if it did not agree to an armistice in the fighting. Alongside General Douglas MacArthur, who urged direct threats of such bombings, Eisenhower was a model of restraint, as he was again during the French collapse at Dien Bien Phu in Vietnam in 1954 when suggestions arose of using atomic bombs against the Viet Minh Communists.

The Cuban missile crisis in October 1962, which triggered a heightened defense alert in the United States and brought the world to the brink of a nuclear exchange, gave fresh meaning to the dangers of nuclear war. After the crisis ended, President John Kennedy, commenting to an aide on air force general Curtis LeMay's pressure for an air strike that would have likely provoked a Soviet missile response, said, "Can you imagine LeMay saying a thing like that? These brass hats have one great advantage in their favor. If we listen to them, and do what they want us to do, none of us will be alive later to tell them that they were wrong."

The 1964 presidential election, which pitted Republican senator Barry Goldwater against President Lyndon B. Johnson, sent another wave of fear through the world: Goldwater joked that we should consider lobbing the bomb into the men's room of the Kremlin, and the Johnson campaign responded with the "daisy girl" ad, suggesting that Goldwater might destroy every youngster's future by reckless use of nuclear weapons. Bumper stickers declaring, "In Your Heart, You Know He Might," "In Your Gut You Know He's Nuts," and "Stamp Out Peace—Vote Goldwater" reflected the conviction that, as president, Goldwater might trigger a nuclear conflict.

Once Johnson involved the country in the Vietnam War, the temptation to rely on a nuclear attack became a part of the conversation during Johnson's presidency. As the war settled into a stalemate and Johnson lost credibility with the public, Texas governor John Connally advised him to consider using a tactical nuclear weapon. When Johnson resisted, Connally wondered about having these weapons if we could not use them to win a war.

Despite doubts that nuclear missiles could be a rational alternative in any conflict, the conviction that they could deter an attack by an adversary fueled their expanded development. In the 1960s and '70s, the nuclear arms race gave birth to submarine-launched ballistic missiles (SLBMs), multiple independently targeted reentry vehicles (MIRVs), missiles capable of carrying several bombs aimed at separate targets, SS9s, intercontinental ballistic missiles (ICBMs), and antiballistic missile systems (ABMs), meant to counter the ICBMs by guarding missile sites. National security officials conceded that the expansion of these nuclear arsenals provided no advantage to one side or the other, and, as one critic said, the only function these weapons could serve was "to make the rubble bounce." After all, it was accepted wisdom that just one sixteen-megaton nuclear bomb exploded one mile above Manhattan would turn everything from the tip of the island to 110th Street, the northern reaches of Central Park, into molten ash. And the United States had over thirty thousand of these weapons.

A second Cold War nuclear alert in 1973, eleven years after the Cuban crisis, further underscored the dangers of weapons of mass destruction. When the Soviets threatened to parachute forces into the Sinai Desert during the Yom Kippur War between Israel and Egypt to rescue Egypt's Third Army, Secretary of State Henry Kissinger and General Al Haig, President Richard Nixon's chief of staff, forced Moscow to back down by raising the country's nuclear alert or Defense Condition from DEFCON IV to DEFCON III, "the highest stage of readiness for essentially peacetime conditions." Because Nixon, who was under great stress during the Watergate scandal and threats of impeachment, was sedated or drunk during this crisis, Kissinger and Haig made the decision in conjunction with five other national security officials, all of whom were unelected presidential appointees. Only the rational good sense of Eisenhower in 1953–54, John Kennedy and Nikita Khrushchev in 1963, Johnson in 1967, and the Soviets responding to the Kissinger-Haig alert in 1973 averted a nuclear holocaust.

Because the danger of a nuclear conflict was never far from the thinking of scientists and public officials in postwar America, discussions of how to contain the danger formed a significant part of the national dialogue in 1945–46. Sixty-five years after the bomb became a part of every nation's consciousness, people around the world take nuclear weapons for granted, believing that somehow we will not see another mushroom cloud. True, governments fret over proliferation, and U.S. officials in particular, especially after the terrorist attacks on September 11, 2001, sound repeated warnings about the dangers of rogue states or radical groups acquiring and using weapons of mass destruction.

Nevertheless, the sense of urgency about countering the dangers to civilization from "nukes" is nowhere near what it was in 1945–46. Shortly after the Hiroshima bombing, the Danish physicist Niels Bohr publicly sounded the alarm about "the crisis of humanity" that nuclear weapons posed. As early as 1944, Bohr had used his prominence in the Anglo-American effort to split the atom and build a bomb to lobby Roosevelt and Churchill against a future arms race by planning for international control. Where Roosevelt had encouraged Bohr's hopes with an ambiguous response, Churchill rebuffed Bohr's overture in a face-to-face conversation and convinced the president to include a provision in a 1944 aide-mémoire agreeing to guard against any leak of atomic information to the Russians, with whom Bohr had contacts at their London embassy.

The agreement signaled the difficulties in the way of international control. But postwar pressures for inhibiting the spread of nuclear weapons were too great to be ignored. The popular *Ladies' Home Journal* counseled its readers to make the prevention of an atomic war a matter of constant concern: it was "the thought you should wake up to, go to sleep with, and carry with you all day." The subject dominated the print media and radio during the last months of 1945 and throughout 1946.

The novelist Norman Mailer, who was serving in the Pacific, wrote to his wife two days after Hiroshima that "the news of the atom bomb has created more talk out here than the news of V-E day, and as much as President Roosevelt's death." Although he approved of anything that would shorten the war and get him home sooner, the bomb was "a terrifying perspective," and he could imagine "humanity destroying itself." He saw it as the "final victory of the machine. . . . The vista is horrifying. There will be another war, if not in twenty years, then in fifty, and if half of mankind survives, then what of the next war." He expected "the world cities of tomorrow" to be "built a mile beneath the earth. . . . He [man] will have descended a thousand fathoms nearer to Hell."

At the end of 1945, concerned scholars established the Federation of Atomic Scientists (FAS). In order to prevent an arms race, they described the dangers to humankind and urged United Nations control of the fissile material required to build the bomb. When U.S. military and defense chiefs encouraged congressional action to put all atomic research and development in their hands, the FAS lobbied the White House and Congress to assure civilian dominance. The result was a division of control between civil and military authority vested in an Atomic Energy Commission. The commission was ostensibly a civilian agency with David Lilienthal, a nonmilitary chief, as director, but the final legislation in July 1946 established a Military Liaison Board with power to review any issue involving atomic weapons.

The public fears persuaded the Truman administration to work for some kind of restraint, not only because it seemed essential to human survival but also because it was good politics. In January 1946, after the United Nations agreed to establish its Atomic Energy Commission to work for international control, the State Department announced the appointment of a high-level committee chaired by Undersecretary Dean Acheson and including establishment figures— former assistant secretary of war John J. McCloy, prominent scientists Vannevar Bush and James Conant, and the Manhattan Project's military chief, General Leslie R. Groves—to prepare a proposal for submission to the UN.

Because Acheson believed it essential on so important an issue to have expert advice in crafting committee recommendations, he asked five "wise men" to become committee consultants: most prominently David Lilienthal, then chairman of the Tennessee Valley Authority, a major FDR program that had employed numerous engineers; Robert J. Oppenheimer, the country's most famous atomic scientist; and the corporate chiefs at General Electric, Monsanto Chemical, and New Jersey Bell.

Despite the committee's determination to reduce or eliminate dangers of future nuclear competition, hopes of international control were doomed from the start. Stalin's February 9 speech, coupled with the revelations about the Ottawa spy ring, had aroused too much fear in the United States to allow the Truman administration to come forward with a selfless proposal that might have convinced the Soviets that the United States was determined to forego a nuclear monopoly or international dominance of the technology to produce and warehouse weapons. Numerous members of the U.S. Congress and those responsible for the country's national security in the War, Navy, and State departments believed that even the most generous offer to transfer control of atomic energy to an international agency would not deter Moscow from trying to develop a bomb. They saw an unqualified giveaway of America's atomic advantage as a naive action that would leave the United States vulnerable to Soviet nuclear blackmail.

The dilemma for what became known as the Acheson-Lilienthal committee was how to come up with something that both protected U.S. interests and convinced Moscow and other nations that Washington had no malign intentions or plans to use its nuclear advantage to advance America's global economic and political control. But a workable solution was out of reach.

The committee's one-hundred-plus-page report of March 28, 1946, included an apocalyptic warning: "Only if the dangerous aspects of atomic energy are taken out of national hands . . . is there any reasonable prospect of devising safeguards against the use of atomic energy for atomic bombs." Acheson called the document "brilliant and profound." It was, but excellence could not overcome suspicions and assumptions about self-interest.

Principally drafted by Oppenheimer, the report called for the establishment of an International Atomic Development Authority that would control all "uranium mines, atomic power plants and laboratories." Nations would give up the possibility of building bombs, and nuclear materials could only be used for peaceful purposes. The report proposed no inspection regime, since it would be impossible to assure against rogue actions by this means, or so Oppenheimer and his colleagues believed. The United States would retain control of its handful of atomic bombs until the agency could be up and running. The report included no sanctions against nations violating the terms of the agreement, relying instead on the faith in every nation's understanding that a world ultimately free of nuclear weapons served all countries' national security.

The report could not disarm mutual Soviet-American distrust. Stalin assumed that even if the United States dismantled its handful of atomic bombs, it would still have the wherewithal to build new ones, giving it an advantage over a Soviet Union that forswore developing the technology.

Doubts in the United States about Soviet intentions were a match for those in Moscow. In March 1946, Winston Churchill publicly counseled Americans not "to entrust the secret knowledge or experience of the atomic bomb . . . to the world organization, while still in its infancy. It would be criminal madness to cast it adrift in this still agitated and un-united world." While people everywhere could sleep soundly as long as the United States held a monopoly over bomb technology, it would be different if "some Communist or neo-Fascist State" had this power. Only "when the essential brotherhood of man is truly embodied and expressed in a world organization with all the necessary practical safeguards to make it effective, these powers would naturally be confided to that world organization."

Truman and most of his advisers had no intention of reducing America's military advantage over the Soviet Union or any other nation that might try to exceed American power. Although White House public pronouncements could not have been more supportive of the Acheson-Lilienthal proposals, the president's actions belied his rhetoric. He approved a proposal from military chiefs for atomic tests in July that promised "rapid engineering breakthroughs." The White House indicated that the coming talks on international control would be no deterrent to "American testing, production, and stockpiling" of atomic weapons.

As revealing, Truman asked the seventy-five-year-old Bernard Baruch, someone with no scientific expertise but with considerable influence with Congress, to lead the American delegation to the UN Atomic Energy Commission talks. A millionaire financier with close ties to Secretary Byrnes and members of both political parties, to whom he had made generous campaign contributions, Baruch eased conservative fears that the administration was intent on some pie-in-the-sky arrangements with the world organization that would ultimately undermine U.S. national security. It was quickly evident that Baruch would reflect the views of America's military chiefs in the coming talks and fulfill Truman's private comment that the United States "should not under any circumstances throw away our gun until we are sure the rest of the world cannot arm against us."

Baruch's appointment distressed Acheson and Lilienthal, who saw him as entirely unqualified to discuss atomic energy or exhibit the skills needed in difficult negotiations with the Russians. Lilienthal complained that Baruch would convince the Russians that his only objective was "to put them in a hole, not caring about international cooperation." Truman didn't much care for Baruch either, saying after a conversation with him about chairing the delegation that he "wants to run the world, the moon and maybe Jupiter—but we will see." Despite Truman's complaint, Baruch was clearly an instrument of the president's purposes. Knowing full well that Baruch would insist on inspections of potential nuclear plants in Russia and elsewhere as well as sanctions against any nation violating restrictions on atomic development, conditions that seemed certain to antagonize Moscow and undermine prospects for an agreement, Truman gave him the freedom to shape the U.S. proposal at the UN.

Baruch, who was an effective showman, launched America's part in the discussions at the UN in June with a dramatic speech: the world needed to choose between "the quick and the dead," he declared. Just what that meant was never clear, but the substance of what Baruch presented left no doubt that the AEC deliberations were a contest between American and Soviet power. Baruch insisted that any control agreement had to include inspections, sanctions against violators, no Security Council veto of UN-voted punishment of rogue nations, and an effective limitation accord before the United States relinquished control of its atomic weapons. The Soviets responded with demands for a prompt end to every nation's acquisition, stockpiling, or use of atomic bombs. No demand was made for elimination of a veto over sanctions against any nation breaching the agreement, since the only country with the wherewithal to violate the agreement was the United States.

Although negotiations would continue for months, it was a foregone conclusion that the United States and the Soviet Union would fail to find common ground on how to rein in the building of revolutionary weapons of mass destruction. The culprits in this escalation of human capacity to produce unprecedented destruction in another total war were initially Hitler and the Japanese militarists, who drove the world into the 1939–45 conflict that led to the manufacture of nuclear bombs. After the war, neither Russians nor Americans could put aside their suspicions of each other; it drove them to see possession of such weapons as essential for their survival. The British, French, Chinese, Indians, Pakistanis, and Israelis would follow suit in the postwar decades, with the North Koreans and Iranians hoping to assure their security and gain international status by joining the twenty-first-century nuclear club.

It is sobering to recognize that the controlling personalities and circumstances of early 1946 made any sort of accommodation between East and West that could have headed off a long-term cold war nearly impossible. By giving his speech of February 9 and instructing his subordinates to strike similar chords in their subsequent talks, Stalin had to understand that he was challenging Truman and Britain's leaders to answer in kind. But he had faced down Hitler, and he had every confidence that he could outlast the Americans and British in a contest of wills. In fact, a tough response from Washington and London was not without appeal to him. To provoke his former comrades in arms into an open contest for world domination was the sort of grandiose contest that gave meaning to his life.

Stalin saw the emerging tensions as an inevitable part of some grand historical struggle between Marxism and capitalism, outwardly depicting himself as no more than an agent of forces beyond any individual's control. It is hard to believe, however, that he didn't privately view himself as more than a part of some impersonal historical development—more, in fact, a shaper of history than a passive actor in its grand designs. And indeed, if individuals have any impact on human affairs, Stalin is a prime example of someone who changed things for the worse because of an inability to rise above his paranoia about enemies at home and abroad. To be sure, Stalin had real opponents eager to bring him down, but much of the animosity toward him was the consequence of ruthless initiatives. A different man with a different outlook might have sought different outcomes. But this implies an alternate history than that produced by the rise and course of Stalin and Soviet Russia.

Churchill, like Stalin, lived for the grand gesture—the dramatic confrontation that could shape the movements of peoples and nations. Consequently, when an invitation came to him from the obscure Westminster College in Fulton, Missouri, to speak in March 1946, he seized the opportunity to have an American pulpit from which he could once again influence public affairs, especially because his absence from his former high position meant less opportunity to assert himself.

Truman was very enthusiastic about the proposal for Churchill to speak. When the president of the college saw Truman at the White House with a copy of the invitation to Churchill, the president wrote in longhand: "This is a wonderful school in my home state. Hope you can do it. I'll introduce you." Churchill responded: "Under your auspices anything I say will command some attention and there is the opportunity for doing some good to this bewildered, baffled and breathless world."

Since he was out of office, Churchill had nothing to lose politically by speaking forcefully about Stalin's challenge to the West. For Truman, however, any association with an attack on Moscow, which continued to have strong sympathizers in the United States, had domestic political consequences he tried to mute. Behind the scenes, he was entirely ready to join Churchill in designing a tough response. While vacationing in Florida, Churchill used two visits to Washington to discuss his intentions with Truman and Admiral William D. Leahy, FDR's former chief of staff, to call for a "full" Anglo-American "military collaboration" against Moscow's threat to world peace. The president and Leahy had no objection to Churchill's proposed remarks, and they, along with a coterie of other White House aides and a large contingent of journalists, escorted Churchill by train to Missouri. As they rode through the American heartland, Churchill polished his speech, which he distributed in advance to the press. Truman told him that it would capture wide attention and "do nothing but good."

It certainly commanded headlines, as Churchill hoped it would. "The President has traveled a thousand miles to dignify and magnify our meeting here today," Churchill declared in his opening remarks to the college audience assembled in the main campus auditorium, "and to give me an opportunity of addressing this kindred nation, as well as my own countrymen across the ocean, and perhaps some other countries too," pointedly suggesting that he hoped the Soviets would pay heed to what he had to say. Lest his pronouncements be seen as official policy or a statement of hostile intent toward the Communists by the American and British governments, Churchill declared that he had "no official mission or status of any kind, and that I speak only for myself." Moreover, he declared that "we aim at nothing but mutual assistance and collaboration with Russia."

Yet he did not mince words about his objective—which was "to try to make sure . . . that what has [been] gained with so much sacrifice and suffering shall be preserved for the future glory and safety of mankind." America's newfound power made it the world's defender against "two giant marauders, war and tyranny," he said. Eventually, he hoped that a world army or United Nations force would become the international peacekeeper. When the UN's military might had matured into a reliable defender, it could be armed with nuclear weapons or have exclusive control of these weapons of mass destruction. In the meantime, his advice about a U.S. monopoly on the atom bomb should hold. Moreover, it seemed wise to expand Anglo-American military cooperation—not as an alternative to the United Nations but as a supplement to international stability.

It was "tyranny," however, on which he felt compelled to dwell—the abuse of those freedoms that were the hallmarks of the Anglo-American democracies. He saw no "duty . . . to interfere forcibly in the internal affairs of countries which we have not conquered in war," but he saw an obligation "to proclaim in fearless tones the great principles of freedom" that "are the joint inheritance of the English-speaking world." In short, Washington and London had no military plans to strike the Soviet Union or its satellites, he assured Moscow, but a verbal assault on their repressive governments was another matter.

"It is my duty to place before you certain facts about the present position in Europe," Churchill announced, famously explaining, "From Stettin in the Baltic to Trieste in the Adriatic an iron curtain has descended across the Continent. Behind the line lie all the capitals of the ancient states of Central and Eastern Europe. Warsaw, Berlin, Prague, Vienna, Budapest, Belgrade, Bucharest and Sofia, all these famous cities and the populations around them lie in what I must call the Soviet sphere, and all are subject to one form or another, not only to Soviet influence but to a very high and, in some cases, increasing measure of control from Moscow. . . . Police governments

are prevailing in nearly every case, and so far, except in Czechoslovakia, there is no true democracy. . . . Whatever conclusions may be
drawn from these facts—and facts they are—this is certainly not the
Liberated Europe we fought to build up. Nor is it one which contains
the essentials of permanent peace."

The danger now was to other countries around the world from
Communist subversion directed from Moscow, though not in either
the British Commonwealth or the United States, "where communism
is in its infancy. These are somber facts," Churchill declared, "but we
should be most unwise not to face them squarely while time remains."
None of this was meant to suggest that "a new war is inevitable" or
even imminent. He had every confidence that America and Britain
had the power "to save the future." Moreover, he was convinced that
the Soviets did not desire war. "What they desire is the fruits of war
and the indefinite expansion of their power and doctrines." The goal
now was not to show weakness; "nothing for which they [the Rus-
sians] have less respect . . . especially military weakness." Rather, it
was to demonstrate strength or resolve to stand together against tyranny with all Anglo-American "moral and material forces and convictions"; then "the highroads of the future will be clear, not only for
our time, but for a century to come."

The reaction in the United States was general approval. Numerous Americans, like the administration, were receptive to Churchill's
tough talk about Russia. Seventy-one percent of responders to a
Gallup survey said they disapproved of Soviet foreign policies, and
two-thirds in another poll favored a continuing U.S. monopoly of
atomic bombs: they expressed opposition to having representatives
of other nations observe or learn anything from atomic tests scheduled for the summer.

At the same time, a substantial minority of Americans on the left,
led by Secretary of Commerce Henry Wallace, deplored Churchill's
call for an Anglo-American military alliance, seeing it as an attack on
the former Soviet ally by someone who could not free himself "from

the roll of the drums and the flutter of the flag of Empire." They also saw the speech as an assault on the United Nations and international cooperation other than that between America and Britain. When Churchill showed up for a speech in New York the following week, pickets greeted him with chants of "Winnie, Winnie, go away, UNO [United Nations Organization] is here to stay," and "Don't be a ninny for imperialist Winnie!"

However eloquent, Churchill's speech had a quality of bombast to it that raised concerns beyond liberal circles. Yet the stubborn refusal of people like Henry Wallace to see that the Soviet Union was not a benign force for universal economic equality but an imperial aggressor intent on securing itself from foreign dangers provoked American conservatives into excessive fears of U.S. vulnerability to subversion at home and Soviet ambitions and capacity for world domination abroad. Left naiveté and right militancy now fed on each other, opening up a division in the United States that would make it difficult for any administration to respond realistically to problems overseas. For the left, the Truman White House's expressions of compromise toward Moscow were now seen as insufficient to assure the peace, while tough talk and actions could not satisfy the right that the administration was doing enough to fend off disaster.

Truman now found himself caught between left and right. To counter concerns in Moscow and the United States that he had aligned himself with Churchill's forceful criticism of the Russians, Truman denied that he had read Churchill's speech before its delivery or was endorsing his remarks. His presence on the stage at the college signaled otherwise, however, giving some comfort to anyone eager for a tough response to Soviet aggression. Yet his refusal openly to align himself with Churchill's tough talk angered conservative critics.

In Moscow, Churchill's speech provoked a heated response from Stalin, who was quoted in *Pravda*, the official Soviet newspaper, as saying that Churchill was laying claim to Anglo-American moral superiority, which Stalin likened to Hitler's "racial theory." He also denounced the speech as "a dangerous act" that signaled an inclination to fight a war against the Soviet Union.

Prospects for long-term peace following the end of the war in 1945 were now, to borrow Shakespeare's phrase, "a fleeting shadow" that was "seen no more."

PART II

STATE OF WAR

Cold War Illusions— and Realities

Convictions are more dangerous enemies of truth than lies.
—Friedrich Nietzsche

On his return from the United States, Churchill felt compelled to prod the Labor government and all of Britain toward an understanding of the dangers the Western democracies now faced from Russia's postwar ambitions for international control. As important, he wished to underscore his message to Stalin that he was risking the future of his country and of European recovery if he kept on the path he had taken since the end of the war.

In a speech to the House of Commons, Churchill "venture[d] to give this friendly hint to my old wartime comrade, Marshal Stalin. . . . Soviet propaganda has been steadily making headway backwards. I would not have believed it possible that in a year, the Soviets would have been able to do themselves so much harm, and chill so many friendships in the English-speaking world." The "despotic" rule imposed on part of Europe by "the Commissars in the Kremlin" was sowing "the seeds of a new world war. . . . We may be absolutely sure that the Sovietising and, in many cases, the Communising of this gigantic slice of Europe . . . will not be achieved in any permanent manner without giving rise to evils and conflicts which are horrible to contemplate," Churchill told the Parliament.

Because Britain was "exhausted physically, economically, and, above all, financially," Churchill believed that the United States, increasingly irritated by Moscow's behavior, would in time be stirred to respond. "The American eagle sits on his perch, a large, strong bird with formidable beak and claws," Churchill declared. "There he sits motionless, and Mr. Gromyko [the Soviet Ambassador] is sent day after day to prod him with a sharp pointed stick—now his neck, now under his wings, now his tail feathers. All the time the eagle keeps quite still. But it would be a great mistake to suppose that nothing is going on inside the breast of the eagle."

By the summer of 1946, Churchill believed that the West would fight a war with the Soviet Union and its East European satellite countries in seven or eight years. "We ought not to wait until Russia is ready. I believe it will be eight years before she has these [atom] bombs. . . . America knows that fifty-two percent of Russia's motor industry is in Moscow and could be wiped out by a single bomb. It might mean wiping out three million people," he told his physician, Lord Moran, but he justified this by saying that the Russians "would think nothing of that. They think more of erasing an historical building like the Kremlin."

It was an astonishing confession of acquiescence in the possibility of a nuclear war that would indiscriminately kill millions of civilians. After the unprecedented destruction of so many lives in the century's two world wars, the deaths of millions more seemed less like an impermissible alternative than an almost natural outcome to irrepressible human conflict. Yet it is difficult to square Churchill's readiness to fight with his onetime observation that it is better to jaw, jaw, jaw than to war, war, war. He had grown so apprehensive about Moscow's reach for world control, however, that he was ready to consider another international cataclysm and to assume that the United States would take the lead in answering the Soviet threat. Indeed, his "Iron Curtain" speech had been an overt attempt to shape America's response to Soviet aggression. For Churchill, it was nothing more than what he had been doing since 1940, when the Canadian industrialist William Stephenson had set up the British Security Coordination (BSC) in New York with Churchill's blessing to encourage anti-Nazi and pro-British sentiment.

Churchill's warnings were heard in Washington and Moscow, and both could imagine a war in seven or eight years, as Churchill had predicted. But neither felt compelled to initiate the fighting; certainly not in the immediate future. Each was confident that it could hold off the other for the time being.

In 1946, Stalin saw little risk in defying the United States. Despite Churchill's description of the eagle's limited patience, Stalin believed that American indebtedness to the Soviet Union for its wartime sacrifices remained a bar to an attack. Moreover, Stalin saw Truman as indecisive and inhibited by unsettling popular divisions centered on the national economy, which Communist doctrine confidently predicted was about to suffer another serious downturn that would temporarily immobilize the Americans from any kind of assertiveness in foreign affairs.

The constraints upon the Americans persuaded Stalin that he didn't need to satisfy their demands for representative governments in Eastern Europe. On the contrary, agreeing to self-determination for Russia's western neighbors seemed like a prescription for hostile nations on Moscow's borders that could undermine communism. The Americans might complain loudly about Soviet aggrandizement, but Stalin did not think Washington's unhappiness would result in war—at least not yet. Eventually, yes, but for the time being the American government was unable to mobilize its people to fight, and by the time it did, he expected Russia to have the bomb.

Although some in the Politburo might disagree with Stalin's assessments, none were powerful enough to shape policy; Stalin's views were Soviet doctrine: "The Russian Government is like the Roman Catholic Church," Churchill said; "Their people do not question authority," or show any doubts about the wisdom of their ideology.

In Stalin's judgment, class warfare in the democracies was more likely in the immediate future than another great conflict between nations. Among Communists, this idea was holy writ. But it had little, if any, basis in reality. Labor and management in the United States might be at odds over a host of issues, but this was not the advance wave of revolution. Moreover, the assumption that class struggles would erupt in the West poorly served the Soviet Union, undermining prospects for better relations abroad.

There was no give or flexibility in Communist thinking about how economic and political interactions worked. After almost thirty years of Communist mismanagement in Russia, the party still could not accept more pragmatic means to achieve economic growth and social peace if these contradicted their ideology. If they had been open to alternative ideas, or to incorporating Western thinking into their economic planning, they could have been more accepting of interactions with the outside world and less aggressive about imposing themselves on other peoples. Such open-mindedness could have brought reconstruction help from abroad and more rapid revival and expansion of Russia's postwar economy.

But paranoia about Western intentions and fears of collapse dominated Soviet thinking and behavior. Stalin believed that any sort of compromise with the capitalists would mean the demise of what he and the Bolsheviks had worked to establish since the Revolution. A severe drought in the Ukraine in the spring of 1946, for example, crimped grain production and caused famines later in the year that forced Moscow to rely on the United Nations Relief and Rehabilitation Administration (UNRRA) to feed part of its population. Food was in such short supply that feeding Soviet troops in Germany became a worry. The famine intensified Stalin's fear that dependence on the West could cripple his regime, and the Soviet press complained that the food shortages were giving Washington a way to exert political pressure on Russia.

At the same time, Stalin was preoccupied with domestic intrigues and fear of colleagues he believed intent on replacing him, a bunker mentality that left no room for flexibility toward outside competitors for international power or consideration of the possibility that the West was ready to live in a world divided between capitalist and socialist camps. In this oversimplified formulation, capitalists were unalterable enemies of socialism and Stalin's rule of a Soviet state. Stalin trusted no one at home or abroad: allies—domestic or foreign—were nothing more than temporary collaborators who were all too ready to exploit any weakness they detected in his and Soviet behavior.

In 1946, Stalin was determined not only to diminish high-ranking collaborators as a way to keep them under control but also to make sure that the educated men and women who could become more distant rivals for power did not stray from his party line. He complained that Russia's "middle intelligentsia, doctors and professors," were without "patriotic education. They have unjustified admiration for foreign culture. . . . This tradition comes from Peter [the Great] . . . admiration of Germans, French, of foreigners, of assholes. The spirit of self-abasement must be destroyed."

Jewish Communist party leaders particularly worried Stalin; he saw them as his most likely internal and foreign enemies. "Jews were 'middlemen, profiteers and parasites,' " Stalin told Roosevelt at Yalta. The influence of American Jews and heightened identification of Soviet Jews with their brethren after the Holocaust intensified Stalin's suspicions of an ethnic group he had always distrusted. The interest of Soviet Jews in establishing a homeland in the Crimea became in Stalin's view "a sinister Zionist/American Trojan horse. . . . Zionism, Judaism and America became interchangeable in Stalin's mind."

In a three-thousand-word cable sent to the Soviet Foreign Office in September 1946, Nikolai Novikov, Soviet ambassador in Washington, confirmed the Kremlin's belief that America was determined to destroy Russia's Communist regime—not at once, through a quick war, but in time. Washington was aiming at "world domination. This is the real meaning of repeated statements by President Truman and other representatives of American ruling circles that the U.S. has a right to world leadership," Novikov explained in what may be seen as the Soviet equivalent of Kennan's February 1946 "Long Telegram" deciphering past, current, and future Soviet policy.

Novikov described a failed wartime U.S. plan to let the European and Asian powers exhaust each other in the fighting while the U.S. stood on the sidelines. Washington now intended to realize its ambitions for international control "through the creation of a system of naval and air bases far from the U.S., an arms race, and the creation of newer and newer weapons." FDR's death meant the rise of Truman, "a politically unstable person with certain conservative tendencies" reflecting "the influence of the most reactionary circles of the Democratic Party on foreign policy."

Novikov's cable bristled with talk of Anglo-American imperial ambitions, plans to divide the world into spheres of influence, and "world domination" that would eventually bring the Soviet Union to its knees by injecting "American monopoly capital" into economies all over the world. The United States aimed to eliminate the veto in the United Nations Security Council as a way to subject Moscow to international sanctions that could force the overthrow of pro-Soviet governments in Eastern Europe. In addition, Washington planned to resurrect German and Japanese power as a prelude to an anti-Soviet war fought with atomic bombs.

Although most of what Novikov wrote was nothing more than the speculations of a suspicious mind that resonated with what Kremlin ideologues were thinking, he could point to Washington's 1946–47 defense budget as giving his argument plausibility: $13 billion for the military, over 36 percent of the national annual spending, was thirteen times what the United States had spent each year on national security before the war. In addition, the postwar presence of American military forces in Europe, the Near East, and Asia aroused Moscow's worst fears.

Novikov saw clear evidence of Washington's anti-Soviet outlook in the Truman administration's decision to force Secretary of Commerce Henry Wallace's resignation in September 1946. To most Americans on the left, Wallace was the representative of a pro-Soviet policy they were convinced FDR would have carried over into the postwar era. Wallace was outspoken in his opposition to what he openly described as the belligerence of those in the United States and abroad who wanted to fight a war with the Soviet Union. He characterized Soviet actions in Europe, Asia, and the Middle East as not acts of aggression but as a response to American hostility to Moscow. He predicted that a return to Roosevelt's friendly dealings with Stalin would assure the future peace and urged Truman to side with friends of Russia rather than the anti-Communists in and out of his administration.

Truman's repudiation of Wallace's public pronouncements on administration policy toward Russia forced him to resign. Privately, he denounced Wallace's irresponsible wish "to disband our armed forces and trust a bunch of adventurers in the Kremlin Politbureau [sic]." He dismissed Wallace and "the Reds, phonies, and 'parlor pinks' " as "a national danger." Because Truman saw Wallace and "the crackpots" supporting him as living in some fantasyland about Stalin and Soviet realities, he was happy to see Wallace go. At the same time, however, he was pained at the fact that Wallace's unrealism allowed right-wing critics to attack the White House as coddling pro-Communist subversives and to win public backing for a more belligerent stance toward Moscow. Justifiably, Truman felt caught between those on the left and the right underestimating and overestimating the Soviet threat.

In 1946 false assumptions in the United States, Russia, China, and Korea put international stability and peace at risk, both in the short and long term. Truman later reflected on the travails of a president weakened by opposition that immobilized him and made it difficult for him to follow a more realistic foreign policy: "Our country has never suffered seriously from any acts of the president that were truly intended for the welfare of the country; it's suffered from the inaction of a great many presidents when action should have been taken at the right time." His experience of that year taught him that a president must not be "afraid of controversy" or of offending groups opposed to his actions. In retrospect, he was convinced that "reasonable people will always go along with a man who has the right ideas and leadership."

It was an idealized picture of what he and perhaps other leaders in other countries might have accomplished for the sake of peace in the year and a half after the war ended. The intense antagonisms in the United States and among so many others abroad, including Russia, made the immediate postwar period more a combat zone than an environment in which sweet reason could have prevailed in charting a foreign policy assuring international harmony. Domestic crosscurrents made Truman's reach for coherent dealings with Soviet Russia a nearly impossible challenge. The response to Churchill's Iron Curtain speech was but one example of how divided the country was about a sensible unified policy.

Much more, however, was at work in limiting Truman's freedom to take bold initiatives in foreign affairs. Polls showed that large majorities favored compulsory military training and a standing army of a million or more men. But pressure on the president to "bring the boys home" and dismantle much of America's wartime force was incessant and politically impossible to resist.

At the same time, public antagonism toward American Communists and Russia had become intense and difficult to alter. In June 1946, 36 percent in a U.S. opinion survey favored *killing* or *imprisoning* all American Communists. Another 16 percent preferred curbing them or making them "inactive"; only 16 percent saw them as relatively harmless and wished to "do nothing" about them. As for Russia, few in the United States any longer held her in high regard: 58 percent believed she aimed "to rule the world," and 71 percent disapproved of her policy in "world affairs."

Views of the United Nations were changing as well. Its initial hold on Americans as a peace engine largely faded during 1946. In April, only 37 percent of the country had much confidence in the world organization's ability to contain national aggression. It was seen as lacking the power to turn nations, especially Russia, away from self-serving actions and toward genuine international cooperation. Only one-third of *Who's Who* Americans had much confidence that the world would avoid a war in the next twenty-five years.

Any attempt Truman might have made to mobilize the public in support of a major peace initiative was hamstrung not only by current feelings about postwar international developments, but also by a loss of general confidence in his handling of the postwar domestic transition.

In 1945–46, inflation spurred by an end to price controls and shortages of housing, automobiles, and consumer goods, which the production of war matériel had replaced after 1939, led to union demands for higher wages and strikes that angered a majority of Americans. Truman, who found himself in the middle of these clashes between industries and blue-collar workers struggling to maintain their living standards, became the focus of public hostility. Reluctant to oppose the unions, which were principal supporters of his Democratic Party, but determined to restrain inflation that was eating away at the country's material well-being, he satisfied neither labor nor business chiefs nor a majority of middle-class citizens.

Tensions over southern lynchings of African Americans, denial of their voting rights across the region, and black inequality in jobs, housing, and economic opportunity nationally spurred pressure for civil rights legislation that put additional strains on the president's party and his image as an effective leader. Demands that Moscow allow the occupied East European countries self-determination provoked Soviet charges of American hypocrisy: a country that denied some of its citizens basic freedoms was in a poor position to complain about democratic rights in Russia's satellites, where Moscow said there was more freedom than in America's southern states.

A rising fear of Communist subversion joined with charges that the Democrats had been coddling Communist sympathizers in the

federal government for years to further undermine Truman's standing as a president who could effectively defend the national security.

In the 1930s anti-Communism had become a conservative political weapon in the fight against growing federal involvement in the
national economy. New Deal programs were denounced as stealth
socialism or an advance wave of communism. By the 1940s, as tensions mounted with the Soviet Union, pressure to ward off Communist subversion by pro-Soviet federal employees allegedly aiming
to overthrow the United States government became a disturbing part
of the national political discussion. White House resistance to blan-
ket investigations of federal workers became a political liability, and
Truman reluctantly agreed to loyalty declarations in which civil servants had to reveal whether they previously or currently favored the
violent overthrow of the American government.

The domestic divisions, dissatisfaction with the state of the economy, and the administration's failure to satisfy hopes for international
harmony jeopardized Democratic Party majorities in both congressional
houses. After fourteen years of largely one-party rule in the executive and legislative branches, the Republicans seized upon the national
discontent to recapture the Congress. Their campaign slogan in the
1946 congressional elections struck exactly the right chord with a
majority of voters: "Had enough?" Had enough inflation, enough
strikes, enough shortages, enough communism? On November 5 the
Republicans turned large Democratic majorities into decisive Republican ones: 246 to 188 in the House, the greatest advantage the Republicans would enjoy in the lower chamber for the next sixty-two
years, and 51 to 45 in the Senate. Arkansas congressman J. William
Fulbright proposed that Truman resign after appointing as secretary
of state Michigan's Republican senator Arthur Vandenberg, who,
without a sitting vice president, would become president. The congressman should be called "Halfbright," Truman remarked.

Yet Fulbright reflected the current view of the president, who now
impressed millions of Americans as not up to the job; he was "the

little man from Missouri." His approval ratings declined by 55 points in fifteen months: from a high of 87 percent in June 1945, to 63 percent in January 1946, to 43 percent in June, and to 32 percent in September. The 3 percent of the public that had disapproved of Truman in the initial 1945 survey had swollen to 45 percent a year later. He now became the object of ridicule with comedians joking, "To err is Truman," and declaring that the popular song "I'm Just Wild About Harry" should be amended to "I'm Just Mild About Harry." When Gallup asked voters which party they thought would win the 1948 presidential election, only 9 percent said the Democrats, with 79 percent naming the Republicans, suggesting that Truman commanded negligible support for a White House campaign.

A congressional race in southern California that elevated Richard M. Nixon to a House seat reflected the current national mood in the second half of 1946. A World War II navy veteran and a resident of California's twelfth congressional district, where he had earned a BA from Whittier College, practiced law, and won the respect of local Republicans with whom he shared a conservative ideology, the thirty-three-year-old Nixon seemed to be a sacrificial lamb in a district that had elected liberal Democrat Jerry Voorhis five times. Voorhis's earlier success had rested on the area's support for Roosevelt's New Deal programs that had aided local farmers and small businesses. Voorhis had also profited from patriotic backing for the administration in wartime.

But the political climate in 1946 formed a sharp contrast with the previous ten years. The economic problems of the last eighteen months and growing fears of Communist aggression abroad and subversion in the United States made close identification with the Roosevelt and now Truman White House more a liability than an asset.

Nixon had a keen feel for the anti-Communist sentiment that was so pronounced in his district and across the United States. He turned the campaign into a contest between patriots and "fellow travelers"— men and women who were too critical of traditional American values and too drawn to alien ideas suspiciously close to Soviet thinking.

Voorhis, a Yale graduate and well-off elitist, who Nixon pictured as out of touch with ordinary small-town citizens, was a perfect target for a candidate promoting the politics of resentment and patriotism. Nixon also described Voorhis as a close ally of unpopular labor unions, a card-carrying radical who "votes straight down the line for the SOCIALIZATION OF OUR COUNTRY." He warned against someone "who would destroy our constitutional principles through the socialization of American free institutions." Voorhis was one of those "who front[s] for un-American elements, wittingly or otherwise"; he would "deprive the people of liberty." As a congressman, he was casting "pro-Russian votes."

Nixon's campaign was essentially a response to current local and national anxieties about the economy and communism. But by exploiting the mood of fear, he gave support to increasingly irrational worries about Communist control of the United States and the impulse to see all left reform movements abroad as a menace to America's national security.

It wasn't only Nixon and conservative Republicans who encouraged a national groundswell of anti-Communist anguish. Some Democrats running for Congress shared the conviction that the "Reds" were an immediate menace to the United States who must be contained at all costs.

Across the United States, for example, in the eleventh congressional district of Massachusetts, which included Cambridge and several Boston wards populated by Irish and Italian dock and factory workers, the twenty-nine-year-old John F. Kennedy was a formidable candidate. Although a political novice with few ties to the district, Kennedy's biography as a navy veteran cited for bravery in the South Pacific and connections to two famous Boston families made him the front-runner in the Democratic primary. His campaign, however, profited less from his pedigree as the grandson of former mayor John "Honey Fitz" Fitzgerald and the son of Joseph P. Kennedy, the former ambassador to Great Britain and Boston's wealthiest native son, than from Kennedy's identity as a war hero and proponent of strong national security policies, which was code for combating communism. With some $250,000 to $300,000 of his father's money to spend in the campaign—a staggering amount in 1946 and six times what future Speaker of the House Thomas "Tip" O'Neill would spend in 1952 to win Jack's open seat—Kennedy flooded the district with his message. He won a decisive victory, gaining twice as many votes as the closest of ten rivals.

The Nixon and Kennedy victories signaled a shift in the American political landscape. Like Nixon, Kennedy emphasized the Communist danger: "The time has come when we must speak plainly on the great issue facing the world today," he declared in a typical stump speech and on the radio. "The issue is Soviet Russia," which he described as "a slave state of the worst sort" engaged in "a program of world aggression." Unless "the freedom-loving countries of the world" stopped Russia now, they would "be destroyed."

Unlike in the 1930s, when the country resisted any suggestion of a major U.S. involvement abroad, and especially in the European war that erupted in 1939, political popularity in the postwar 1940s demanded identification with a military record and unqualified commitments to combating the Communist menace. Lyndon B. Johnson, an ambitious Texas congressman since 1937, understood that a successful political future after Pearl Harbor required military credentials and tough talk about national defense. Taking a leave of absence from his House seat in 1941 to serve as a navy lieutenant commander, Johnson arranged an assignment for himself to the Southwest Pacific, where he briefly participated in a combat mission against Japanese forces in New Guinea. Receiving what was later described as the least deserved and most publicly flaunted medal in the country's military history for his role as an observer in an air raid, Johnson exploited his national security credentials to help propel him into the U.S. Senate in 1948.

No national political figure did more to agitate the anti-Communist issue than Wisconsin senator Joseph R. McCarthy. In 1946, the thirty-seven-year-old World War II Marine Corps veteran won a Senate seat after having served as an intelligence officer in the South Pacific and as an elected circuit judge. During his 1946 campaign, he reinvented himself as a war hero who had flown harrowing missions as a tail gunner and a wounded veteran with a permanent limp. His wartime service had in fact been at a desk, debriefing bomber crews, and his injury was the result of an accident during a drunken spree. Building his campaign around promises to "clean up the political mess" in Washington, particularly the Truman administration's failure to guard against Communist subversion, McCarthy joined the Eightieth Congress ready to exploit the fear and anxiety about the Soviet danger that had become a principal part of the national political mood.

Although Washington correspondents would vote him the worst member of the Senate after his first two years in office, McCarthy would enjoy extraordinary influence. In the words of one contemporary, he held "two presidents captive—or as nearly captive as any Presidents of the United States have ever been held; in their conduct of the nation's affairs, Harry S. Truman and Dwight D. Eisenhower, from early 1950 through late 1954, could never act without weighing the effect of their plans upon McCarthy and the forces he led, and in consequence there were times when, because of this man, they could not act at all. He had enormous impact on American foreign policy at a time when that policy bore heavily on the course of world history, and American diplomacy might bear a different aspect today if McCarthy had never lived." (The reference was to Korea and the war with China.)

A dustup over an alleged espionage case, the *Amerasia* investigation in June 1945, had joined with Soviet aggression in Eastern Europe to make the Communist danger front-page news across the United States and a forceful campaign issue in 1946. The discovery that State Department China experts had provided "secret" documents to the editors of an academic journal about innocuous subjects like Chinese "rice yields in selected provinces, water tables [and] livestock populations" produced Justice Department requests that a grand jury issue espionage indictments. Because the documents had been previously released to the press and were hardly "secret," despite "Confidential" stamps, which were routinely placed on all reports, the indictments were rejected. Nevertheless, in the atmosphere of suspicion that had engulfed the United States after 1945, especially about China, which was locked in a civil war between Nationalists and Communists accused of being Soviet surrogates, the *Amerasia* episode took on exaggerated importance. It diminished any chance of the accommodation with a potential Mao government that might have avoided much of the later Sino-American strife.

The *Amerasia* affair triggered other destructive developments. In response to the accusations of Communist espionage, Truman, who saw the charges of subversives in his government as largely bogus, sought political cover in a commission to study allegations of spying by federal employees. In March 1947, when the commission recommended the creation of a federal employee loyalty program, Truman felt compelled to comply by issuing an executive order encouraging congressional investigators to demand State Department personnel files that, if withheld, would intensify suspicions of a White House cover-up to protect Communist sympathizers. Given Soviet control of Eastern Europe and the growing possibility of a Chinese Communist regime, the State Department became the whipping boy for critics of the Roosevelt-Truman foreign policy.

The myth of a giveaway or appeasement of Stalin at Yalta and Potsdam now became a central part of the anti-Communist attack on both Roosevelt and Truman and their administrations. According to this history, a dying Roosevelt ceded Eastern Europe to the Soviet dictator by accepting a meaningless declaration of freedom for these countries liberated from the Nazis, and agreed to a secret deal giving Stalin Japanese and Chinese territory in return for unneeded Soviet participation in the Pacific War. These commitments were either the product of misjudgments about postwar Soviet intentions or the result of pro-Soviet advisers persuading an impressionable FDR to take these unwise actions. Likewise, Truman endorsed Roosevelt's policies at the Potsdam conference with Stalin by naively trusting Soviet promises.

Members of Roosevelt and Truman's own party, including freshman congressman John Kennedy, repeated this narrative about their failure to exercise appropriate diligence in dealing with ruthless Communists. Kennedy publicly described Roosevelt as too sick at Yalta to act wisely, agreeing to Soviet territorial claims in East Asia and the inclusion of China's Communists in a coalition government with Chiang's Nationalists. "The failure of our foreign policy in the Far East," Kennedy said, "rests squarely with the White House and the State Department. . . . They lost sight of our tremendous stake in a non-Communist China. . . . What our young men had saved [in World War II], our diplomats and our President have frittered away."

Never mind that Soviet troops occupied Eastern Europe, and Roosevelt had no hope of ousting them. Nor could he have known that the atom bomb would end the war without the need for Soviet intervention, which he and his military chiefs assumed was essential to save American lives in an invasion of Japan's home islands. The same held true for Truman, who in fact took a tough line with Stalin at Potsdam. None of these rational considerations counted in a politically heated postwar environment in which Republicans were more focused on breaking the Democrats' fourteen-year hold on the White House and Congress than on realistic assessments of the country's national interest.

The public clamor against the Communist danger was a demonstration of what Alexis de Tocqueville famously described as democracy's weakness in the making of foreign policy: "Foreign policies demand scarcely any of those qualities which are characteristic of a democracy and requires, on the contrary, the cultivation of almost all those it lacks," Tocqueville wrote more than a hundred years earlier.

"Democracy cannot, without difficulty, coordinate the details of a great enterprise [abroad], fix on one plan and follow it through with persistence, whatever the obstacles. It is not capable of devising secret measures or waiting patiently for the result." In sum, it was the predominance of "impulse rather than prudence" and the tendency "to abandon mature design for the gratification of a momentary passion" that he saw as central to America's dealings abroad.

Whether Roosevelt and Truman ever read Tocqueville is uncertain, but they both understood that to secure steady mass support for great foreign policy undertakings, they would need to engage in considerable manipulation of public opinion. Out of a determination to convert the national outlook from isolationism to internationalism at the end of World War II, FDR knowingly encouraged the false belief that Soviet Russia and Nationalist China would be reliable partners in curbing aggression and promoting democracy. His famous pronouncement to a joint congressional session on Yalta as representing the end of traditional power politics was less an exercise in wishful thinking than a calculated effort to draw Americans into international affairs on a false hope.

Truman was more open with intimates about his methods for dealing with possible unpopular foreign policy initiatives. When Truman fired Henry Wallace over their differences about Soviet policy, he purposely deceived the public by pretending not to have known the contents of a Wallace speech beforehand. In fact, he encouraged Wallace to give his speech, not to encourage a debate about administration policy but as a way to bring Wallace down for having spoken against White House intentions. An effective president, Truman told his daughter in reference to the Wallace dispute, needed sometimes to be "a liar" and a "double-crosser."

Yet on January 6, 1947, when Truman gave his second annual State of the Union message before a joint congressional session, he could not have been more straightforward. If nations would cooperate, he saw a chance for "lasting peace." Moreover, he did not view his status as the twentieth president in U.S. history to have an opposition party controlling Congress during a part of his administration as compelling a breakdown in an effective foreign policy or forestalling bipartisanship to serve the national well-being. Indeed, he described bipartisanship as essential for the country's continued prosperity as well as for "political stability, economic advancement, and social progress" abroad.

Truman's hopes of cooperative dealings with the congressional opposition quickly collapsed under the Republicans' determination to undermine the president in the run-up to the 1948 presidential campaign. In foreign affairs, unless Truman could convince his critics that an initiative redounding to his credit was essential to the national security, it was unlikely that they would cooperate with it.

A crisis in the first months of 1947 immediately tested the limits of bipartisanship. In November 1946 Churchill had told the students at England's storied Harrow School, "You will be going forth into the world, and you may find it, if I may say so, full of problems, more baffling problems than it has ever had before." It was a prophesy that events promptly vindicated.

A series of fierce European winter storms at the start of 1947 gave added meaning to Churchill's description of the postwar continent as "a rubble heap, a charnel house, a breeding ground of pestilence and hate." The weather "paralyzed England. Agricultural production dropped below nineteenth-century levels. Industry shut down. Electricity was limited to a few hours each morning, unemployment rose to over 6 million, and rations were tighter than in wartime." In London, the cold burst water pipes all over the city, and Big Ben stood frozen in time. Ice halted rail, road, and river traffic across the continent, and people in Berlin and Paris shivered in their homes without heat, some suffering frostbite.

Although the United States had agreed to a $3.75 billion loan to Great Britain in the summer of 1946, the natural disaster afflicting Europe made the loan little more than a down payment on what

European leaders and administration sympathizers believed would be needed to rescue the continent from a collapse that could throw it into the Soviet orbit. Former president Herbert Hoover, who had administered humanitarian relief in World War I, returned from an assessment of European conditions Truman had asked him to make with forecasts of disaster unless the United States provided food and fuel to suffering civilians.

The first order of business was Greece, which was an area of traditional British concern in the eastern Mediterranean. In fact, in October 1944, when Churchill and Stalin privately mapped out their Balkan spheres of interest, Churchill had assigned 90 percent of foreign control over Greece to London and Washington. Stalin did not object. Nor did he try in 1945–46 to obstruct Britain's military mission to install in Athens a conservative government that inhibited Greece's Communists from a controlling influence. When in March 1946 the left boycotted British-sponsored parliamentary elections that gave the right clear political dominance, the Communists, despite receiving no encouragement from Moscow, resorted to armed opposition. Indeed, fearful that a Soviet hand in a Greek Communist uprising might risk an unwelcome conflict with America and Britain, Stalin had unsuccessfully urged Greece's Communist Party to participate in the 1946 elections.

Where he would not bend on Eastern Europe, which he saw as a vital sphere of Soviet control, Stalin was highly cautious about a country the West considered part of its defense zone. And this was despite worries that the United States was angling to establish a military presence in southeastern Europe that could threaten southern Russia. In his dispatch of September 1946, Ambassador Novikov cautioned that

the visit of an American fleet to Greece, and the great interest which American diplomacy shows in the problem of the Straits have a dual meaning. On the one hand, it means that the US has decided to consolidate its position in the Mediterranean to

support its interests in the countries of the Middle East and
that it has chosen the Navy as the tool of this policy. On the
other hand, these facts are a military and political demonstration against the Soviet Union. The strengthening of the US position in the Middle East and the creation of the conditions to
base the US Navy at one or several places in the Mediterranean
(Trieste, Palestine, Greece, Turkey) will therefore mean the appearance of a new threat to the security of the southern regions
of the Soviet Union.

In the second half of 1946, American representatives in Athens and
State Department officials warned against a successful Communist
uprising as certain to bring a pro-Soviet government to power, and
with it a surge of Communist control across the Balkans. Nevertheless, requests for U.S. aid were turned aside as Britain's responsibility
and as likely to involve the United States in expensive commitments
for which the American public would have little sympathy. The resistance to providing help provoked more heated rhetoric from advocates of aid, who argued that without American support—arms
and money—Greece would collapse and turn into a Soviet satellite,
which would then facilitate Communist dominance in the Middle
East and North Africa.

Although planning for economic and military assistance was now
begun, if only as an unwanted contingency, a British warning about
its incapacity to bear the responsibility forced the issue to the forefront of Truman's attention. On February 21, 1947, the British ambassador informed the State Department and White House that the
winter storms had intensified London's financial and economic crisis
and made it impossible for Great Britain to maintain a presence that
could ward off Communist control in Greece and Turkey.

Truman was entirely receptive to assuming responsibility for a
region of the world most Americans considered removed from the
country's traditional overseas involvements. However eager to help, he

knew he could not proceed without the agreement of the Republican-controlled Congress. But its promises to reduce current deficits and long-term national debt made any outlay for Greece a large question mark. Moreover, Truman appreciated that he would also need to convince the mass public, which preferred to limit overseas commitments and would see any large grant-in-aid to Greece as an unwanted shift in responsibility to the United States.

During a meeting with congressional leaders on February 27, Truman asked Secretary of State George Marshall, who had taken office in January and enjoyed a reputation for nonpartisan defense of the nation's security, to make the case for replacing Britain as the principal defender of Greek and Turkish independence. But Marshall's low-key appeal did not persuade congressional chiefs, who remained reluctant to increase the national debt and become a stand-in for the British in the Near East. Undersecretary of State Dean Acheson rescued the proposal with an apocalyptic monologue on the catastrophe that would befall the United States and all the democracies if Greece succumbed to communism. Acheson predicted that "the corruption of Greece would infect Iran and all the East"; but the contagion wouldn't end there. With Britain and France prostrate, it was up to the United States to stop Moscow's reach for world power.

Senator Arthur Vandenberg, the chairman of the Foreign Relations Committee, urged Truman to make the case to the nation before a joint congressional session. He predicted that Congress would support the president's appeal, but only if Truman spoke in language that would "scare the hell out of the country."

Truman knew smart political advice when he heard it. His speech to the Congress and the country on March 12, which was principally drafted by Acheson, purposely rang alarm bells that challenged Congress and the public to take immediate action to save the United States from a catastrophic defeat in an emerging contest between freedom and totalitarianism. U.S. "assistance is imperative if Greece is to survive as a free nation," Truman declared. Communist rebellion supported by Soviet-style governments in Albania, Bulgaria, and Yugoslavia was threatening the self-determination of the country that had given birth to democracy. Because Great Britain was all but bankrupt and the United Nations lacked the resources to help, it was up to the United States to assume the burden of saving Greece; it would be an act to bolster "the foundations of international peace and hence the security of the United States."

The choice now was between "free institutions, representative government, free elections, guarantees of individual liberty, freedom of speech and religion, and freedom from political oppression" and minority rule relying on "terror and oppression, a controlled press and radio; fixed elections, and the suppression of personal freedoms." For Truman, the choice was clear. The danger was not just to Greece, but to Turkey, "the entire Middle East," and all the peoples of Europe struggling "to maintain their freedoms." Only "immediate and reso-lute action"—$400 million in aid—could save the day. "If we falter in our leadership," the president ominously ended, "we may endanger the peace of the world—and we shall surely endanger the welfare of our own nation."

Truman's speech was an exercise in rhetorical overkill. To be sure, Stalin's pronouncements on Greece and the growing tensions with the West had been highly provocative. But his actions in Greece and Iran bespoke caution and hardly suggested that Britain's retreat from the Middle East would imperil all of Western civilization.

George Kennan, who was now teaching at the War College in Washington and was slated to become the head of a new State De-partment policy planning council, was "extremely unhappy" about the president's apocalyptic language. It was "more grandiose and sweeping than anything" he believed wise. He did not object to the need for a U.S. response to Britain's retreat from the Middle East. But he "did not view the prospect of such a Communist takeover as 'in itself any immediate and catastrophic setback to the Western world.'" He doubted that the Soviets would have the wherewithal to support a Greek Communist government economically, and if they tried, he thought it might cause them problems that the West could "ultimately exploit to good advantage."

Nevertheless, he saw a Greek Communist regime as giving Moscow a long-term regional military or strategic advantage by putting Turkey under considerable pressure that could shake its stability. He doubted, however, that events in Greece and Turkey would presage any significant Communist penetration of the broader Arab world, where Muslims would find no attraction to a godless Communist ideology.

Kennan believed that economic—but not military—aid to Greece and Turkey made perfectly good sense. It would provide assurance to hard-pressed European societies that Communist control of their countries was not inevitable. While he believed that Communist governments in Western Europe would in time be brought down by their ultimate ineffectiveness, he considered it much more preferable for Washington to shore up Greece, Turkey, and all the countries to the west against the sort of economic and political instability that could make them vulnerable to any siren song from the east.

At the same time, however, Kennan saw Truman's universal promise "to support free peoples who are resisting subjugation by armed minorities or by outside pressures" as excessive and unrealistic. "It seemed to me highly uncertain," he wrote later, "that we would invariably find it in our interests or within our means to extend assistance to countries that found themselves in this extremity." He cited China as just one of several possible examples.

An unfortunate result of Truman's impassioned call to universal anti-Communist opposition was its encouragement to the country's most vociferous advocates of repression and intolerance toward anyone even slightly left of center. Mindless conformity and uncritical patriotism were already enough in fashion without a Democratic president giving them a powerful boost by describing a worldwide contest between the forces of good and evil. Truman had little patience with "the Communist bugaboo" or "fear of the Communist penetration of the government." He understood that it was partly a Republican Party strategy for driving the Democrats from power. Joe Martin, the recently installed Republican Speaker of the House, was anything but subtle when he declared, "The long tenure of the Democratic Party had poisoned the air we Republicans breathed."

Truman saw no reason to panic over government officials who were allegedly soft on communism or to think that Communists were about to subvert the country's institutions. America is "perfectly safe so far as Communism is concerned," Truman wrote Pennsylvania's Democratic governor—"we have far too many sane people." Yet nine days after his speech on Greece had added to the growing siege mentality in the United States, Truman felt compelled to establish the Federal Employee Loyalty Program. Whatever its political necessity to keep accusations of White House indifference to the Communist threat to a minimum, it facilitated unproductive investigations of some 3 million federal workers: although 212 employees charged with questionable loyalty would be forced to resign, not a single one was ever "indicted and no evidence of espionage would be found."

Truman's speech had an even more pernicious effect on the country's ability to follow sensible, realistic foreign policies. The declaration of a cold war, as many came to see the president's doctrine, narrowed the country's international options. It fostered a climate of opinion decrying passive acceptance of a Communist government anywhere, making it impossible to discriminate between Soviet rule in Moscow and a Marxist regime in China or Yugoslavia, whose leaders preferred to keep some distance from Russia. National differences that could have been turned to America's advantage were now lost from view in a world of undifferentiated Communists. "Is it excessive to expect such intelligence from one's leaders and such rationality from the public?" Adam Ulam, a critic of Truman's overheated rhetoric, declared.

Truman's speech did not surprise Stalin. He told Yugoslavia's

Milovan Djilas, "The uprising in Greece must be stopped and as quickly as possible. . . . Great Britain and the United States will [not] permit you to break their lines of communication in the Mediterranean Sea." Nevertheless, his public statements on Greece gave the impression that he would back Greece's Communists against the West. But London and Washington couldn't look past the Kremlin rhetoric to its actions to see that Stalin's private reluctance to challenge Britain and America in a contest for control of Athens was the greater reality. To be sure, the Bulgarian and Yugoslav Communist governments provided limited help to their Greek comrades, but it was more a show of Communist solidarity than a decisive infusion of aid. At any rate, what it demonstrated was how a mindset can dominate action, even if the reality is not in sync with the outlook. The same was certainly true of Stalin, as demonstrated by his dealings with the West on Germany and America's Marshall Plan.

In March 1947, another Allies' foreign ministers conference was scheduled in Moscow. The principal topic was Germany's future. George Marshall, who had been secretary of state for only two months, faced his first big challenge in dealings with the Soviets. He entered the negotiations with considerable skepticism that he could overcome Soviet suspicions of Western motives and aims.

His doubts were partly the consequence of his thirteen months trying to mediate the Chinese civil war. As someone with an impeccable reputation as an architect of victory in World War II and unemotional fairness in dealings with friends and foes, he had won unanimous Senate approval as the president's chief diplomat. He also enjoyed the good will of China and of Stalin as an advocate of unconditional victory over Japan and Germany. Yet none of this had been sufficient to disarm the extremists in the Chinese Nationalist and Communist camps. As Marshall complained on leaving China in January 1947, "irreconcilables," men with fixed ideas who could not be budged, had made his task impossible. They cared less about

China's well-being than their own agendas, and unfortunately they had enough power to dwarf the efforts of more flexible realists opposed to the ideologues in both parties.

Marshall had taken away a meaningful lesson from his China mission. Goodwill was not enough to forge a settlement between competing forces if they refused to see compromise as a superior alternative to a continuing conflict they were convinced they could win.

Yet in spite of Marshall's antagonism to ideologues unwilling to bend to imperfect realities, he could not bring himself to counsel a break with Chiang's failing regime. Like the majority of U.S. officials at the time, Marshall resisted the possibility that the United States might be better served by a relationship with the Maoists than the Nationalists; that China's Communists might be willing to stand apart from Moscow if Washington showed itself receptive to a revolution that ousted Chiang for a reform regime—albeit a Communist one with leaders devoted to economic and social arrangements fundamentally at odds with American ideas about free enterprise and individual rights, but one that seemed more likely to command public approval and serve America's international position in the emerging Cold War.

It was not as if American officials were purists about repressive regimes on the right. Spain's Fascist government passed muster as worthy of official relations with the United States, despite its indifference to traditional American ideas about free speech, the press, and elections, as did other undemocratic governments in Latin America. The distinguishing feature that made all the difference in winning U.S. acceptance was anticommunism. Had China's Communists made their resistance to Soviet domination overt, might it have created greater sympathy for their revolution and potential government? Probably not: the right in America undoubtedly would have rejected professions of Chinese Communist tensions with Moscow as a deception. By 1947, anticommunism in the United States was akin to a faith-based movement; a sort of closed thinking that mirrored the

Soviet conviction that there could be no accommodation with capitalists who were determined to destroy communism at all costs.

In Moscow, Marshall met a wall of resistance to American suggestions for the resurrection of German economic self-sufficiency. He came to Russia with no illusions that he could produce a miraculous transformation in Soviet thinking. But he had some hope that he could reduce their suspicions and begin discussions for a later agreement on Germany's future. There was no question about who the Germans preferred as governing authorities: in 1947, Germans joked that in the respective occupation zones, "The Russians promise everything and do nothing. The Americans promise nothing and do everything. The British promise nothing and do nothing."

Marshall and a team of eighty-four aides spent a dreary six weeks in Moscow holding tedious daily meetings with Molotov, British foreign secretary Ernest Bevin, and French foreign minister Georges Bidault and their delegations. Molotov was unrelenting in his insistence that Germany pay $10 billion in reparations. Neither memories of how reparation payments had upended the German economy in the 1920s nor the extent of postwar German destitution moved Molotov to alter his demands. Marshall and the corpulent Bevin, a career labor union anti-Communist, consistently spoke in the same voice for German economic revival that could serve all Europe. Bidault, a slightly built de Gaullist who had distinguished himself in the wartime underground, repeatedly sided with Molotov lest he be accused of having supported a German restoration that could put France in renewed jeopardy. He was also the spokesman for a government that had to accommodate a powerful French Communist Party eager to support the Soviet Union.

The differences over Germany between the Allies extended to the form of government and the extension of traditional American freedoms to all Germans. Molotov dismissed a Marshall plea for democratic rights as "generalities" that were of no interest to the Soviet government. The back-and-forth over arrangements for Germany produced nothing but acrimony. After five weeks of stalemate, Marshall asked to meet with Stalin in the Kremlin.

The Soviet leader could hardly refuse the request of someone with Marshall's credentials as a vital collaborator in "The Great Patriotic War." Though more genial than Molotov, Stalin was no more forthcoming. Marshall tried to play on Soviet fears of German resurgence by warning that divisions between the former Allies might open the way for renewed German power in Europe. He also warned of the dangers to future stability and peace from the economic disarray across the continent. Stalin said he did not share Marshall's concerns. He was confident that in time the Allies would find common ground on Germany. Marshall interpreted Stalin's outward unconcern as a conviction that a European economic crisis would best serve Soviet interests by making countries in the West more vulnerable to Communist takeovers.

Marshall returned to the United States determined to find the means to stabilize Western Europe and insulate it from Communist arguments that their policies were more likely to bring economic revival and political stability. Yet neither Marshall nor Truman saw a clear path to achieving these ends: reviving Europe's economy would require billions of dollars, and the U.S. Congress, which in May 1947 had not yet agreed to fund Truman's $400 million request for Greece and Turkey, seemed unlikely to look favorably on an administration proposal for a multibillion-dollar Europe-wide subsidy. Nor was it possible for the International Monetary Fund or the International Bank for Reconstruction and Development (the World Bank), both of which had been created in 1944 at the Bretton Woods conference in New Hampshire, to foster international prosperity by supplying the $17 billion Europe needed for reconstruction.

Truman and Marshall wisely concluded that any initiative for a broad program should originate with the more credible and less politically controversial secretary of state rather than the president.

Moreover, they agreed that any plan for helping Europe must include direct European participation.

In measured words before the Harvard graduating class of 1947, where Marshall chose to give a speech in the least politically charged setting possible, he described Europe's travails and the American stake in alleviating them: "The consequences to the economy of the United States should be apparent to all," he declared. Unless the world was restored to "normal economic health," there would be "no political stability and no assured peace." But any recovery plan could not be a unilateral American effort, but the product of "some agreement among the countries of Europe as to the requirements of the situation and the part those countries themselves will take in order to give proper effect to whatever action might be undertaken by this government. It would be neither fitting nor efficacious for this government to undertake to draw up unilaterally a program designed to place Europe on its feet economically. This is the business of the Europeans."

The cooperative effort, Marshall pointedly told the Soviets, should be "directed not against any country or doctrine but against hunger, poverty, desperation, and chaos. . . . Any government that is willing to assist in the task of recovery will find full co-operation, I am sure, on the part of the United States government. Any government which maneuvers to block the recovery of other countries can not expect help from us. Furthermore, governments, political parties, or groups which seek to perpetuate human misery in order to profit therefrom politically or otherwise will encounter the opposition of the United States."

Marshall's words were not those of a politician or an imperialist seeking a special advantage for his country, but of a statesman who saw the economic health of all Europe as a boon not only to the United States, which anticipated selling billions of dollars of American goods in Europe, but to impoverished Europeans across the entire Continent—East and West. U.S. economic interests and international well-being, however, were not Marshall's only motives; he and State Department colleagues understood that Soviet acceptance of the secretary's proposal could have a destabilizing impact on Moscow's control of its East European satellites.

Stalin and the Soviets refused to accept the U.S. initiative as anything but another demonstration of capitalist determination to destroy Communist regimes everywhere. At least that was the ultimate response in July 1947 after Molotov had conferred with Bevin and Bidault in Paris for five days.

The fact that Molotov had agreed at all to discuss the possibility of Soviet participation in the U.S.-proposed European Recovery Plan (ERP) signaled initial Kremlin indecision about a response to Marshall's offer. If they agreed to join in, the Soviets could imagine that the U.S. Congress would balk at helping Moscow with a share of the billions the Americans would be providing. It would be a way to kill the program and leave Europe vulnerable to the Communist parties seeking power in the West. On the other hand, if the program went forward, it would compel Moscow to reveal all sorts of economic data that would demonstrate its weakness and long-term inability to compete with the West. Moreover, participation in ERP would mean the renewal of Soviet and East European exposure to Western influences that Stalin feared could topple Communist control.

The irony is that Marshall's largely constructive proposal, which might have raised living standards in Soviet-bloc countries and muted some of the East-West tensions, became the occasion for a Soviet campaign of vilification against the capitalists that made the Cold War irreversible. As the Kremlin now saw it, Marshall's plan was nothing less than a declaration of war on the "anti-imperialist and democratic camp" by what was described as the last "remnants of fascism" reaching for worldwide control. Not surprisingly, the Kremlin now projected onto opponents their most steadfast intentions. It was the ultimate solipsism: they flattered themselves by thinking that everyone was just like them.

WAR BY OTHER MEANS

A great empire and little minds go ill together.
—Edmund Burke

*How good bad music and bad reasons sound
when we march against an enemy.*
—Friedrich Nietzsche

B y the middle of 1947, an East-West struggle for what each saw as the survival of their respective economic, political, and social systems was in full motion. Both sides described themselves as defending against the other's aggression. The Soviets were convinced that the United States was determined to destroy communism, but not necessarily by military action, and certainly not in the short term. To be sure, they viewed America as preparing for a possible armed conflict that could include the use of atomic bombs, but they strongly believed that Washington hoped to win a cold war by economic means: the hidden aims of the Truman Doctrine and the proposed Marshall Plan were to make all of Europe dependent on the United States for its survival.

"Whereas the Truman Doctrine was to terrorize and intimidate these [pro-Soviet] countries," Andrei Zhdanov, Stalin's Politburo spokesman on foreign affairs, said, "the 'Marshall Plan' was designed to test their economic staunchness, to lure them into a trap and then shackle them in the fetters of dollars 'assistance.' " Had the Soviet

Union and the Eastern European "democracies" signed on to the American proposal, he added, they would have found themselves subjugated to Washington.

The Americans might ultimately feel compelled to resort to military aggression against the "anti-imperialist" East. But according to Soviet thinking, the militarists in the West understood that left-leaning parties in America, Britain, and France, which were currently opposed to another war, especially against a Soviet Union for which they continued to have high regard, were too strong to be ignored. The "fascists" hoped to silence these sympathetic elements and prepare their general populations for warfare "by slanderously accusing the Soviet Union and the new democracies of aggressive intentions." These propagandists, Zhdanov declared, "fully realize that long ideological preparation is necessary before they can get their soldiers to fight the Soviet Union."

In seeing the Truman administration as intent on bringing down Communist regimes, the Soviets seemed to be mesmerized by their own rhetoric. They had enough insight to understand that persuading a majority of Americans to attack Russia was not realistic in 1947, or for as long as the Communists did not provoke a military confrontation by aggression against the West. The Soviets believed, however, that if economic imperialism failed to force Communist countries into Washington's orbit, the United States would provoke a war. In the meantime, it was important to educate Soviet citizens about American intentions. This served not only to foster support for defense outlays but also to unify the country behind Stalin and put pressure on East European satellites to comply with Moscow's demands. As Plato explained in *The Republic*, "When the tyrant has disposed of foreign enemies by conquest . . . then he is always stirring up some war or other, in order that the people may require a leader."

Indisputably, some Americans and West Europeans, especially in Germany, where hopes of liberating their eastern provinces from Russia were a constant in postwar affairs, supported any actions needed to destroy Communist governments. These devout anti-Communists shared a conviction that Moscow was intent on imperial expansion and that the East and the West were irreconcilable foes. Yet these war hawks were a distinct minority, though they were vocal enough to intensify Soviet paranoia. Nevertheless, it reveals more about the Soviet state of mind than about the realities of Western intentions that Moscow would now consistently denounce the United States and its allies as a menace to world peace. Having imposed their rule on the Baltic and Balkan countries, the Soviets could readily imagine U.S. reliance on its greater power to overturn these Communist governments.

Countering affinity among some in the West for military action against the Soviet Union was an understanding in the highest reaches of the U.S. government that Moscow was in no condition to start a war in Europe or Asia that provoked a fight with the United States. "None but mad men . . . would undertake war against us," Ferdinand Eberstadt, the wartime director of the U.S. Munitions Board, told secretary of the navy James Forrestal in November 1946. After British Field Marshal Bernard Montgomery visited the Soviet Union at the end of the year, he told Eisenhower that "devastation in Russia is appalling and the country is in no fit state to go to war."

Yet even the officials who had the strongest doubts about Soviet war making capacity did not rule out the possibility and even the likelihood of eventual aggression. In July 1947, assistant secretary of war Howard C. Petersen concluded that "the time element permits emphasis on strengthening the economic dikes against Soviet communism rather than upon preparing for a possible eventual, but not yet inevitable war." Confident that Moscow would develop the bomb, the atomic scientist J. Robert Oppenheimer began to think of the United States and Russia, as "two scorpions in a bottle, each capable of killing the other, but only at the risk of his own life."

The danger of so much talk about war was that neither side could see the other as on the defensive. What one country saw as protective measures registered on the other as aggressive actions. Professions of good intentions could not generate the sort of trust friendly nations feel toward each other. Both sides felt embattled. To cast aside suspicions seemed like the worst kind of folly—a betrayal of the nation's fundamental interests.

The object now for each nation was to contain the other, or restrain it from imperial overreach that could prompt a military conflict. In July 1947 Kennan published an article in *Foreign Affairs*, "The Sources of Soviet Conduct," under the pseudonym "X." As the head of the State Department's policy planning staff, his anonymity was meant to discourage conclusions that the article represented an official statement of policy. But this is exactly what it was; indeed, it had originated as a paper written for Navy Secretary James Forrestal, and the State Department's committee on unofficial publication had approved its appearance in *Foreign Affairs*. Few could doubt that the author's concealed identity signaled that he was a high official stating government policy.

Kennan described Soviet rule as the product of an unrestrained drive for worldwide control. Moscow's stress on external dangers was "founded not in the realities of foreign antagonism," Kennan asserted, "but in the necessity of explaining away the maintenance of dictatorial authority at home. . . . The semi-myth of implacable foreign hostility" fostered a "state of siege" mentality. Undergirding this was the conviction that "the aims of the capitalist world are antagonistic to the Soviet regime." While manifestations of this outlook may occasionally be muted, it is a fixture of Soviet ideology, Kennan said. Moscow had no terminal date for the defeat of capitalist adversaries, but it was an imperishable goal that Western leaders should not ignore or lose sight of.

"In these circumstances," Kennan declared, "it is clear that the main element of any United States policy toward the Soviet Union must be that of long-term, patient but firm and vigilant containment of Russian expansive tendencies. . . . It is clear that the United States

Winston Churchill, Franklin Roosevelt, and Josef Stalin at Yalta, February 1945, discussed postwar plans, which were dictated more by conditions on the ground than anything they pledged to do.

A German general, who committed suicide in the Leipzig city hall in April 1945 as U.S. troops were about to capture the city, clutches a torn picture of Hitler, symbolizing the anger toward the Fuehrer for leading Germany into a disaster.

A German photograph of the evacuation of Jews, helpless victims of Hitler's paranoid fantasies about World Jewry's power to destroy Germany.

Bodies of dead children found in the concentration camp at Nordhausen lie in mass burial grave.

The Dock at Nuremberg, where Herman Göring, Rudolf Hess, Joachim von Ribbentrop, Wilhelm Keitel in the front row and Karl Doenitz, Erich Raeder, Baldur von Schirach, and Fritz Sauckel seated behind them were tried as war criminals.

Churchill, Truman, and Stalin at the Potsdam Conference, July 23, 1945. The smiles of satisfaction hid the rising tensions among the allies, who argued over end of war arrangements for Europe.

Truman addressing the United Nations Conference, June 26, 1945. The devastation of the war spurred renewed hope that the world might achieve a peaceful future through a new international organization replacing Woodrow Wilson's League of Nations.

CONFERENCE OF BIG THREE POWERS AT POTSDAM, NEAR BERLIN, GERMANY, 7 JULY THRU 2 AUGUST 1945, TO DEMAND THE SURRENDER OF JAPAN. Generalissimo Josef Stalin, facing camera, shakes hands with Secretary of State James F. Byrnes near the conference table just before the opening of the third day's session. 7/19/45

In which I tell Stalin we expect to drop the most powerful explosive ever made on the Japanese. He smiled and said he appreciated my telling him — but he did not know what I was talking about — the Atomic Bomb!

HST

Truman's handwriting on the back of a Potsdam photograph describing telling Stalin about the atomic bomb. Truman naively believed that Stalin did not know what he was talking about.

The first atomic bomb test, Alamogordo,
New Mexico, July 16, 1945.

Aerial view of Hiroshima demonstrating the devastation of the atomic
bomb blast, August 1945.

MacArthur, standing in the foreground, during Japanese surrender ceremonies on the USS *Missouri* in Tokyo Bay, September 2, 1945.

MacArthur, who administered the occupation of Japan, receives a precedent-shattering visit from the Emperor Hirohito, July 1946. MacArthur presided over the transformation of Japan from a military dictatorship into a modern democracy.

Truman and de Gaulle during a welcoming ceremony at the White House, August 22, 1945. De Gaulle was determined to reestablish France as a great power, including the restoration of her colonial empire—a decision that would cost his country considerable blood and treasure.

This idealized, undated portrait of Chiang Kai-shek masked his repressive wartime rule in China that alienated millions of Chinese, who supported the Communists as an alternative postwar government.

Chinese Communist party leaders Mao Tse Tung, second from left, and Chou En-lai, far right, meet with U.S. Ambassador Patrick Hurley, fourth from left, August 27, 1945, in Yenan, China, in hopes of heading off a civil war.

U.S. efforts, including a mediating mission by General George C. Marshall, failed to prevent a civil war. This is a photo of a Communist ammunition train destroyed by the Nationalists in 1946 in Manchuria, where the two sides fought for control.

Truman meets with Nationalist China's Ambassador to the United States, V. K. Wellington Koo, and other Chinese officials in July 1947 to show support for Chiang's government. Nationalist defeat in 1949 provoked bitter criticism of Truman's China policy, which the administration answered with the *China White Paper*.

Churchill and Truman at Westminster College, Fulton, Missouri, on March 5, 1946, for Churchill's "Iron Curtain" speech, marking the start of the Cold War.

George C. Marshall taking the oath of office as secretary of state, January 21, 1947. Truman considered Marshall the greatest general in U.S. history and brought him out of retirement to help the country fight the Cold War.

Truman mobilized U.S. public opinion and challenged Congress to meet the Soviet challenge with his March 12, 1947, Truman Doctrine speech proposing aid to Greece and Turkey.

George F. Kennan, who shaped U.S. Cold War policy with his famous "Containment" article in the summer of 1947, struggled to keep the competition with the USSR from turning into a hot war.

Planes lined up at Berlin's Templehof Airport, August 1948, were part of an airlift that rescued West Berlin from a Communist blockade and settled a conflict that could have become a Soviet-American war.

Dean Acheson being sworn in as secretary of state in January 1949. Acheson successfully advocated the creation of NATO to deter Moscow from any attack on Western Europe and the United States.

General Dwight D. Eisenhower saying good-bye to Truman, Acheson, and Marshall, January 1951, as he prepared to fly to Europe to inspect NATO forces, of which he had become supreme commander.

Dean Acheson and Paul G. Hoffman, the director of the European Recovery, or Marshall Plan, present Marshall, April 1950, with a plaque citing the success of the plan and, implicitly, the success of containment.

Acheson with India's Prime Minister Jawaharlal Nehru, October 1949. The division of the subcontinent into India and Pakistan in 1947 created a host of problems for the United States in trying to keep the peace in South Asia and counter Soviet efforts to exert influence in the region.

Truman with Israel's Prime Minister David Ben-Gurion and Ambassador Abba Eban, May 8, 1951. Truman's decision to support the creation of Israel in 1948 launched an enduring partnership with the Jewish state.

The physicist J. Robert Oppenheimer, who played a pivotal part in developing the atomic bomb, doubted the wisdom of building hydrogen bombs, describing a war between nuclear powers as suicidal for both sides.

Senator Joseph McCarthy of Wisconsin, pictured here in 1952, stirred irrational fears of Communist subversion in the United States and belittled containment as a prescription for defeat in the Cold War.

General MacArthur, who defeated the initial North Korean invasion of the South, presides over a ceremony restoring South Korean President Syngman Rhee's rule in Seoul, September 29, 1950.

Truman and MacArthur meet at Wake Island, October 14, 1950, where MacArthur confidently predicted the liberation of North Korea from Communism if his forces crossed the 38th Parallel.

President-elect Dwight D. Eisenhower visited Korea in December 1952 to decide how to end the fighting. He is pictured with President Rhee and General Omar Bradley, Chairman of the Joint Chiefs, far right.

cannot expect in the foreseeable future to enjoy political intimacy with the Soviet regime. It must continue to regard the Soviet Union as a rival," an adversary that should be "contained by the adroit and vigilant application of counterforce at a series of constantly shifting geographical and political points."

Ironically, Kennan, who pictured Soviet Russia as a messianic society intent on defeating capitalism, ended his article with a messianic note of his own: "The thoughtful observer of Russian-American relations will find no cause for complaint in the Kremlin's challenge to American society," he counseled. "He will rather experience a certain gratitude to a Providence that, by providing the American people with this implacable challenge, has made their entire security as a nation dependent on their pulling themselves together and accepting the responsibilities of moral and political leadership that history plainly intended them to bear."

When the article produced widespread public attention, Kennan felt "like one who has inadvertently loosened a large boulder from the top of a cliff and now helplessly witnesses its path of destruction in the valley below." Not the least of his concerns was the interpretation of containment as the reliance on "military means" to inhibit a "military threat" rather than "political containment of a political threat." He also subsequently lamented the conclusion that his urging of the "application of counterforce at a series of constantly shifting geographical and political points" meant worldwide, rather than in the five select regions—"the United States, the United Kingdom, the Rhine Valley with adjacent industrial areas, the Soviet Union, and Japan"—that he considered most vital to America's national security.

Within days of the article's publication, *New York Times* columnist Arthur Krock identified Kennan as the author, instantly underscoring the official nature of Kennan's assertions and intensifying feelings in Russia and the United States that Moscow and Washington were moving toward a military confrontation.

In response, America's most influential syndicated columnist, Walter Lippmann, published a series of articles that shortly appeared as a book, *The Cold War: A Study in U.S. Foreign Policy*. Lippmann took strong exception to Kennan's proposed indiscriminate military containment of the Soviets around the world as a reckless policy that could provoke a catastrophic war. Soviet actions in Eastern Europe were not the product of a messianic drive for worldwide control, he argued, but the result of victory in World War II. They were also the consequence of a long-standing Russian fear of invasion from the West, which Hitler's devastation of the Russian homeland had amply justified as not paranoid but a reality that no Russian government could exclude from its calculations.

Lippmann also disputed Kennan's call for containment of all alleged Soviet efforts at expansion. The cost to the United States of stopping Soviet advance everywhere would be incalculable, and ultimately destructive to U.S. interests. Instead, Washington would do better to reach a settlement with Moscow in Europe, where American security was directly involved. Lippmann chided Kennan for failing to propose a diplomatic solution to current Soviet-American differences through an agreement to protect Moscow from German military revival, and encourage Soviet withdrawal from Eastern Europe.

Kennan later described himself as mortified by the "egregious" errors that led Lippmann to challenge the assertions in his article. Like Lippmann, he later made clear that he had no sympathy with a strictly military containment of the Soviet Union. To the contrary, he saw Lippmann as espousing "a concept of American policy so similar to that which I was to hold and to advance in coming years that one could only assume I was subconsciously inspired by that statement of it. . . . He [Lippmann] urged a concentration on the vital countries of Europe; he urged a policy directed toward a mutual withdrawal of Soviet and American (also British) forces from Europe; he pointed with farsighted penetration to the dangers involved in any attempt to make of a truncated West Germany an ally in an anti-Soviet coalition. All these points would figure prominently in my own later writings."

Yet Kennan did not issue any corrective at the time, he said, "because of my official position." But his excuse seems unconvincing. His article was all too clearly an expression of current thinking by the country's foreign policy establishment. In May, when Robert Lovett, who was about to become Marshall's undersecretary of state, conferred with foreign policy experts at the Council on Foreign Relations in New York, they unanimously urged opposition to Soviet expansionism everywhere. "Clear priorities," they advised Lovett, "included the Western Hemisphere, Greenland, Iceland, the United Kingdom, the West European rim land, and Japan. But notwithstanding these priorities, initiatives everywhere, except perhaps Korea, had to be contemplated." These establishment experts on international relations saw a bleak future for the United States unless its governing authorities accepted "that there would be a severe and persistent competition of ideologies."

Kennan's failure to express any regrets about the "errors" (his word) Lippmann had criticized in the X article was not the result of a misjudgment at the time but of a conviction that the article's conclusions were more in line with U.S. national interests than Lippmann's assertions.

In the summer of 1947, following the Truman Doctrine and the Marshall Plan, which made economic aid the vehicle for combating Communist advance, the emphasis in the U.S. government had shifted to America's military capacity to meet the Soviet challenge. For Kennan or any high government official to have made the case at this point for diplomacy would have provoked complaints of naiveté comparable to Henry Wallace's soft view of Moscow's intentions.

As Kennan warned in his article, the Soviets were capable of temporary agreements that gave the appearance of long-term accommodation, but their "duplicity" and "unfriendliness of purpose" were immutable, or at least "there to stay for the foreseeable future." When

Moscow showed a friendly side, "there will always be Americans who will leap forward with gleeful announcements that 'the Russians have changed,'" Kennan said, ". . . but we should not be misled by tactical maneuvers. These characteristics of Soviet policy, like the postulate from which they flow, are basic to the internal nature of Soviet power, and will be with us, whether in the foreground or the background, until the internal nature of Soviet power is changed."

In the meantime, U.S. officials believed that they had no choice but to develop a national security apparatus that would discourage Moscow's reach for greater power and prepare the United States for a war if economic and political containment didn't work. A pervasive sense of Soviet Russia as the heir to Hitler's global ambitions now became the conventional wisdom in the highest reaches of the American government as well as in all circles of informed opinion. They thought communism was like a virus spreading around the globe, threatening to infect not only poor nations but millions of well-off men and women in advanced industrial societies naive enough to believe that Moscow was a sincere advocate of social justice and peace.

The two world wars had stimulated discussions in the United States about the need for a more coherent defense establishment than the War and Navy departments, which were traditional rivals for military appropriations. As early as 1943, General Marshall had suggested that the existing departments be brought under a civilian cabinet secretary of the armed forces who would preside over army, navy, and air force branches. The navy's resistance to giving up its separate identity frustrated the plan until Truman persuaded Congress to enact a National Security Act in July 1947: the law created a secretary of defense responsible for the "National Military Establishment." The new defense arrangement provided for Army, Navy, and Air Force departments, a National Security Council (NSC), which was to act as an advisory body to the president, and a Central Intelligence Agency (CIA), which was to gather and evaluate information about foreign dangers and stand as a shield against a future Pearl Harbor or surprise attack by an adversary.

Truman's fear that he might be creating an American "Gestapo" or secret police that would foster a "military dictatorship" reflected the long-standing national reluctance to have anything resembling the powerful military establishments that existed in European and Latin American countries. But the fear generated by competition with a nation like the USSR, which had elevated control of every aspect of its society to a science, encouraged the belief in the United States that it desperately needed military might and counterespionage by agencies that could outdo the Soviet spymasters.

Dean Acheson "had the gravest forebodings" about the CIA, and "warned the President that as set up neither he, nor the National Security Council, nor anyone else would be in a position to know what it was doing or to control it." But to resist the agency's creation seemed close to treason. Kennan said that Russia's "almost psychotic preoccupation . . . with secrecy appeared to many, not unnaturally, to place a special premium on efforts to penetrate that curtain by secretive methods of our own," and led "to the creation here of a vast bureaucracy dedicated to this particular purpose."

Clark Clifford, Truman's White House counsel, had no doubt but that "a great nation must have the capacity to defend its own interests, and this includes a first-rate intelligence service. I believed that a limited number of covert programs, tightly controlled by the President and the NSC, would be a necessary part of our foreign policy. But over the years, covert activities became so numerous and widespread that, in effect, they became a self-sustaining part of American foreign operations. The CIA became a government within a government, which could evade oversight of its activities by drawing the cloak of secrecy around itself." As a consequence, it undermined America's good name as a democratic republic that honored the rule of law at home and abroad. Sixty-plus years after its founding, we remain in the dark about many, if not most, of its past activities.

In September 1947, Truman appointed Secretary of the Navy James Forrestal as the first secretary of defense. His selection was well received as an acknowledgment of current conservative thinking about America's tensions with the Soviet Union and communism more generally.

Although slightly built at five foot nine inches, Forrestal was a pugnacious character who had devoted himself from early in life to building his physical constitution with boxing, wrestling, tennis, and golf. A broken nose he had suffered in a boxing match, joined to his deep-set eyes and pursed lips, gave him a puglike appearance or the look of a cocky bantamweight fighter. Most people described him as fiercely competitive, combative, and tough.

Forrestal's background as a self-made Wall Street investment banker, head of the Navy Department during and after World War II, where he had fought numerous bureaucratic battles with admirals and other defense chiefs, recommended him to Truman as a wise choice for the Defense Department. The sixty-five-year-old Forrestal was a conservative Democrat whose clashes with army and air force officials over the division of defense funds and programs had given him an understanding of the challenges facing a secretary charged with developing an effective military establishment—not only in knitting the competing armed services into a unified fighting force but also in overcoming congressional and public resistance to devoting large national resources to the country's security.

Forrestal's credentials as an anti-Soviet, anti-Communist defender of the nation's security were common knowledge. He was famous for his anecdote about the U.S. official who asked Stalin whether Soviet fighting men ever failed to perform their duties as ordered by commanders. No, Stalin replied; "It would take a brave man to be a coward in the Soviet Army." Forrestal used the story to explain that if the United States were to win the Cold War, it "would also require an Army in which cowardice was more hazardous than combat duty." Among Forrestal's other homilies was the assertion that world peace depended upon American military strength, which he openly and repeatedly stated was essential to combat Soviet ambitions. It was Soviet Russia, he consistently declared, which posed "the most formidable threat in history to American interests."

During the summer and fall of 1947, publicly and privately, Moscow and Washington seemed to edge toward war. The announcement of the Marshall Plan in June and the passage of the National Security Act in July drew fire from the Soviets. An anti-American "propaganda barrage climaxing in a diatribe equating Truman with Hitler" preceded the establishment of the Cominform in September, which prodded the Communist parties of France and Italy to become more aggressive in battling their pro-American governments. In response, they unleashed labor walkouts in key industries that produced violence and forced Paris and Rome to call elections that might give the left enough power to block participation in Washington's recovery plan.

The Soviet objective was not a set of Communist governments in Western Europe, which might provoke U.S. military intervention, but turmoil and resistance to Marshall Plan aid that would deter Western countries from becoming models of freedom and democracy for Moscow's East European satellites.

At the same time, Truman and U.S. national security officials engaged in some rhetorical overkill of their own. In July, Undersecretary of State Robert Lovett described the Marshall Plan as "the last clear shot we will have at finding a [peaceful] solution to the Soviet threat in Europe." He privately told the industrialist Henry Ford that "war could come at any time."

Truman used the White House bully pulpit to pressure congressmen reluctant to appropriate the billions needed for Marshall's European Recovery Program. During a White House meeting at the end of September, he warned that "we'll either have to provide a program of interim aid relief until the Marshall program gets going, or the governments of France and Italy will fall, Austria too, and for all practical purposes, Europe will be Communist. The Marshall Plan goes out the window, and it's a question of how long we could stand up in such a situation. This is serious. I can't overemphasize how serious."

U.S. Air Force chiefs, convinced that they alone among America's military held the means to save the United States in a future conflict, began planning for an all-out war with Moscow. In September, General Carl Spaatz told an air policy commission that Truman had set up in July, "The low grade terror of Russia which paralyzes Italy, France, England, and Scandinavia can be kept from our own country by an ability on our part to deliver air atomic destruction. If Russia does strike the U.S., as she will if her present frame of mind continues, only a powerful air force in being can strike back fast enough, and hard enough, to prevent the utter destruction of our nation." How Moscow, without the air power to reach the United States or the atomic bombs that could destroy American cities, was to fulfill Spaatz's prediction formed no part of the discussion.

George Marshall was skeptical of the rush to consider military solutions against the Soviets. "Gentlemen," he told his State Department colleagues, "let us not discuss this as a military problem; to do so turns it into a military problem." Instead, Marshall asked Kennan for an overview of Soviet-American relations, which he assumed would be more judicious than anything he heard from the military. Kennan did not disappoint him: on November 6, he advised Marshall that "the danger of war is vastly exaggerated in many quarters"; the Soviets "neither expected nor wanted war." The political containment of communism was succeeding, as demonstrated by the diminished popularity in national elections of the French and Italian Communist parties, which had antagonized millions of their countrymen with disruptive strikes and protests. The key now, Kennan said, was to carry forward Marshall's recovery program, but with the cooperation of the Europeans, who would need to assume a part of the financial burden and take responsibility for planning how the ERP would improve their respective economies.

The two most pressing problems Kennan saw in future dealings with Moscow were Czechoslovakia and Germany. With the Soviets facing diminished influence across Western Europe, they would feel compelled to strengthen their hold on the eastern portion of the continent. Czechoslovakia was their biggest worry: the country enjoyed a degree of autonomy from Moscow's control that "could too easily become a path of entry for truly democratic forces into Eastern Europe generally." Kennan cautioned against using a Soviet decision to "clamp down completely on Czechoslovakia" to trigger a U.S. military response. The repression of Czech freedoms should not be seen as an initial act of aggression against Western Europe, but as "a purely defensive move." Moreover, while the Soviets would be able to maintain their hold on Eastern Europe "for some time," they would be hard pressed to assure themselves of permanent control. There were limits to how long 100 million Russians could keep 90 million more advanced Europeans, "with long experience in resistance to foreign rule," in thrall.

As for Germany, Kennan warned that the Soviets would use an upcoming foreign ministers' conference in London, beginning on November 25, to work toward expanded Communist influence in all parts of the country. Sharing Kennan's concern, Marshall intended to resist any Moscow scheme to make West as well as East Germany part of its postwar empire.

First, however, he tried to forestall a Soviet reach for German domination by disabusing them of malign U.S. intentions. In a Chicago speech, a week before traveling to London, Marshall scolded Moscow for its "calculated campaign of vilification and distortion of American motives in foreign affairs." There was no truth whatsoever to charges of "imperialistic design[s], aggressive purposes, and . . . a desire to provoke a third world war." The United States aimed not to fill a power vacuum in Europe, as Moscow said, but to help rebuild its economy as a prelude to ending aid, which was a burden on the American people.

Marshall had no realistic expectation of a positive Soviet response. *Pravda* confirmed his assumption by dismissing his defense of U.S. motives as "the clearest hypocrisy": the Americans favored a divided Germany as a prelude to unifying the western zones and integrating them into an anti-Soviet coalition. *Pravda* had it right, but for the wrong reasons; in the West, it was seen as a defense against Soviet imperialism, not as a ploy for destroying communism.

Predictably, the conference became an exercise in political posturing: Molotov rejected Marshall's proposals for a reunited but demilitarized Germany organized along genuine democratic lines as a ploy for securing American control. Molotov instead urged a united, disarmed Germany free of occupation forces, but only if Moscow could share control over production in the industrial Ruhr and receive $10 billion in reparations from current German output. Because Molotov's proposals would have given Russia a say in governing West Germany and would have compelled the United States to bear the cost of reparations in the years before German production would be able to pay it, Marshall rejected the Russian plan. Molotov then excoriated the Americans as the unacknowledged proponent of a neo-imperialism meant to "enslave" vulnerable countries. Marshall coldly called Molotov's remarks undignified and unjustified propaganda.

It's conceivable that Moscow and Washington could have found common ground by showing greater flexibility. But the distrust between them was already too pronounced for any compromise to work. Neither side could convince the other that it was defending itself from aggression rather than maneuvering to conquer the world.

After seventeen unproductive sessions over three weeks, both delegations agreed to an adjournment with no plans for future meetings. The absence of even ceremonial demonstrations of regard for one another and collapse of any ostensible hope for constructive exchanges at another conference created a mood of apprehension in the West. "There was no country on the Continent that had any confidence in the future," British foreign secretary Bevin told Marshall the day after the conference ended. Marshall saw no recourse but to suggest consideration of a military alliance to assure Western Europe's security.

The collapse of the conference left both sides self-righteously proclaiming their innocence and denouncing each other's motives and intentions. From Moscow's perspective, its desire for a unified pro-Soviet Germany was nothing more than an assurance against another devastating attack on its homeland. From Washington's vantage point, an integrated grouping of Western zones signaled not a plan to reestablish German military power to overturn Communist rule in Eastern Europe and Russia but a means of reestablishing German economic autonomy and freeing the United States from a heavy burden of aid. Ironically, Germany, which had brought Russia and the Western democracies into a temporary alliance against Hitler, now became the decisive catalyst for tearing the Allies apart.

Shortly after the conference, when U.S. ambassador Walter Bedell Smith met with Deputy Foreign Minister Andrei Vyshinsky in Moscow about some minor custom procedures, Vishinsky "departed from the usual attitude of personal friendliness regardless of official subject and showed irritability and antagonism. It is quite obvious that he had received instructions to make no concessions whatever." Unable to find common ground on the major differences facing them, U.S. and Soviet representatives saw themselves as adversaries waiting to see which one would feel compelled to attack the other with arms rather than words.

In December, when Truman submitted a detailed request to Congress for Marshall Plan appropriations, he resorted to rhetoric similar to that he had used in his earlier appeal for Greek-Turkish aid. He once more described the Soviet-American confrontation in apocalyptic language: Europe's recovery, he said, was "essential to the maintenance of the civilization in which the American way of life is rooted."

Nothing less was at stake than "peace and stability in the world." America's "economic system" and its national security, with "our freedoms and privileges," were in jeopardy as well.

A crisis over Czechoslovakia beginning in February 1948 became the impetus for consideration of a Western military arrangement. The Czech government, which included a number of Communists freely elected in 1946, began a purge of non-Communist officials to strengthen their hold on power. Countermoves by center-right parties precipitated a political crisis that compelled President Edvard Beneš to give the more numerous Communists majority control. Two weeks later, after the pro-Western foreign minister Jan Masaryk leaped or was thrown to his death (almost certainly the latter) from a window in his ministry residence, Western capitals exploded with indignation at the demise of Czech democracy.

The death of Czech independence, especially Masaryk's alleged suicide, which seemed like an all too convenient development favoring Communist power, understandably frightened people in the West. Rumors that Masaryk intended to resign as foreign minister and live in exile in London, where he had resided during World War II as a symbol of Czech independence from Nazi rule, may have been too threatening to the Communists: an exile proponent of Czech freedom could have been too much of a rallying point against Soviet domination of Czechoslovakia and other East European countries for Moscow to allow Masaryk to live. As it was, undisclosed tensions with Tito in Yugoslavia, joined to prospects of German and West European revival, put the Kremlin on edge about its capacity to sustain its hold on its East European empire.

In Moscow's view, forcing Prague into the Soviet camp was a strictly defensive action. But Stalin should have understood that making Czechoslovakia a Soviet satellite was bound to stir war talk in Western Europe and the United States, where the "Czech Coup" was only seen as an act of aggression reminiscent of Hitler's prewar actions. A cable from General Lucius Clay, the commanding U.S.

officer in Berlin, who had considered war unlikely with Russia "for at least ten years," now predicted that a conflict "may come with dramatic suddenness."

Kennan was chagrined not only by Clay's "error of interpretation" but also by the readiness of the State Department and the rest of official Washington to accept Clay's warning as gospel. They "would have done better," Kennan wrote in his *Memoirs*, "to rely on the judgment of some of us who knew something about Russia." Although Kennan remonstrated against Clay's overreaction at the time, "a real war scare ensued, the intensity of which may be judged from the fact that on March 16 the Central Intelligence Agency thought it necessary to hand to the President an estimate saying that war was 'not probable within sixty days.' " When U.S. Air Force chiefs were urged to consider extending this time period by another two weeks, they refused. Remembering the fate of the brass at Pearl Harbor, they did not wish to take the fall for an unanticipated attack.

Stalin's clamp-down on the Czechs and Eastern Europe was so "abrupt and clumsy" that few could doubt his aggressive intentions, or think of him as mainly defending his homeland against a future German or Western invasion. Anti-Communist purges across Eastern Europe and the creation of economic agencies in Bulgaria, East Germany, Hungary, Rumania, and Poland that transferred their agricultural and industrial wealth to Russia added to impressions of ruthless Soviet rulers seizing everything they could for their own benefit. Seventy-seven percent of Americans told pollsters that "Russia is trying to build herself up to be the ruling power of the world." Only 12 percent thought that her move against Czechoslovakia could be seen as "protection against being attacked in another war."

Kennan understood the limits of Soviet capacity to turn its fears of the West into military expansion, but his subtlety of comprehension was beyond the grasp of almost all political leaders across the West and threw them, especially the French, into frenzied efforts to build a military wall that would prevent the sort of defeat Hitler inflicted on them at the start of World War II. "I regarded the anxieties of the Europeans as a little silly," Kennan wrote later. "This was not . . . the time to start talking about military defenses and preparations." He "saw dangers in any form of . . . reassurance that would encourage them in their military preoccupations." He accurately foresaw that unneeded military steps would provoke counterreactions leading to an unpredictable cycle of defense preparations that could result in another European war.

But Kennan's rational calculations were of no consequence in shaping current events. Fears of Russian power and longer-term German revival haunted the French. They imagined Russian control of all Germany followed by an invasion of France, and saw the United States abandoning Western Europe to the Soviets, with "Russian hordes" occupying "the area raping women and deporting the male population for slave labor in the Soviet Union." They expected the U.S. to retaliate with atomic bombs that would devastate Western Europe.

Despite an understanding in both European and American military circles that the Soviet Union was in no position to begin an offensive war any time soon against Western Europe or certainly the United States (it was economically weak, lacked the air power to sustain a successful campaign, and had no atomic weapons), Britain, France, the Netherlands, Belgium, and Luxemburg felt compelled to sign a mutual defense agreement, the Brussels Pact, which the United States endorsed as essential to their long-term security.

Like the Europeans, Truman now saw Stalin and the Soviets as another Hitler and the Nazis. "We are faced with exactly the same situation with which Britain and France were faced in 1938–9 with Hitler," he wrote his daughter on March 3. It was an imperfect analogy: although the Russians were as ruthless in their disregard for free expression as the Nazis, their military strength compared to Western adversaries was nothing like Hitler's advantage on the eve of World War II. But the memories of appeasement at Munich seemed too compelling to ignore. Marshall counseled the president against over-stating the dangers, but Truman told some of his aides that the secretary's advice "stank."

In an appearance before a joint congressional session on March 17, Truman "felt it necessary to report to the nation . . . on the grave events in Europe [that] were moving so swiftly." He pointedly upbraided the Soviet Union as the "one nation" that "has not only refused to cooperate in the establishment of a just and honorable peace, but—even worse—[it] has actively sought to prevent it. . . . The Soviet Union and its agents have destroyed the independence and democratic character of a whole series of nations in Eastern and Central Europe. It is this ruthless course of action, and the design to extend it to the remaining free nations of Europe, that have brought about the critical situation in Europe today." The Brussels Pact, Truman concluded, was "a notable step in the direction of unity in Europe for protection and preservation of its civilization."

That night, in another speech in New York before a St. Patrick's Day group, Truman reiterated his concerns and repeated a call for Congress to fund the Marshall Plan, extend the military draft, and pass a law requiring universal military training (UMT) for every able-bodied male turning eighteen. Canadian prime minister Mackenzie King read the president's pronouncements as an expression of U.S. readiness to rely on force in any future confrontation with the Soviets.

In the spring of 1948, if doubts had existed among Washington policymakers about a defensive alliance, a crisis over Berlin put them to rest. During the first months of 1948, London and Washington agreed to the creation of a West German state with a separate currency from that of the Soviet occupation zone. Concessions to Paris assuring it protection against a remilitarized Germany won French support for the plan. At the same time, American and British military planners began secret discussions that leaked to the Russians on how to meet the Soviet threat with expanded production of atomic bombs and promises of support for the Western union should it face a Soviet attack.

The prospect of a West German state incorporated into a Western bloc that would directly threaten the Soviet Union convinced Stalin that he needed to thwart Washington's plans for Germany. He ordered a shutdown of Anglo-American access to West Berlin from West Germany through the 110 miles of rail lines stretching through Soviet-controlled East Germany. Because a loss of West Berlin seemed likely to demoralize all Western Europe, Washington and London decided to defend its rights of access and the freedom of West Berliners, even at the possible cost of war. Stalin saw the limited blockade not as a pretext for war but as a bargaining chip to deter the creation of a West German state. The fear of a revived Germany was greater in Russia than the worry that limits on Western access to Berlin would touch off an East-West war.

Although neither side wished to use force, the stakes for both were high enough to provoke discussions of a military clash. To make clear the U.S. determination not to back down, the Senate passed a bipartisan resolution in June, named for Republican senator Arthur Vandenberg, pledging American backing for the Brussels Pact. (Domestic politics, especially in a presidential election year, were never absent from foreign policy and national security decisions. Having already credited the Democratic administration with the Truman Doctrine and the Marshall Plan, Republicans insisted on attaching a prominent Republican senator's name to assure bipartisan support for another major overseas initiative.)

When the Western occupiers formally declared the creation of a West German state with a new currency at a London conference in June, the Russians expanded the rail-line disruption, which they had temporarily suspended for the sake of possible negotiations, into a full-scale blockade of West Berlin, closing off all rail and highway traffic through its East German zone.

For the sake of his standing at home and in Eastern Europe, Stalin felt he could not afford to let the move toward a Western German state go unanswered. True, he and all Russia trembled at the thought of another confrontation with a rearmed Germany, but Stalin's hold on his own government and his satellites also seemed imperiled by Western defiance of his wishes.

In significant part, Stalin's power continued to rest on intimidation and terror. Anecdotes about the fears of anyone brought into Stalin's presence abounded: the first time the young diplomat Anatoly Dobrynin encountered him, surrounded by personal bodyguards in the halls of the Kremlin, Dobrynin cringed with his back to the wall and hands thrust forward to show that he had no weapon as the great man approached. Stalin stopped to ask who he was and, sensing the young man's fright, declared: "Youth must not fear Comrade Stalin. He is its friend." Dobrynin remembered that he "shuddered."

In the spring of 1948 Stalin was clearly in declining health, and several members of the Politburo were vying for his endorsement as his successor. Because Stalin had no intention of relinquishing his power before physical incapacity or death compelled him to, he encouraged competition among those believed to be contenders for his replacement as the Communist Party's general secretary. To head off any premature attempts to oust him, Stalin struck these men down before they could act. The Politburo men around him described Stalin's "intellectual decline and dangerous unpredictability," and said that he showed "conspicuous signs of senility." But he remained as ruthless and driven as ever. His systematic elimination of his oldest Politburo comrades, like Molotov and Anastas Mikoyan, from influence reflected the actions not of someone who had lost his mental faculties but of a tyrant clinging to power by crushing those most likely to succeed him.

Soviet general V. N. Gordov, a decorated hero of the Stalingrad fighting, said in December 1946 that everybody was "fed up with his life, people say so quite openly—on the trains—in the Metro, everywhere, they come straight out with it." He told his wife of his contempt for Stalin: "I can't bear to look at him, I can't breathe the same air. . . . It's just like the Inquisition, people are just dying. . . . I'm not the only one . . . not by a long shot." Gordov and his wife were arrested and executed in 1947.

It was all part of Stalin's campaign to terrify dissidents or anyone suspected of dissension. But "the idea that they [high ranking officials around Stalin] could engage in intrigues of their own is laughable," one commentator said. "It was he [Stalin] who organized them in rival groupings and egged them on to destroy each other. One man and one man only stood behind each and every one of the Kremlin cliques: the Boss."

An attempt to destroy Yugoslavia's Marshal Tito was another part of Stalin's effort at this time to sustain his hold on power. In Stalin's view, Tito was a defiant upstart whose independence threatened his control at home and abroad. Against Stalin's wishes the Yugoslav president, who enjoyed enormous popularity in his country as a result of his organized resistance to Nazi occupation during World War II, had aided the Greek Communists, clashed with Anglo-American forces in attempts to wrest Trieste from Italy, and established a Yugoslav-Bulgarian federation. Having avoided any significant reliance on Soviet military intervention to free Yugoslavia from Nazi control and having achieved the nearly impossible in unifying his nation's competing ethnic groups, Tito had no intention of submitting to Stalin's dictates. He was determined to preserve his country from the fate Stalin meted out to Balkan neighbors.

Stalin wished to make Tito an example of how Moscow dealt with governments that put their national interest above the Communist party line written in Russia. On June 19, 1948, five days before Stalin imposed the Berlin blockade, he instructed his deputies at the second Cominform meeting in Bucharest to expel the Yugoslav president as "an Imperialist spy." Stalin told one Politburo member, "I'll shake my little finger and there'll be no more Tito." But Tito was not so easy to bring down: mindful of other foreign visitors to the Kremlin who never returned home or were heard from again, Tito refused a February 1948 invitation to visit Stalin and then foiled two assassination attempts by Kremlin agents who could not penetrate the shield Tito put up against Stalin. Stalin's inability to work his will against the defiant Yugoslav became another reason for the Berlin blockade: it seemed essential for Stalin to demonstrate his power on the larger problem of West Germany.

The blockade suggested that conditions were ripe for a full-blown confrontation with the West. But neither Moscow nor Washington saw the clash of wills as a reason for war. The Russians did not try to starve West Berlin into submission, allowing its occupants to buy foodstuffs, petrol, and coal from the East. They also did nothing to close or imperil the air corridors between West Germany and West Berlin. As a consequence, U.S. air forces were able to begin an around-the-clock airlift of basic supplies for West Berliners. Some 130 large air transports began making 250 daily round trips into the Berlin Tempelhof airfield.

Similarly, while Truman made it clear that the United States would "stay in Berlin," he took care to avoid provocations that could trigger a military clash. He rejected proposals from General Clay for armed surface convoys into the city, insisted on exclusive White House control of atomic bombs, and declared his determination to use all possible diplomatic means to resolve the crisis. During a meeting in Moscow in August between the American, British, and French ambassadors and Stalin and Molotov, all of them made clear that they wanted to reach a settlement, though neither side was ready to concede enough to bring an end to the impasse.

Kennan, who had a better understanding of the Kremlin's motives and intentions than anyone else in the U.S. government, was incensed at the inclination of the Europeans and Americans to use the crisis to rattle sabers. He saw the Czech coup and the Berlin blockade as "just the predictable 'baring of the fangs.' Nor did I see any reason why the development of military strength on our side, and particularly the development of new relationships of alliance between this country and European countries, was required to meet that behavior."

The lack of response to his warnings puzzled him: he wondered "why so much attention was paid in certain instances, as in the case of the telegram of February 1946 from Moscow and the X-Article, to what I had to say, and so little in others. The only answer could be that Washington's reactions were deeply subjective, influenced more by domestic-political moods and institutional interests than by any theoretical consideration of our international position." He saw himself as naive "in the assumption that the mere statement on a single occasion of a sound analysis or appreciation, even if invited or noted or nominally accepted by one's immediate superiors, had any appreciable effect on the vast, turgid, self-centered, and highly emotional process by which the views and reactions of official Washington were finally evolved."

Like any assertive personality ambitious for influence in the highest councils of government, Kennan was sensitive to anything he considered a slight by his superiors, who were erratic in their responses to his advice. But he glimpsed the truth when he surmised that more than strict theoretical calculation and personal disregard for him went into the making of foreign policy in response to the Czech and Berlin crises.

To be sure, Soviet behavior seemed unnecessarily provocative, stimulating fears of a Soviet Russia following the example of Hitler and the Nazis in 1939–40, when they recklessly went to war. Images of Moscow relying on force to intimidate opponents into conceding political and territorial advantages that could give Russia an upper hand in a struggle for European control understandably came to mind.

But more than World War II memories shaped Truman's response to the Berlin crisis. Domestic politics were also at work in his show of determination against Soviet actions. How could it be otherwise?

Although presidents always deny that political considerations or anything other than strict national security calculations shape their foreign policy decisions, they are ever mindful of how any foreign affairs action will register on public opinion. And they should be. After all, a president who loses public backing for steps abroad is implementing a foreign policy that is unsustainable. An overseas action that costs the nation blood and treasure or opens the prospect of such losses may cost a president not only his office but also the national embarrassment produced by a retreat.

Franklin Roosevelt and Harry Truman were both mindful of how the loss of domestic political support had played havoc with Woodrow Wilson's postwar foreign policies. The defeat of Wilson's party in the 1918 congressional elections had resulted in the Senate's refusal to ratify the Versailles Treaty and agree to U.S. participation in the League of Nations. By the end of World War II, a majority of Americans believed that rejection of the treaty and league had contributed to the onset of the century's second great war. Whether this belief was accurate or not, the lesson seemed to be that domestic political support was inseparable from effective implementation of wise foreign policy. Certainly Franklin Roosevelt's caution in leading the United States into the war had rested on an understanding that a congressional declaration of war that did not enjoy widespread and strong public backing was too great a danger to the all-out effort that would be needed to win a global conflict. Moreover, Roosevelt's overstated hopes for postwar harmony were part of a domestic political campaign to ensure that internationalism would replace traditional isolationism at the end of the fighting.

In 1948, Harry Truman believed that his containment policy was essential to the country's future safety and well-being. If political rivals to his left or right defeated him in that year's election, he thought, it would be disastrous for the nation. Political opponents urging greater accommodation to Moscow or tougher steps that could precipitate a war impressed him as offering dangerous alternatives.

The likelihood of a Truman defeat in 1948 overshadowed these concerns. Clark Clifford, the president's White House counsel, who had also become his principal campaign adviser, remembers that his hopes of Truman's election "went up and down. At times I thought the president was either fooling himself or putting forward a brave front to keep *our* spirits up." The truth is that few, if any, close observers thought that Harry Truman had much of a chance. After losing control of both houses of Congress in 1946, Truman seemed to be a president with little public backing. In the spring of 1948, a Gallup poll recorded only 36 percent approval and 50 percent disapproval. In the "solid Democratic South," Truman had just a 35 percent favorable rating, with 57 percent holding negative views of him. In straw polls matching him against the Republican nominee, New York governor Thomas Dewey, Truman trailed through the summer and fall by between 6 and 12 percentage points. A late October survey had voters predicting a Dewey victory by a two-to-one margin.

But Truman carried off the greatest election upset in presidential history. Several elements contributed to his success: an unqualified appeal to New Deal liberals, the cultivation of African American voters, a whistle-stop cross-country train trip in which the president endeared himself to voters by his plain speaking, and an uninspired Republican campaign from the lackluster Tom Dewey, whose stiff formality gave him a reputation as the only man who could strut sitting down.

In a time of international crisis, the public wanted strong executive leadership. When the president took a firm stand on a divisive issue, it encouraged people to see him as an officeholder with integrity, who was willing to speak his mind regardless of the political consequences. Truman's 1947–48 stand on civil rights, a highly controversial issue, was an ideal case in point. His speaking out for equal treatment under the law of all Americans, regardless of race, gender, or ethnic origin, was calculated to raise the president's reputation for courage with voters.

In 1947–48, Truman spoke out against civil rights abuses of blacks as no president had since the civil war. There was unquestionably some political calculation in the president's public identification with African American demands for legislation that would end lynching, increase black access to the polls, require fair employment practices, and end discrimination in the armed services. On matters of race, Truman, a native of western Missouri, where segregation and bias against blacks was commonplace, grew up with the shared convictions of his time and place that blacks were inferior to whites.

But anecdotes about physical attacks on returning black veterans by southern racists, who in one instance beat up and blinded a black sergeant in one eye, genuinely incensed Truman. He concluded that "the main difficulty with the South is that they are living eighty years behind the times." Unpunished killings of blacks in Deep South states convinced him that the "country is in a pretty bad fix from the law enforcement standpoint." To remedy these abuses, in February 1948 Truman asked Congress to pass a civil rights law that enforced the equal treatment clauses of the Constitution, but control of key committees by southern congressmen and senators blocked passage of such legislation.

Stalin, Soviet actions, and alleged Communist subversion served Truman's political appeal as well. The president's firm response to the Czech crisis and the Berlin blockade, tied to his successful bipartisan appeal in 1947 for the Truman Doctrine and the Marshall Plan, gave him standing as an effective leader intent on containing communism by economic and political means rather than by war. And though Americans were not happy with Soviet control of Eastern Europe and the Communist insurgency that threatened to topple the pro-American Nationalists in China, they were content with the rescue of Greece, Turkey, Western Europe, and West Berlin from Soviet domination without resorting to the horrors that an atomic conflict would bring.

Truman's attentiveness to national anxiety about Communist

subversion also struck resonant chords with voters. The Communist takeover in Prague without overt Soviet intervention, as well as accusations in August 1948 by Whittaker Chambers that Alger Hiss, a former colleague in the Roosevelt-Truman State Department, had passed secret documents to the Russians, made Communist spying a campaign issue. In his March speeches about the Czech coup, Truman had denounced Henry Wallace and his Progressive Party, which were running against him, saying that he "did not want the support of 'Henry Wallace and his Communists.'"

Something more seemed to be needed, however, after the president said during a campaign talk in June, "I like old Joe," explaining that Stalin "is a decent fellow [who] is a prisoner of the Politburo." Truman's remarks caused an embarrassing uproar over his naiveté in believing that the Politburo rather than Stalin dictated Soviet policy. Truman privately acknowledged his error, telling aides, "Well, I guess I goofed."

He found himself in political hot water again when he dismissed as "a red herring" the spy scare on Capitol Hill that followed Chambers's testimony. When one of Clark Clifford's aides told him that domestic communism was the "Administration's most vulnerable point," the White House felt compelled to hit back at Republican charges of being soft on the Communist threat.

Clifford was a hard-nosed political operator who had few qualms about cutting political corners to win an election. Like de Gaulle, Clifford's physical appearance gave him an instant advantage over almost everyone he dealt with. At six feet, with broad shoulders, a full head of blond hair that gave him a boyish appearance, and a soft voice, he was as glamorous as a movie actor. His appearance discouraged some people from taking him seriously. But he was exceptionally shrewd and effectively manipulative: anyone approaching him with a request would have to work the levers of influence to gain access. On being ushered into his office, a visitor would find him hunched over his desk, pretending to study some document, while he waited until he acknowledged their presence. It was a trick he used to establish control of a meeting and the conversation.

Clifford counseled Truman to counter charges of being soft on communism by giving a national radio speech in September that pilloried the Republicans for diverting attention from the "real danger" of Soviet expansionism to bogus warnings about Communist espionage. But it was not the complaint about false warnings that registered on voters as much as Truman's assertion that "the Democratic party has been leading the fight to make democracy effective and wipe out communism in the United States," essentially acknowledging the greatly exaggerated threat of Communist subversion. The real enemies of domestic security, Truman said, were the Republicans and the Wallace progressives: the latter hoped that they could win enough votes to ensure a Dewey victory, which would then result in "reactionary policies" that could foster "confusion and strife on which communism thrives. . . . There is nothing that the communists would like better than to weaken the liberal program that are our shield against communism."

Truman's response was calculated less to argue against overblown fears of Communist spying than to suggest that Wallace and his supporters were wittingly or unwittingly serving the Communist cause. In Truman's formulation, unwise Republican policies would create a similar result: implementing their reactionary ideas would make the country more vulnerable to domestic agitation from discontented radicals who sympathized with the Communists. However much Truman despised the unrealistic attacks against anyone even faintly vulnerable to charges of fellow traveling, his counters to their smears gave their false warnings a measure of credibility that would continue to promote a Red scare among millions of gullible Americans.

No foreign policy issue more directly influenced the election than Truman's decision to give prompt recognition to the state of Israel in May 1948. It is true that significant political considerations entered into the president's decision, and they so angered Secretary of State

Marshall—who, like others in the State Department, believed that less overt backing for Israel was in America's best interest—that he never spoke again to Clark Clifford, who pushed recognition as essential to the president's election.

For Truman, who accepted the political necessity of overtly supporting the new Jewish state, there was nothing untoward about doing so: not only would it help him politically, but he believed it was the right and realistic policy. He fully accepted the moral claims for a Jewish homeland in Palestine, and Clifford convinced him that Israel would come into existence with or without America's immediate backing.

When he won election in November, Truman believed that he had both made a smart political decision on Israel and acted in concert with larger moral and historical forces. Israel's successful resistance to the Arab League armies in 1948 vindicated Clifford's prediction that an Israeli state would come into being regardless of initial outside reactions. When the chief rabbi of Israel told Truman during a visit to the White House, "God put you in your mother's womb so you would be the instrument to bring the rebirth of Israel after two thousand years," Truman started to cry. Such are the fictions by which men sometimes take comfort from their actions. Neither the rabbi nor the president reflected on the potential for continuing violence created by the irreconcilable differences between Israelis and Palestinians over land and survival in the Holy Land.

THE MILITARY SOLUTION

War is Peace.
—George Orwell, *1984*, (1949)

At the start of 1949, as President Truman began his full term, he understood that heightened tensions with the Soviet Union following the Czech coup and Berlin blockade made foreign affairs his foremost concern. Compounding his worries was the need to replace George Marshall, who at sixty-nine was in declining health as a result of surgery to remove a kidney with a benign cyst. Although he would live for another ten years and would perform one last tour of duty as secretary of defense between 1950 and 1951, Marshall urged the president to replace him with a younger, more vigorous man who could deal with the urgent challenges of the next four years. Truman, who viewed Marshall as one of the greatest public servants in the country's history, reluctantly let him go, appreciating that the general had given more of himself to the nation than anyone in his generation.

In choosing a new secretary, Truman recalled his personal tensions with James Byrnes and the satisfaction he had from the mutual regard he and Marshall had shown each other. Where differences with Byrnes had been over his failure to show proper deference to the president's authority, the Truman-Marshall conflicts had been strictly over policy, particularly toward the emerging state of Israel. Truman wanted a new secretary who not only had the expertise to provide wise counsel on foreign affairs but would also accept that the president had the final say on all major policy matters without being a cipher. Truman, whose popular approval stood at 69 percent at the start of his new term, was free to choose almost anyone he liked. But the decision was comparatively easy.

Dean Acheson was the president's first choice. He had a long history of government service, beginning with Roosevelt's Treasury Department in 1933. His work for Truman as undersecretary of state and acting secretary during Marshall's absences abroad included major contributions to the president's doctrine for Greece and Turkey and the Marshall Plan.

But, as two people from greatly different backgrounds, would they be able to work comfortably together? Truman, the Missouri farmer and Democratic Party wheelhorse, had little in common with the northeastern elite Acheson represented. The son of the Episcopal bishop of Connecticut, schooled at Groton, FDR's prep school, Yale, and Harvard Law School, Acheson was known for his brilliance and sense of superiority. Everything from his erect posture and mustache to his pinstripe suit and homburg hat bespoke self-confidence and authority; this was someone who expected others to defer to him.

Although Acheson and Roosevelt shared a class identity and privileged schooling, the president expected the thirty-nine-year-old Acheson to show a proper regard for his higher station and demonstrate unquestioned loyalty as undersecretary of the treasury. Acheson, however, resented what he saw as FDR's patronizing behavior toward subordinates, especially himself. It was "not gratifying to receive the easy greeting which milord might give a promising stable boy and pull one's forelock in return," Acheson recalled.

When he and the president differed on a currency issue—no small matter in the midst of the Great Depression—Acheson stubbornly held his ground. During a heated argument in the Oval Office, Roosevelt imperiously told him: "That will do!" When the president suspected that Acheson continued to defy him by offering surreptitious critical comments to the press, Roosevelt demanded his resignation. Acheson complied by writing a respectful letter saying he understood the president's need to have "complete freedom of choice as to whom you will place in charge at the Treasury." It was a belated expression of recognition that the president was the boss, despite Acheson's undiminished personal annoyance at Roosevelt's imperious manner. Appreciating Acheson's willingness to resign like a "gentleman," Roosevelt told him: "I have been awfully angry at you. But you are a real sportsman. You will get a good letter from me in answer to yours." Roosevelt never followed through on his promise.

Acheson learned a valuable lesson from his conflict with Roosevelt. He later concluded that he had shown "stubbornness and lack of imaginative understanding of my own proper role and of the President's perplexities and needs." He belatedly understood that he should have put aside personal considerations for the sake of larger public ones.

He did not make the same mistake with Truman. From the first, he thought of Roosevelt's successor as "straight-forward, decisive, simple, entirely honest." Moreover, he believed it "a blessing that he is the President and not Henry Wallace," who would have plunged the country into "bitter partisan rowing." It may be that unlike Roosevelt's treatment of him—demands for the sort of courtier's deference Acheson resisted giving—Truman's respectful regard made Acheson partial to him. But whatever Acheson's motives, he had genuine respect for Truman as a man of intelligence and integrity who was devoted to serving the country as best he could.

Although Truman never insisted on the sort of deference Roosevelt demanded, he was no less sensitive to demonstrations of personal regard. In 1946, after the Democrats had lost control of the Congress in the November elections and Truman's prospects of winning in 1948 seemed bleak, the president, who had been in Missouri to vote, returned by train to Washington, where the only government official on the platform at Union Station was Undersecretary of State Acheson. "It had for years been a Cabinet custom to meet President Roosevelt's private car on his return from happier elections and escort him to the White House," Acheson recalled. "It never occurred to me that after defeat the President would be left to creep unnoticed back to the capital." Truman never forgot the gesture, and on that occasion, he invited Acheson to join him for a drink at the White House.

In choosing Acheson, Truman risked congressional defiance. While the president had Democratic majorities in both houses in 1949, the fear of Communist subversion cast a shadow over Acheson's Senate confirmation hearings. The Whittaker Chambers–Alger Hiss controversy in the summer of 1948 had embarrassed Acheson. Hiss, who Chambers had fingered as a Soviet agent, was described as an Acheson State Department assistant.

Although Acheson would make clear at his confirmation hearings that his assistant had been Alger's brother, Donald, who was then a law partner, and that testimony by former assistant secretary of state Adolph Berle before the House Un-American Activities Committee about his ties to Alger Hiss was inaccurate, the Senate committee insisted on publishing a statement emphasizing Acheson's anticommunism. Acheson, who had been an architect of Truman's Cold War opposition to postwar Soviet aggression, was made to reaffirm his hostility to Communist ideology: "It is my view that communism as a doctrine is economically fatal to a free society and to human rights and fundamental freedom. Communism as an aggressive factor in world conquest is fatal to independent governments and to free peoples," Acheson was quoted as telling the Senate Committee on Foreign Relations.

It was an exercise in political theater propelled by the growing national fear of Communist subversion that the most patriotic and consistent anti-Communist members of the government had to deny any connection to Stalin. Everyone in the Politburo must have taken satisfaction and hope for their cause from the idea that Americans distrusted officials as outspokenly anti-Communist as Dean Acheson, who some on the right accused of being a Soviet spy. It told the Kremlin that millions of Americans doubted the capacity of their government to stand up to the Communist challenge.

On taking office, Acheson confronted a world beset by troubles and dangers. Closest to home, Latin America, the neglected stepchild of U.S. foreign policy, seethed, he said, with "an explosive population, stagnant economy, archaic society, primitive politics, massive ignorance, illiteracy, and poverty." Acheson believed that conditions in Central and South America and the Caribbean were an invitation to Communist takeovers.

Likewise, a Chinese civil war that threatened to replace a pro-American Nationalist regime with a hostile Communist one, joined with anticolonial revolutions against Dutch and French rule in Indonesia and Indochina, seemed likely breeding grounds for Soviet influence. North Africa, where French control in Algeria seemed equally vulnerable to collapse, was another worry for Washington. The competition for hearts and minds in emerging nations raised fears of long-term defeat for the West. The outlook, except in Europe, Acheson recalled, was "one of deterioration and gloom."

The irony is that the Truman administration's principal anti-Communist initiative came not in Latin America or Asia or Africa but in Europe, where the democracies were in the ascendancy. True, Truman proposed Point Four, a major program for technological assistance to developing countries—helping suffering peoples by giving them the know-how to increase food production, shelter, and energy that could "lighten their burdens." But the program never gained significant traction because, as its intended recipients declared, what was most needed in Third World nations was not technological instruction but capital to build infrastructure. Western leaders disputed this conviction, arguing that without "technological and managerial competence," capital infusions would fall short of expectations. But whatever the superior formula for promoting advance in the Third World, Washington's principal effort to combat communism was a European defensive alliance.

It was the least effective way to defend the West against Communist gains. But the mindset in Western Europe and the United States was fixed on building military might against Soviet aggression. The North Atlantic Treaty Organization (NATO) was the product of outsize fears of Russia and Germany in France, Holland, Great Britain, and the United States. Never mind that U.S. troops remained as an occupying force in West Germany, with no suggestion that they would be withdrawn at any time in the foreseeable future—a deterrent to any Soviet plans to expand its control westward or to any likelihood that an emerging West German state would pose a threat to its neighbors in the West or farther to the East.

But governments everywhere were held fast by false analogies with the past. America's isolationist history made its current allies fearful that public opinion in the United States might force a sudden withdrawal from Europe and leave Germany's former victims vulnerable to another round of attack by that country's virulent nationalist forces. Similarly, leaders in the West saw Stalin as another Hitler, who burned with ambition to conquer all of Europe in order to create a thousand-year Communist empire. Stalin may well have yearned to impose communism on all of Europe, but the backwardness of the Soviet economy and the limits of its capacity to extend its control beyond Eastern Europe made any such wish an unrealizable dream.

Moreover, if Stalin were another Hitler, he was a much more cautious aggressor. In the first four months of 1949, as the NATO treaty moved to completion, Stalin signaled his willingness to end the Berlin blockade, which in fact occurred in May. It was a prelude to another Council of Foreign Ministers meeting in Paris to discuss differences over Germany and Berlin in particular. Stalin's back-down on Berlin was seen not as an indication that he was loath to risk war with the West, but as a reason to believe that the Allies had learned how to deal with a ruthless dictator: firm action, including a readiness to take up arms, as demonstrated by the airlift and the emerging NATO alliance, were the proper answers to Soviet aggressors intent on exploiting any sign of weakness. A more rational calculation in Europe's Western capitals would have been: Stalin feared war with a nuclear-armed United States and was acting not out of aggressive ambition to roll his tanks into their countries but from fear of a revived Germany, which would use NATO to avenge its defeat in World War II.

The great majority of Americans made their own miscalculations about what would best serve the country's national security. Between two-thirds and three-quarters of Americans favored NATO, the first offensive-defensive alliance in U.S. history since the agreement with France in 1778. Although most supporters of the pact believed it was strictly for defensive purposes, they saw this U.S. military commitment as a belated effort to do what they should have done in the 1930s—join Britain and France in an alliance that might have prevented the outbreak of World War II.

Without NATO, as Kennan believed, the Warsaw Pact was unlikely, and massive economic resources could have been available for more productive purposes. But spending money on combating potential Communist threats elsewhere than Europe did not have much appeal. Setting up a military alliance that directly confronted Soviet power in Eastern Europe had far greater attraction than countering potential Communist subversion in the Third World. Most Americans could identify more comfortably with combating the Communist threat in Europe, where most of their ancestors had lived, than in Asia or Africa, which seemed remote. A Communist regime in North Africa or South or Southeast Asia, while unwelcome, seemed less threatening than one in Paris, Rome, or Berlin, however unlikely that might be without a military alliance.

Despite the receptivity to leadership of NATO, the U.S. Congress was less enthusiastic about giving substance to the commitment by appropriating the billion-plus dollars needed to build the alliance's military muscle. At least, that was so until news of a Soviet atomic bomb test arrived in September 1949, sending a chill of fear through the U.S. political establishment that spurred agreement on finding the money to fund a military assistance program.

After Potsdam, Stalin had made the bomb's development his highest military priority. It was named "Task Number One," and Stalin told the lead scientist, "If a child doesn't cry, the mother does not know what she needs. Ask for whatever you like. You won't be refused." Between 330,000 and 460,000 people were assigned to the project, including 10,000 technicians. Although the scientists were given special treatment, living well above the standard of the average Soviet citizen, they operated in an atmosphere of terror enforced by Lavrenty Beria, who told one manager, "You're a good worker, but if you'd served six years in the camps, you'd work even better." When one scientist had the nerve to tell Beria that his work might improve if he were free, Beria replied: "Certainly. But it would be risky. The traffic in the streets is crazy and you might get run over."

Beria could be even more threatening: "Don't forget we've plenty of room in our prisons," he told members of the production team. It was more a verbal spur to keep everyone in line than a prelude to punishment. His advice to Stalin about complaints from the scientists: "Leave them in peace. We can always shoot them later." When the bomb was tested successfully, Beria was ecstatic, menacingly declaring, "It would have been a great misfortune if this hadn't worked out."

Although Truman and Acheson were more than willing to use the Soviet A-bomb test to prod the Congress into passing a military appropriations bill, the president was reluctant to announce the Soviet achievement. Moscow's nuclear capacity seemed too likely to stir anxieties in Europe and America, and intensify accusations about Soviet agents stealing atomic secrets from Democratic administrations infiltrated by Communist sympathizers. How otherwise could Moscow have built the bomb more quickly than anyone in the West anticipated? When Truman was warned that news of the Soviet A-test would leak regardless of what he did and could undermine public confidence in him, he announced the Soviet success. The public did not overreact to the information. In the fall of 1949, a majority of Americans did not believe that the Soviet bomb would significantly change international affairs.

Few in either the Soviet Union or the United States saw Russia's greater armed might as increasing the likelihood of a third world war. The accepted Soviet wisdom was that the capitalist countries, locked in competition for international economic resources, would inevitably fight each other. Reluctant to further unite the West against the Communist East, Stalin and the Soviet press issued reassuring statements of peaceful intent about its nuclear capacity. Moreover, Stalin privately expressed the belief that an atomic war would run counter to what "people" would allow. He told one of his courtiers, "If war broke out, the use of A-bombs would depend on Trumans and Hitlers being in power. The people won't allow such people to be in power. Atomic weapons can hardly be used without spelling the end of the world." By lifting the Berlin blockade, Stalin hoped to leave the "natural" fissures in the West more room to grow. He was confident that eventually Britain and France, as well as a resurrected Germany, would rise up in competition with the United States and fight another "capitalist war."

Moscow's warnings of America's war preparations and devotion to a showdown with the East were meant less to prepare Soviet citizens for a military conflict with the United States than to entice Westerners to support a pro-Soviet peace movement. A World Peace Congress representing 600 million peace advocates was part of a Moscow campaign to encourage antiwar activism in capitalist countries that might limit defense budgets and inhibit military buildups in response to Soviet efforts to outdo the West in an arms race.

Few in the West took Soviet propaganda at face value. Stalin's speculation on a war among the capitalists—like Soviet boasts about inventing the telephone, air flight, and the radio, and claims to higher living standards than those in the West—was the sort of nonsense that made people outside the Eastern bloc dismiss communism as a crack-pot ideology. Stalin registered on most people in the democracies as a cautious Hitler—a power-hungry dictator ready to exploit any show of weakness, but intimidated by America's greater might and unwillingness to appease him.

Although Moscow now had the bomb, Americans remained confident that the United States continued to enjoy military advantages: more and bigger bombs in its arsenal and the new NATO alliance. Nonetheless, Americans were divided on what made greatest sense in dealing with the Communist threat. Some favored a war while the United States held a military edge that seemed to promise a quick and relatively inexpensive victory. Others preferred clandestine action that could destabilize and subvert communism outside of Russia as a prescription for destroying the Soviet empire and eventually bringing down the Soviet Union itself. Yet others believed that Russian communism was so economically unproductive that it would self-destruct in time, and that the best strategy was to reach an accommodation with Moscow by creating a neutral zone in Central and Eastern Europe.

It is remarkable how much distorted thinking dominated the governments and populations of the two most important powers in the postwar world. The Soviet belief that capitalist competition would inevitably produce war between the Western democracies was as gross a distortion of reality as the German belief in Hitler's Thousand-Year Reich.

Americans had good reason to assume implacable hostility toward the West from Moscow. But the conviction that a buildup of military might was the most vital element in restraining the Soviets from running roughshod over Western Europe was a miscalculation that did more to extend the Cold War than to shorten and end it.

In May 1949, when the Council of Foreign Ministers met in Paris—the price the Allies had agreed to for an end to the Soviet blockade of Berlin—it quickly became clear that neither side was ready to concede anything on its basic positions about Germany. The West remained eager to reestablish a self-governing and prosperous Germany among the family of nations, and the Soviets aimed to keep Germany divided and weak as a defense against another German drive to the east in search of renewed European dominance.

Yet despite Soviet intransigence, Soviet foreign minister Andrei Vishinsky, a slim, slight man, unlike the heavyset Soviet officials and secret police agents who surrounded him, came across to Acheson as not a skilled, worldly diplomat but a dull mechanical bureaucrat, who tediously espoused predictable Communist propaganda. British foreign minister Bevin opposed evening meetings because, he said, Vishinsky's long-winded speeches put him to sleep. Vishinsky observed that Bevin had the habit of sleeping during afternoon sessions. Unembarrassed, Bevin recommended it as a useful device for getting through the meetings, in which both sides talked past one another.

The meeting in Paris convinced Acheson that the Marshall Plan had revived Western European confidence and optimism. By contrast, the Soviet pronouncements on Germany convinced Acheson that Moscow had moved "from an offensive attitude in 1947 to a defensive one in 1949"—a conclusion that seemed to suggest that the NATO pact was superfluous.

No one in Washington or in any of the other Western capitals took strong issue with the prevailing wisdom of what must be done to secure the democracies against the Soviet danger—except George Kennan. In 1946–47, his brilliance as an analyst of Soviet behavior and how the West could limit further expansion of postwar Soviet power was recognized and rewarded by his appointment to the directorship of the State Department's newly created Policy Planning staff. By 1949, however, he had become something of an outsider—an independent thinker who proposed long-term policies for Germany and Europe that were at variance with the thinking of most policymakers, including Secretary of State Acheson, as sensible means of guarding the West from the Communist menace.

Kennan described himself as trying "to look ten to twenty years into the future. My friends in Washington, London, Paris, and The Hague were thinking of the problems we had immediately before us. . . . I did not believe in the reality of a Soviet military threat to Western Europe. . . . I was concerned not so much to provide protection against the possibility of such an attack . . . as to facilitate the retirement of Soviet forces, and with them dominant Soviet political influence, to limits closer to the traditional boundaries of the Russian state. My friends, less concerned about the division of Europe, and indeed in many instances quite content with it, were thinking of how to deter—and if it could not be deterred, how to withstand—a Soviet attack envisaged by the military planners as likely to ensue in the early 1950s."

Although Kennan had ideas that might have changed the course of the Cold War, his views were considered interesting but impractical— the ruminations, in Kennan's words, of "a court jester, expected to enliven discussion, privileged to say the shocking things, valued as an intellectual gadfly on hides of slower colleagues, but not to be taken fully seriously when it came to the final, responsible decisions of power." By the end of 1949, Kennan, sensing his negligible impact as a dissenting insider, decided to resign from the State Department and take up residence at Princeton University's Institute of Advanced Study, where he would be freer to speak his mind in the hope of having a greater impact on the direction of U.S. foreign policy.

But the political climate in which Kennan and official Washington lived at the time made bold initiatives at variance with formulaic anticommunism unpopular and suspect. Paranoia and messianic thinking were hardly the exclusive preserve of Moscow and other Communist capitals.

In the United States, the belief that communism everywhere was tied to Moscow and an unquestionable threat to U.S. security was a distortion that no rational discussion of Soviet power and Communist intentions in other countries could alter. Single-minded anticommunism in the United States impeded the wiser course of trying to reduce tensions by neutralizing Europe and wooing nonaligned and Communist regimes outside of Russia. Of course, Soviet bombast about capitalist war plans could not help but agitate fears in the United States of universal Communist determination to destroy Western governments and social systems by political subversion or direct military conflict if necessary. But the failure to see this as rhetoric that outran capacity or as talk from Moscow that masked national tensions in the Communist camp was a misreading of political and international realities that ill served U.S. national security.

No greater blunder occurred in this regard than U.S. dealings with the Chinese Communist government that established the People's Republic of China (PRC) on October 1, 1949, after driving Chiang Kai-shek's Nationalists off the mainland to the island of Taiwan. The Communist victory, though increasingly evident in 1948 and 1949, came as a shocking defeat for the United States. It had refused to abandon Chiang, despite his widely unpopular government and mismanagement of military campaigns against initially less numerous and less well equipped Communist forces.

The Truman administration understood how hopeless the Nationalist cause was after Marshall returned from China in 1947, and how little it could do to preserve Chiang's regime without introducing massive U.S. forces. But this was an unacceptable alternative: it seemed likely to do no more than create a stalemate that would involve the United States in a drawn-out war on the Asian mainland. The administration understood that the cost of such a conflict in blood and money would quickly test the limits of public support and create demands for atomic attacks that would not assure victory and would saddle the United States with a reputation for indiscriminate slaughter of Asian enemies.

Besides, a Chinese Communist victory seemed more worrisome for its negative political repercussions in the United States than as a genuine threat to U.S. national security. To counter the predictable political attack on the administration for having "lost China," Truman and Acheson agreed to publish a State Department white paper in August 1949 explaining Chiang's self-inflicted defeat. This 1,079-page volume of annotated documents included a six-thousand-word letter of transmittal from Acheson to Truman, making the case for the administration's reasonable handling of relations with China from 1944 to 1949.

Although Acheson acknowledged that the volume was an incomplete history of U.S.-China relations, he described it as "a frank record of an extremely complicated and most unhappy period in the life of a great country." He reminded readers that the U.S. and Russia were allies during the war and that a determination to speed victory over Japan and save American lives had moved military planners to assure Soviet involvement in the Far Eastern fighting after victory in Europe with territorial concessions that unintentionally shielded China's Communists from Nationalist attacks.

Soviet control of Manchuria at the end of the fighting, however, could not explain Mao's victory. Postwar developments in China were the consequence of conditions and actions beyond either Moscow's or Washington's power to control. The results of the civil war could be found in China itself: the Nationalist failure to solve China's age-old problem of feeding its massive population and the transparent corruption of Chiang's government, joined with Communist promises to transform the country into a modern society, sapped Nationalist appeal and made Mao's party the popular alternative.

The United States had three choices at the end of the Pacific fighting: abandon China to its fate; intervene in the Chinese civil war on the side of the Nationalists on a major scale; or assist the Nationalists at the same time we worked to arrange a compromise between the two sides. Neither of the first two alternatives was acceptable to the American public or made sense in terms of existing conditions in China. Truman considered Chiang's government the "rottenest" in the world.

It was run by "grafters and crooks," and sending them aid was comparable to "pouring sand down a rat hole." While mediating China's differences seemed like the only viable option, it failed not because of American shortcomings but because of Nationalist-Communist unwillingness to reach a mutually agreeable settlement.

In the final analysis, the collapse of the Nationalist regime was an entirely self-inflicted failure. "The unfortunate but inescapable fact," Acheson concluded, "is that the ominous result of the civil war in China was beyond the control of the government of the United States. Nothing that this country did or could have done within the reasonable limits of its capabilities could have changed that result; nothing that was left undone by this country has contributed to it. It was the product of internal Chinese forces, forces which this country tried to influence but could not."

The backdrop to the preparation of the white paper was a debate in the administration about future relations with Mao's regime. The Communists assumed that the greatest likelihood of future stability for their government required help from Moscow for reconstruction and support against Western threats of intervention to overturn the PRC. As late as the spring of 1949, however, Stalin had refused to invite Mao to Moscow or to promise future economic aid. He also discouraged him from crossing the Yangtze River and occupying all of China as a way to avert U.S. intervention. He urged Mao to be content with ruling northern China, while leaving the south to Chiang.

Because Stalin was so unforthcoming, Mao did not rule out a relationship with the United States. But he made clear to U.S. envoys in China that any ties would depend on an end to American support of Chiang, promises of nonintervention in Chinese affairs, the abrogation of earlier unequal treaties, and trade on mutually agreeable terms.

Buffeted by reluctance to see Communists in control of so large a country and convictions that shaping China's future was beyond American power, the Truman administration was erratic in response. National security considerations dictated that Washington do what it could to prevent a Sino-Soviet alliance that would threaten wider Communist control in Asia. As a consequence, in the first half of 1949, Truman and Acheson did not rule out official relations with a Chinese Communist government.

By June, however, as the Nationalist collapse became a matter of time, Truman backed away from any secret dealings with the Communists. When Ambassador John L. Stuart, a China-born missionary and president of Yenching University, proposed to visit Peking for the University's graduation, Mao and Chou signaled their readiness to talk with him. But Truman instructed Stuart not to go to Peking nor suggest any U.S. intention to recognize Mao's government. Acheson underscored the administration's opposition to the new regime by declaring in his letter of transmittal that the Communists represented not independence for China but the establishment of imperial control by Moscow as part of its drive for worldwide dominance. Future American policy toward China would "be influenced by the degree to which the Chinese people come to recognize that the Communist regime serves not their interests but those of Soviet Russia and the manner in which, having become aware of the facts, they react to this foreign domination."

The depiction of China under Soviet control partly resulted from a Mao declaration on July 1 that China "must lean to one side. . . . Not only in China but throughout the world, one must lean either to imperialism or to socialism." For Truman to have allowed his ambassador to travel to Peking would have been seen as appeasement of a Communist government that had no good intentions toward the United States. Private assurances from Mao that his speech was aimed at members of his party most determined to align China with Moscow could not combat the certain outburst of criticism from America's ardent anti-Communists should it become known that Truman had opened secret talks with Mao.

In fact, the 1949 white paper, like the reluctance to test a possible Sino-American relationship after Chiang was ousted and before a firm Sino-Soviet alliance was established, largely rested on domestic political considerations. But the publication of the State Department's defense of U.S. China policy did more to intensify an attack on the administration for having "lost" China than to convince the mass of Americans that Truman had acted wisely. Former ambassador Patrick Hurley described the white paper as "a smooth alibi for the pro-Communists in the State Department who had engineered the overthrow of our ally, the Nationalist Government of the Republic of China." Conservative Republican senators, seizing on the chance to pillory Truman's White House, attacked the State Department volume as a "1,054-page whitewash of a wishful, do-nothing policy which has succeeded only in placing Asia in danger of Soviet conquest."

Having subscribed to the idea that a Peking Communist government was a smokescreen for Soviet control of China and all Asia, the Truman administration could not dispute the Republican conclusion about the dangers posed by Mao's takeover. Moreover, with Chiang's Nationalists on Taiwan still describing themselves as the government of all China, it was nearly impossible for Truman to raise the possibility of accepting Mao as the legitimate ruler of the mainland.

American public opinion was also decidedly hostile to any friendly dealings with China's Communists. Of the 36 percent of Americans who said they had heard of the U.S. government's report on China, 53 percent rejected the argument that the administration could not have done anything more to save the Nationalists. Of the three-quarters of the public who said they knew about the Chinese civil war, only 20 percent wanted the United States to extend recognition to the new Communist regime.

Because Truman and Acheson believed that Mao would oust the Nationalists from Taiwan and definitively end Chiang's claims to being the legitimate government of China, Acheson rejected State Department proposals for putting the island under UN control or occupying it with U.S. troops. The White House secretly accepted the likelihood that the island would fall to the Communists as a prelude to U.S. recognition of Mao's government, which would follow wide acceptance of the regime by America's European allies. "Mao is not a true [Soviet] satellite," Acheson told the Joint Chiefs of Staff at the end of 1949, "in that he came to power by his own efforts and was not installed in office by the Soviet Army." But fearful that an invasion of Taiwan might provoke the United States into an attack on his forces and willing to have the Nationalists as a threat that remained useful in unifying the mainland population, Mao did not move against Chiang.

Mao, Stalin, and the Americans, driven by irrational fears, now acted in ways that added to international tensions, shed the blood of their fellow citizens, and led to wasteful defense costs.

Mesmerized by his own rhetoric about American imperialism and convinced that the United States—not without reason—would make every effort to bring down his regime, Mao decided to court Soviet support. In December 1949 he traveled by train to Moscow, where he was subjected to humiliating treatment by Stalin, who did not meet him at the station and kept him at arm's length for two months while their representatives negotiated a treaty of "friendship." At a time when Mao's new government faced huge tasks in launching the transformation of China's half-billion population, he felt compelled to sit in Moscow—where, he complained, he had "nothing to do . . . but eat, sleep and shit"—until Stalin granted him some meager concessions.

The Sino-Soviet Treaty of Friendship, Alliance, and Mutual Assistance of February 14, 1950, ceded to the Chinese control over the Manchurian Railway and Port Arthur, which the Yalta agreements had granted to the USSR, but not until 1952—time enough to see if Mao's regime would maintain its hold on power. The Chinese would also regain control of Darien, the warm-water port on the Kwantung Peninsula Stalin had won the right to lease at Yalta. But the lease would not be terminated until after a Soviet-Japanese peace treaty in the indeterminate future. A provision of the treaty promising mutual support against Japanese aggression—hardly a likely prospect anytime soon—said nothing about a possible attack launched from Taiwan with American aid. Finally, the Soviets pledged $300 million in credit at 1 percent interest for a period of five years—a pathetically small loan that did not match the amounts provided to the East European satellites or come anywhere near meeting the needs of a China emerging from more than a decade of invasion and civil war.

The Mao-Stalin encounter and the 1950 treaty signaled grudging ties between the two Communist giants. Stalin, who did not think the Chinese were true Marxist-Leninists but what he called radish Communists—red on the outside but white on the inside—feared the Chinese as a competitor for world leadership of communism. Mao, who distrusted Soviet support for a united, powerful China that could defend its territorial integrity and promote anti-imperial revolutions around the world, piled up resentments during his Moscow visit that would find full expression in the next twenty years.

Stalin, who was busy purging Soviet leaders in Leningrad he believed were trying to replace him, could not bring himself to anything more than friendly gestures toward the Chinese. He saw them as competitors for current and future power, who were forcing him to give up some of his postwar Asian gains. The possibility of a genuine friendship that might bolster the long-term stability of Russian communism through economic exchange and defense against threats from the West never occurred to Stalin. Similarly, Mao could not see himself turning away from Moscow to court Washington, either because he believed his own rhetoric about international communism being incompatible with capitalist nations or because he assumed that ideologues in his party would rebel against any hint of a preference for a capitalist foe over Soviet comrades.

Nor was flexible good sense at the forefront of American thinking about the Cold War—and especially about the threat the new Chinese Communist regime posed to U.S. national security interests.

The greatest beneficiary in the United States of Mao's victory was McCarthyism—the idea that communism in China had been made possible by members of the State Department, who either by design or naiveté colluded with Moscow to bring down Chiang Kai-shek's government. Because of these witting or unwitting "traitors," the United States had "lost" China, was the constant refrain of administration critics. "Was there ever an odder flight of the imagination?" George Kennan wondered. How could one nation lose another it had never owned or governed?

Such an attitude sprang from the arrogance of power, the feeling at the end of the war that the United States was the anointed nation, the country that God had brought into existence to save mankind from itself, as Woodrow Wilson had suggested when he described America's role in World War I as making this the war to end all wars, making the world safe for democracy. China's turn to Communism seemed to refute not only Henry Luce's wartime prediction that this would be the American century but also the widely held American assumption that China would eventually be remade in America's image. As Nebraska senator Kenneth Wherry said in 1940, "With God's help, we will lift Shanghai up and up, ever up, until it is just like Kansas City."

In January 1950, three months after the PRC's declaration of statehood and with Mao in Moscow negotiating the Sino-Soviet treaty, Alger Hiss was convicted of perjury and sentenced to a prison term. When asked at a press conference about Hiss's conviction, Acheson courageously, but foolishly, gave brooding anti-Communists like McCarthy a political opening when he declared, "I do not intend to turn my back on Alger Hiss."

McCarthy, who was looking for a reelection campaign issue that could generate support in Wisconsin, seized upon a suggestion by Father Edmund A. Walsh, a Georgetown University priest, to focus on Communist subversion. In response to Acheson's statement, McCarthy rose in the Senate to ask if the secretary was prepared to defend other unidentified Communists in the government as well. On February 9, in a speech before the Wheeling, West Virginia, Republican Women's Club, McCarthy claimed that he had a list of 205 known Communist State Department employees Acheson was protecting.

Although the number on the list would change repeatedly over the next several months—from 205 to 57, back up to 81, down to 10, and as high again as 121—McCarthy's evasiveness did nothing to bring him down. On the contrary, the charges stuck, despite McCarthy's changing numbers: memories of Nazi subversives in Norway—Quislings—and other European countries; Soviet puppet governments in Eastern Europe; the spying that had facilitated Soviet development of an A-bomb; and Russia's alleged control of China's new Communist government gave credibility to charges of American Communists working to give Moscow control of the United States. There were of course Soviet spies in Britain, Canada, and the United States, but the fears of their capacity to bring down Western governments were wildly out of proportion to the actual threat.

Something more was at work here: cynical political aspirations to bring down the Democrats. But there was also genuine anger at those who had been responsible for governing the country for the last eighteen years. Why was America so threatened? After all, it had emerged from World War II with unparalleled power; now, suddenly, it found itself vulnerable in a world besieged by Communists who, by their own acknowledged purpose, intended to destroy capitalism everywhere.

The Democrats were an easy target, and the aristocratic Acheson was a perfect whipping boy. Nebraska's Republican senator Hugh Butler, a conservative self-made seventy-two-year-old businessman, expressed popular suspicions and antagonism toward the secretary of state when he said, "I look at that fellow. I watch his smart-aleck manner and his British clothes and that New Dealism in everything he says and does, and I want to shout, 'Get out, Get out. You stand for everything that has been wrong with the United States for years!' "

McCarthy, exploiting Acheson's identification with Hiss, another "elitist," convicted of perjury and condemned as "disloyal" to the United States, echoed Butler's complaints: "When this pompous diplomat in striped pants, with the phony British accent, proclaimed to the American people that Christ on the Mount endorsed Communism, high treason, and betrayal of sacred trust, the blasphemy was so great that it awakened the dormant indignation of the American people."

In April 1950, in a speech before the American Society of Newspaper Editors, Acheson replied to what he called "this filthy business." He declared that the press, "by reason of your calling, are . . . unwilling participants" in this ugly assault on honorable men whose reputations were being smeared.

Truman privately denounced McCarthy as "just a ballyhoo artist who has to cover up his shortcomings by wild charges." Truman believed that McCarthy's accusations were another episode in a history of "hysterical stages" that temporarily seized hold of the country and then faded from view as earlier outbursts had. He saw them as part of the 1950 congressional campaign, which politically frustrated Republicans were desperate to win.

But when McCarthy's appeal seemed to grow in the first half of 1950, and he charged that Moscow's "top espionage agent" in the United States had ties to the State Department, Truman saw himself dealing with a greater problem than he had anticipated. He wrote a cousin: "I am in the midst of the most terrible struggle any President ever had. A pathological liar from Wisconsin and a blockheaded undertaker from Nebraska [Kenneth Wherry, a licensed embalmer] are trying to ruin the bipartisan foreign policy. Stalin never had two better allies in this country." Truman went after McCarthy in a press conference, saying that he was the Kremlin's "greatest asset" in trying "to sabotage the foreign policy of the United States." But the attack only added to McCarthy's notoriety and credibility; by responding to McCarthy, Truman suggested to millions of Americans that the senator had struck a raw nerve and deserved a hearing.

As later Senate majority leader Lyndon Johnson would tell liberal Minnesota senator Hubert Humphrey, who was eager to hit back at McCarthy, "He just eats fellows like you. You're nourishment for him." Johnson considered McCarthy "the sorriest senator up here. Can't tie his goddamn shoes. But he's riding high now, he's got people scared to death some Communist will strangle 'em in their sleep, and anybody who takes him on before the fevers cool—well, you don't get in a pissin' contest with a polecat."

The problem in the meantime was the damage to those whose reputations had been sullied and, more broadly, to the country, which was unable to consider a more rational foreign policy or take its distance from a doctrinaire anticommunism. The president and the public could not free themselves from thinking that fostered an arms race and a preference for military responses to challenges that diplomacy could have made less costly in lives and treasure.

The decision to build the hydrogen bomb, "the super," as those who understood its potential for destruction called it, is a telling case in point. The same national mood that gave birth and credibility to McCarthy gave life to the belief that the United States could not avoid arming itself with thermonuclear weapons.

In September 1949, the Truman administration had decided to counter Russia's capacity to build A-bombs by expanding America's nuclear arsenal from about fifty Hiroshima-strength bombs to about three hundred. But some in the government, led by Atomic Energy Commissioner Lewis Strauss, believed that the country's margin of safety now required it to rush to develop a hydrogen bomb that would be a thousand times more powerful than the atomic bomb.

A debate erupted in the government between advocates and opponents of a building program. Those in favor, supported by physicists Edward Teller and Ernest Lawrence and MIT president Karl T. Compton, believed that the United States had no alternative but to go ahead. The Soviets, they said, who would see an H-bomb as an opportunity to eclipse the West in military power, were surely already planning to develop such a weapon. The only alternative the bomb's proponents saw was a preventive war against the Soviet Union, and nobody wanted that.

Harvard president James Conant, Oppenheimer, and Lilienthal lined up against trying to build a bomb that could annihilate millions of people in a matter of minutes. "It is not a weapon which can be used exclusively for the destruction of material installations of military or semi-military purposes," Oppenheimer explained. "Its use therefore carries much further than the atomic bomb itself the policy of exterminating civilian populations. . . . A super bomb might become a weapon of genocide." These opponents hoped that the Soviets could be approached about an agreement of mutual restraint. The possibility that the Soviets would go ahead even if the United States didn't was not absent from the discussion. The anti–H-bomb advocates believed that America's arsenal of atom bombs was a sufficient deterrent that Moscow would never consider a thermonuclear attack on the United States.

In November 1949, when the AEC voted 3 to 2 against building an H-bomb, supporters began a drumbeat of complaint that persuaded Truman to ask a three-member committee made up of Lilienthal, Acheson, and Secretary of Defense Louis Johnson to review the matter and give him a recommendation by January. With the question of whether to develop the "super" becoming a matter of public debate, the Joint Chiefs of Staff and conservative senators stirred public fears with warnings that not to go ahead would be irresponsible. "It's either we make it or we wait until the Russians drop one on us without warning," the navy's representative on the Joint Chiefs said.

The committee met only twice during its two months of deliberations. Bitter exchanges between Lilienthal and Johnson on these occasions made additional discussion pointless. Although Acheson held a more middle-ground position, he concluded that Truman had no choice but to approve a development program.

Kennan tried to convince Acheson otherwise. In a seventy-nine-page memorandum entitled "The International Control of Atomic Energy," he argued that the United States should set an example by restraining its hand and declare itself "prepared to go very far, to show considerable confidence in others, and to accept certain risk for ourselves" in hopes of persuading the Russians to avoid an arms race with no foreseeable limits in dangers and costs. Kennan considered this advice the most important he ever provided as a public official

In response, Acheson declared, "How can you persuade a paranoid adversary to 'disarm by example'?" Acheson urged Kennan to leave the government, telling him, "If that was his view he ought to resign from the Foreign Service and go out and preach his Quaker gospel but not push it within the department. He had no right being in the Service if he was not willing to face the questions as an issue to be decided in the interests of the American people under a sense of responsibility."

But was it really "the [best] interests of the American people" that Acheson and H-bomb advocates represented? Political considerations muted Acheson's doubts about the wisdom of building the bomb. By the end of January, when Truman received the committee's two-to-one report in favor of a development program, the political climate in the country made it impossible for him to disagree, or so Acheson and Johnson told him. "The American people simply would not tolerate a policy of delaying nuclear research in so vital a matter," they advised. "We must protect the President," Johnson told Lilienthal, meaning that Truman would be politically ruined if he decided against the bomb. The recommendation might have been the best political advice for the president and the Democratic Party, but was it the best advice for the nation?

Truman shared the view that the country's political mood left him no alternative but to see if a hydrogen bomb was possible. When the advisory committee presented the report to him on January 31, he asked, "Can the Russians do it?" The predictable yes from all three committee members moved Truman to say, "In that case, we have no choice. We'll go ahead." Lilienthal complained to his diary that it had taken all of seven minutes for the president to reach this monumental decision. It was a foregone conclusion, however, what Truman would do, as was made clear by a radio address he gave that evening to announce the plan to explore the "feasibility of a thermonuclear weapon."

While politics certainly played a part in Truman's decision (he would not let the Republicans outflank him on a crucial national security issue), he genuinely believed that the country's future safety depended on staying ahead of the Soviet Union in nuclear weapons. Since the United States and its European allies could not match Moscow's ground forces, it seemed essential to maintain an edge over them in air power and weapons that could be delivered from bombers stationed in Europe and Asia.

Yet in committing the United States to the development of H-bombs in 1950, Truman, Acheson, and the great majority of Americans misread what would best serve the national and international well-being. The nuclear arms race between the United States and the Soviet Union over the next forty years and the acquisition of these weapons of mass destruction by at least seven other nations—Britain, France, Russia, China, Israel, India, and Pakistan—with two more, North Korea and Iran, developing them, unquestionably made the world more dangerous. A war between any of the nuclear powers promised to not only decimate their populations and economies but also inflict unprecedented misery on the rest of the world. The concern in the first years of the twenty-first century that terrorists might acquire the wherewithal to smuggle a hydrogen bomb into the United States and detonate it in a heavily populated city adds to current doubts about the wisdom of having been the first to build such a weapon of mass destruction.

Was there an alternative to the nuclear arms race? Possibly. If the United States had proposed a summit meeting between Truman and

Stalin in a middle ground like, say, Austria, the president could have candidly explained America's reluctance to build weapons of such destructive power and invited the Soviets to join him in a shared effort to ban their development and deployment. Any summit had to be outside of the Soviet Union, lest it evoke memories of Britain's Neville Chamberlain and France's Edouard Daladier going to Munich to appease Hitler.

It is certainly true, as Acheson said, that Stalin was the paranoid head of a paranoid government, but at the same time, he feared the prospect of another war that could inflict even greater damage on his country than had Hitler. A chance to avoid investing in a thermonuclear program so much wealth and energy that could instead be used to increase the painfully low standard of living that the world war and the system of state economic control had inflicted on Russia might have been enough to draw Stalin into an arms limitation commitment.

But even if a Soviet promise to hold their hand proved false, their testing of an H-bomb would have been immediately detected, and could have triggered initial warnings. America's greater capacity to use its atomic arsenal against Soviet targets would make any suggestion of an attack on America or its allies an act of folly that would cost Russia millions of lives and the end of their Communist experiment. Nothing would then preclude the United States from a thermonuclear building program of its own.

Kennan certainly seemed to have it right when he said that war for Stalin "was not just a glorified sporting event, with no aim other than military victory; he had no interest in slaughtering people indiscriminately, just for the sake of slaughtering them; he pursued well-conceived, finite purposes related to his own security and ambitions. The nuclear weapon could destroy people; it could not occupy territory, police it, or organize it politically. He sanctioned its development, yes—because others were doing so, because he did not want to be without it, because he was well aware of the importance of the shadows it could cast over international events by the mere fact of its inclusion in a country's overt national arsenal." But he had no intention of using such a lethal weapon and inviting the kind of devastation on his country it was certain to bring.

American political and military chiefs, however, could not accept the assumption that the Soviets saw their military might as a deterrent to a Western attack rather than as a preparation for an assault on those they saw as eager to bring them down. In American eyes, the Soviet Union was simply an "Evil Empire," as Ronald Reagan would later describe it, which would strike at the first sign of weakness. Only the strongest possible United States would be able to survive the Communist challenge.

The argument for all-out mobilization just short of war against the Soviet threat expressed itself in National Security Council Report 68 (NSC-68), *United States Objectives and Programs for National Security,* a document largely prepared by the State Department's Policy Planning staff, which upon Kennan's retirement was headed by Paul Nitze, and presented to the president in April 1950. A wealthy forty-three-year-old Harvard-educated Wall Street banker who had served in a variety of defense and economic planning posts during and after World War II, including as a principal author and advocate of the Marshall Plan, Nitze had been at the forefront of those arguing for a firm U.S. stance against postwar Soviet expansion.

The Soviet acquisition of the atomic bomb had confirmed Nitze's conviction that nothing short of an all-out American military buildup could assure the future security of the United States. As NSC-68 explained, the Soviet Union was an adversary with "a new fanatic faith, antithetical to our own." Its objective was nothing less than "absolute authority over the rest of the world." Nitze believed that the "Kremlin's design for world domination" depended on "the ultimate elimination of any effective opposition." U.S. military planners needed to assume that the Soviets hoped to obtain "a sufficient atomic capability to make a surprise attack on us . . . swiftly and with stealth."

Nitze's description more accurately described the plans of a Hitler and the Nazis than a Stalin and the Communists. And someone as high in U.S. national councils as Acheson saw Nitze's warnings as hyperbolic. But "the purpose of NSC-68," he said, "was to so bludgeon the mass mind of 'top government' that not only could the President make a decision but that the decision could be carried out." In short, Nitze was calling for at least a threefold expansion of defense expenditures, which Congress and Defense Secretary Johnson and even Truman would resist. The path to "sufficient" defense, as those most on edge about Moscow's threat saw it, was through overheated rhetoric about America's potential demise at the hands of a nuclear-armed Soviet Union. Moreover, it was not enough to think of containing Soviet power; it must be countered in ways that would eventually sap its strength and bring an end to its rule in Eastern Europe and Russia.

Acheson, Nitze, and others in the government were not primitives like McCarthy and Wherry and Butler, whose parochialism and impulsive response to the Communist threat drew them into an uncritical militancy. Truman's national security advisers were well educated, sophisticated, and knowledgeable about the world. But they were held in thrall by the experience of World War II and the failed appeasement policies that gave the Nazis and the Japanese license to run wild in Europe and Asia—at least until they confronted superior force. Any thoughts of reaching out to Stalin echoed the failures of British and French actions and America's shortsighted isolationism of the 1930s.

History had taught Truman and his counselors that measured toughness was the only language that a dictator understood, and the best means by which the United States and its allies could avoid not only defeat but the need to fight another war. Increasing America's atomic arsenal, building hydrogen bombs, and expanding the country's military might as proposed in NSC-68 were prescriptions that might have worked well against Berlin and Tokyo, but the Soviet Union and the weapons of mass destruction available by 1950 required other policies than the ones that could have been effective at an earlier time.

The military buildup proposed in 1950 rested on a misreading of history. This is not to suggest that Hitler and Stalin had nothing in common; they shared an affinity for power and a ruthless disregard for the humanity of anyone opposing them. But Stalin had a much more realistic grasp of his and Russia's limited capacity to defeat external enemies, as his back-down on Berlin had demonstrated. It was no small distinction, and one Stalin's Western adversaries would have done well to take more fully into account in responding to his reach for global dominance. A firm approach to the Soviets certainly made good sense, especially against the backdrop of Joe McCarthy's popular appeal for a no-holds-barred fight against communism at home and abroad. It was one thing, however, to describe a "completely irreconcilable moral conflict" with Moscow—and even to call upon the Soviets to free their East European satellites and end their campaign of subverting other democratically elected governments, as Acheson did in a series of speeches in the spring of 1950—and entirely another to call for the H-bomb and a massive expansion of military might.

LIMITED WAR

War always finds a way.
—Bertolt Brecht, 1939

B y the middle of 1950, East-West tensions in Europe had sta-
bilized. Soviet control of Eastern Europe, including an East
German Communist state, balanced by an American-led alliance of
Western Europe, with a democratic West Germany contributing to
an economic revival, seemed like fixtures for the foreseeable future.
The Communist coup in Czechoslovakia and the Berlin blockade
had made fear of Soviet aggression a constant concern in the West.
But Stalin's retreat on Berlin and the creation of NATO had generated considerable confidence that the continent might be facing a
lengthy Cold War standoff rather than a violent showdown.

Conditions in Asia were in greater flux. Mao's Communists had
won control of mainland China, but Chiang's Nationalists, who
had taken refuge on Taiwan, seemed to be facing an uncertain future.
Would Mao's forces try to seize the island and eliminate Chiang once
and for all as a rival for power? And though the Truman administration seemed little inclined to interfere should Mao's armies assault
the Nationalists on their island retreat, speculation abounded that
Washington could not let its Chinese ally suffer a final defeat.

Similarly, Japan was showing signs of recovery from the devastation of the wartime bombing and collapse. Moreover, the American
occupation was turning its arch Asian rival into a friend, and a peace

treaty that would restore a measure of Japanese autonomy was under discussion. Nevertheless, no one was ready to describe Tokyo as a reliable ally in the emerging Asian cold war or to suggest that Japan should be rearmed as a counter to a Communist China. Memories of Japanese aggression and atrocities were too fresh to reestablish Tokyo as a dominant Asian power.

In South Korea, where the United States had ended its military presence by 1950 and turned the caretaker's role over to the United Nations, tensions between the Soviet-sponsored Communist regime in the North and Syngman Rhee's pro-American government in the South threatened to erupt into a civil war. Washington, however, hoped that U.S.-trained and -equipped Republic of Korea forces, joined to the possible intervention of a UN army, would be enough to deter Kim Il Sung's government in Pyongyang from unleashing its Soviet-trained forces against the South.

Among the last things American planners in Washington antici-pated was a war involving a large commitment of U.S. troops and matériel to a conflict in Korea. In the spring of 1947, when Un-dersecretary of State Robert Lovett had consulted members of the foreign policy establishment at the Council on Foreign Relations in New York, they had urged initiatives to forestall Soviet adventurism almost everywhere around the world, except possibly in Korea, which was sandwiched between the Soviet and Chinese Communist giants and would not be a priority in a global war.

To be sure, some American national security officials believed that a Korean Peninsula under Communist control would represent a threat to Japanese security and wished to discourage Communist convictions that America would passively accept the North's absorption of the South. But with so many demands on U.S. resources in Europe and Japan, Korea did not stand out as a likely field of combat for U.S. forces, especially after refusing to fight Mao's armies in China. To the White House, the ideal compromise was the mutual withdrawal of American and Soviet troops from the peninsula, simultaneous with

UN-supervised elections that could unite North and South Korea under a representative government.

Although both Moscow and Washington agreed to withdraw their troops, the Soviets would not support peninsula-wide elections that seemed certain to give the more populous pro-American South, where two-thirds of Koreans lived, control of its client in the North. Washington's alternative was an independent South Korea supported by U.S. aid that would remain a buffer for Japan against the North Korean and Chinese Communists. In addition, the emergence of a pro-Western South Korea could help quiet complaints in the United States that the White House was too passive in dealing with Communist aggression and needed to reverse the pattern of recent Soviet advances and U.S. retreats.

Despite the decision to support an independent Seoul, by 1950 Korea was largely lost in the daily catalogue of East-West tensions. When Dean Acheson spoke at the National Press Club in Washington on January 12 about U.S. national security concerns in Asia, Korea was notable for its absence. In line with the Joint Chiefs and MacArthur in Tokyo, Acheson omitted South Korea from his description of a "defensive perimeter" running from the Aleutian Islands through Japan, Okinawa, and the Philippines. Congress matched White House reluctance to make South Korea a priority in the emerging Asian cold war by voting only limited financial support.

The principal object of Acheson's speech was to discourage continuing talk of U.S. intervention on the mainland to oust Mao's government, calling it "the folly of ill-conceived adventures on our part" and predicting that any such action would "deflect from the Russians to ourselves the righteous anger, and the wrath, and the hatred of the Chinese which must develop. It would be folly to deflect it to ourselves."

The possibility of an assault on South Korea by Pyongyang wasn't entirely missing from discussions about the Communist threat. At the close of Acheson's speech, a reporter asked how it would be possible to defend the South against an attack by the North. In response,

Acheson referred the journalist to the Pentagon's assumption that Seoul could hold its own against the Communists and that the United Nations, which had taken responsibility for South Korea's elections, would meet its commitment to repel aggression, as its Charter had intended. Nothing was said about Moscow's veto power in the Security Council, where a vote would need to precede any UN military action.

That neither Acheson nor anyone else made this a part of the calculations about Korea is understandable. The disinclination even to think about a U.S. military role in a conflict on the peninsula was matched by an equal reluctance to involve ourselves in the political war of words between North and South or the intrapolitical clashes swirling around Rhee's coalition government. Given the multiple political worries facing the Truman administration—building the European alliance, combating the domestic outcry over the "loss" of China, determining how to meet pressures from Chiang and the China lobby should Mao's forces move against Taiwan—Korea was a side show that commanded minimal attention.

Perceptions in North Korea, Moscow, and Peking about conditions in the South and American detachment from developments on the peninsula encouraged the Communists to think that if Kim Il Sung's forces crossed the parallel, it would not provoke a U.S. military response and might well generate an outpouring of support from dissidents being suppressed by Rhee.

By June 1950, anyone focusing closely on events of the previous two years—or, for that matter, since 1945—should not have been surprised that a civil war was in the offing. The governments in both the North and the South were notable for their militant rhetoric about unifying all Korea under their respective regimes.

In the North, Kim Il Sung was a thirty-six-year-old firebrand. In 1929, as a seventeen-year-old student in Manchuria, where he and his family had moved to escape the oppressive Japanese occupation of Korea, he had joined the Communist Party. Between 1930 and 1945, he moved back and forth between China and Russia and gained distinction among Communists in both countries as a commander of Korean troops fighting the Japanese. His devotion to independence for Korea from Tokyo's control and to revolutionary Marxist doctrines made him an attractive candidate for head of a provisional government in Pyongyang, where he reflected Moscow's determination to impose a Communist government on all of Korea.

In 1948, after the Soviets rejected calls for UN-supervised elections as a prelude to Korean unification, Moscow rewarded Kim's loyalty by making him North Korea's prime minister. It was the culmination of a personal campaign to make himself the ultimate ruler of all Korea, if possible, and at a minimum, the all-powerful leader of a North Korean state.

He succeeded beyond anything Stalin and Mao—two of the most storied autocrats of the twentieth century—achieved as authoritarian heads of their parties and countries. Kim elevated himself to a figure of transcendent importance in North Korea. Over forty-six years he created a cult of personality that seems comparable only to a religious movement whose devoted worshipers give unquestioned loyalty to their leader. Monuments to the "Eternal President," as the country's constitution described Kim, made him a constant presence in every city and hamlet. A sixty-six-foot bronze statue occupies a prominent place in Pyongyang, to which his adoring countrymen could come to worship their Great Leader.

Like other authoritarian figures of his generation—Hitler, Stalin, and Mao—Kim was a man of contradictions. Despite the murderous impulses that Hitler visited on his millions of victims, he could show kindness to children and displayed great affection for his dogs. According to Averell Harriman, one of the westerners who saw Stalin up close most often and knew him best, he was a difficult character to pigeonhole: "It is hard for me to reconcile the courtesy and consideration that he showed me personally with the ghastly cruelty of his wholesale liquidations. Others, who did not know him personally, see only the tyrant in Stalin. I saw the other side as well—his high intelligence, that fantastic grasp of detail, his shrewdness and his surprising human sensitivity."

Kim could also show people a kindly side. One South Korean who repeatedly visited Pyongyang as Kim's guest had no illusions about his ruthless treatment of his countrymen. "There was no such thing as a conversation with Kim Il Sung," he said. "If he spoke to a North Korean, that person stood up, in effect at attention, to receive instructions or orders." By contrast, Kim showed his guest special regard, calling him every day to ask about his well-being and personal comfort. New York congressman Stephen J. Solarz, the first elected American official to meet with Kim in 1980, described him as avuncular, a burly, heavyset man eager to convince a U.S. official that he was no ogre but an approachable statesman principally concerned with the happiness and welfare of his people.

From the moment the Soviets installed him as North Korea's prime minister in 1948, Kim built a military force that would allow him to defend against a possible invasion from the South and prepare for a move across the thirty-eighth parallel to bring all of Korea under his control. Kim's concern that South Korean forces might attack his country before he attacked them was not simply the speculations of a paranoid mind. From the start of his election as South Korea's president in 1948, Syngman Rhee openly favored a "march north" to rid the peninsula of Communist influence and achieve a lifelong dream of governing a single Korean nation.

Like Kim, Rhee had spent most of his life before 1945 in exile. Born in 1875, Rhee was already seventy when he returned to his homeland. Given his age, he had a sense of urgency about unifying Korea. He also felt that the hardships he had endured as a nationalist forced to live abroad entitled him to become the first president of a modern Korean state. As a young man, between 1897 and 1904, he had spent seven years in prison for opposing Japanese control of his country. Upon his release, he went to the United States, where he studied at George Washington University in Washington, D.C., Harvard, and Princeton, earning a PhD in international law at the latter institution. Rhee returned to Korea for three years between 1910 and 1913, before his renewed political opposition to Japanese control of his homeland forced him to flee again to the United States, where he settled in Hawaii as the principal of a Korean school.

In 1919 Rhee was elected president of a provisional Korean government formed by pro-independence factions based in Shanghai. Unable to assert himself effectively against the divisive groups that made up the coalition, however, he was ousted from the presidency in 1925 amid charges of abuse of power by opponents who saw him as too dictatorial—a prelude to what occurred when he became South Korea's first president in 1948. The same divisive factionalism would plague the South after 1945, when 205 groups asked for recognition as political parties. As one member of the U.S. occupying force would jest, "Every time two Koreans sit down to eat they form a new political party."

A Rhee campaign to remove all leftists from political influence in Seoul, as well as his unconstitutional actions, including arbitrary arrests, detentions, and torture of opponents, provoked divisions and tension across South Korea, spawning an armed rebellion and encouraging Kim to believe that should his armies cross the parallel, they would be welcomed as a genuine unifying force.

It was the Truman administration's misfortune to have two such autocratic and self-righteous figures vying for power in Korea. Each man's interest in unifying the country under his exclusive control exceeded any genuine regard for the well-being of the Korean people. If Kim and Rhee had to shed blood and repress dissent by any and all means, they considered this a small price to pay for fulfilling their grandiose dreams of becoming the founder of a modern Korean nation. With such leaders, the Korean people didn't need foreign occupiers who treated them badly.

The clash of wills between Kim and Rhee was a prelude of sorts for what the United States would have to deal with later in negotiations to end the war between South and North Vietnam. As Kissinger privately told a reporter in 1972 about the representatives of the two countries, "when you meet with two groups of Vietnamese in the same day, you might as well run an insane asylum." He called them "tawdry, filthy shits" who "make the Russians look good." Nguyen Van Thieu, the president of South Vietnam, was "an insane son-of-a-bitch," and the North Vietnamese were a bunch of "bastards" who "have been screwing us."

The Koreans and the Vietnamese shared an aversion to representative government; kings and despots were the traditional rulers of the peasant farmers who peopled their countries. Democracy was an exotic import the Americans, speaking from their own experience, hoped both Asian cultures would see fit to embrace. The solution to political problems this latest foreign occupier of Korea asked them to accept was reasoned discussion of their differences. But in 1950 neither Kim nor Rhee saw any solution to their opposing national visions except force of arms. Although their disagreements would precipitate a war, they shared an affinity for repression and control that made them more alike than either would have cared to admit.

The outbreak of the Korean conflict on June 25, 1950, was the result of an extraordinary combination of events in at least five countries: North and South Korea, the Soviet Union, China, and the United States. Each played a significant part in moving the divided Koreans toward bloodshed.

In the South, in 1949, Rhee's government had initiated a series of attacks on North Korean forces stationed along the thirty-eighth parallel. Because his forces were insufficient in numbers and equipment to stage an effective advance north, Rhee provoked the fighting as a way to command Washington's attention and stimulate military and financial aid the Americans were reluctant to provide. The clashes with the Communists also gave Rhee an excuse to crack down on political opponents on the left and stimulate greater unity

of support for his government, which was threatened by destabilizing factionalism.

Conditions in the South had encouraged Kim to believe that Rhee's
republic was too divided to resist an invasion and absorption into
his Communist regime. Because Rhee was making progress in suppressing insurgents, who might overturn his government in response
to an invasion, and was developing a relationship with Japan that
could strengthen South Korea's economy, Kim was eager to strike as
quickly as possible.

In 1949 Kim pressed Stalin for permission to invade the South.
But the Soviet dictator equivocated, urging Kim instead to support
armed insurgents who might topple Rhee's government without an
invasion. At the beginning of 1950, however, with the acquisition
of the A-bomb, Mao's victory in China, the emerging alliance with
Peking, and the conviction that Washington would shortly reach a
peace agreement with Tokyo that would station U.S. forces in Japan
indefinitely and threaten Moscow's Far East possessions, Stalin's opposition had softened. An East-West stalemate in Europe had shifted
his focus to Asia, where opportunities for Communist gains seemed
greater. Specifically, believing that the United States would stand aside,
as it had in China, and as Acheson's description of a northeast Asian
defense perimeter seemed to confirm, Stalin viewed South Korea as
vulnerable to an attack from the North. He also saw potential benefits from a U.S. intervention in a Korean civil war: it might slow a
military buildup in Europe and limit the West's capacity to threaten
the Soviet Union's dominance in Eastern Europe.

Yet Stalin had qualified his approval of an attack by instructing Kim to seek Mao's support before he acted. The Chinese might
oppose a war on the peninsula out of concern that it could lead to
U.S. intervention, North Korean defeat, and jeopardy to Mao's control of the mainland—developments that would reverse Moscow's
recent advances in Asia.

But the Chinese did not resist Kim's war plans. Like Kim and

Stalin, Mao doubted that the Americans would fight to prevent North Korea's unification of the peninsula. When chairman of the U.S. Senate Foreign Relations Committee Tom Connally, a Democrat allied with Truman, publicly acknowledged in May 1950 that the United States would probably be unable to prevent a Communist takeover in Seoul, Acheson, reiterating the administration's Korean policy, rejected suggestions that the United States would intervene to prevent such an outcome, reinforcing Communist convictions that South Korea would be abandoned by its sponsor.

Although the Chinese were reluctant to see a war erupt in Korea before they had ousted Chiang from Taiwan, they could not deny Kim's request for moral and material backing and a commitment to join the conflict should U.S. forces threaten Pyongyang with defeat. Saying no would have made the Chinese seem less committed to the fight against international capitalism and less militant in revolutionary zeal than the USSR, with which they already had a keen, if muted, rivalry. Moreover, a sense of obligation to North Korea's Communists, who had fought in Mao's armies against Chiang, made it difficult for Peking to discourage Kim from fighting his own civil war.

In the final analysis, the war was the result of poor leadership and misjudgments by the heads of government in Pyongyang, Moscow, Peking, Seoul, and Washington, none of whose calculations proved prescient. If Stalin, Mao, and Kim had had a better understanding of the political pressures on the Truman administration, they would have assessed the likelihood of U.S. intervention in the fighting more realistically. If Rhee and U.S. military planners had recognized just how weak Rhee's armed forces were, and if Truman and Acheson had anticipated the irresistible pressure to intervene in the fighting, they would have promised support for Seoul against any attack and warned North Korea not to test America's resolve.

American interest in preventing small or large wars should have made Washington more active in dissuading the Koreans, North and South, from an all-out military conflict. This was essential because the two Koreas, China, and the Soviet Union were never as put off by the prospect of a civil war as Washington.

The autocrats in those countries operated with a casualness about potential war costs that set them apart from the Truman administration and Americans as a whole. Kim, Rhee, and Mao rationalized their actions as serving their countrymen, and when these actions resulted in painful losses, they lauded the sacrifice, as essential to the national well-being. Stalin could feel less troubled about a Korean outbreak than Peking, Pyongyang, or Seoul, since Soviet troops were not fighting, and the deaths of Koreans, Chinese, and Americans did not trouble his sleep. Having shed so much Soviet blood by mistakenly aligning himself with Hitler in 1939, and by purging ethnic and political opponents of his rule, he was indifferent to the death of others in what he saw as the service of his country and personal power. As the North Koreans began to pay a heavy price for the war, Stalin said that they "lose nothing, except for their men."

The news of Kim's invasion of the South shocked the White House—less because a civil war on the peninsula had seemed so unlikely than because a South Korea forcefully brought under Communist control would undermine America's international position and public confidence at home.

In the four days after the North Korean attack began in the early morning of June 25, Rhee's armies suffered a series of defeats. In less than forty-eight hours, Kim's forces were moving on Seoul, and General MacArthur, America's principal military chief in the Far East, began predicting South Korea's collapse. Despite support by U.S. air and naval units of the hard-pressed Republic of Korea (ROK) armies, North Korean troops seemed poised to overrun the peninsula. In response, on June 30, President Truman ordered U.S. ground forces in Japan to enter the fighting and the U.S. Seventh Fleet to take up positions in the Taiwan Strait, where it would stand guard against any Chinese attempt to invade Taiwan. South Korea's possible fall compelled a dramatic shift in thinking about saving Chiang's Nationalists.

The outbreak of the fighting had unanticipated and unwelcome consequences for every nation the war touched—except for Chiang Kai-shek, for whom it meant a last-minute reprieve from a final defeat by the Communists.

A key element in Truman's decision to rescue South Korea was the conviction that North Korea's aggression was Soviet-inspired, and if unresisted would become a prelude to other attacks by Communist forces in Europe and Asia. The lesson of World War II was central to White House thinking: memories of how Munich in 1938 had created conditions leading to a Europe-wide war made Truman determined not to repeat Chamberlain's ill-fated appeasement. To the president, Acheson, and all their national security advisers, to allow South Korea to be overrun by Communist armies acting as surrogates for Moscow was tantamount to inviting the Soviets and Chinese to commit future acts of aggression. Indeed, the North Korean attack was seen in Washington as a renewed Russian drive for world conquest.

On the face of it, the assumption made little sense. A Soviet Union that lacked the wherewithal to strike the United States with atomic bombs—or any weapons at all—was hardly about to unleash an attack on Western Europe that could bring a devastating response from U.S. air forces with nuclear armaments. The Truman administration should have understood that Stalin, however much he matched Hitler in his ruthlessness toward dissenters at home and in satellite countries, was not about to repeat the Nazi mistake of starting a war he might lose.

While the White House genuinely believed that intervention in Korea was essential to prevent a third world war, domestic politics also played a part in Truman's decision, though he refused to acknowledge it. On the day after the fighting began, during a discussion at Blair House, where Truman convened a meeting of his advisers, Undersecretary of State James Webb said, "I'd like to talk about the political aspects of the situation." Truman decisively vetoed the request: "We're not going to talk about politics. I'll handle the political affairs."

In the spring of 1950, Communist advances in the Cold War had dropped the president's approval rating to 37 percent, with 44 percent disapproving of his performance. National eagerness for someone with stronger credentials as a military leader gave General Dwight Eisenhower a 60 to 31 percent advantage over Truman in a poll about a 1952 presidential contest.

Truman was under the gun to satisfy public eagerness for a firm stand against North Korea's aggression. Once the president had deployed troops to fight in Korea, 65 percent surveyed said it was the right decision, even though 57 percent of the country thought it meant we were already in World War III. The bad news for the White House was that 50 percent of the country thought that the nation was poorly prepared to fight such a war, which, by a three-to-one margin, the public blamed more on the Democrats than the Republicans.

In refusing to acknowledge that domestic politics had contributed to his Korean decision, Truman was reluctant to concede that he was in any way countering right-wing complaints about "losing" China and "allowing" Soviet spies to steal atomic secrets. Yet Truman understood that another setback in the Cold War could decisively cripple his capacity to govern eighteen months into his four-year term. To be sure, Truman and Acheson believed it essential to stand up to aggression if they were to avert a world war. And in fact, it made a great deal of sense to counter Kim's attack and block Mao from invading Taiwan if the United States were to sustain a balance of power in the Far East and convince European allies that it would defend them against aggression. As important, if the United States was to have an effective governing authority during the remaining two and a half years of Truman's presidency, it was essential to assuage the country's anxiety about the Communist threat by meeting it head-on in Korea and the Taiwan Strait.

However popular the administration's response to North Korea's

aggression, this did not excuse the Truman-Acheson failure to forestall Pyongyang's attack by making clear that South Korea would
not be another Czechoslovakia forced into the Communist sphere.
America's inattentiveness to developments on the Korean Peninsula
had given license to the Communists to attack. And while no one
should absolve the Communists of prime responsibility for the fighting, Washington's overt passivity toward Korea before June 1950 contributed to the conditions that led to war.

Moreover, however wise the determination to halt North Korea's
onslaught might have been, the means by which the Truman administration acted is open to question. To downplay the belief that the
world was on the verge of a worldwide conflict between the United
States and the Soviet Union, Truman sensibly described America's
military intervention as a "police action" under the auspices of the
United Nations. A resolution presented to the UN Security Council on June 27 to defend South Korea from Pyongyang's aggression
passed by a vote of seven to one. The Soviet delegation, which had
been boycotting Security Council meetings as a protest against the
UN's refusal to replace Chiang's representative with Mao's, was not
present to exercise its veto.

The Soviet absence was not the result of an oversight on Stalin's part.
He was content to have the UN, led by American forces, take up the
fight against Kim's troops. As Stalin told Klement Gottwald, Czechoslovakia's Communist president, he did not object to the UN action: a
United States "entangled in the military intervention in Korea" would
"squander its military prestige and moral authority." He also believed
that U.S. involvement in Korea would reduce the likelihood of an
American attack against Soviet armies in Germany. A long, drawn-out
conflict that eventually pitted China against the United States would
further "distract the United States from Europe to the Far East. And
the third world war will be postponed for the indefinite term, and this
would give the time necessary to consolidate socialism in Europe." It
also gave the Soviets time to develop a hydrogen bomb, now that their

spy Klaus Fuchs, who the Soviets playfully called Santa Klaus, had
secretly given them the American design Edward Teller had developed
in 1946.

Stalin neglected to say that a Korean civil war, which threatened
to become a wider conflict, was also a valuable tool for suppressing
his domestic opponents—the men and women in his inner circle he
saw as angling to replace him and the ethnics he continued to distrust as intent on subverting his rule. He could more easily execute
them or send them to the gulags without exciting protest if external
dangers continued to make him the country's indispensable leader, as
in World War II. It was a confirmation of James Madison's prophetic
observation that it is a "universal truth that the loss of liberty at home
is to be charged to provisions against danger, real or pretended, from
abroad."

The Korean conflict had long-term domestic consequences for
the United States as well. Truman's decision to describe the war as
a "police action" conducted under binding treaty obligations to the
United Nations was a wise means of averting a greater sense of crisis
at home and abroad. To have asked Congress for a declaration of war
against North Korea could have raised questions about China's obligations to Pyongyang. And if China had chosen to enter the conflict
because of treaty commitments to North Korea, it could in turn have
triggered discussion of mutual Sino-Soviet defense pledges under the
Peking-Moscow pact of January 1950. In short, making American
intervention other than an outright act of war averted the sort of crisis
that had preceded the outbreak of World War I, when each of the
European powers mobilized their armies in response to one another
and then found it impossible to step back from an all-out war.

But Truman's commitment of U.S. forces to fight in Korea without congressional authorization set a precedent for the unilateral
presidential decisions Lyndon Johnson, Richard Nixon, and George
W. Bush made to fight in Vietnam, Cambodia, and Iraq, respec-
tively, in 1964, 1970, and 2003. It is true that the State Department

gave Truman a memo listing eighty-seven instances in which earlier presidents had sent troops into combat without congressional authorization. It is also true that the Congress would pass resolutions supporting military actions in Vietnam in 1964 and Iraq in 1991 and 2003. But the pre-1950 military interventions cited by the State Department were typically limited forays to protect and remove U.S. citizens from war zones. And the acts of congressional approval were essentially rubber stamps for prior presidential commitments.

At a minimum, as Truman ordered U.S. forces into combat, he could have asked Congress for a supporting resolution that was not a declaration of war but an acknowledgement that the war-making authority in the Constitution remained with the legislature. It would not have precluded Johnson, Nixon, and George W. Bush from using their authority as commanders in chief to fight in Vietnam, Cambodia, and Iraq, but it might have compelled them to have involved the Congress more fully in the decisions. A vigorous debate on the wisdom of military action might have reduced the human, financial, and political costs to the country and the presidents of these largely unilateral commitments to fight.

Because Congress never speaks with one voice, it is vulnerable to the "imperial presidency" in times of crisis. Nevertheless, the legislature's failure in 1950 to assert itself more forcefully against the executive's preemption of its war-making power was an invitation to future presidents to fight wars without the sort of democratic debate the founders of the republic considered essential to the long-term national well-being. The misadventures we associate with the Korean, Vietnam, Cambodian, and Iraq conflicts are, or should be, cautionary tales about the need to return to more robust debates in and between the two branches of government responsible for decisions to fight.

U.S. involvement in the Korean fighting increased national militancy. A series of Gallup polls during the summer and fall of 1950 revealed a nation committed to battling and defeating Communism with every tool at its command: 61 percent favored using atomic bombs in another world war, ostensibly against the Soviet Union; 68 percent said it was more important to "stop Russian expansion" than "keep out of war"; 79 percent wanted the United States to fight if Russian troops attacked West Germany; 50 percent endorsed the idea of reorganizing the UN without Russia and all Communist-dominated countries; and 64 percent wanted United Nations forces not only to drive North Korean troops out of South Korea but also to cross the thirty-eighth Parallel into North Korea, where the Communists should be forced to surrender.

In a chilling demonstration of intolerance or the "tyranny of the majority," as Tocqueville called it, only 1 percent of Americans believed that members of the U.S. Communist Party should remain free. Forty percent wished to see them interned; 28 percent thought they should be exiled, with about half this number suggesting they be sent to the Soviet Union; while 13 percent were ready to have them shot or hanged.

With the onset of the Korean War, the goals described in NSC-68, which was first put before Truman in April 1950, suddenly became more urgent. Expanding the atomic arsenal, building the hydrogen bomb, establishing larger and more powerful armed forces, and developing covert operations and psychological warfare to destabilize and overturn Soviet-backed regimes in Eastern Europe and undermine communism in Russia, China, and the Third World became national security priorities. The increased costs of implementing the directive was calculated at more than three times the $14 billion the president had included in his budget for fiscal 1951 or an increase on defense spending over five years from 5 to 20 percent of gross national product (GNP). Acheson recalled that "it is doubtful whether anything like what happened over the next few years could have been done had not the Russians been stupid enough to have instigated the attack against South Korea and opened the 'hate America' campaign."

The Korean attack stimulated not only a wide-ranging defense buildup but more immediately a commitment of the bulk of America's available ground forces, a quarter of a million troops, to fight on the peninsula. The success of the North Korean armies, which by the end of August had driven hard-pressed ROK troops and American infantry units into a defensive perimeter around Pusan, South Korea's southernmost port, made Pyongyang's defeat of the South even more likely.

MacArthur, who had added to his luster as a military chief in World War II by his effective command of America's occupation forces in Japan, was charged with reversing ROK-U.S. battlefield fortunes. Truman had his doubts about MacArthur, who at seventy may have been too old for such a demanding assignment. Truman also recalled MacArthur's retreat to Australia from the Philippines in 1942, which the president saw as an inappropriate surrender of his command and a reason to question his reputation as a great field general. Privately, Truman berated him as a "supreme egoist who regarded himself as a god," calling him a "dictator in Japan."

Truman had considered recalling MacArthur, whose independence from Washington had irked him, but the likely political outcry from Republicans, who shared MacArthur's outspoken determination to save the world from communism, impressed Truman as too high a political price to pay. He foresaw "a tremendous reaction in the country where he [MacArthur] had been built up to heroic stature." Moreover, his standing as the architect of victory in the Pacific made it difficult for the president to bypass him as the commander of U.S. and UN forces in Korea.

In August 1950, after Truman had made him field commander in Korea, MacArthur publicly challenged the administration's China policy as too weak and lauded Chiang as an essential U.S. ally in the struggle for Asia, suggesting that his return to the mainland should be a high priority. Fearful that MacArthur's endorsement of Chiang might be seen in Peking as a statement of official policy and could provoke Chinese involvement in Korea, Truman rebuked MacArthur for creating false impressions that the United States intended

to help Chiang overturn Mao's government. The president's repri-
mand brought an apology from MacArthur that muted their differences and persuaded Truman not to force the general's retirement for
insubordination. Besides, with the war going so badly, MacArthur
seemed like the country's best hope for turning defeat into victory.
Recalling him risked a political firestorm Truman remained unprepared to accept.

In September, MacArthur rewarded the faith in his leadership
by beating back the North Korean offensive. At the beginning of
the month, after his forces had halted the Communist advance at
Pusan and built a defensive perimeter that the North Koreans seemed
unable to breach, MacArthur's troops found themselves in a stalemate reminiscent of the trench warfare that had dragged on for so
long in World War I.

MacArthur had no intention, however, of settling for a draw that
would leave Pyongyang in control of most of South Korea. To break
the impasse, he planned a daring offensive behind North Korean lines
at Inchon, a port city on the west coast of South Korea within easy distance of Seoul. Defying the difficulties of the tides and terrain, which
convinced the North Koreans that Inchon was an unlikely place for
an amphibious assault, MacArthur surprised the enemy when 70,000
marines and army troops came ashore on September 15. In a matter
of days, they had routed some 30,000 to 40,000 defenders at a cost
to American forces of "536 dead, 2,550 wounded, and 65 missing."
Caught between MacArthur's troops to the south around Pusan and
to their rear at Inchon, the North Koreans began a retreat that took
them back above the thirty-eighth parallel by the end of September.
Recapturing Seoul and clearing the South of Kim's armies fifteen
days after assaulting Inchon, MacArthur's armies suddenly seemed
invincible. The victory gave him renewed standing as a brilliant field
commander who was indispensable to the war effort.

Suddenly an invasion of North Korea, with the destruction of Kim's
regime and the incorporation of the North into the South under the

authority of the United Nations, seemed within reach. On September 11, the president approved a National Security Council directive instructing MacArthur to cross the thirty-eighth parallel—but only if neither Soviet nor Chinese forces had entered North Korea from Siberia or Manchuria or showed themselves prepared to intervene.

On September 27, as the Communists retreated, the Joint Chiefs gave MacArthur a green light to destroy what was left of Kim's armies, with the only limitations being that no U.S. planes were to violate Chinese or Soviet airspace, and only ROK troops were to approach the Yalu River, which formed the border between Korea and China. Two days later, George Marshall, as secretary of defense, with Truman's approval, cabled MacArthur, advising him "to feel unhampered tactically and strategically to proceed north of the thirty-eighth parallel." MacArthur saw the instruction as countering earlier limits on U.S. troop movements above the parallel. "Unless and until the enemy capitulates, I regard all Korea as open for our military operations," MacArthur replied. By October 7, when the UN General Assembly voted in favor of a U.S. resolution calling for "a unified, independent, democratic [Korean] government," ROK troops were already on the outskirts of North Korea's east-coast port of Wonsan.

Almost everything now encouraged Truman and his advisers to see invading North Korea to destroy Kim's armies and end his rule as a realizable goal. To leave the North under Communist control was considered a victory of sorts for Moscow. It would suggest that Kim's act of aggression, though not successful, nevertheless would go unpunished. Instead, elections that could unite the peninsula under a UN-sponsored democratic government would not only assure Korea's self-determination but also signal a reversal in the Cold War from defeat to advance.

Initially, American planners saw little evidence that either the Russians or the Chinese would join the fighting to prevent Kim's defeat. At the end of September, as UN forces cleared the South and ROK troops entered North Korea, Soviet officials at the UN went out of their way to be conciliatory by signaling an interest in peace talks to end the Korean fighting. Soviet apprehensions about a NATO buildup that would include German forces also seemed to make them less belligerent. In brief, no one saw signs that Moscow was intent on risking a war with the United States over Korea.

Chinese intentions seemed less predictable. While reports that Peking was moving troops to the Manchurian border could be read as preparation for saving North Korea's Communist government, other evidence indicated that the Chinese were not planning a major effort and might only follow a policy of "indirect intervention" or limited backing for Kim's forces. At least, that was what diplomats in China were reporting. By the beginning of October, however, the Chinese began issuing warnings that if American forces entered North Korea, they would be compelled to join the fighting. Reports now reached Washington of Chinese mechanized units already moving across the Yalu into Korea.

Between October 2 and 18, the Chinese debated the advantages and disadvantages of entering the war. At the same time they pressed Stalin, who was urging them to fight in defense of their national security and the Communist world revolution, to promise supplies and Soviet air support if they became a belligerent. On October 4 and 9, as they considered their options, the Chinese issued additional threats if MacArthur's American troops crossed the thirty-eighth parallel in force. By the ninth, however, U.S. forces were already across the Korean dividing line. Moreover, despite doubts that the Soviets were as interested in helping them in Korea as in distracting the Americans from a NATO buildup with a punishing war in Asia, the Chinese felt compelled to join the Korean fighting. They hoped not only to prevent an American military presence on their Manchurian border, save Kim's Communist regime, and inspire other Third World revolutionaries to continue their struggles against Western imperialism, but also to bolster a domestic campaign to suppress "reactionaries and reactionary activities."

By sending U.S. troops into North Korea, Truman understood that he might be risking a war with China, which could escalate into a wider conflict with the Soviet Union. Yet he and his advisers believed otherwise. True, an occupation of North Korea would bring American troops within hailing distance of China's Manchurian border. But since Washington had given every indication that it would not support Chiang's return to the mainland, Truman hoped that Peking would not see an American presence above the thirty-eighth parallel as a threat to its rule. He assumed that the Communist government, for all its revolutionary rhetoric, understood that the United States had a history of friendly dealings with China and that Russia was its more natural rival. Moreover, if the Chinese knew anything at all about American politics, they would understand that no current Washington administration could let another Communist act of aggression go unpunished. A Democratic, liberal Truman government had to take account of the conservative outcry against a president who could be seen as soft on communism.

While Truman's views on America's China policy and the constraints on his administration from domestic politics were realistic, his assumption that China's Communist leadership shared his outlook was wishful thinking. Understandably, Peking viewed the United States as unfriendly to a Communist victory in the civil war and to Communist governments everywhere. Consequently, a U.S. occupation of the Korean peninsula was likely to be seen as threatening communism's survival in Korea and China. Truman wasn't blind to these Chinese concerns, but the domestic pressures on him to win a "victory" in the Cold War by overturning a Communist regime were too compelling for him and Acheson to limit the fighting to South Korea's rescue. After so many perceived setbacks in the Cold War— Soviet domination of Eastern Europe, including East Germany and East Berlin, the Soviet A-bomb, communism's triumph in China, and threats of additional conquests in Asia and Africa—pressure for a rollback or defeat of one Communist regime, however limited a victory it might be, seemed irresistible.

Because conquering North Korea risked a wider war with China, Truman wished to give himself some political cover from Republican attacks. He was eager to fully identify MacArthur, who enjoyed iconic status among American conservatives and remained a military hero to millions of Americans, with decisions to occupy North Korea and bring the peninsula under UN control. If such ambitious policies provoked a wider conflict, it could not then be seen as simply Harry Truman's war. In addition, with congressional elections less than a month away, regardless of what happened in the fighting, Truman saw political advantage in associating himself with so popular a general.

On October 12, three days after U.S. troops had crossed into North Korea, Truman invited MacArthur to meet him on October 15 either at Oahu or at Wake Island, if the general felt he could not be absent from his command for the time required to travel to Hawaii. MacArthur chose Wake.

Both men approached the meeting suspicious of the other's motives. Truman saw MacArthur as a potential political adversary, whose highest priority was self-aggrandizement. "Have to talk to God's right-hand man tomorrow," Truman scathingly wrote a friend as he flew across the Pacific. MacArthur saw the conference as orchestrated for "political reasons" or as nothing more than a "political junket" and resented the distraction from his duties that compelled him to make an eight-thousand-mile round trip.

It was far less than Truman's journey, which was nearly twenty-nine thousand miles across seven time zones. The president obviously saw compelling strategic and political reasons for making so long a trip.

MacArthur, who had never met the president, did not make the best of first impressions: dressed informally in a shirt open at the neck and a much-traveled garrison cap, he did not salute the president

as he descended from his plane but warmly grasped his hand and
gripped his right arm with his left hand—what MacArthur called
his number-one handshake. Truman reciprocated the general's warm
welcome. But on a car ride from the plane to a nearby Quonset hut,
where the two would speak alone for half an hour, Truman immediately came to the principal point for the conference: his worry about
Chinese intervention in the war. Accompanied on the trip by General Omar Bradley, the only high-ranking military man the president brought along, and three State Department officials—Averell
Harriman, Dean Rusk, and Phillip Jessup—Truman was most concerned not with battlefield maneuvers but with the possibility that
seizing North Korea might result in a bigger war.

At a subsequent meeting with Truman's and MacArthur's aides
that lasted less than two hours in a one-story civil aeronautics building at the airfield, Truman came back to his fear of a larger conflict.
MacArthur could not have been more reassuring: he saw an end to
formal resistance in five or six weeks, by Thanksgiving, predicting
that the Eighth Army could return to Japan by Christmas and U.S.
troops could be out of Korea by January 1951, after countrywide
Korean elections. When the president reiterated his interest in keeping this a limited war, MacArthur saw "very little" chance of either
Soviet or Chinese intervention. Should Chinese troops, who lacked
air cover, enter the fighting and try to recapture Pyongyang, "there
would be the greatest slaughter."

MacArthur, who described himself as eager to return to his duties
in Japan and Korea, declined the president's invitation to lunch and
flew away after Truman had pinned a Distinguished Service Medal—
the fifth in his military career—on his chest. Truman flew back to
San Francisco, where he gave a speech carried around the world by
the Voice of America. In it he described MacArthur's greatness as a
soldier and the "unity in the aims and conduct of our foreign policy."
If anything were to go wrong now, was partly the president's unstated
message, the responsibility lay in a shared decision that relied on the

judgments of the field commander as well as the policy makers in Washington.

Despite MacArthur's assurances about Chinese or Soviet non-intervention, Truman would have done better to trust his concerns about a larger war. But the optimism generated by MacArthur's rout of the North Koreans was combined with concerns about a campaign of vilification if the president halted the offensive at the thirty-eighth parallel. For Kennan, who had confidently assured NATO ambassadors in Washington that the United States "had no intention of doing more than to restore the *status quo ante*," it was a shock to see U.S. forces moving north of the dividing line.

Truman couldn't resist the assumption in U.S. military and diplomatic circles that there would be an easy victory over Pyongyang. Such a victory would not only buoy American spirits, which Communist gains had dimmed, but also send a forceful message to Moscow, Peking, and foes everywhere that the United States was determined to stand its ground in the Cold War at whatever cost in blood and treasure.

The Korean War now became a toxic brew for everyone who supported it. No one—not the Koreans, North and South, nor the Chinese, the Soviets, or the Americans—could escape the negative consequences of extended fighting on the peninsula.

During the last week of October, advance South Korean units ran into resistance from some 200,000 Chinese troops, who had crossed from Manchuria into Korea. And by the first week of November, though MacArthur asked permission to bomb the bridges over the Yalu River to halt the flood of Chinese men and matériel, he continued to insist that a quick victory was within easy reach and would result from an end-the-war offensive beginning in mid-November.

By November 28, however, with Chinese infantry and armor staging a massive assault on ROK and U.S. troops that drove them back below Pyongyang in less than two weeks, MacArthur had to concede that his command "now faced . . . conditions beyond its control . . . an entirely new war." He rationalized his misleading predictions about an easy conquest of North Korea by asserting that China's large-scale involvement in the fighting had resulted from Mao's understanding through British spies that the United States would confine its combat to Korea and not carry the war into China. Although it was evident to MacArthur that Washington had no appetite for a larger conflict with China, which might trigger a world war with the Soviet Union, this was not clear to Peking; its decision to engage the Americans in a full-blown ground war was accompanied by considerable anxiety that U.S. air forces might strike Chinese cities with atomic bombs.

The fear was well advised. In June and July, National Security Council and State Department officials discussed not whether to use nuclear weapons but what conditions might make their use acceptable—to avert defeat, or if they would not result in "excessive destruction of noncombatants." No one discussed what "excessive" might mean— more than the numbers that had perished at Hiroshima and Nagasaki? Shortly after the Chinese successfully intervened in the fighting, MacArthur asked permission to drop thirty-four atomic bombs on Manchuria that could create a radioactive belt of cobalt that would last for at least sixty years and provide a defense against any invasion of Korea from the north.

The Chinese willingness to fight nevertheless rested on the belief that Washington would be reluctant to risk a world war with a nuclear-armed Russia by striking directly at China. Peking also assumed that its greater manpower would prevent U.S. domination of the peninsula, from which it could threaten stability in China, and that it could use the war to eliminate remaining domestic pockets of resistance to Communist rule. In November and December, Stalin encouraged Mao to defeat U.S. aggression in Korea and promised to support his war effort with supplies and Soviet air cover over Manchuria. As from the beginning of the fighting, Stalin was less interested in driving the Americans off the peninsula than in tying them down in a war that would limit their military presence in Europe and force them to take account of Soviet and Chinese opposition to U.S. bases in Japan.

The miscalculations on the part of all the leaders who facilitated the Korean fighting inflicted a heavy price on each of their countries. Not surprisingly, the loss of military personnel and civilians from the ground and air campaigns on the peninsula that lasted over three years destroyed a generation of Koreans—about 3 million, approximately 10 percent of the population, north and south, were killed, missing, or wounded, with another 5 million displaced or forced to become refugees. The United States had over 36,000 dead, and over 90,000 wounded.

The Chinese suffered as many as 900,000 killed in combat. In November and December, they drove U.S. and South Korean troops back to the parallel, but at a huge cost in troops and matériel. And although China's population, exceeding 550 million, gave it seemingly endless reinforcements, the U.S. advantage in airpower and weaponry threatened to increase China's battlefield casualties to unbearable levels and to turn North Korea into a wasteland. Surely, the Chinese and Korean militaries knew the extent of the devastation from World War II's conventional bombs and napalm. Nor could Mao be confident that Washington wouldn't resort to atomic weapons if it faced defeat in Korea. Yet the initial success of the Chinese armies had deluded Mao into thinking that he could expel the Americans from the peninsula and trumpet a people's victory over imperialism. Consequently, he dismissed ceasefire proposals that assured South Korea's autonomy and halted the Chinese advance at the thirty-eighth parallel.

Mao's refusal to settle for a negotiated peace that rescued North Korea was a miscalculation for which his troops would pay dearly. Judging from the millions who perished in famines and the Cultural Revolution of the late 1960s, Mao, like Stalin, didn't hesitate to sacrifice lives for the sake of communism and his personal rule. "The more people you kill, the more revolutionary you are," he said.

The Soviets, who had hoped to reduce U.S. militancy by trapping it in a debilitating conflict, were anguished by the opposite result. In response to the war, the Americans not only vastly expanded their defense preparedness, increasing the size of their armed forces and constructing a larger, more powerful nuclear arsenal, but also built NATO, partly with German units beginning in 1955, into a formidable defense arm and signed a Japanese peace treaty that included long-term U.S. bases in the islands. These unwanted developments, especially the prospect of a rearmed Germany, made Moscow less secure and more driven to invest scarce resources in its defense.

China's entrance into the fighting, which now dramatically increased U.S. casualties, demoralized Americans and made them more vulnerable to the exaggerated fears and remedies for world problems favored by right-wing politicians. In the early weeks of 1951, hopes of overturning Kim's regime and preserving South Korea from Communist control faded as Chinese forces captured Seoul and pushed the defenders into a new perimeter above Pusan, forcing plans to evacuate the peninsula.

At the end of the month, however, U.S.-led UN forces regained the initiative when General Matthew Ridgway replaced General Walton Walker, who had been killed in a jeep accident, as field commander. A tough, determined World War II paratrooper, who dismissed warnings that his troops would have to flee Korea, Ridgway, Joint Chiefs chairman Omar Bradley said, provided "brilliant, driving, uncompromising leadership." He sparked a new offensive that inflicted large losses on the Communists, recaptured Seoul, and drove the Chinese back above the parallel by the end of March.

Yet even with these victories, Americans had lost faith in the wisdom of fighting in Korea, and in Truman's leadership. Initially, 65 percent in a poll thought it a good idea for the United States to have entered the war. By January, at the low ebb of battlefield fortunes, 66 percent of a survey wanted the president "to pull our troops out of Korea as fast as possible." Forty-nine percent now believed

U.S. participation in the war a mistake, with only 38 percent endorsing it as a wise policy. Even after Ridgway had launched his winter offensive, 50 percent said the war was an error, and just 36 percent favored a second invasion of the North. By better than a three-to-one margin—30 percent to 9 percent—Americans thought that Russia was defeating the United States in the Cold War.

The Korean defeats dropped Truman's standing to new lows, and the country favored reckless actions to beat the Communists. The president's approval ratings fell from 43 percent in the summer to 36 percent in January and a miserable 26 percent in February, with 57 percent negative about his performance. By a margin of 64 to 28 percent, Americans said that in the future the Congress rather than the president should decide when soldiers should be sent "overseas." As in 1946, political commentators joked, "To err is Truman."

Americans knew that the best way out of foreign dangers was the assertion of the country's superior military power. At a press conference on November 30, Truman responded to a reporter's question about using atomic bombs against the Chinese in Korea by saying that this was under consideration and that the field commander had the freedom of decision. Although Truman undoubtedly was only trying to frighten the Chinese, the American public, unlike governments in Europe and Asia, did not take exception to his comments.

The Cold War had frightened the country into favoring extreme actions to preserve the nation's security. Sixty-one percent supported using atomic bombs in a world war to stop Communist expansion, saying we should hit them with nuclear weapons before they struck us. A majority of Americans thought that the fighting in Korea meant we were already in World War III; 81 percent believed it was a war we had to fight if Russia were not to become the "ruling power of the world." Fearful that a full-scale conflict with China could last four years, about the length of World War II, a plurality of Americans supported using atomic bombs against her as well. The dread of a nuclear war, which had been so prominent immediately after 1945,

had given way to the conviction that using nuclear arms against ruthless Communists was essential to America's survival.

A bitter divide now opened up in the United States about future
policy in Korea. Because conservatives led by MacArthur and Joe
McCarthy believed that the fighting on the peninsula was the opening round in a global showdown with the Communists, they urged
an attack on mainland China, including the use of Chiang's forces
on Taiwan, to bring down Mao and free Korea from Communist
power. By contrast, Truman and Acheson favored a ceasefire that
reestablished South Korea's autonomy and left Kim in control of
North Korea. China's insistence that an end to the fighting include a
U.S. removal of the Seventh Fleet from the Taiwan Strait, leaving the
island vulnerable to a Communist attack, and that the Peking government replace Chiang's as China's UN representative undermined
prospects for a quick end to the war.

By March 24, when it was clear that Washington would not aim
to unify the peninsula through fresh offensive operations above the
parallel, MacArthur underscored his differences with the president
in a statement that enraged the Chinese and assured the continuation of the fighting. Pointing to recent UN battlefield gains, he dismissed China's military capacity to win an extended conflict against
the UN and urged Peking to concede its defeat in Korea or face a
wider war that would bring an "imminent military collapse." The
Chinese, who did not see themselves as losing the war by any means,
dismissed MacArthur's pronouncement as propaganda and prepared
themselves for a spring offensive.

MacArthur's statement provoked not only the Chinese but also
the White House. Having blundered in crossing the parallel once,
Truman had no intention of making the same mistake again. His
willingness to return to the status quo ante risked, as it had earlier,
a political firestorm in the United States. But having propelled the
United States into a larger conflict and increased the likelihood of

an even bigger, more destructive war, Truman now concluded that the political explosion at home was a lesser evil than the dangers resulting from another attempt to eliminate North Korea's Communist regime.

To keep domestic divisions over Korea from intensifying, however, Truman muted his response to MacArthur's new attack on his strategy. MacArthur followed with yet a second challenge to White House policy in a letter House Republican minority leader Joseph Martin read into the congressional record on April 5: MacArthur found it "strangely difficult for some to realize that here in Asia is where the Communist conspirators have elected to make their play for global conquest." He warned that "if we lose the war to communism in Asia the fall of Europe is inevitable. . . . We must win. There is no substitute for victory."

Truman thought him dead wrong and felt compelled to dismiss him. The Joint Chiefs agreed with the president. As the chairman, General Omar Bradley, would famously tell a Senate inquiry into MacArthur's removal, "Red China is not the powerful nation seeking to dominate the world. Frankly, in the opinion of the Joint Chiefs, this strategy would involve us in the wrong war, at the wrong place, at the wrong time, and with the wrong enemy."

In firing MacArthur, Truman believed that the general had left him no choice. By endorsing Martin's recommendation of a Nationalist invasion of the mainland that he hoped could topple Mao's government, win the war in Korea, and defeat the Soviet reach for global power, MacArthur was assuming the role of commander in chief; it was a breach of the president's constitutional authority. As Truman later told Merle Miller, his oral biographer, "I didn't fire him because he was a dumb son of a bitch, although he was. . . . I fired him because he wouldn't respect the authority of the president."

Truman also retired him because he believed that MacArthur was no longer "right in the head." It was Truman's way of saying that

MacArthur's proposal to destroy communism in China was reckless and could get the United States into a third world war, which fighting in Korea was meant to avoid.

From the perspective of more than fifty years after Truman ended MacArthur's military career, the president has all the better of the argument. Attacking China would have dragged the United States into an impossible struggle to determine China's political future and would have tested Moscow's fear of allowing Washington to dominate East Asia and all that might mean to the survival of Soviet communism. The Truman-Acheson-Kennan strategy of containing Communist advance by defending South Korea from Kim's aggression made eminent good sense. But the more aggressive policy of rolling back post-1945 Communist gains in North Korea or Eastern Europe would have risked the global conflict the containment strategy so successfully averted.

As MacArthur himself would acknowledge in a 1961 speech, "Global war has become a Frankenstein to destroy both sides. , . . If you lose, you are annihilated. If you win, you stand only to lose. No longer does it possess even the chance of the winner of a duel. It contains now only the germs of double suicide."

ELUSIVE PEACE

We must be patient—making peace is harder than making war.
—Adlai Stevenson, 1946

Harry Truman paid a heavy political price for MacArthur's firing. Predictably, the right wing was apocalyptic over the removal of one of the few U.S. officials they believed determined to defeat communism. Their agitation over the general's ouster became a vicious ad hominem attack on Truman's competence as president.

Joe McCarthy denounced the president as drunk on "bourbon and Benedictine" when he recalled the general. Senator William Jenner of Indiana joined McCarthy in calling for Truman's impeachment, saying that he was part of "a secret inner coterie which is directed by agents of the Soviet Union." Whether Jenner actually believed that Truman was a traitor or was posturing for political gain is less interesting than the fact that any number of people in the country were receptive to such an outlandish charge; the frustration with a limited war that might end in defeat enraged people, who turned their anger against a president they blamed for timid leadership. The *Chicago Tribune* was relatively restrained in describing Truman as "unfit, morally and mentally for his high office."

Although most Americans were not ready to dismiss the president as unable to handle his job, two-thirds disapproved of his treatment of MacArthur, less because they continued to have great faith in the general's leadership than because of how Truman had dismissed him.

The controversy further undermined Truman's sagging approval ratings; toward the end of the year, he fell to an all-time low of 23 percent. But the president's unpopularity did not translate into political capital for MacArthur: a majority of potential voters opposed a MacArthur bid for the White House, which some commentators believed he envisioned as a capstone to his storied military career.

As with any member of the military who had devoted years of his life to defending the country—and especially one as revered as MacArthur—millions of Americans believed that the general should have been allowed to retire in a more decorous fashion. An outpouring of regard for him in parades and at an appearance before a joint congressional session more than made the point. In New York, where millions of people lined the nineteen-mile route the motorcade took almost seven hours to travel, the parade greatly exceeded the 1945 celebration of Eisenhower's return from victory in Europe. MacArthur was an American hero, and in a time of war when so many Americans saw a threat to the country's long-term survival, they wished to pay homage to the general best known for his contributions to Japan's defeat and rebuilding. They were also showing him the regard they believed Truman had denied him.

The expressions of respect for MacArthur were as much an attack on Truman as a fêting of the general. It was the Republicans who arranged MacArthur's appearance before the joint session, knowing that the White House and congressional Democrats would not risk a political backlash by blocking it. A MacArthur speech would embarrass the president by underscoring differences between a general who wanted victory in Korea and a White House willing to settle for a standoff.

MacArthur's appearance on April 19, 1951, could have been orchestrated by a Hollywood producer: his march down the aisle before a cheering audience of congressmen and senators, his pronouncements on selfless duty to country, his calls for victory in Korea, and a promise not to seek any grander role for himself in public life but to "just fade away" struck all the right chords in a time of national anxiety. His delivery was pitch-perfect, his voice rising and falling in a melodic rhythm that seemed to hypnotize his listeners. His "gallant men" asked, "Why . . . surrender military advantages to an enemy in the field?" Pausing to let the gravity of the question sink in, he responded, "I could not answer." When he finished, some in the audience sobbed openly and jostled each other as he came up the aisle to touch his hand or arm. A congressman, carried away by the emotions of the moment, declared: "We heard God speak here today, God in the flesh, the voice of God!"

Yet for all the adulation, MacArthur's championship of a wider, decisive war fell flat. Privately, White House aides belittled MacArthur's self-importance and appetite for public drama with gallows humor: they suggested that the general should have led a parade to the capital riding on an elephant, and that a proper sequel to his congressional address should have been the burning of the Constitution, the lynching of Secretary Acheson, and a twenty-one-atomic-bomb salute. Truman declared MacArthur's speech "a hundred percent bullshit," and marveled at the "damn fool Congressmen crying like a bunch of women."

What principally dampened enthusiasm for MacArthur was his testimony before a Senate committee looking into his dismissal and "the military situation in the Far East." Although radio and television were not allowed in the hearing room, daily transcripts of the proceedings were distributed to the press, which featured them prominently on the front pages of their newspapers and on the airwaves. MacArthur had ample opportunity over three days between May 3 and May 6 to make his case. Sensing that MacArthur's best critic would be his own words, Senate opponents gave him all the time he wanted to demonstrate that he was a reckless advocate of a war against China and Soviet Russia, if necessary. When asked what his strategy would be should we get into a global war, he skirted the question: "That doesn't happen to be my responsibility," he said.

Truman answered some of his critics and dampened the enthusiasm for MacArthur when he said of the general's testimony, "We are right now in the midst of a big debate on foreign policy. A lot of people are looking at this debate as if it were just a political fight. But . . . the thing that is at stake in this debate may be atomic war. . . . It is a matter of life and death."

While the public was not eager to follow MacArthur into a nuclear war, it did share his concerns about the Korean fighting: "What are you going to do to stop the slaughter in Korea?" he asked. "Does your global plan for defending these United States against war consist of permitting war indefinitely to go on in the Pacific?"

Like the Joint Chiefs, the public had no appetite for the expanded fighting MacArthur favored to defeat the Communists in Peking and Pyongyang and, if necessary, in Moscow too. But it was in sync with MacArthur's demand for an end to the fighting in Korea—only not in the way he envisioned. Initial majority support for crossing the parallel and destroying Kim's regime had collapsed with China's entrance into the fighting and the prospect of a drawn-out stalemate. Most Americans now preferred a negotiated settlement that divided the peninsula along prewar lines and left the Rhee and Kim governments in place rather than an all-out struggle to inflict a decisive defeat on the Communists. MacArthur's eagerness for a full-scale war with China frightened people, who thought he might lead them into a nuclear holocaust.

In July both sides in the Korean fighting, implicitly acknowledging that neither was likely to win a clear victory, agreed to open truce talks at Kaesong, a city just below the parallel. Seventy-four percent of Americans thought the discussions a good idea. When an unidentified U.S. senator declared the Korean conflict "an utterly 'useless war,' " a telling 56 percent of Americans agreed. Remembering Roosevelt's effective dealings with Stalin during World War II, 70 percent of a survey favored a U.S.-Soviet summit that might ease differences between Moscow and Washington.

While the White House was receptive to talks, it was eager to salvage something more than South Korea's autonomy from the negotiations. Given the success of the winter–spring offensive in 1951 that had driven the Communists back above the parallel, Washington demanded more at the negotiating table than a return to the prewar dividing line, as the Chinese proposed. The United States pressed Peking to give the South a swath of territory above the parallel that was then under Communist control. U.S. negotiators argued that their dominance in the air over Korea and the surrounding waters entitled them to push South Korea's boundary north of where it used to be. Having dropped their demands for discussions of U.S. evacuation of the peninsula, removal of the Seventh Fleet from the Taiwan Strait, and a say in negotiating the Japanese peace treaty as part of Korean armistice talks, the Chinese refused to concede anything else, especially any North Korean territory, which could be interpreted as an acknowledgment of defeat.

With both sides primarily concerned to represent any settlement as a victory, neither would alter their positions. Never mind that Peking could describe its rescue of Kim's regime from an American occupation as a triumph over the imperialist West or that Washington could claim the defeat of North Korea's aggression against the South. Each side wished to convince domestic and international observers that they were militarily stronger and politically more resolute than their adversary. But it was their home audiences that the Chinese and American governments were most eager to impress. Mao needed to convince his mass public that its sacrifices in the war and for the revolution were essential to preserve the nation from a new era of foreign imperial control, which would squelch promises of better days ahead. Truman felt compelled to fend off attacks on his administration and party as weak leaders, or maybe even closet Reds, reluctant to defeat the Communist threat.

The preoccupation with perceptions of winners and losers, regardless of realities on the ground, was central to the armistice talks. At the conference table, the Chinese and North Koreans insisted that Admiral Turner Joy, America's chief negotiator, sit facing north. Mindful that victors in Asian cultures always sat facing south, the Communists positioned themselves accordingly. Moreover, they arranged to make their chief delegate appear taller and more dominant than Joy at the initial session of the talks by having the latter sit in a smaller and lower chair. To avoid being caught on Communist cameras looking less imposing than the Chinese delegates, Joy insisted on chairs of equal size and height to those of his counterparts.

The negotiations, which affected so many lives, were inextricably bound up with public posturing. Since neither side was going to emerge from the fighting with any clear advantage, the belligerents were as attentive to appearances as to battlefield results. It was a formula for stalemate rather than an end to war making.

In August 1951, two military clashes in the neutral zone around Kaesong increased tension in talks already notable for their acrimony. The Chinese, for example, had responded to American boundary demands as "incredible," "naive and illogical." Their chief negotiator asked: "Seeing that you make such a completely absurd and arrogant statement for what have you actually come here?" Joy replied: "Rudeness such as you have displayed will lead . . . the United Nations Command delegation . . . to conclude you have no serious or sincere purpose at this conference."

The violations of the neutral zone became an excuse for the Communists to suspend the negotiations in late August. They blamed the interruption on their adversaries and demanded concessions from them before they would resume talks. To both sides, the negotiations had become a form of alternate warfare or "war by other means."

American opinion now hardened against the Communists. The great majority of the country already saw the Soviets and the new Chinese regime as driven, ruthless ideologues who only understood military might. And while the Russian and Chinese Communists were also seen as indifferent to their people's lives, all too ready to sacrifice their populations in the service of their ambitions, Americans believed that only their determination to preserve their respective governments in Pyongyang, Peking, and Moscow could push the Communists into any kind of settlement with the West.

The unproductive talks at Kaesong, however, convinced two-thirds of Americans in a Gallup poll that the Chinese were uninterested in peace and that a new round of talks would not end the conflict. A majority in the United States concluded that only the most drastic measures would force the Chinese into a truce: 51 percent in one poll favored use of atomic bombs against enemy targets in Korea; only 37 percent thought it a poor idea.

During the two months following the breakdown in negotiations, both sides in Korea tested each other's resolve with military probes. At the same time, the Soviets increased tensions in Germany, where the Communists put new restrictions on road traffic into West Berlin, and the United States signed a peace treaty with Tokyo that convinced Peking and Moscow of American determination not to leave Japan or the peninsula but to establish permanent bases from which it could threaten China's Communist regime and Soviet East Asian interests.

Because a complete breakdown in settlement talks threatened unacceptable losses to the Americans in stepped-up fighting, Washington favored a prompt return to the peace table. The Chinese, who privately acknowledged that the war was putting unbearable strains on their domestic economy, shared an interest in renewed negotiations. A rising concern that a prolonged conflict might trigger a U.S. nuclear attack on China's principal cities created an added inducement for Peking to restart the discussions. At the end of October, to give the talks a fresh sense of momentum and both sides a greater sense of control over the meeting site, they agreed to resume the negotiations at Panmunjom, another border city southeast of Kaesong.

In the course of a month, the negotiators agreed to compromise on the dividing line between North and South Korea, accepting the demarcation or battlefield positions at the end of November as the new state boundaries. The agreement, which expanded the South just north of the thirty-eighth parallel, gave the United States some of the border changes it had originally asked, but not enough to suggest a major Chinese concession on the disputed point.

During the second week in December, the negotiators began to focus on what no one foresaw as a stumbling block to a final settlement—the exchange of prisoners of war. The American decision to make repatriation voluntary among the 116,000 Chinese and North Korean POWs, however, became an intolerable political condition for the Chinese. Washington had every confidence that the 16,000 U.S. and South Korean POWs would eagerly seek repatriation. But if many of the Chinese and North Korean internees would not, it would be a propaganda victory. Washington also saw an "all-for-all" exchange as calculated to boost Communist troop concentrations that could destabilize existing battle lines.

Insisting that the prisoner exchange should be an unrestricted swap of all POWs, the Chinese saw the U.S. proposal as creating "a serious political struggle." But with the Chinese consumer economy continuing to suffer severe strains from demands for war production and a weather-induced famine in north China threatening the stability of Mao's regime, he became eager to refocus national energies on internal growth rather than defense needs. Yet he would not end the conflict under what he described as "bullying . . . by foreign imperialists."

While eager to gain a propaganda victory over Peking as well as avert the sort of tragedy that had occurred at the end of World War II when some Soviet POWs had committed suicide rather than return home, the United States searched for a formula that would allow the Chinese to accept voluntary repatriation. To soften the blow to Peking from a mass refusal of their internees to go home, the United States promised to return at least 70,000 POWs. In July 1952, three months after this initial proposal, Washington increased the number to 83,000.

But when Washington described the POW exchange as a human rights issue, the dispute became too great a potential embarrassment to Peking for it to agree to a compromise. The Chinese denounced the U.S. plan as "absolutely" unacceptable, calling it "a brutal and shameless proposition."

Despite the Chinese response, Truman refused to budge on freedom of choice for POWs. In December and January, 1951–52, when the issue threatened to stalemate the talks, the president told State and Defense department advisers that more was at stake than just the freedom of some Chinese and North Korean POWs: he feared that an armistice in Korea would prove to be only a temporary pause in the fighting that could eventually topple South Korea and spur isolationist sentiment in the United States. Moreover, he worried that an end to the war would undermine support for the country's rearmament program under NSC-68.

Nevertheless, Truman was painfully ambivalent about continuing the war. He couldn't let go of the conviction that anything short of a perceived victory over the Communists would be destructive to America's long-term prospects in the Cold War. At the same time, however, it was costing the country precious lives and tax dollars that could go to domestic programs—health insurance for seniors and federal aid to education—that he had promised to enact under his Fair Deal. In addition, the war was undermining his popularity and playing havoc with his freedom to lead the country in both domestic and foreign affairs.

At the end of January 1952, Truman's frustration at being trapped in a war that he had no clear way to end and that was destroying his presidency found expression in a private diary entry that would not see the light of day until decades later. "Dealing with communist governments is like an honest man trying to deal with a numbers racket king or the head of a dope ring," he complained. The Communists were entirely without a "moral code." Their criminality allowed him to imagine sending "an ultimatum with a ten day expiration limit, informing Moscow that we intend to blockade the China coast from the Korean border to Indo-China." He wished to threaten to "destroy every military base in Manchuria, . . . and if there is any interference we shall eliminate any ports or cities necessary to accomplish our peaceful purposes. . . . We are tired of these phony calls for peace when there is no intention to make an honest approach to peace. . . . This means all-out war." After ticking off Russia's and China's principal cities that "will be eliminated," he concluded, "This is the final chance for the Soviet Government to decide whether it desires to survive or not."

Truman's apocalyptic fantasy rested on a conviction that it was the Soviets who were calling the shots in the Korean fighting by using the Chinese and North Koreans to do their bidding without direct sacrifice by their own citizens. And as in every war, where adversaries dehumanize each other in order to justify mass killing, Truman pictured the Communists as ruthless enough to continue fighting even if it meant annihilation for their governments and societies. Killing great numbers of Russians and Chinese could be rationalized as not the fault of Americans dropping atomic bombs on their cities but the consequence of the policies imposed on their countries by madmen.

At the same time that Truman ventilated his rage at Moscow and Peking for forcing him and the United States into a debilitating and demoralizing conflict, he could not bring himself to issue such an ultimatum out of fear that he might have to act upon it. It would then burden him and the United States with the guilt of having slaughtered millions of innocent people, exceeding the mass destruction in Hiroshima and Nagasaki. Paraphrasing Woodrow Wilson's initial response to World War I, that America was too proud to fight, Truman saw himself as too civilized to act as the Nazis had and the Communists might if they were in America's advantaged position. Besides, if he unleashed nuclear attacks on Russia and China, it would be no more or less than what he had dismissed MacArthur for suggesting—an all-out war to end the Communist threat.

The tensions at the negotiating table increased in the first half of 1952. Partly to counter the propaganda advantage the United States gained from its support for voluntary repatriation, the Chinese began hammering on charges of biological warfare by the Americans against North Korean and Chinese troops and civilians in Manchuria. Although none of these assertions has ever been proved, archival evidence indicates that the Chinese genuinely believed that American pilots were dropping bombs containing infected insects on noncombatants, and they did all in their power to disseminate the information to domestic and international audiences.

These charges, coupled with China's unbending stance on POWs, incensed U.S. officials. General Ridgway denounced the Chinese as "treacherous savages" with no regard for human life or "sense of honor." Peking's claims suggested that the Americans, who had used atomic bombs against the Japanese, were racists ready to exterminate other Asians with biological weapons.

The POW issue, on which a majority of Americans supported the administration, nevertheless put Truman in a difficult position. The continuing incarceration of U.S. prisoners for the sake of their Chinese and North Korean counterparts, who had fought against the United States, but whose freedom was the sticking point in the negotiations, was not likely to sit well indefinitely with most Americans. Truman also resented having to defend the United States from what he saw as unsubstantiated complaints about germ warfare, which found receptive audiences in many "neutral" Third World countries. The accusations gave Peking a political counter to attacks on it as afraid to let its POWs choose between going home and taking refuge in the "free world."

Truman continued to blame the war and its physical losses and political dilemmas on the Russians. In another private outburst in May 1952, he recorded in a diary that he would like to tell Stalin and his Politburo: "You have broken every agreement you made at Teheran, Yalta and Potsdam. You have no morals, no honor. . . . Now do you want an end to hostilities in Korea or do you want China and Siberia destroyed? You may have one or the other, whichever you want. . . . You either accept our fair and just proposal or you will be completely destroyed." He signed the diary entry: "C. in C," Commander in Chief, rationalizing such drastic action as a military imperative. But again, it was a step too far: an act of mass destruction that other countries would see as unjustified and would open the United States to accusations of ruthlessness exceeding anything the Communists did. Besides, it remained too much like MacArthur's solution to the conflict for Truman to have followed through on such extreme measures.

Nevertheless, he was determined to take a hard line with the Chinese short of using nuclear weapons. He would not compromise on the principle of voluntary prisoner returns. And since the Communists were also unwilling to bend on the issue, Truman believed that the best course to an armistice was through renewed attacks on their troops in Korea with beefed-up and better-equipped U.S. forces. With the November 1952 elections on the horizon, he was not going to undermine Adlai Stevenson, the Democratic Party's presidential candidate, or his party's hold on the Congress by showing any weakness in his dealings with Peking and Pyongyang. On October 8, after three months of sporadic talks when the Chinese had rejected the latest U.S. proposal for prisoner exchanges, the U.S. delegation announced an indefinite recess in the negotiations.

The hope that a renewed offensive against Chinese forces could bring Peking back to the negotiating table quickly lost credibility. The Chinese had dug in so effectively along the existing combat lines, increasing their armies to 1.35 million men, stockpiling ample amounts of food and ammunition, and developing North Korean coastal defenses against an Inchon sort of landing, that prospects of routing them faded fast. To be sure, a stepped-up air war leveled cities and towns in North Korea. And according to the U.S. Air Force, it took control of a hundred-mile area behind enemy lines by day-and-night saturation bombing. Although air force planners believed that this sort of attack could prove decisive in the war, the prompt rebuilding of roads, bridges, and rail lines demonstrated otherwise.

By the fall of 1952 the war had turned into a stalemate, and the belligerents could only look forward to more loss of life in the maneuvering for advantage on the ground and the destruction of North Korea's infrastructure from the air, especially its irrigation dams and its rice crops, the country's principal food staple. The Chinese now hoped to outlast the Americans, whose patience with a war of attrition seemed distinctly limited. In a conversation Chou En-lai had with Stalin in August 1952, Chou confidently described the conflict as "getting on America's nerves" and a clear demonstration that "the USA is not ready for the world war."

Stalin encouraged Chou to see the United States as a paper tiger, saying, "The Americans are not capable of waging a large-scale war at all. . . . All of their strength lies in air power and the atom bomb. . . . America cannot defeat little Korea. . . . Americans are merchants. Every American soldier is a speculator, occupied with buying and selling. . . . It's been already two years and USA has still not subdued little Korea. What kind of strength is that? . . . They are pinning their hopes on the atom bomb and air power. But one cannot win a war with that. One needs infantry, and they don't have much infantry; the infantry they do have is weak. They are fighting with little Korea, and already people are weeping in the USA."

For all the brave talk about American weakness, Stalin counseled caution, advising against Chinese air raids on South Korea or any sort of offensive while armistice negotiations were continuing. Chou agreed about holding off on an offensive while truce talks went forward, but said that "China is preparing for the possibility of another 2–3 years of war."

The Truman administration also believed that the war might continue for quite a while. But it was determined not to show any signs of weakness by giving in on the POW issue, despite mounting convictions that the conflict was becoming a repeat of the deadlocked trench warfare of World War I.

The Republican presidential campaign by Dwight Eisenhower and vice presidential nominee Richard Nixon made it especially difficult for Truman to yield anything in the negotiations. It would confirm the Republican assault on the president and his party as naive and unreliable in the contest with communism for national survival.

Nixon, who had established a reputation as a fierce anti-Communist through his pursuit of Alger Hiss, was the campaign's point man for attacking the Democrats as having failed to defend the country from the Communist menace at home and abroad. New Deal appointees were depicted as subversives, especially in the State Department, where they had allegedly allowed Mao's Communists to seize control of China. Adlai Stevenson, the Democratic nominee, was described as a brainy Ivy League type who lacked the military training and hardheaded realism held by "Ike" to deal with the fundamental dangers posed by the plotters in the Kremlin and Peking reaching for world control.

Nixon summed up the campaign's assault on Stevenson and the Democrats when he said that the Illinois governor was a graduate of (in some versions, held a PhD from) Dean Acheson's "Cowardly College of Communist Containment." The phrase effectively announced the campaign's principal message: Stevenson and the Democrats are elite intellectuals who are either covert Communist sympathizers or too soft-minded to do more than contain rather than defeat the Communists.

Although Eisenhower came to the campaign as an apolitical military hero, who had never voted and had no party affiliation (at the beginning of 1952, some Democrats, including Truman, hoped Ike might run on their ticket), the general proved to be a savvy politician.

Less acerbic than Nixon or other right-wing Republicans like McCarthy, Jenner, and Robert Taft of Ohio, Eisenhower nevertheless exploited the national mood about the Democrats' failure to meet the Communist challenge, especially in Korea. When he campaigned in Indiana, Jenner's home state, Eisenhower did not resist having Jenner on the platform with him, where the senator would grab Ike's arm and thrust it skyward in a show of unity at each applause line. Jenner's attack on George Marshall, Ike's mentor, as a "front man for traitors" and "a living lie" did not deter Eisenhower from standing shoulder to shoulder with Jenner. In private, Eisenhower complained that Jenner's touch made him feel dirty, but he gave no sign in public of being at odds with him.

The general further compromised himself when he traveled through Wisconsin with McCarthy at his side. Ike had contempt for McCarthy's unsubstantiated charges of Communist ties to bring down opponents. But he believed that the Democrats had given McCarthy credibility by their "neglect, indifference and arrogance," which had allowed communism to penetrate "dangerously into important regions of our government and our economic life." Eisenhower condemned "un-American practices applied against the individual," but he wholeheartedly accepted McCarthy's objective of removing subversive elements from power in Washington. In a speech in Montana, the general promised that his administration would "find the pinks; we will find the Communists; we will find the disloyal." His language reflected the exaggerated fear of Communist subversion that had become accepted understanding.

To put some distance between himself and McCarthy during his campaign through Wisconsin, Eisenhower included a paragraph in a major speech at Milwaukee praising George Marshall, who, like Jenner, McCarthy had made the focus of anti-Communist attacks. But when pressured by aides to drop the positive references to his former mentor, Eisenhower agreed. Although he had given McCarthy a private dressing-down for his abuse of due process in going after "subversives," Ike refused to take him on publicly in Wisconsin. In fact, the most he did in a speech at Green Bay was say that he did not share McCarthy's methods, but agreed with his purposes in aiming to rid the government of "the incompetents, the dishonest and above all the subversive and disloyal."

Despite Eisenhower's public complaint about McCarthy's methods, the impression he gave was of someone more concerned with removing the Reds in government than with how it was done. In his Milwaukee speech, he echoed the cry of the Republican right that the loss of Eastern Europe and China had been the result of betrayal in Washington. Communist penetration of the American government, he said, "meant—in its most ugly triumph—treason itself." To right this wrong, he promised to "aid by peaceful means, but only by peaceful means, the right to live in freedom." He gave no encouragement to those who favored military steps to free Soviet satellite countries, but implied that he would go beyond containment to liberate the "enslaved" peoples of Eastern Europe.

Korea was the greatest source of voter concern and Eisenhower's most effective campaign issue. The eagerness among Americans for an end to a war that had already cost some 35,000 lives and close to 90,000 wounded was palpable. Although Eisenhower offered no specifics on how he would achieve an honorable peace, his military credentials and a promise to travel to Korea for a firsthand assessment of the fighting convinced voters that he had an unstated plan for ending the conflict. On October 24, he announced his first post-election priority as "ending the Korean War. . . . That job requires a personal trip to Korea. . . . Only in that way could I learn how best to serve the American people in the cause of peace."

Truman, who saw Eisenhower's pledge to go to Korea as nothing more than a campaign tactic and as "demagoguery . . . almost beneath contempt," publicly dismissed Ike's statement on Korea by saying that the general had been in agreement with everything the administration had been doing there, and told voters that "no professional general has ever made a good President. The art of war is too different from the art of civilian government." Truman's warning was of no consequence. Eisenhower won decisively—55 percent of the popular vote and a five-to-one margin in the Electoral College.

Because Truman understood that public sentiment was on Eisenhower's side and that conceding anything to the Chinese would have increased the animus toward him and the Democrats, he refused to bend on the POW exchange. He also viewed POW freedom to choose as humane and a defeat for the Communists, which he was avid to achieve for the thousands of Americans who had sacrificed their lives in the fighting. He considered any sort of victory a warning to the Soviets and Chinese not to test the United States in combat again. Since the outcome in Korea would form a significant part of his presidential legacy, he was determined not to change policy.

To be sure, had Truman accepted the Chinese proposal on prisoner exchange, he would have lost some additional public support and the sense of satisfaction from forcing the Communists into an embarrassing concession, but he probably could have ended the war and spared the country continuing losses. Instead, he allowed the politics of foreign policy and the reach for a more positive legacy than the rescue of South Korea to take precedence. As a consequence, he continued what had already become a pointless war from which nothing more was to be gained.

It was left to Eisenhower to end the conflict. A war-weary public and a military commander's understanding of battlefield possibilities dictated his actions. True to his word following his election, he traveled to Korea at the end of November 1952 to gain a firsthand impression of possible benefits from a fresh offensive. His designated secretary of state, John Foster Dulles, as well as Mark Clark, the commander of U.S. forces in Korea, and Syngman Rhee, urged an all-out offensive that could drive the Chinese out of North Korea and unify the peninsula under Rhee's control. But the president-elect's visit to Korea, where he spoke with front-line troops and flew a reconnaissance mission over the dividing line between entrenched forces, convinced him that an assault on well-fortified Chinese positions would result in terrible casualties and little gain. He concluded that "small attacks on small hills would not end this war."

Eisenhower did not see a major offensive with nuclear weapons as the right answer either. MacArthur urged him to drive the Chinese and North Korean troops off the peninsula with atomic bombs and then threaten China with a bombing campaign if it refused to abandon its war of "aggression." Some in the Republican Party, who believed their own rhetoric about rollback and liberation in Korea, China, and Eastern Europe by all means, were disappointed at Eisenhower's restraint.

Although unwilling to resort to MacArthur's drastic measures, Eisenhower did not discount the value of threats in forcing the Chinese to resume negotiations. He gave every indication that he was considering an escalation of military actions in Korea and against China's mainland: an announcement that he was removing the Seventh Fleet from the Taiwan Strait, which freed Nationalist troops on Taiwan to attack the Communists, a reversal of the original rationale for having it there to prevent a Communist invasion of the island; his visit to Korea; a well-publicized consultation with MacArthur on how to end the war; and congressional testimony by the new secretary of defense, Charles Wilson, who hinted at stepped-up military actions in Korea, were all intended to scare the Chinese into a new round of negotiations that could lead to an armistice.

Mao, however, was not intimidated. He correctly believed that China's defensive lines in Korea would hold against any new assault, and that Eisenhower would not resort to atomic bombs because of the certain condemnation by world opinion and the danger of a nuclear exchange with Moscow. Mao calculated that Eisenhower's public descriptions of the war as "intolerable" meant not an all-out campaign to win but an indication that the Americans would be the first to offer an olive branch, which the Chinese could then agree to as a face-saving way to return to the peace table. Consequently, in February 1953, when Mark Clark proposed an exchange of sick and wounded POWs as a first step toward renewed discussions, the Chinese were ready to accept.

At the end of March, Peking agreed to a mutual repatriation of wounded and sick POWs. The Chinese followed this announcement with a proposal that prisoners who refused repatriation should be transferred to a neutral state, where the question of their ultimate location could be settled without continuing pressure from any of the belligerents. Peking tied this proposal to a resumption of the armistice talks at Panmunjom.

Eisenhower was ready to accept and told his National Security Council on April 8 that he would settle for an armistice that divided the peninsula along current North-South lines, which meant largely a return to the prewar status quo. Dulles and Wilson opposed a truce that left a Communist regime in the North. Dulles thought that the United States could not "get much out of a Korean settlement until we have shown—before all Asia—our clear superiority by giving the Chinese one hell of a licking." An armistice conceding North Korea to Communist control was an affirmation not of rollback or liberation, as promised in the campaign, but of Truman's containment policy.

Having considered a Dulles proposal for an offensive aimed at occupying about a third of all North Korea, the area below Pyongyang and Wonsan, Eisenhower concluded that the cost of such an attack would be too high and was more likely to prolong than end the war. On April 16, 1953, in a speech before the American Society of Newspaper Editors, he rejected counsels of renewed military action and urged an end to the U.S.-USSR arms race: They were a formula for "perpetual fear and tension. . . . Every gun that is made," he asserted, "every warship launched, every rocket fired signifies, in the final sense, a theft from those who hunger and are not fed, those who are cold and are not clothed." Coming from a general who could not be dismissed as a soft-minded pacifist opposed to all wars, Eisenhower's preference for negotiations over expanded combat in

Korea carried exceptional weight with all but the most doctrinaire anti-Communists at home and abroad.

His speech was a prelude to renewed truce talks at the end of April. It would take three more months before both sides could find common ground for an armistice. During that time, Eisenhower struggled against right-wing Republicans and South Korea's Rhee, who opposed a settlement that could not be described as a decisive defeat of the Communists: militants in his party and Rhee complained that leaving Kim in power was appeasement of an aggressor and a prescription for another future attack on the South by the Communist North. Conservative Republican opponents of Ike's policy privately observed that if Truman had done what Eisenhower was doing, he would have been impeached. Counterpressures from American public opinion, which was eager to end the fighting (84 percent of an April 1953 poll favored a settlement), and from NATO allies, who considered the war a distraction from the larger issue of European security, gave Eisenhower leverage to move forward in the peace talks.

At times, however, it seemed as if the president, in the words of one American diplomat, was "trying to reconcile the irreconcilable." Syngman Rhee was especially difficult to bring in line with Eisenhower's decision to end the fighting. In mid-June, the South Korean president released some 27,000 Communist POWs, who took refuge in South Korea. It was an embarrassment to both Pyongyang and Peking that so many of their citizens would refuse repatriation. Rhee's action, tied to the possibility that he might reject any final settlement and continue fighting, jeopardized prospects for an armistice.

To prevent Rhee, whose troops manned two-thirds of the front lines, from blocking a truce, Eisenhower agreed to a mutual defense treaty between Washington and Seoul, promising to defend South Korea against any future attack, pledged economic assistance to rebuild the South, and agreed to support a postwar political conference that would seek ways to unify the peninsula. Despite these commitments, Rhee, a reckless nationalist single-mindedly committed to over-throwing Kim and unifying all Korea under his rule, refused to sign a truce, though he agreed not to obstruct it. He did, however, threaten to resume fighting if a post-armistice conference failed to bring uni-fication. The reality, however, that the United States and other UN allies would not fight with him made this an empty threat. Moreover, Eisenhower made clear to Rhee that any decision he made to go it alone would be an act of national suicide.

Were it not for Eisenhower's determination to end the war, the conflict might have continued indefinitely, though the settlement was as much dependent on Chinese agreement as that of Washington. Like Eisenhower, Mao saw more to be gained from ending the war in July 1953 than from additional fighting. Having reduced the em-barrassment of some 14,000 Chinese and 8,000 North Korean POWs refusing repatriation by transferring them to United Nations supervi-sion, where their decisions to go to Taiwan and South Korea could not be so readily exploited by the United States or Seoul, and having launched successful last-minute offensives against South Korean po-sitions that brought the truce line closer to the thirty-eighth parallel, Peking could end the war with plausible assertions of victory. Where the United States' willingness to fight in Korea gave it greater cred-ibility with NATO and Japan as a reliable ally, the Chinese emerged from the conflict with higher standing as a nation able to mount an effective resistance to the world's principal superpower. A Chinese general announced shortly after the armistice went into effect, "The time has gone forever when the Western powers were able to conquer a country in the East merely by mounting several cannons along the coast."

The war was a demonstration of poor leadership by all the bel-ligerents. Kim and Rhee had been equally determined to destroy the other's power and unify the peninsula under his rule; neither could imagine a coalition government for the good of the country. Nor did either of them foresee the sort of mass destruction of life and infrastructure with no discernible gain at the end of the fighting. Their respective convictions that only their kind of governance would serve Korea blinded them to the horrors of the civil war.

By the close of the conflict, neither Truman nor Mao had done much better than Kim or Rhee. Truman's initial decision to respond to Kim's aggression made eminent good sense. To stand aside would have carried unacceptable political consequences at home and abroad. But crossing the parallel proved to be reckless, serving neither the United States in general nor the White House in particular: it cost thousands of additional American lives, provoked antagonisms with China for another twenty years, and largely destroyed Truman's capacity to lead. The only initial gain for his administration was in quieting political attacks from the American right, which would have pilloried the president and Acheson for missing a chance to liberate North Korea from communism. But the invasion of the North bought Truman only six months of bipartisan support. Once he rejected MacArthur's ill-advised strategy for a wider war with China and, if necessary, a showdown with Soviet Russia, he became the object of a renewed right-wing campaign of vilification.

Mao cannot be seen as any wiser than Truman or the Koreans for having entered the conflict. China's battlefield casualties were horrendous—more than a million—and the war delayed badly needed investments in the domestic economy to raise the country's miserably low standard of living. The alternative of a Korea under United Nations control would have posed no significant threat to Peking and would have freed it from the difficulties that reclusive North Korean regimes continued to pose to peace in northeast Asia. (Pyongyang's reach for nuclear weapons fifty years later became an obstacle to China's improved dealings with the United States, Japan, and South Korea.) The United States had no intention of making Korea into a permanent outpost of anticommunism from which it would work to destabilize Mao's regime. But all the apocalyptic talk in the United States and Peking and Moscow about destroying communism and capitalism made more rational considerations on both sides all but impossible. It is an object lesson in why public officials should speak softly, especially when they have the where-withal to strike with a big stick.

Stalin's Russia did not escape the negative consequences of the war either. Although Stalin made only limited commitments of men and matériel to the fighting, he was a prime mover in causing and con-tinuing the war for three years. His hopes of seeing a Communist regime across the entire Korean Peninsula and of negotiating an end to the U.S. occupation of Japan by making it a neutral country in the Cold War were disappointed when Truman decided to resist Kim's invasion of the South and make a separate peace agreement with Tokyo that included U.S. bases in the home islands.

Only with Stalin's death from a stroke at the age of seventy-three did Moscow weigh in on ending the Korean conflict. The new Soviet leaders—the troika of Nikita Khrushchev, Lavrenty Beria, and Georgy Malenkov—fearful of a war with the United States, for which they felt unprepared, launched a peace campaign. "There is not one disputed . . . question that can not be decided by peaceful means on the basis of mutual understanding of interested countries," Malenkov declared in a well-publicized speech on March 15, 1953, ten days after Stalin had died.

The world was fortunate to have escaped a Soviet-American con-flict in Stalin's last days. The gamble he and Mao had made that the United States would not resort to nuclear weapons to end the Korean War and destroy Communist rule in Korea and China had succeeded. But Soviet advocacy of peaceful coexistence after Stalin's death was evidence of how doubtful the government's new leaders were about Stalin's foreign policies toward Europe and Asia. "In the days leading up to Stalin's death we believed that America would invade the Soviet Union and we would go to war," Khrushchev recalled.

In the last months of his life, Stalin continued to hold extraordi-nary power through the continuing intimidation of everyone inside and outside of his government, including even his closest associates. No one felt safe from his wrath, which could explode against the most loyal of his subordinates: if they were lucky, they would find themselves in exile; if unlucky, imprisoned, tortured, and executed for crimes they never committed. The men most directly around him saw Stalin as now "more capricious, irritable, and brutal" than ever. At all-night bacchanalias, he would take pleasure in humiliating guests by making them sing or dance. Khrushchev remembered that "when Stalin says dance, a wise man dances."

Stalin saw conspiracies everywhere. "I trust no one, not even myself," he said in front of two associates, who he seemed not to notice. Perhaps it was his way of warning those around him that he could not control his paranoia, which could victimize anyone who had close contact with him. Before he ate or drank, a food tester would consume some of the food and drink to assure it was not poisoned.

In 1953, the principal target of Stalin's suspicions was Jewish doctors, who he believed were trying to kill him—or at least, so he said. It was a renewal of the anti-Semitic outburst that had resulted in the persecution of the wartime Jewish Anti-Fascist Committee in 1948. Stalin accused the doctors of being pro-Zionist traitors more loyal to the new state of Israel than to the Soviet Union, pawns of Wall Street Jewish bankers and of American agents working to destroy Soviet Russia's Communist rule.

The Jewish wives of top Soviet officials like Foreign Minister Vyacheslav Molotov and Mikhail Kalinin, the head of state, were imprisoned for crimes against the Soviet government. The chairman of the Jewish Anti-Fascist Committee, Solomon Mikhoels, a leading actor and director of the Moscow Yiddish Theater who had entertained Stalin with private performances of *King Lear* and other Shakespearean dramas, was assassinated in 1948, alleged to have been killed in a car accident. In August 1952, in what came to be known as "the Night of the Murdered Poets," twenty-four Jewish writers and poets were executed in the basement of Moscow's infamous Lubyanka prison.

The alleged doctors' plot may have arisen from Stalin's need for a domestic crisis that would continue to make him the indispensable chief. When he distributed the transcripts of the Jewish doctors' confessions to his associates, Stalin told them, "You are blind like young kittens; what will happen without me? The country will perish because you do not know how to recognize enemies." In January 1953, as the likelihood of a settlement in Korea promised to remove international tensions that Stalin used to sustain his reputation as the nation's best defender—the man who had rescued Soviet Russia from Nazi conquest and now protected it from American capitalists— he went public with the doctors' conspiracy, which allegedly served American-Zionist interests intent on destroying communism.

Stalin's last hours were a window on the terror he had instilled in everyone—from the ordinary citizen to the highest officials. On March 1, 1953, at the height of the so-called doctors' plot, after he had suffered a stroke, Stalin's guards and closest Kremlin associates resisted calling a physician; they feared that he might see it as an attempt to kill him and would retaliate against them if he recovered. When doctors were finally summoned, the physicians, according to one of the guards, "were all trembling like us. . . . Their hands were trembling so much that they could not even get his shirt off." They were "terrified to touch Stalin," to take his pulse.

Felled by a massive stroke or "cerebral catastrophe," Stalin lingered for three days, falling in and out of consciousness. His incapacity brought forth an explosion of invective from Beria, who seemed elated at the imminent death of his tormentor and protector. During moments of waking when it seemed that Stalin might recover, Beria would kneel beside him and kiss his hand. The "magnates," the Politburo insiders who took up the death watch, exhibited feelings of elation and grief at the dictator's passing.

Although the full extent of Stalin's crimes—some 20 million people killed and additional millions exiled to the gulag—would not be fully revealed until after his death, it was an open secret among attentive citizens. No one in the Soviet Union could doubt that they lived in a police state, where the slightest dissent could cost them their life or, at a minimum, the freedom to enjoy the meager Third World existence socialism had inflicted on the country. Yet open protests against Soviet rule were unheard of. Victory in the war and a long history of paternalistic governance by monarchs—whether czars or Soviets—joined with a sense of permanent foreign danger to give Stalin an unshakable hold on his people. Were it not for the regime's terror tactics, which made opposition life-threatening, a reach for a different kind of government that reduced the likelihood of a cold war is imaginable.

Despite the East-West split that put the world constantly on edge and contributed to the onset of the Korean fighting, Russia and the United States managed to avert a third twentieth-century conflict that would have been even more devastating than the century's two earlier wars of mass destruction. The end of the Korean conflict, however, did not call a halt to the fighting between Communists or Soviet-Chinese surrogates, as Washington saw them, and the United States. The Korean armistice temporarily ended America's use of combat forces to fight Asian Communists. But events in Indochina posed new challenges to Washington's determination to halt the advance of communism in Asia, and once again tested Moscow's and Washington's hopes of averting a larger, unprecedented nuclear exchange.

De Gaulle's decision to reestablish France's colonial rule in Indochina had provoked an immediate confrontation with Ho Chi Minh's aspirations for an independent Communist Vietnamese government. And though the United States had supported Ho against the Japanese during the war and even had military representatives on a reviewing stand in Hanoi when Ho declared Vietnamese independence in September 1945, Washington quickly deferred to French insistence on support for control of its Indo-Chinese colonies—Cambodia, Laos, and Vietnam. From September 1945 to November 1946, an uneasy truce marked Ho's relations with the French: they controlled Vietnam south of the seventeenth parallel, and Ho enjoyed limited dominance in the north, where he governed a nominally independent state as part of the French Union.

Neither side, however, was content with the arrangement. Paris would not agree to anything that meant independence for Vietnam or an end to colonial rule, while Ho was determined to achieve full sovereignty for his country. In November 1946, after a series of attacks by insurgents aiming to compel a grant of independence, a French naval bombardment of Haiphong, the principal port city in the north, triggered a full-scale rebellion against French rule.

Although unable to suppress Ho's insurgency, the French created a puppet government under Bao Dai in Saigon, which depended on French military power to hold off Ho's Viet Minh Communist opposition. At the end of 1949, however, when the Chinese, eager to expand Communist rule to Indochina, began providing advisers and increased military aid to Ho's forces, it threatened to end French control. Having already spent $1.5 billion trying to suppress the rebellion, Paris resolved to meet the challenge and lobbied Washington for financial and military aid.

In 1950, the outbreak of fighting in Korea strengthened Mao's determination to aid Ho's rebellion in order to ensure a friendly regime on China's southern border. Over the next two years Ho's Viet Minh, supported by continuing advice and matériel from the Chinese, fought a series of engagements that gave the Communists substantial control of northeast Vietnam. Expanding their operations to northwest Vietnam in the first half of 1953, the Viet Minh and Chinese saw the end of the Korean fighting in July as an opportunity to focus on ousting France from all of Southeast Asia.

At the start of 1950, the Communist victory in China had convinced American planners that the defense of Southeast Asia was vital in the worldwide contest with Moscow and Peking. If the Communists were to seize control of the region, a National Security Council directive declared, "we shall have suffered a major political rout the repercussions of which will be felt throughout the world." In January 1950, Soviet recognition of the Viet Minh as the legitimate government of Vietnam confirmed Washington's view that France's battle against Ho's insurgents was crucial to preserving all of Southeast Asia from Communist domination. In March, the Truman administration began an expanded program of aid to France in its battle for control of Indochina, especially Vietnam, much of which was now under Viet Minh control.

During the next three years, neither Paris nor Washington could find a solution to France's eroding power in the region. While determined to maintain colonial rule in Southeast Asia as a demonstration of its standing as a world power, France had neither the resources, the unity of purpose, nor the strategic plan to maintain its hold on a Vietnamese population eager to rid itself of a Western colonial master. The Truman and then Eisenhower administrations saw saving Vietnam from a Communist takeover as essential to preserving from communism not only all Southeast Asia but also other Third World countries in Asia, Africa, and the Middle East.

Yet, like the French, the United States could not find the means to reach its goals. Washington wanted no part of continued French colonial rule, which Paris refused to relinquish, and which U.S. policymakers believed would undermine America's appeal as an advocate of self-determination for all peoples. Consequently, neither Truman nor Eisenhower would agree to take over the fighting from the French. Pleas from Paris for the use of U.S. airpower and, at the last moment, ground forces to rescue the French from defeat were ruled out as too likely to involve the country in another unpopular conflict like Korea and give Moscow and Peking talking points with other colonies battling to free themselves from Western colonialism.

The struggle for control of Vietnam was the object of distorted assumptions by all the belligerents. The Vietnamese Communists sold support for their cause to the Chinese by promoting the belief that their victory against the French and the Americans, who, in spite of everything, were financing and supplying French forces, could be seen as a triumph over all Western colonial control and for Communist insurgency everywhere.

The Chinese did not need much prodding from Ho to see Communist rule in Vietnam as not simply a defensive barrier on their southern border but as having the wider implications Ho suggested. Having fought the United States to a standstill in Korea, the Chinese now hoped to build on that with a Communist victory in Vietnam and possibly Cambodia and Laos. More importantly, they assumed that Communist success in Southeast Asia would stand as a clarion call to all Asians to follow China into the socialist camp. The Soviets, though less invested in the Korean and Vietnamese conflicts, nevertheless shared the hope that world revolution was a distinct possibility and that preserving Kim's Communist regime in Korea and helping Ho claim victory in Vietnam were part of the larger proletarian reach for world power.

The dream of communism spreading around the globe was a grand illusion: the sort of false belief that revolutionaries, whose auto-intoxication is essential in motivating them to risk their lives for a cause outside themselves, always cling to. It is the conviction of those promoting the true religion, the ultimate answer to human dilemmas, the triumph of man over his own nature and the failed forms of governance that have been tried throughout history.

The French and Americans weren't much different from the Chinese or the Soviets in their illusory thinking. For French citizens, struggling to regain their sense of national pride after their humiliating defeat in World War II, holding on to their empire seemed essential if they were to maintain any sort of standing as a great power. For the Americans, who saw Communist gains in Europe and Asia as an indication that democracy and capitalism were in retreat and faced catastrophic losses everywhere, Vietnam and Southeast Asia took on exaggerated importance.

Neither the Vietnamese nor the Chinese nor the Soviets nor the French nor the Americans were realistic about what a Communist government in Vietnam would ultimately mean. It did not signal the collapse of French power; to the contrary, France's release from its military and economic burdens in Asia and Africa freed it to be a more productive and prosperous society. De Gaulle's conviction that the loss of empire would threaten France with a renewed sense of defeat that would make it vulnerable to Communist control proved to be dead wrong. It was a misreading of events that he himself came to acknowledge.

Moreover, Ho's victory in Vietnam did not presage Communist rule across all of Southeast Asia or any other part of the world. It was strictly a homegrown movement that could not even extend its influence to its closest neighbors.

Like so much else in the years after World War II, assumptions by the world's most astute and powerful leaders were deeply flawed. Churchill, who had his share of misjudgments, sensed the missteps animating the postwar generation when he said in 1947, "It would be a great reform in politics if wisdom could be made to spread as easily and as rapidly as folly."

EPILOGUE

Dost thou not know, my son, with what
little wisdom the world is governed?
—Count Oxenstierna, Swedish statesman, 1648

Almost four hundred years later, Oxenstierna's query seems rhetorical. The more perplexing question is: Why can't a world with so many intelligent and thoughtful people do better? Part of the answer may be that people do not want to face up to how badly their leaders performed or how much people believe that national failings by their leaders reflect poorly on themselves: Holocaust deniers, a Russian government currently trying to depict Joseph Stalin as the architect of victory in World War II without reference to his annihilation of opponents, real and fancied, and Japanese nationalists refusing to acknowledge the Nanjing massacres or the grievances of Korean "comfort women" are cases in point.

A collective amnesia or reluctance to learn from past miscues is another part of the equation. Was the German philosopher Hegel right when he said that the only thing we learn from history is that we never learn? His cynicism seems largely vindicated by the history of the first half of the twentieth century. Political leaders and governments around the world certainly did not take much knowledge from the horrors of the two world wars.

Hitler, delusional to the end, could not imagine how universally despised he would be. And the German masses marched in lockstep with him until their country lay in ruins and they had suffered total defeat. Even the military plotters of 1944 who tried to assassinate the Führer and fend off Germany's collapse acted not out of protest against Hitler's crimes but to spare the Fatherland from additional suffering.

Stalin went to his grave with no misgivings about the horrors he had perpetrated against his own people, let alone the misery he had inflicted on all Europe by facilitating Hitler's initial aggression in 1939–40. His postwar crimes were continuing acts of faith in his messianic convictions about communism and Russia. And the passivity of the Soviet masses in stoically accepting the fictions Stalin and his Politburo collaborators presented as gospel remain puzzles no historian probably will ever fully explain.

Nor have only villains like the Führer and the Red Czar, as some called Stalin, been excoriated for policies and actions that produced so much human suffering. China's lethal combination of Chiang and Mao cost the lives of millions as well. Lesser dictators like Kim Il Sung and Syngman Rhee, who were also architects of national and international misery, albeit on a smaller scale, have come in for their share of justifiable opprobrium.

The desolation caused by far more honorable and well-meaning leaders like Charles de Gaulle and Harry Truman should not be overlooked: de Gaulle's efforts to reestablish France's colonial empire and Truman's decision to cross the thirty-eighth parallel in Korea led to bloodshed and losses that could have been avoided. These leaders' affinity for earlier truths or misappropriations of history—national standing measured by its global reach and the need to see every aggressor as another Hitler—were of limited use in deciding what would serve their national interests post-1945.

The distressing news is that wretched acts of leadership did not abate entirely in the years after 1953, when Stalin's death and the end of the Korean War gave the world glimmers of hope for a better future. To be sure, nations have not had another catastrophic worldwide conflict since then. Ironically, the deterrent has been less an aversion to war than the existence of nuclear weapons that could destroy nations and jeopardize human survival. But despite the documented crimes of Hitler and Stalin, mass killings have not disappeared. Earlier offenses against humanity formed no inhibition on Cambodia's killing fields, for example.

The men at the helm of several countries in the last six decades have taken a number of wrong turns. France's misadventures in Algeria; the Anglo-French-Israeli missteps in the Suez attack; Nikita Khrushchev's provocation of the Cuban missile crisis, which brought the world to the brink of a nuclear war; the Chinese Communist government's Cultural Revolution and the repression of dissidents in Tiananmen Square; the failure of Pakistan and India to avoid the 1971 conflict, and subsequent tensions that led them to build nuclear arsenals; the Soviet Union's destructive intervention in Afghanistan; the Balkan strife of the 1990s, with its episodes of ethnic cleansing; the unresolved Israeli-Palestinian conflict that has made the Middle East a constant source of world troubles; the 1994 Rwandan genocide visited on Tutsis by Hutu militias, and the world's failure to intervene; the more recent genocide in Darfur, Sudan; and the Iranian and North Korean obsessions with acquiring nuclear weapons that pose threats to international stability are some of the most glaring examples of the disasters and difficulties more rational leadership and better understanding of past missteps by government chiefs might have prevented.

The United States, the dominant global power for the last sixty-five years, has not been innocent of actions that violate human rights and cause suffering: Eisenhower's use of the CIA to topple popular governments in Iran and Guatemala; John Kennedy's unleashing of Cuban exiles at the Bay of Pigs to bring down Fidel Castro; Lyndon Johnson's failed war to rescue South Vietnam from Communist control; Richard Nixon's and Henry Kissinger's four-year extension of the Vietnam War and their aid in ousting Salvador Allende's democratically elected government in Chile; Ronald Reagan's machinations supporting the contras in Nicaragua; and George W. Bush's determination to spread democracy across the Middle East by overturning Saddam Hussein's rule in Iraq are case studies in actions that ultimately served neither American nor international well-being.

It would be extraordinary if we could discern a common pattern in all these miscalculations by U.S. and foreign leaders. But the best we can say is that these disasters were not the result of inevitable forces beyond human control; rather, they were the consequence of bad judgments and a misuse of historical experience by decision makers, who more often than not acted with the support of national majorities.

The errors of the pre-1953 years, however, have not gone entirely unrecognized. To the contrary, U.S. and foreign leaders since that time have partly compiled a record of sensible actions that rested on rational calculation and a realistic reading of the past and the present. A balanced assessment of these recent years makes it clear that blunders were not the only distinguishing feature of the period. A recounting of some of the brighter moments may provide clues to what has gone into wise governance.

John F. Kennedy's successful resolution of the Cuban missile crisis is a striking example of effective and constructive leadership. Kennedy's military advisers favored a bombing campaign and an invasion to assure the elimination of the missile sites Khrushchev had decided to build in Cuba. Because the emplacement of nuclear missiles on the island would reduce America's significant advantage in the nuclear arms race with Russia and incidentally undermine the president's political standing at home and abroad, Kennedy could not allow it to go forward. Persuading the Russians to remove the missiles without military action that could lead to a wider war presented Kennedy with a grave challenge. Just how grave would only become known later, when it was learned that U.S. military steps would likely have led to a nuclear exchange costing millions of lives and devastation to a part of the United States and most of Russia's principal cities.

Kennedy saw military action as a desperate last resort. He believed trying a blockade of Cuba or a "quarantine," which was less likely to be described as an act of war, should be a first step. The Joint Chiefs were dead set against it. Maxwell Taylor, chairman of the Joint Chiefs, warned that without a military response, the United States would lose credibility with its allies. Air Force Chief of Staff Curtis LeMay dismissed a blockade as "a pretty weak response," which provoked Kennedy's dismissive remark about the "brass hats" and their affinity for a war that would kill all of them.

When Khrushchev backed down, Kennedy wisely instructed his staff not to betray any hint of gloating—a provocation to Soviet credibility and pride could lead to a later war. Similarly, he rejected additional plans for an invasion, which Secretary of Defense Robert McNamara put before him in case the Soviets did not honor a promise to remove their missiles. Kennedy continued to see an invasion as carrying huge risks: "Consider the size of the problem," he told McNamara, "the equipment that is involved on the other side, the Nationalists['] fervor which may be engendered, it seems to me we could end up bogged down. I think we should keep constantly in mind the British in the Boer War, the Russians in the last war with the Finnish and our own experience with the North Koreans." Given his concerns about getting "bogged down" only ninety miles from U.S. shores, would Kennedy have been as ready as Lyndon Johnson to put hundreds of thousands of ground troops into Vietnam?

Kennedy has been much praised for his resistance to using unnecessary force and his rational decision making, which resolved the crisis and spared the world from a nuclear holocaust. It was a model of wise statesmanship. But it is not a blueprint for how to act in some future crisis with its own special attributes—except to emphasize that the components of Kennedy's success were a realistic grasp of current considerations and of relevant historical analogies.

Richard Nixon and Henry Kissinger were similarly rational in reducing the long-standing tensions between the United States and

China by traveling to Beijing for reconciliation talks. Nixon, the principal architect of the policy shift, had a personal history as a tough-minded anti-Communist. His understanding that no one in the United States, including the conservatives most likely to object to a conciliatory initiative toward Beijing, could accuse him of appeasement was a piece of political realism that made all the difference in allowing him to go forward with so bold a move. In addition, his realistic assessment of the advantages and disadvantages of continuing hostilities with a nation of over 800 million people, who were at odds with America's other great Communist adversary, the Soviet Union, was crucial in convincing him that improved relations with China carried substantial benefits for the United States.

Expanded trade with China was one goal of a new day in dealings with Mao's government. But more important in Nixon's thinking was the strategic value the United States could gain from better relations with Beijing: Nixon shrewdly calculated that Moscow was bound to see friendlier U.S. dealings with China as a threat to Soviet security, which was jeopardized by severe tensions with a nuclear-armed China allied to the United States. Nixon's understanding that Sino-Soviet differences contributed to a long history of tensions between the two countries convinced him that the Soviets would respond to his China initiative with proposals for reduced Soviet-American tensions. Within months of traveling to China, Nixon went to Moscow, where he and Soviet leaders reached arms control and trade agreements that amounted to a détente in their formerly strained relations.

The dramatic developments in U.S. relations with the two Communist giants aimed not only to improve America's national security but also to advance a structure of international peace: an end to the war in Vietnam, greater European harmony, reduced tensions in the Middle East, and a return to something resembling Franklin Roosevelt's Good Neighbor policy in Latin America. While Nixon and Kissinger fell short of their grand design, their recognition that nuclear weapons had made great power wars unacceptable and their realistic assessment of the limits of American power sensibly advanced international stability. Moreover, they provided a model of realistic dealings that future American presidents and foreign leaders could consult in serving every nation's quest for peace.

The model of rational behavior informed by a grasp of recent history resonated during George H. W. Bush's presidency in the Gulf War of 1990–91. Iraq's invasion of Kuwait in August 1990 triggered a coalition of forces led by the United States to compel Saddam Hussein to relinquish his conquest and desist from further aggression against its neighbors. In a brief air and land campaign in January and February 1991, the coalition forced Hussein to retreat from Kuwait. Remembering Harry Truman's problems after he decided to cross the thirty-eighth parallel to topple North Korea's Communist regime, Bush called a halt to the fighting at Iraq's borders. He believed that an invasion of Iraq would cost the United States and its allies unacceptable casualties and would burden his administration with responsibility for a fractious society. In his words, we would become "an occupying power in a bitterly hostile land."

As the Iraq War initiated by George W. Bush has demonstrated, his father's outlook was prophetic. With relatively narrow majorities supporting the 1991 war—52–47 in the Senate and 250–183 in the House—the first President Bush feared an expanded conflict with increased casualties and "no viable 'exit strategy.' " He worried that the United States would become trapped in an unpopular conflict that neither coalition partners nor congressional or public majorities would support, a repetition of the domestic responses to the Korean and Vietnam wars that did so much to undermine the Truman and Lyndon Johnson presidencies. Bush described the Gulf War as an indication that the United States had kicked the Vietnam syndrome. An invasion of Iraq would have repudiated his assertion.

In the twentieth century, successful rational calculation in international dealings, however noteworthy, was never the consistent rule, even for presidents like Kennedy, Nixon, and the first George Bush, whose prescience did not translate into wisdom in response to all their foreign policy challenges. Yet the inconsistency in performance of most leaders is no reason for despair. Given the uncertainties in human affairs and the many regrettable decisions highlighted in this book, it would be easy enough to succumb to Plato's observation that "only the dead have seen the end of war." Or to indulge our pessimistic side with Mark Twain's wry observation, "When we remember we are all mad, the mysteries disappear and life stands explained."

But in spite of painful misjudgments, good sense and courageous determination to muster renewed hope have been an enduring force in world affairs. That the countries of Eastern Europe and Russia emerged from decades of miserable Soviet control with a new spirit of eagerness to build better societies; that Germany and Japan could break with their pasts to establish functioning democracies; that racial segregation in the United States has come to seem so foreign alongside current accepted norms, all suggest an optimism about human progress, not perfection, to be sure, but slow steady movement toward sensible regard for life and liberty, that should make even the sourest of pessimists marvel at the capacity for change.

The missteps recounted in this book, then, should be taken not as an admission of hopelessness but as a reminder that the flawed leadership of the past was less the consequence of circumstances than of choice. Just as war among Western Europe's nations has become an anachronism, so power in the hands of ruthless leaders willing to abuse individual and collective rights can be made an artifact of the past, or at least more the exception than the rule. A world with wise leadership is not easily achieved, but it is not beyond imagining.

ACKNOWLEDGMENTS

This book rests in significant part on the pioneering scholarship of journalists and historians who have written so perceptively about the end of war and immediate postwar years. I am especially indebted to the masterful accounts of events in Germany, the Soviet Union, China, and Korea that are central to any understanding of this period's troubles. The book's notes and bibliography reflect the specifics of my obligation to existing studies.

None of this is to suggest that the books and articles I have mined for information bear any responsibility for my interpretations and conclusions. This is not to suggest that earlier writers are without influence on my thinking, especially George F. Kennan, whose contemporary critiques of policy decisions I found highly convincing. Nevertheless, my judgments are the result of my own considered opinions, developed from many years of teaching and writing about the events covered in the book.

I am grateful to several people for taking time from their busy schedules to read and suggest revisions of my chapters. Andrew J. Bacevich, Matthew Dallek, Stephen Krasner, and John W. Wright gave me the benefit of their keen judgments on what I had written. Kai Bird, Peter Kovler, and Martin Sherwin responded to numerous lunchtime discussions of my ideas with encouragement and thoughtful critiques. All their suggestions helped me sharpen my arguments and make the writing more accessible to a wider audience.

At an early stage in my thinking about the book, Elisabeth Sifton encouraged me to broaden my focus from 1945 to the seven years between the end of the war and the beginning of the Eisenhower presidency, the time frame I have covered. I greatly appreciate her suggestion.

Tim Duggan, my editor, provided a superb critique after reading the first half of the manuscript. It led me to rethink some of what I had done, and it helped shape the whole book. His wise counsel has been a constant source of support, for which I am most grateful.

Allison Lorentzen, Tim Duggan's right hand, and Lydia Weaver, the production editor, were essential collaborators in turning the manuscript into a finished book. I am grateful to them, as I am to Miranda Ottewell, whose excellence as a copy editor saved me from numerous errors; I am most appreciative of her help.

As with everything I have written over the last forty years, my wife, Geraldine Dallek, brought her keen editorial skills to bear on my prose. She has made me a better writer and a better historian, or at a minimum, a scholar who constantly keeps in mind that the best history engages an educated public eager to learn the lessons of the past. She has been an indispensable helpmate in all I have achieved.

NOTES

Introduction

1 **At the start of 1945**: Winston S. Churchill, *The Second World War: The Gathering Storm* (New York: Bantam Books, 1948), vii–viii.

2 **At the start of the twentieth century**: James J. Sheehan, *Where Have All the Soldiers Gone? The Transformation of Modern Europe* (Boston: Houghton Mifflin, 2008), chap. 1.

2 **Yet while national leaders**: Ibid., 105–7. The Clemenceau quote can be found at "Quotations by Subject: War," The Quotations Page, http://www.quotations page.com/subjects/war/.

3 **Although a formidable**: George Mosse, *Fallen Soldiers: Reshaping the Memory of the World Wars* (New York: Oxford University Press, 1990), 6–7.

3 **This pride, combined with**: See Geoffrey Wheatcroft, "Europeans Are from Venus," review of Sheehan, *Where Have All the Soldiers Gone? New York Times Book Review*, February 10, 2008, pp. 26–27.

3 **World War II consumed**: John W. Dower, *War without Mercy: Race and Power in the Pacific War* (New York: Pantheon Books, 1986), 22, 51–52, 90–93, 328 n. 47; David M. Kennedy, *Freedom from Fear: The American People in Depression and War, 1929–1945* (New York: Oxford University Press, 1999), 530–31, 811.

4 **Japanese troops**: Kennedy, *Freedom from Fear*, 812.

5 **Although Germany's Nazis**: Dower, *War without Mercy*, 34–35; Pyle is quoted on pp. 78, 140.

5 **The perception about**: Saul Friedlander, *Nazi Germany and the Jews: The Years of Persecution, 1933–1939* (New York: HarperCollins, 1997), 1; Lucy S. Dawidowicz, *The War against the Jews, 1933–1945* (New York: Holt, Rinehart and Winston, 1975), provides a numerical, country-by-country capsule account of the Holocaust in appendixes A and B.

5 **Allied victory in 1945**: Marshall is quoted in the *Dartmouth Review*, February 8, 2008. For the polls, see George H. Gallup, *The Gallup Poll: Public Opinion, 1935–1948* (New York: Random House, 1972), 497 and 517.

6 **And yet leaders**: Suzy Platt, ed., *Respectfully Quoted: A Dictionary of Quotations* *from the Library of Congress* (Washington, D.C.: Congressional Quarterly, 1992), 194, 332.

6 **Alexis de Tocqueville**: Daniel Jonah Goldhagen, *Hitler's Willing Executioners* (New York: Vintage Books, 1997), frontispiece.

6 **Winston Churchill**: Anthony Jay, ed., *The Oxford Dictionary of Political Quotations* (New York: Oxford University Press, 1996), 88–89; Platt, *Respectfully Quoted*, 291. On Lincoln and Washington, see *Gallup Poll, 1935–1948*, p. 489.

7 **Churchill understood**: Einstein is quoted in "Quotations by Subject: War."

8 **"peoples' peace"**: Arthur Schlesinger Jr. and Fred L. Israel, *The State of the Union Messages of the Presidents, 1905–1966* (New York: Chelsea House, 1966), 2890–94.

8 **General Douglas MacArthur**: William Manchester, *American Caesar: Douglas MacArthur, 1880–1964* (Boston: Little, Brown, 1978), 448–54.

9 **The horrors**: Simon S. Montefiore, *Stalin: The Court of the Red Tsar* (New York: Vintage Books, 2005), 491–92.

11 **"Now the trumpet"**: For the JFK quote, see Robert Dallek, *An Unfinished Life: John F. Kennedy, 1917–1963* (New York: Little, Brown, 2003), 326.

12 **"I had a part"**: Gordon M. Goldstein, *Lessons in Disaster: McGeorge Bundy and the Path to War in Vietnam* (New York: Times Books, 2008), 21.

Chapter 1: London, Moscow, and Washington: Friends in Need

16 **Churchill's life**: A. J. P. Taylor, Robert Rhodes James, and J. H. Plumb, *Churchill: Four Faces and the Man* (Middlesex, England: Penguin Books, 1968), 50.

16 **From his earliest**: The details of Churchill's early life can be found in Roy Jenkins, *Churchill: A Biography* (New York: Farrar, Straus, and Giroux, 2001). There is also a detailed chronology of Churchill's life in Taylor, James, and Plumb, *Churchill*, 247–52. The quote "military glory" is on p. 226. "Bolshevism should have been" is quoted by Jeffrey Wallin in an interview with Juan Williams, September 4, 2001, Fox News Channel. Churchill's description of Mussolini is in Churchill, *Gathering Storm*, 13–14.

18 **In the 1920s**: On Spain, see Churchill, *Gathering Storm*, 190–93, 219–23. "Defeat without a war": Taylor, James, and Plumb, *Churchill*, 250. "You were given": "Winston Churchill," Wikipedia, http://en.wikipedia.org/wiki/Winston_Churchill.

19 **Churchill wisely**: Churchill, *Gathering Storm*, 349–52.

19 **For Churchill, the 1930s**: See Anthony Storr, "The Man," in Taylor, James, and Plumb, *Churchill*, 206–7, on how Churchill's life story translated into a rallying cry for all Britain.

20 **In rallying the nation**: Winston S. Churchill, *The Second World War: Their Finest Hour* (New York: Bantam Books, 1962), 13. See Storr, "The Man," 232, on Hitler as Churchill's ideal enemy.

21 **In June 1941**: Winston S. Churchill, *The Second World War: The Grand Alliance* (New York: Bantam Books, 1962), 313–15.

21 **In December 1941**: Martin Gilbert, *Winston S. Churchill: The Road to Victory, 1941–1945* (Boston: Houghton Mifflin, 1986), 16.

21 **Yet in October 1944**: On the Balkans, see Winston S. Churchill, *The Second World War: Triumph and Tragedy* (New York: Bantam Books, 1953), 196–202; and Alexander Werth, *Russia at War, 1941–1945* (New York: Avon Books, 1964), 828–29. On atomic power, see Robert Dallek, *Franklin D. Roosevelt and American Foreign Policy, 1932–1945* (New York: Oxford University Press, 1995), 416–18, 470–71.

24 **Roosevelt's suspicions**: See "Prologue: An American Internationalist," in Dallek, *Roosevelt and American Foreign Policy*, 3–20.

26 **Although he devoted**: On FDR's reaction to the Red scare, see Jean Edward Smith, *FDR* (New York: Random House, 2007), 171–73.

26 **Six months after**: On Russian recognition, see Dallek, *Roosevelt and American Foreign Policy*, 78–81. Howard is quoted in Smith, *FDR*, 342. Also see Frank Freidel, *Franklin D. Roosevelt: A Rendezvous with Destiny* (Boston: Little, Brown, 1990), 171–75.

27 **Roosevelt saw**: Freidel, *Roosevelt*, 175; Dallek, *Roosevelt and American Foreign Policy*, 80–81.

27 **Although Roosevelt's hopes**: Dallek, *Roosevelt and American Foreign Policy*, 196, 208–212; Freidel, *Roosevelt*, 319, 324–25.

28 **When Hitler invaded**: Dallek, *Roosevelt and American Foreign Policy*, 278–81, 292–96; Susan Butler, *My Dear Mr. Stalin* (New Haven, Conn.: Yale University Press, 2005), 3–5, 33–39.

29 **In the spring and summer of 1942**: For the descriptions of Molotov, see Montefiore, *Stalin*, 39–40. Also see "Vyacheslav Molotov," Wikipedia, http://en.wikipedia.org/wiki/Vyacheslav_Molotov.

30 **Although Roosevelt understood**: Dallek, *Roosevelt and American Foreign Policy*, 339–51.

30 **Hopkins took it**: Arthur M. Schlesinger Jr., *The Age of Roosevelt: The Coming of the New Deal* (Boston: Houghton Mifflin, 1959), 265–66; Dallek, *Roosevelt and American Foreign Policy*, 279–80.

31 **Churchill's agitation**: Gilbert, *Road to Victory*, 171–72. The general's quote is in "Dividing the World," episode 3 of the BBC documentary *World War II: Behind Closed Doors*, broadcast May 20, 2009.

31 **The Soviet leader**: For the exchange between Churchill and Stalin, see BBC, "Dividing the World." For the rest, see Montefiore, *Stalin*, 6–7.

32 **Born in 1878**: Stalin's early history: Montefiore, *Stalin*, chaps. 1–3.

32 **The man Churchill**: Ibid., 27, 55–57, 301, 335, 394–95, 477, 665 n. 1.

34 **The three men**: The anecdote about the cigarette case was told to me by George Kennan at a panel on World War II during a meeting of the Organization of American Historians. Stalin's comment on the English is in BBC, "Dividing the World." For the rest, see Gilbert, *Road to Victory*, 171–72, 176–79, 180–82, 184–87, 189, 192, 195, 204–05, 208; Warren F. Kimball, *Churchill and Roosevelt:*

Their Complete Correspondence (Princeton, N.J.: Princeton University Press, 1984), 1:560–61, 564–72.

36 **In fact, he and Roosevelt**: Butler, *My Dear Mr. Stalin*, 84–105; Gilbert, *Road to Victory*, 274, 279–82; Dallek, *Roosevelt and American Foreign Policy*, 368–69. For the cartoon, see BBC, "Dividing the World."

37 **Churchill and Roosevelt**: Dallek, *Roosevelt and American Foreign Policy*, 369–72; Gilbert, *Road to Victory*, 307.

38 **To soften the blow**: Dallek, *Roosevelt and American Foreign Policy*, 363–66, 373–76; Gilbert, *Road to Victory*, 312–13; Butler, *My Dear Mr. Stalin*, 112–22.

39 **During April**: Churchill on Smolensk is in BBC, "Dividing the World"; Butler, *My Dear Mr. Stalin*, 122–29.

39 **Roosevelt hoped**: Kimball, *Churchill and Roosevelt*, 2:283.

40 **In addition**: Robert Dallek, "World War II: E Pluribus Unum," chap. 5 in *The American Style of Foreign Policy: Cultural Politics and Foreign Affairs* (New York: Alfred A. Knopf, 1983).

40 **Despite initial receptivity**: Butler, *My Dear Mr. Stalin*, 136–39, 141–47.

41 **Although less important**: Dallek, *Roosevelt and American Foreign Policy*, 362–66, 376–79; *The Complete War Memoirs of Charles de Gaulle* (New York: Simon & Schuster, 1972), 382–99.

42 **Churchill's dealings**: Gilbert, *Road to Victory*, 275–78, 305–06.

43 **Churchill and Roosevelt were at odds**: On FDR's anticolonialism, see Dallek, *Roosevelt and American Foreign Policy*, 459–61.

43 **Despite their differences**: Butler, *My Dear Mr. Stalin*, 149–57.

Chapter 2: From Tehran to Roosevelt's Death

45 **By September 1943**: Dallek, *Roosevelt and American Foreign Policy*, 414–18.

45 **The meeting from November 28 to December 1**: *Ibid.*, 430–38; Gilbert, *Road to Victory*, 570–93.

46 **Churchill was wisely**: Butler, *My Dear Mr. Stalin*, 131–32, 159.

47 **Stalin flew**: Montefiore, *Stalin*, 463–66.

47 **Stalin worked hard**: Ibid., 469–70; Gilbert, *Road to Victory*, 576, 580–81.

48 **Roosevelt left the meetings**: Dallek, *Roosevelt and American Foreign Policy*, 431–41.

50 **For Roosevelt, an essential**: Freidel, *Roosevelt*, 512–18.

51 **Despite his health problems**: Dallek, *Roosevelt and American Foreign Policy*, 463–67.

52 **After Tehran**: Gilbert, *Road to Victory*, 651–52, 671–76, 699–700.

53 **During the rest of 1944**: Ibid., chap. 53, quotes on p. 1000.

53 **For Stalin**: Werth, *Russia at War*, 696–97.

53 **The victories**: Edward Radzinsky, *Stalin* (New York: Anchor Books, 1997), 500–04; Montefiore, *Stalin*, 472–73. Beria's statement is in "Lavrenty Beria," Wikipedia, http://en.wikipedia.org/wiki/Lavrenty_Beria. For more on Beria, see

I. C. B. Dear, *The Oxford Companion to the Second World War* (New York: Oxford University Press, 1995), 123–24; and Amy Knight, *Beria: Stalin's First Lieutenant* (Princeton, N.J.: Princeton University Press, 1993).

54 **Whatever the appearance**: Werth, *Russia at War*, 700–01, 826–31.

54 **All three leaders**: Gilbert, *Road to Victory*, 1064–66, 1069–70, 1078, 1095, 1101, 1105, 1137, 1143–44, 1159, 1214. FDR's suggested toast: Dallek, *Roosevelt and American Foreign Policy*, 509. "The Riviera of Hades": Montefiore, *Stalin*, 480. The best book on Yalta is S. M. Plokhy, *Yalta: The Price of Peace* (New York, Viking, 2010).

56 **Roosevelt shared Churchill's**: Dallek, *Roosevelt and American Foreign Policy*, 503–08.

58 **The Big Three convened**: Gilbert, *Road to Victory*, 1163–70; Anthony Eden, *The Memoirs of Anthony Eden, Earl of Avon: The Reckoning* (Boston: Houghton Mifflin, 1965), 511; U.S. Department of State, *Foreign Relations of the United States: The Conferences at Malta and Yalta, 1945* (Washington, D.C.: Government Printing Office, 1955), 540–46.

59 **The Yalta conference**: Dallek, *Roosevelt and American Foreign Policy*, 520. Churchill's recollection: Gilbert, *Road to Victory*, 1173–74.

60 **Yet however much**: Dallek, *Roosevelt and American Foreign Policy*, 521. The British observer: Gilbert, *Road to Victory*, 1175.

60 **For Churchill, the conference**: Gilbert, *Road to Victory*, 1172, 1182, 1195–96.

61 **Churchill was certainly**: Ibid., 1179–94, 1198, 1206–09.

61 **At the same time, however**: Ibid., 1194, 1196.

61 **For Stalin, the conference**: De Gaulle, *Complete War Memoirs*, 736–37, 751, 757.

63 **In the two months following Yalta**: Butler, *My Dear Mr. Stalin*, 310–12.

64 **At the same time, a Soviet-American clash**: Ibid., 313–15.

65 **Churchill's distress**: Kimball, *Churchill and Roosevelt*, 3:609–13, 617, 630.

65 **Stalin would not reward**: Gilbert, *Road to Victory*, 1291–92.

67 **"Stalin's fondness"**: Montefiore, *Stalin*, 466, 486.

Chapter 3: Collapse and Renewal

68 **Roosevelt's death**: Churchill, *Triumph and Tragedy*, 410–11. The Ickes quote is in Dallek, *Roosevelt and American Foreign Policy*, vii; Montefiore, *Stalin*, 498.

69 **It was easy**: David McCullough, *Truman* (New York: Simon & Schuster, 1992), 105, 281, 324–25.

70 **The trajectory**: Robert Dallek, *Harry S. Truman* (New York: Times Books, 2008), chap. 1.

71 **Truman's sudden elevation**: Gilbert, *Road to Victory*, 1294–95.

71 **Truman's assumption**: Butler, *My Dear Mr. Stalin*, 324.

72 **The only ones**: Ian Kershaw, *Hitler, 1936–1945: Nemesis* (New York: W. W. Norton, 2000), 791–92.

72 **It was a characteristic**: For a detailed reconstruction of Hitler's early life and rise to power, see Ian Kershaw, *Hitler, 1889–1936: Hubris* (New York: W. W. Norton, 2009). The Friedlander quotes are in Friedlander, *Nazi Germany and the Jews: The Years of Extermination, 1939–1945* (New York: HarperCollins, 2007), xix.

74 **His brief imprisonment**: On *Mein Kampf,* see Dawidowicz, *War against the Jews,* 18, 150–51, 156–57; Goldhagen, *Hitler's Willing Executioners,* 455–56.

75 **The onset and spread**: Kershaw, *Hubris*; Ian Kershaw, *Hitler, 1936–1945: Nemesis* (New York: W. W. Norton, 2000). See *Nemesis,* pp. 183–88, for the rise of the "Führer cult"; the young girl's quote is on p. 184.

76 **Hitler's manipulation**: See Friedlander, *Years of Extermination,* 657–58.

76 **Although blind faith**: The fighting is well recounted in Kershaw, *Nemesis,* chaps. 11–14, also pp. 687–95, "His left hand trembled" on 797, "The Führer was sent" on 685.

77 **It was not Providence**: Kershaw, *Nemesis,* 728.

77 **The last four months**: Ibid., 761–63; Gilbert, *Road to Victory,* 1219–20; Werth, *Russia at War,* 806–7.

78 **On the battlefields**: Stephen E. Ambrose, *Eisenhower: The Soldier and Candidate, 1890–1952* (New York: Simon & Schuster, 1983), 371.

78 **Eisenhower had reason**: Werth, *Russia at War,* 806–7; Deborah E. Lipstadt, *Denying the Holocaust: The Growing Assault on Truth and Memory* (London: Penguin Books, 1993); and Lipstadt, *History on Trial: My Day in Court with a Holocaust Denier* (New York: Harper Perennial, 2005).

79 **Well after it was clear**: Kershaw, *Nemesis,* 687–88, 746–47, 754–55, 779–80, 822, 829–41.

81 **In the end**: Gilbert, *Road to Victory,* 1273–76, 1278–81, 1289, 1299; Ambrose, *Soldier and Candidate,* 368–74.

82 **In the first months of 1945**: Robert Dallek, *The American Style of Foreign Policy: Cultural Politics and Foreign Affairs* (New York: Alfred A. Knopf, 1983), 138–40.

82 **But it wasn't only Americans**: Werth, *Russia at War,* 848–54.

83 **In the spring of 1945**: A. Russell Buchanan, *The United States and World War II* (New York: Harper & Row, 1964), vol. 1, chaps. 3, 4, and pp. 214–17. The Churchill quote is in Gordon Wright, *The Ordeal of Total War, 1939–1945* (New York: Harper & Row, 1968), 41.

84 **The only satisfactions**: Manchester, *American Caesar,* 3–9, 213, 248–68. Dallek, *Roosevelt and American Foreign Policy,* 36; William E. Leuchtenburg, *Franklin D. Roosevelt and the New Deal, 1932–1940* (New York: Harper & Row, 1963), 96.

85 **The following month**: Dallek, *Roosevelt and American Foreign Policy,* 334–35; Buchanan, *United States and World War II,* 1:219–20.

86 **Symbolic slaps**: The Pacific fighting is described in Buchanan, *United States and World War II,* vol. 1, chaps. 10–13, especially pp. 273–78, 280–87, and vol. 2, chaps. 24–26, especially pp. 550–57, 559–67.

87 **Japanese determination**: Dower, *War without Mercy,* 52–53, 57–60, 232–33,

300; John Dower, *Embracing Defeat: Japan in the Wake of World War II* (New York: W. W. Norton, 1999), 87, 156.

87 **To Americans, the quintessential**: Dower, *War without Mercy*, 141.

88 **It was not Tojo's**: For details on Hideki Tojo, see I. B. C. Dear, ed., *The Oxford Companion to the Second World War* (New York: Oxford University Press, 1995), 1116–18, which includes the quote. Also see John Toland, *The Rising Sun: The Decline and Fall of the Japanese Empire* (New York: Random House, 1970); and Herbert Bix, *Hirohito and the Making of Modern Japan* (New York: HarperCollins, 2000).

88 **The vicious Pacific**: Buchanan, *United States and World War II*, 2:568–80; Dower, *Embracing Defeat*, 44–46; Dower, *War without Mercy*, 40–41.

89 **Although U.S. military**: For a biographical sketch of LeMay, see Thomas M. Coffey, *Iron Eagle: The Turbulent Life of Curtis LeMay* (New York: Crown, 1986).

89 **Among the many frustrations**: Barbara W. Tuchman, *Stilwell and the American Experience in China, 1911–1945* (New York: Macmillan, 1971), 187–88; Dallek, *Roosevelt and American Foreign Policy*, 328–30, 355, 384.

91 **If Roosevelt had any doubts**: Dallek, *Roosevelt and American Foreign Policy*, 385–91.

93 **By 1944–45**: Ibid., 398, 422, 485–502, 516–19.

94 **By the time of Roosevelt's death**: See Dear, *The Oxford Companion to the Second World War*, for casualties. For the quote, see Wright, *Ordeal of Total War*, 263–64.

95 **Only the United States**: See the entries on China, Germany, Japan, United Kingdom, USA, and USSR in Dear, *The Oxford Companion to the Second World War*. The U.S. economic statistics are on pp. 1180–82.

96 **It was not just optimism**: Robert Divine, *Second Chance: The Triumph of Internationalism in America during World War II* (New York: Atheneum, 1971), 6–12, 24–25, 57, 68–70, 168–71.

97 **Ever attentive to**: Dallek, *Roosevelt and American Foreign Policy*, 342, 434–35, 466–67, 482, 508; Divine, *Second Chance*, 85–86, 114–15; Gilbert, *Road to Victory*, 471, 1198–99, 1279; William Taubman, *Stalin's American Policy: From Entente to Détente to Cold War* (New York: W. W. Norton, 1982), 88–90; Stephen C. Schlesinger, *Act of Creation: The Founding of the United Nations* (New York: Westview, 2003), 61.

98 **Roosevelt saw agreement**: Dallek, *Roosevelt and American Foreign Policy*, 510–12; Taubman, *Stalin's American Policy*, 92–93, 95–96; Butler, *My Dear Mr. Stalin*, 302–03, 305; Schlesinger, *Act of Creation*, 61–62.

100 **After Roosevelt died**: Butler, *My Dear Mr. Stalin*, 323; Taubman, *Stalin's American Policy*, 97–100; Schlesinger, *Act of Creation*, 87–91; McCullough, *Truman*, 382.

101 **Truman's tough response**: Schlesinger, *Act of Creation*, 91–92.

102 **American optimism**: On Truman's pre-presidential history, see McCullough, *Truman*, pts. 1, 2. On HST's view of Stalin, see Taubman, *Stalin's American Policy*, 100–101. On Stettinius, see Schlesinger, *Act of Creation*, 73–77.

103 **It was a daunting**: Harriman is quoted in Taubman, *Stalin's American Policy*, 106. The deliberations in San Francisco are covered in Divine, *Second Chance*,

chap. 11; and Schlesinger, *Act of Creation*, White quote on 156. Dallek, *An Unfinished Life*, 114–16.

105 **Kennedy and White**: Schlesinger, *Act of Creation*, 286–87, 294.

Chapter 4: Hope and Despair

107 **The end of the war**: Milovan Djilas, *Conversations with Stalin* (New York: Harcourt, Brace, 1962), 73–74.

108 **The establishment of**: Gilbert, *Road to Victory*, 1299, 1306, 1320, 1334–35. For the war plan against Moscow, see BBC Documentary: *World War II: Behind Closed Doors*, Episode Five.

109 **Truman saw the need**: Harry S. Truman, *Memoirs*, vol. 1, *Year of Decisions* (Garden City, N.Y.: Doubleday, 1955), 256; Ralph Keyes, ed., *The Wit and Wisdom of Harry Truman* (New York: Gramercy Books, 1995), 124; McCullough, *Truman*, 404, 409–11.

110 **To ease his fears**: Merle Miller, *Plain Speaking: An Oral Biography of Harry S. Truman* (New York: Berkeley Medallion Books, 1973), 237.

110 **Truman took some comfort**: Truman, *Memoirs*, 340; Churchill, *Triumph and Tragedy*, 538; Alonzo Hamby, *Man of the People: A Life of Harry Truman* (New York: Oxford University Press, 1995), 327–28; McCullough, *Truman*, 333, 368, 406–09, 412.

112 **Truman also found**: Miller, *Plain Speaking*, 85; Keyes, *Harry Truman*, 124.

112 **After their morning meeting**: Churchill, *Triumph and Tragedy*, 538–39; Truman, *Memoirs*, 1:341.

112 **The scenes of destruction**: "What a pity" is quoted in Alonzo Hamby, *Man of the People*, 328.

112 **As Truman and Churchill saw**: McCullough, *Truman*, 407, 416; Montefiore, *Stalin*, 496.

113 **Churchill and Truman were sympathetic**: Montefiore, *Stalin*, 498; Churchill, *Triumph and Tragedy*, 541–42.

114 **Truman also saw Stalin's**: Truman, *Memoirs*, 1:341–42; McCullough, *Truman*, 417–18, 451; Hamby, *Man of the People*, 328–29, 331.

115 **Truman's inclination**: Charles E. Bohlen, *Witness to History, 1929–1969* (New York: Norton, 1973), 340.

116 **On July 17**: McCullough, *Truman*, 425–26.

116 **It was not misperceptions**: The Potsdam conference is covered in Truman, *Memoirs*, 1:332–412; McCullough, *Truman*, 420–52. "Iron fence" and "Fairy tales": Montefiore, *Stalin*, 499. HST on Attlee and Bevin: McCullough, *Truman*, 447–48. "Pig-headed" and "police government": Truman, *Memoirs*, 402.

118 **During the conference**: Martin J. Sherwin, *A World Destroyed: Hiroshima and Its Legacies*, 3d ed. (Stanford, Calif.: Stanford University Press, 2003). The Groves and Farrell reports are on pp. 308–14.

120 **Truman was "immensely pleased"**: Ibid., 223–24.

120 **Some of the scientists**: Kai Bird and Martin Sherwin, *American Prometheus: The Triumph and Tragedy of J. Robert Oppenheimer* (New York: Alfred A. Knopf, 2005), 309, 314, 323.

120 **Truman was not unmindful**: McCullough, *Truman*, 443–44; Hamby, *Man of the People*, 332.

121 **But how?**: Churchill, *Triumph and Tragedy*, 546–47.

121 **Truman preferred**: Ibid., 572–73; McCullough, *Truman*, 442–43.

122 **Churchill and others watching**: Anthony Beevor, *The Fall of Berlin, 1945* (New York: Penguin Books, 2003), 138–39; Montefiore, *Stalin*, 499–501.

122 **The Anglo-American-Soviet**: Michael Ignatieff, "Getting the Iraq War Wrong: What the War Has Taught Me about Political Judgment," *New York Times Magazine*, August 5, 2007, 28.

125 **Stalin told the president**: Manchester, *American Caesar*, 437; McCullough, *Truman*, 425.

126 **The Japanese in fact**: Dower, *Embracing Defeat*, 27–28.

126 **In a pronouncement**: The Potsdam Declaration: Truman, *Memoirs*, 391–92. The Japanese response: Sherwin, *A World Destroyed*, 236. MacArthur's view: Manchester, *American Caesar*, 437.

126 **Unless the Japanese**: McCullough, *Truman*, 456–58; Bird and Sherwin, *American Prometheus*, 315–16, 320–21.

127 **Were the atomic bombings**: Churchill, *Triumph and Tragedy*, 546; Dower, *Embracing Defeat*, 44, 569 n. 12, 570 n. 13; Dallek, *Truman*, 25–28.

129 **On August 15**: Dower, *Embracing Defeat*, 34–36.

129 **However absurd**: Ibid., 25, 29–30.

130 **It was not as**: Bird and Sherwin, *American Prometheus*, 291–300, 302; Montefiore, *Stalin*, 502. On Stalin, also see Vladimir O. Pechatnov, "The Soviet Union and the Outside World," in *The Cambridge History of the Cold War*, ed. Melvyn Leffler (Cambridge, England: Cambridge University Press, 2010). Leffler gave me a copy of Pechatnov's manuscript.

131 **In September**: George F. Kennan, *The Nuclear Delusion: Soviet-American Relations in the Nuclear Age* (New York: Pantheon, 1983), 72, 175–79; Arnold A. Offner, *Another Such Victory: President Truman and the Cold War, 1945–1953* (Stanford, Calif.: Stanford University Press, 2002), 106–10.

133 **Because such a prospect**: Taubman, *Stalin's American Policy*, 116–20; Offner, *Another Such Victory*, 101–05; Hamby, *Man of the People*, 339.

135 **Soviet-American tensions**: Taubman, *Stalin's American Policy*, 114–15, 119–20; Manchester, *American Caesar*, 439; Dower, *Embracing Defeat*, 73.

135 **The decision to have**: Dower, *Embracing Defeat*, 69–73, also chaps. 6–7; Manchester, *American Caesar*, 441–48.

136 **MacArthur's famous**: Manchester, *American Caesar*, 466–74; Dower, *Embracing Defeat*, 223.

138 **In the summer of 1945**: *Gallup Poll, 1935–1948*, 517, 530, 535.

139 **Korea was a minor**: Melvyn P. Leffler, *A Preponderance of Power: National Se-*

curity, the Truman Administration, and the Cold War (Stanford, Calif.: Stanford University Press, 1992), 88–90.

139 **Indochina**: William Appleman Williams et al., eds., *America in Vietnam: A Documentary History* (Garden City, N.Y.: Doubleday, 1985), 30–32, 39–41, 61–62; Lloyd C. Gardner, *Approaching Vietnam: From World War II through Dienbienphu* (New York: W. W. Norton, 1988), 58–62; de Gaulle, *Complete War Memoirs*, 926–31.

141 **It was, however, a bitter**: Gardner, *Approaching Vietnam*, 62–72; Robert D. Schulzinger, *A Time for War: The United States and Vietnam, 1941–1975* (New York: Oxford University Press, 1997), 19–22.

142 **China was another matter**: See John K. Fairbank, *The United States and China* (New York: Viking Press, 1958), 308, 313; and Tuchman, *Stilwell*, 460, for the White quote. See also the fine discussion of these China dilemmas in Offner, *Another Such Victory*, 307–21.

144 **Nevertheless, by the summer**: Michael Schaller, *The United States and China in the Twentieth Century* (New York: Oxford University Press, 1979), 98–103.

145 **After Potsdam**: *Gallup Poll, 1935–1948*, 508, 525, 536, 564.

Chapter 5: Irrepressible Conflicts?

146 **In late August 1945, Charles de Gaulle**: De Gaulle, *Complete War Memoirs*, 905–08; *Gallup Poll, 1935–1948*, 550.

148 **In the fall of 1945**: *Gallup Poll, 1935–1948*, 534–35; Leffler, *Preponderance of Power*, 40–48; Offner, *Another Such Victory*, 23–24.

149 **Truman tried**: Offner, *Another Such Victory*, 107–09.

149 **Stalin was never**: George F. Kennan, *Russia and the West: Under Lenin and Stalin* (New York: New American Library, 1962), 361; Montefiore, *Stalin*, chap. 46, pp. 514 and 531 for the quotes.

150 **In October:** Montefiore, *Stalin*, 532–37; Kennan, *Russia and the West*, 235.

151 **Although his ruthless**: Kennan, *Memoirs*, 279.

151 **During the all-night**: Kennan, *Russia and the West*, 241; Montefiore, *Stalin*, 524, 526.

152 **A more important question**: For Kennan's early life, see his *Memoirs, 1925–1950* (Boston: Little, Brown, 1967). The quote is in Kennan, *Russia and the West*, 244–45. On Stalin's response to the outbreak of the war and his ultimate realism, see Montefiore, *Stalin*, 363–83, especially 374–77.

153 **My point here**: Robert L. Messer, *The End of an Alliance: James F. Byrnes, Roosevelt, Truman, and the Origins of the Cold War* (Chapel Hill, N.C.: University of North Carolina Press, 1982), 134–35.

154 **Mindful that Byrnes**: Kennan, *Memoirs*, 284.

154 **Kennan**: Ibid., 286–88.

155 **Kennan's observations**: Offner, *Another Such Victory*, 112–24; Leffler, *Prepon-*

derance of Power, 47–49; McCullough, *Truman*, 356. See also Messer, *End of an Alliance*, chaps. 8 and 9.

156 **Truman's personal antagonism**: Offner, *Another Such Victory*, 111, 117, 121.

157 **By the time Byrnes**: Ibid., 113–14, 120; Leffler, *Preponderance of Power*, 79–81.

157 **The differences over Iran**: Leffler, *Preponderance of Power*, 78–79; Offner, *Another Such Victory*, 84–85, 112–13, 120.

158 **American sleight of hand**: Messer, *End of an Alliance*, 132, 150.

158 **While the United States**: U.S. Department of State, *The China White Paper: August 1949*, 2 vols. (Stanford, Calif.: Stanford University Press, 1967), 1:64–65, 96–100, 108–10, 131–32; Kennan, *Memoirs*, 236–39; Forest C. Pogue, *George C. Marshall: Statesman, 1945–1959* (New York: Penguin Books, 1987), 56, 59–60; Offner, *Another Such Victory*, 309–21.

160 **At the end of November**: U.S. Department of State, *China White Paper*, 2:581–84.

161 **The overt sympathy**: Dallek, *Truman*, 30.

161 **Eager for both**: Pogue, *George C. Marshall*, 525, 597, 685; McCullough, *Truman*, 472, 534–35, 794, 862.

162 **Marshall's instructions**: For Marshall's mission, see Pogue, *George C. Marshall*, chap. 4. On Dies, see Richard Gid Powers, *Secrecy and Power: The Life of J. Edgar Hoover* (New York: Free Press, 1987), 231, 256, 281. On Dewey, see James MacGregor Burns, *Roosevelt: Soldier of Freedom* (New York: Harcourt Brace Jovanovich, 1970), 529.

163 **The tensions with**: Dallek, *Roosevelt and American Foreign Policy*, 502; Kennan, *Memoirs*, 373–74; Kennan, *Russia and the West*, chaps. 18 and 24; Pogue, *George C. Marshall*, 86–90. For the views of leading scholar Chen Jian, see *Mao's China and the Cold War* (Chapel Hill: University of North Carolina Press, 2001), chap. 2, especially 38.

165 **In going to China**: Pogue, *George C. Marshall*, 107.

165 **After Marshall arrived in China**: Ed Cray, *General of the Army: George C. Marshall: Soldier and Statesman* (New York: W. W. Norton, 1990), 562–63.

166 **Although Marshall**: Ibid., 570.

166 **The temporary gains**: Ibid., 566, 572–73.

167 **The forty-seven-year-old Chou**: Pogue, *George C. Marshall*, 84–85; Henry A. Kissinger, *White House Years* (Boston: Little, Brown, 1979), 743–46.

169 **As World War II ended**: See Stanley Wolpert, *Roots of Confrontation in South Asia: Afghanistan, Pakistan, India and the Superpowers* (New York: Oxford University Press, 1982), 96, 116.

169 **In the 1920s and '30s**: Ibid., chap. 7; Stanley Wolpert, *Jinnah of Pakistan* (New York: Oxford University Press, 1984), chaps. 17–21, especially pp. 258–60, 265–68, 316–18, 321, and 326.

171 **"The greatest menace"**: Herbert Butterfield, *Christianity, Diplomacy and War* (London: Epworth Press, 1953), cited in Platt, *Respectfully Quoted*, 47.

172 **After World War II, the Middle East**: Jehuda Reinharz, *Chaim Weizmann*, 2 vols. (New York: Oxford University Press, 1993). Conversation between Weizmann and Balfour cited from *Current Biography Yearbook, 1942* (New York: H. W. Wilson, 1942), 877–80.

174 **The United States**: Miller, *Plain Speaking*, 230–32; Dallek, *Truman*, 63–65.

177 **The partition and British withdrawal**: Leffler, *Preponderance of Power*, 237–46.

Chapter 6: The Triumph of Fear

179 **For a country**: Stalin quoted in Montefiore, *Stalin*, 539.

180 **Andrei Zhdanov**: Ibid., 136–39, 540–44, 547; Isaac Deutscher, *Stalin: A Political Biography* (New York: Oxford University Press, 1966), 558–64, 577–78. For the Soviet joke, see Lawrence W. Levine, *The Unpredictable Past: Explorations in American Cultural History* (New York: Oxford University Press, 1993); Kennan, *Memoirs*, 541.

182 **On February 9, 1946**: *Vital Speeches of the Day* 12 (March 1, 1946): 300–04.

183 **Stalin's principal associates**: U.S. Department of State, *Foreign Relations of the United States, 1946: Eastern Europe* (Washington, D.C., Government Printing Office, 1969), 694–96.

184 **Whether Stalin actually thought**: Walter Bedell Smith, *Moscow Mission, 1946–1949* (London: Heinemann, 1950), 51–65; Taubman, *Stalin's American Policy*, 133–34; Montefiore, *Stalin*, 556–57.

185 **The response in the United States**: Robert J. Donovan, *Conflict and Crisis: The Presidency of Harry S. Truman, 1945–1948* (New York: W. W. Norton, 1977), 187; Offner, *Another Such Victory*, 128–29; James Chace, *Acheson: The Secretary of State Who Created the American World* (New York: Simon & Schuster, 1998), 148–49; Kennan, *Memoirs*, 539.

187 **Soviet preoccupation**: *Gallup Poll, 1935–1948*, 555, 557, 564.

187 **This outlook existed**: Donovan, *Conflict and Crisis*, 170–71; Offner, *Another Such Victory*, 126.

188 **The revelations**: *Gallup Poll, 1935–1948*, 564–67.

189 **As the war ended**: Kennan, *Memoirs*, 532–46.

190 **Kennan worried**: Ibid., 292–95; 547–59.

192 **The hysterical anticommunism**: Ibid., 407–14, 462–63.

193 **Domestic dislocations**: *Gallup Poll, 1935–1948*, 557, 587; Dallek, *Truman*, 31–34.

193 **Like the president**: Paul Boyer, *By the Bomb's Early Light: American Thought and Culture at the Dawn of the Atomic Age* (New York: Pantheon Books, 1985), chaps. 1 and 4.

194 **By 1981**: Stephen E. Ambrose, *Eisenhower: The President* (New York: Simon & Schuster, 1984), 34–35, 51–52, 184, 205–06.

194 **The Cuban missile crisis**: For these crises in the 1960s and 1973, see Dallek, *An Unfinished Life*, 545–74, JFK quote on 555; Robert Dallek, *Flawed Giant: Lyndon*

Johnson and His Times, 1961–1973 (New York: Oxford University Press, 1998), 131–35, 168–76, and 444; Robert Dallek, *Nixon and Kissinger: Partners in Power* (New York: HarperCollins, 2007), 136–37, 530–31.

196 **Because the danger**: Boyer, *Bomb's Early Light*, 50; Dallek, *Roosevelt and American Foreign Policy, 1932–1945*, 470–72.

197 **The agreement signaled**: Boyer, *Bomb's Early Light*, 29–32.

197 **The novelist Norman Mailer**: *New Yorker*, October 6, 2008, 51–52.

197 **At the end of 1945, concerned scholars**: Ibid., 51–53; Offner, *Another Such Victory*, 145–46; Bird and Sherwin, *American Prometheus*, 339–40.

198 **Despite the committee's determination**: Bird and Sherwin, *American Prometheus*, 341–42; Robert L. Beisner, *Dean Acheson: A Life in the Cold War* (New York: Oxford University Press, 2006), 33–34.

200 **The report could not disarm**: On Stalin's distrust, see Nicholas Thompson, *The Hawk and the Dove: Paul Nitze, George Kennan, and the History of the Cold War* (New York: Henry Holt, 2009), 44–45; Winston S. Churchill, Iron Curtain speech, March 5, 1946, reproduced as "Sinews of Peace," Wikipedia, http://en.wikisource. org/wiki/Sinews_of_Peace; Leffler, *Preponderance of Power*, 114–16.

201 **Baruch's appointment**: Offner, *Another Such Victory*, 144–52.

202 **It is sobering**: Montefiore, *Stalin*, 536.

203 **Churchill, like Stalin**: Donovan, *Conflict and Crisis*, 190–91; McCullough, *Truman*, 486–88.

204 **It certainly commanded**: Churchill, Iron Curtain speech.

206 **The reaction in the United States**: *Gallup Poll, 1935–1948*, 562, 567; John L. Gaddis, *The United States and the Origins of the Cold War, 1941–1947* (New York: Columbia University Press, 1972), 308–09; Martin Gilbert, *Winston S. Churchill: Never Despair, 1945–1965* (Boston: Houghton Mifflin, 1988), 203–06.

207 **However eloquent**: McCullough, *Truman*, 489–90.

207 **In Moscow**: Donovan, *Conflict and Crisis*, 192; Leffler, *Preponderance of Power*, 136–37.

Chapter 7: Cold War Illusions—and Realities

211 **On his return from the United States**: The Churchill quotes are in Gilbert, *Never Despair*, 233, 238–39, 258. On Stephenson, see William Stevenson, *A Man Called Intrepid* (New York: Lyons Press, 2000). On Soviet thinking, see Adam B. Ulam, *Expansion and Coexistence: The History of Soviet Foreign Policy, 1917–1967* (New York: Frederick A. Praeger, 1968), 414–20.

214 **In Stalin's judgment**: "Moscow Hints Lag in Main Granaries," *New York Times*, November 25, 1946, p. 13. Also see David Christian, *Imperial and Soviet Russia: Power, Privilege and the Challenge of Modernity* (London: Macmillan, 1997); N. M. Dronin and E. G. Bellinger, *Climate Dependence and Food Problems in Russia, 1900–1990* (Budapest: Central European University Press, 2005). On feeding Soviet troops, see Montefiore, *Stalin*, 556.

214 **At the same time, Stalin**: Montefiore, *Stalin*, 538–49, 556–57, quotes on 543, 547, 558–59. See also Adam B. Ulam, *The Rivals: America and Russia since World War II* (New York: Viking, 1971), 112–13.

215 **In a three-thousand-word cable**: Cable of September 27, 1946, available on the Internet at the Cold War International History Project of the Woodrow Wilson International Center for Scholars.

216 **Novikov saw**: Dallek, *Truman*, 46–48.

217 **In 1946 false assumptions**: Ibid., 42.

218 **Much more, however, was at work**: *Gallup Poll, 1935–1948*, 544–46, 549, 567, 575–76, 581–82, 587, 589, 591, 601, 615.

219 **Any attempt Truman**: On HST's domestic difficulties, see Donovan, *Conflict and Crisis*, chaps. 18–19, 22–24; and McCullough, *Truman*, 520–24.

220 **Yet Fulbright reflected**: *Gallup Poll, 1935–1948*, 512, 587, 604, 613.

221 **A congressional race**: Dallek, *Nixon and Kissinger*, 12–15.

222 **It wasn't only Nixon**: Dallek, *An Unfinished Life*, 122–33.

223 **Unlike in the 1930s**: Robert Dallek, *Lone Star Rising: Lyndon Johnson and His Times, 1908–1960* (New York: Oxford University Press, 1991), 230–41.

223 **No national political figure**: William Manchester, *The Glory and the Dream: A Narrative History of America, 1932–1972* (Boston: Little, Brown, 1973), 246, 394, 512; Richard Rovere, *Senator Joe McCarthy* (New York: Meridian Books, 1960), 5–6.

224 **A dustup**: Manchester, *Glory and the Dream*, 489–90.

225 **The *Amerasia* affair**: Ibid.

225 **The myth**: Dallek, *An Unfinished Life*, 159–60.

226 **The public clamor**: Alexis de Tocqueville, *Democracy in America* (New York: Alfred A. Knopf, 1945), 1:234–35, and English ed. (London: Penguin, 2003), 267–68.

227 **Whether Roosevelt and Truman**: Dallek, *Roosevelt and American Foreign Policy*, vii; Dallek, *Truman*, 47–48.

227 **Yet on January 6, 1947**: Schlesinger and Israel, *State of the Union Messages*, 2939, 2947.

228 **Truman's hopes**: Gilbert, *Never Despair*, 290.

228 **A series of fierce**: Donovan, *Conflict and Crisis*, 272–75. "Paralyzed" is quoted in Manchester, *Glory and the Dream*, 434–36.

229 **The first order of business**: Offner, *Another Such Victory*, 193–99. Novikov's warning is in the cable of September 27, 1946.

231 **Truman knew**: Truman Doctrine address, March 12, 1947, http://avalon.law.yale.edu/20th_century/trudoc.asp.

232 **George Kennan**: Kennan, *Memoirs*, chap. 13.

233 **An unfortunate result**: McCullough, *Truman*, 550–53.

234 **Truman's speech had**: Ulam, *Rivals*, 126.

234 **Truman's speech did not surprise**: Taubman, *Stalin's American Policy*, 150–51.

235 **In March 1947**: Cray, *General of the Army*, 583–85.

236 **Yet in spite of Marshall's**: Ibid., 598–606.

238 **Marshall returned**: George C. Marshall, "The Marshall Plan," June 5, 1947, available on the History Place Web site, http://www.historyplace.com/speeches/marshall.htm. The best account of the origins and consequences of the plan is in Greg Behrman, *The Most Noble Adventure: The Marshall Plan and the Time When America Helped Save Europe* (New York: Free Press, 2007). Also see Niall Ferguson, "Dollar Diplomacy: How Much Did the Marshall Plan Really Matter?" *New Yorker*, August 27, 2007.

239 **Marshall's words**: Ulam, *Expansion and Coexistence*, 432–40; Taubman, *Stalin's American Policy*, 172–79.

Chapter 8: War by Other Means

241 **"Whereas the Truman Doctrine"**: The quotes are in Taubman, *Stalin's American Policy*, 176–77.

242 **In seeing the Truman**: Plato is quoted in Jay, *Dictionary of Political Quotations*.

243 **Countering affinity**: Leffler, *Preponderance of Power*, 148–49; J. Robert Oppenheimer, "Atomic Weapons and American Policy," *Foreign Affairs*, July 1953, 529.

243 **The danger**: Taubman, *Stalin's American Policy*, 178.

244 **The object now**: "The Sources of Soviet Conduct," *Foreign Affairs*, July 1947.

245 **When the article produced widespread**: Kennan, *Memoirs*, 354–59.

245 **Within days of the**: Walter Lippmann, *The Cold War: A Study in U.S. Foreign Policy* (New York: Harper and Brothers, 1947). Also see Ronald Steel, *Walter Lippmann and the American Century* (Boston: Little, Brown, 1980), 443–46.

246 **Kennan later described**: Kennan, *Memoirs*, 357–67.

247 **Yet Kennan did not**: Leffler, *Preponderance of Power*, 180–81.

247 **As Kennan warned**: Kennan's quote is in *Foreign Affairs*, July 1947.

248 **In the meantime**: See Steel, *Lippmann*, 487–88.

248 **The two world wars had**: "The NSC and CIA did not create Truman's feared 'Gestapo' or military dictatorship. But together they gave the military pervasive and profound influence from preparation to execution of foreign policy, for both overt and covert activities." See Offner, *Another Such Victory*, 187–93.

249 **Dean Acheson**: Dean Acheson, *Present at the Creation: My Years in the State Department* (New York: W. W. Norton, 1961), 214. Kennan is quoted in the *New York Times*, May 18, 1997. Clark Clifford, *Counsel to the President: A Memoir* (New York: Anchor Books, 1991), 170.

250 **In September 1947**: Arnold A. Rogow, *James Forrestal: Study of Personality, Politics and Policy* (New York: Macmillan, 1963), especially 55–56, 155–56, 247–49.

251 **During the summer and fall of 1947**: Taubman, *Stalin's American Policy*, 175–77; Ulam, *Expansion and Coexistence*, 436–40.

251 **At the same time, Truman**: Daniel Yergin, *Shattered Peace: The Origins of the Cold War and the National Security State* (Boston: Houghton, Mifflin, 1977), 327–29, 339–41.

252 **George Marshall**: Quoted in Cray, *General of the Army*, 591.

252 **Instead, Marshall asked**: Kennan, *Memoirs*, 378–79; Taubman, *Stalin's American Policy*, 170; Offner, *Another Such Victory*, 233.

253 **As for Germany**: Cray, *General of the Army*, 638–43; Leffler, *Preponderance of Power*, 198–99; Offner, *Another Such Victory*, 233; Ulam, *Rivals*, 122–23.

255 **The collapse of the conference**: Taubman, *Stalin's American Policy*, 179–80.

255 **In December, when Truman**: Truman is quoted in Leffler, *Preponderance of Power*, 199–200.

256 **A crisis over Czechoslovakia**: Offner, *Another Such Victory*, 236.

256 **The death of Czech**: Kennan, *Memoirs*, 399–400.

257 **Stalin's clamp-down**: Deutscher, *Stalin*, 583–88; *Gallup Poll, 1935–1948*, 721.

257 **Kennan understood the limits**: Kennan, *Memoirs*, 399.

258 **But Kennan's rational**: Quoted in Leffler, *Preponderance of Power*, 202.

258 **Despite an understanding**: Kennan, *Memoirs*, 400–01; Leffler, *Preponderance of Power*, 210–12; Offner, *Another Such Victory*, 237–40; Truman, *Memoirs*, 2:241–43.

259 **In the spring of 1948, if doubts**: See Offner's excellent discussion of the Berlin crisis in *Another Such Victory*, chap. 10. On Stalin and Dobrynin and Stalin's dealings with rivals and problems with Tito, see Montefiore, *Stalin*, 515, 575–76, 578, 628, 631, 635; and Radzinsky, *Stalin*, 517–27, "idea" quote 526–27.

263 **Kennan, who had a better**: Kennan, *Memoirs*, 403–04.

266 **The likelihood**: *Gallup Poll, 1935–1948*, 724, 727, 745, 749–51, 753, 757, 759, 761, 764–65.

266 **But Truman carried off**: Clifford, *Counsel to the President*, 189–94, 200–02, 230–32; Offner, *Another Such Victory*, 238–39, 241–42, 245–46, 264–65. On civil rights, see McCullough, *Truman*, 247, 532, 569–70, 586–90. On Clifford's appearance, see McCullough, *Truman*, 502. Clifford's technique of intimidation was related to me by Brian VanDeMark, who assisted Clifford and Richard Holbrooke in preparing Clifford's *Counsel to the President*.

269 **No foreign policy issue**: McCullough, *Truman*, 599–620, quote on 620.

Chapter 9: The Military Solution

271 **In choosing a new secretary**: George H. Gallup, *The Gallup Poll: Public Opinion, 1949–1958* (New York: Random House, 1972), 784.

272 **Dean Acheson**: Chace, *Acheson*, chaps. 1–7, especially pp. 62–67; Beisner, *Dean Acheson*, 1–12, 15.

273 **Acheson learned**: Chace, *Acheson*, 68; Acheson, *Present at the Creation*, 104, 200.

274 **In choosing Acheson**: Acheson, *Present at the Creation*, 250–53.

275 **On taking office**: Ibid., 257–58, 259, 264–66.

276 **It was the least effective way**: Ibid., 267–75; *Gallup Poll, 1949–1958*, 800 and 815.

277 **Without NATO**: Montefiore, *Stalin*, 502–04, 539, 599.

278 **Although Truman and Acheson**: Acheson, *Present at the Creation*, 307–13; Leffler, *Preponderance of Power*, 9, 116, 312–13, 325–27; David E. Lilienthal, *The Journals of David Lilienthal, 1945–1950: The Atomic Energy Years* (New York: Harper & Row, 1964), 570–71; *Gallup Poll, 1949–1958*, 867, 869.

279 **Few in either**: Taubman, *Stalin's American Policy*, 206–211, 222–26; Stalin quote in Montefiore, *Stalin*, 601.

279 **Few in the West**: For a discussion of the tensions in postwar U.S. foreign policy, see Scott Lucas and Kaeten Mitry, "Illusions of Coherence: George F. Kennan, U.S. Strategy and Political Warfare in the Early Cold War, 1946–1950," *Diplomatic History* 33, no. 1 (January 2009): 39–66.

280 **In May 1949**: Acheson, *Present at the Creation*, 291–301.

281 **No one in Washington**: Kennan, *Memoirs*, chaps. 18 and 19 on "Germany" and "The Future of Europe," but especially 426–27, 464–65.

283 **Besides, a Chinese Communist**: U.S. Department of State, *China White Paper*, vol. 1. The letter of transmittal is on iii–xvii. HST's views on the Nationalists is in Offner, *Another Such Victory*, 307.

285 **The backdrop to**: Offner, *Another Such Victory*, chap. 12, especially pp. 324–25, 330–36. The quote is from Acheson's letter, in U.S. Department of State, *China White Paper*, xvi–xvii.

286 **The depiction of**: Offner, *Another Such Victory*, 334–35.

286 **In fact, the 1949 White Paper**: Chace, *Acheson*, 218–20.

287 **American public opinion**: *Gallup Poll, 1949–1958*, 852–53, 868–69.

287 **Because Truman and Acheson**: Chace, *Acheson*, 220–22.

288 **Mesmerized by**: Ulam, *Expansion and Coexistence*, 492–95; Montefiore, *Stalin*, 603–07.

289 **Stalin, who was busy**: Kennan, *Nuclear Delusion*, 33–34.

290 **In January 1950**: The Wherry quote about Shanghai: Eric F. Goldman, *The Crucial Decade—and After: America, 1945–1960* (New York: Vintage Books, 1960), 116. The LBJ quote about McCarthy: Dallek, *Lone Star Rising*, 452–53. For the rest, see Chace, *Acheson*, 225–40; Robert J. Donovan, *Tumultuous Years: The Presidency of Harry S. Truman, 1949–1953* (New York: W. W. Norton, 1982), 162–70.

293 **The decision to build**: Kennan, *Nuclear Delusion*, xvi; McCullough, *Truman*, 756–58; Bird and Sherwin, *American Prometheus*, 416–30.

296 **Was there an alternative**: Kennan, *Nuclear Delusion*, 32–33. Also see "Interview with Herbert York," November 15, 1998, National Security Archive, George Washington University; and Thompson, *The Hawk and the Dove*, 105–09.

298 **The argument for all-out**: Fred Kaplan, "Paul Nitze: The Man Who Brought Us the Cold War," *Slate*, October 21, 2004, http://slate.msn.com/id/2108510/; Leffler, *Preponderance of Power*, 355–60.

300 **The military buildup**: For Acheson's speeches, see Beisner, *Dean Acheson*, 248–51.

Chapter 10: Limited War

302 **In South Korea**: For the Council on Foreign Relations discussion, see chap. 7 of this book.

302 **To be sure, some American**: Leffler, *Preponderance of Power*, 167–68, 251–53.

303 **Despite the decision**: Chace, *Acheson*, 222–23; Beisner, *Dean Acheson*, 326–29.

304 **Perceptions in North Korea**: See Don Oberdorfer, *The Two Koreas: A Contemporary History* (Reading, Mass.: Addison-Wesley, 1997), 16–23; Suh Dae-Sook, *Kim Il Sung: The North Korean Leader* (New York: Columbia University Press, 1998); and Andrei Lankov, *From Stalin to Kim Il Sung: The Formation of North Korea, 1945–1960* (New Brunswick, N.J.: Rutgers University Press, 2002).

305 **Like other authoritarian**: W. Averell Harriman and Elie Abel, *Special Envoy to Churchill and Stalin, 1941–1946* (New York: Random House, 1975), 535–36. My thanks to Professor Melvyn Leffler for calling Harriman's quote to my attention. On Kim's behavior, see Don Oberdorfer, *Two Koreas*, 21. Discussion with retired Congressman Stephen Solarz, March 11, 2009.

306 **From the moment**: On Rhee, see "Syngman Rhee (Yu Sungman, 1875–1965)," *The Encyclopedia of Asian History* (New York: Charles Scribner's Sons for the Asia Society, 1988); Oberdorfer, *Two Koreas*, 8; William Stueck, *The Korean War: An International History* (Princeton, N.J.: Princeton University Press, 1995), 14–15, 20–21, 24, 27–28, 30, 32, 36–37. The quote about the two Koreans sitting down to eat is on 21.

307 **The clash of wills**: On Kissinger and the Vietnamese, see Dallek, *Nixon and Kissinger*, 444.

308 **The outbreak of the Korean conflict**: On the run-up to the war, see Bruce Cumings, *The Origins of the Korean War*, vol. 1, *Liberation and the Emergence of Separate Regimes, 1945–1947*, and vol. 2, *The Roaring of the Cataract, 1947–1950* (Princeton, N.J.: Princeton University Press, 1981 and 1990); Bruce Cumings and Kathryn Weathersby, "An Exchange on Korean War Origins," in *The Cold War in Asia: New Evidence on the Korean War*, Cold War International History Project Bulletin no. 6–7 (Winter 1995/1996): 120–22; Kennan, *Memoirs*, 395–96; Stueck, *Korean War*, 31–41; Chen, *Mao's China*, 54–55; Vladislav M. Zubok, *A Failed Empire: The Soviet Union from Stalin to Gorbachev* (Chapel Hill: University of North Carolina Press, 2007), 78–81; Pechatnov, "Soviet Union and the Outside World." The Stalin quote is in Vladislav M. Zubok and Constantine Pleshakov, *Inside the Kremlin's Cold War: From Stalin to Khrushchev* (Cambridge, Mass.: Harvard University Press, 1996), 71, 299.

311 **The news of Kim's invasion**: For the U.S. decision to enter the fighting, see Glenn D. Paige, *The Korean Decision, June 24–June 30, 1950* (New York: Free Press, 1968), Webb-Truman exchange on 141 and 304. Also see Kennan, *Nuclear Delusion*, xiii–xiv, 34, 36; Stueck, *Korean War*, 41–44.

313 **In the spring of 1950**: *Gallup Poll, 1949–1958*, 903, 905, 933, 941–42.

313 **In refusing to acknowledge**: Offner, *Another Such Victory*, 372–74.

314 **The Soviet absence**: Zubok, *Failed Empire*, 80–81. On the H-bomb, see Jeremy Bernstein, "He Changed History," *New York Review of Books*, April 9, 2009, 33.

315 **Stalin neglected to say**: Montefiore, *Stalin*, 607–11. Madison is quoted in Arthur M. Schlesinger Jr., *War and the American Presidency* (New York: W. W. Norton, 2004), 47.

315 **The Korean conflict**: Arthur M. Schlesinger Jr., *The Imperial Presidency* (Boston: Houghton Mifflin, 1973), 132–35. See also Schlesinger, *War and the American Presidency*, 53–54.

316 **U.S. involvement**: *Gallup Poll, 1949–1958*, 929–35, 943.

317 **With the onset of the Korean War**: Acheson, *Present at the Creation*, 73–81, quote on 374; Offner, *Another Such Victory*, 365–67.

318 **MacArthur**: Michael Schaller, *Douglas MacArthur: The Far Eastern General* (New York: Oxford University Press, 1989), 184–98. See also Manchester, *American Caesar*, 561–71.

319 **In September**: Manchester, *American Caesar*, 571–81.

319 **Suddenly an invasion of North Korea**: Ibid., 583–87; Acheson, *Present at the Creation*, 453; Stueck, *Korean War*, 88–96; Chen, *Mao's China*, 55–59.

322 **By sending U.S. troops**: Manchester, *American Caesar*, 588–96; McCullough, *Truman*, 800–08.

325 **Despite MacArthur's assurances**: Kennan, *Memoirs*, 487.

325 **The Korean War now**: Stueck, *Korean War*, 111–30. On U.S. consideration of using A-bombs, see Marilyn Young, "Bombing Civilians: An American Tradition," History News Network, April 13, 2009, http://hnn.us/articles/67717.html, which is drawn from Yuki Tanaka and Marilyn Young, eds., *Bombing Civilians: A Twentieth-Century History* (New York: New Press, 2009). On casualties, see Stueck, *Korean War*, 361; Oberdorfer, *Two Koreas*, 9–10. For Mao's comment, see Roderick MacFarquhar and Michael Schoenhals, *Mao's Last Revolution* (Cambridge, Mass.: Harvard University Press, 2006), 102.

328 **China's entrance into the fighting**: Ibid., 167–68; McCullough, *Truman*, 831–35.

328 **Yet even with**: On Truman's press conference, see Stueck, *Korean War*, 131; *Gallup Poll, 1949–1958*, 929–30, 933, 939, 942, 949–51, 958, 960–61, 963–65, 968, 970. On the change in national mood about nuclear weapons, see Boyer, *Bomb's Early Light*, chap. 9.

330 **A bitter divide**: Stueck, *Korean War*, 135, 142.

330 **By March 24**: John W. Spanier, *The Truman-MacArthur Controversy and the Korean War* (New York: W. W. Norton, 1965), 197–202; Stueck, *Korean War*, 174–75.

330 **MacArthur's statement provoked**: Spanier, *Truman-MacArthur Controversy*, 202–07 and chap. 8, especially 247; Truman, *Memoirs*, 2:436–50; Miller, *Plain Speaking*, 308, 312–13.

332 **As MacArthur himself**: MacArthur's speech before a joint session of the Philippines Congress is quoted in Platt, *Respectfully Quoted*, 239.

Chapter 11: Elusive Peace

333 **Harry Truman paid a heavy political price**: Manchester, *American Caesar*, 647–72, provides a detailed account of the response to MacArthur's firing. Also see Hamby, *Man of the People*, 557–58; and Schaller, 242–44; *Gallup Poll, 1949–1958*, 981–82, 988–89, 993–95, 998–99, 1007, 1019–20, 1029, 1032.

337 **While the White House**: On the negotiations, see Stueck, *Korean War*, chap. 6, especially pp. 222–24 and 227; Chen, *Mao's China*, 97–107; *Gallup Poll, 1949–1958*, 1017, 1027.

339 **During the two months**: Stueck, *Korean War*, 230–35.

339 **Because a complete breakdown**: Ibid., 236–38, 247.

339 **In the course of a month**: Chen, *Mao's China*, 106–07.

340 **During the second week in December**: Stueck, *Korean War*, 244–45, 247–48; Chen, *Mao's China*, 107–09.

341 **But when Washington**: Stueck, *Korean War*, 250–52.

341 **Nevertheless, Truman was painfully**: Ibid., 258–59; Hamby, *Man of the People*, 574.

343 **The tensions at the negotiating**: Stueck, *Korean War*, 271–72; Chen, *Mao's China*, 109–10; Hamby, *Man of the People*, 574.

344 **Nevertheless, he was determined**: Stueck, *Korean War*, 287–89, 305–06; Chen, *Mao's China*, 110–12; and Young, "Bombing Civilians."

345 **By the fall of 1952**: On the air war, see Young, "Bombing Civilians." For the Chou-Stalin conversation, see Cold War International History Project, *Cold War in Asia*, 10–14.

346 **The Republican presidential campaign**: For the Eisenhower-Nixon campaign, see Ambrose, *Soldier and Candidate*, chap. 27, from which are taken the quotes from Nixon and Eisenhower.

348 **Truman, who saw Eisenhower's pledge**: McCullough, *Truman*, 912.

349 **Because Truman understood**: Ambrose, *President*, 30–32, 34–35, 51–52; Stueck, *Korean War*, 305–07; Chen, *Mao's China*, 111–12.

351 **At the end of March**: Stueck, *Korean War*, 308–11; Chen, *Mao's China*, 112.

352 **His speech was**: *Gallup Poll, 1949–1958*, 1140.

352 **At times, however, it seemed**: Ambrose, *President*, 99–107; Stueck, *Korean War*, 313–47, is a detailed account of the end-of-war negotiations.

353 **Were it not for Eisenhower's**: On China's receptivity to a truce, see Chen, *Mao's China*, 112–16. The general is quoted in Stueck, *Korean War*, 362.

353 **The war was a demonstration**: Ibid., 308–09; Alan Bullock, *Hitler and Stalin: Parallel Lives* (New York: Vintage Books, 1993), 941; Zubok, *Failed Empire*, 86.

355 **The world was fortunate**: Nikita Khrushchev, *Khrushchev Remembers: The Last Testament*, trans. and ed. Strobe Talbot (Boston: Little, Brown, 1971), 100–01, 272–73; Bullock, 357, 951–53, 955–65; Joshua Rubinstein and Vladimir P. Naumov, eds., *Stalin's Secret Pogrom: The Postwar Inquisition of the Jewish Anti-*

Fascist Committee (New Haven, Conn.: Yale University Press, 2001), 1–64, especially 2.

357 **The alleged doctors'**: Montefiore, *Stalin*, 962; Jonathan Brent and Vladimir P. Naumov, *Stalin's Last Crime: The Plot Against the Jewish Doctors, 1948–1953* (New York: HarperCollins, 2004), 1–10, 330–36.

357 **Stalin's last hours**: Montefiore, *Stalin*, 638–50.

358 **De Gaulle's decision**: George McTurnan Kahin and John W. Lewis, *The United States in Vietnam* (New York: Dell, 1969), 23–40; George C. Herring, *America's Longest War: The United States and Vietnam, 1950–1975* (New York: Alfred A. Knopf, 1986), 3–42; Chen, *Mao's China*, 118–38.

Epilogue

366 **John F. Kennedy's successful**: Dallek, *An Unfinished Life*, 554–55, 572.

367 **Richard Nixon and Henry Kissinger**: Dallek, *Nixon and Kissinger*, especially chaps. 10–12.

369 **The model of rational behavior**: See Schlesinger, *War and the American Presidency*, 31–33.

BIBLIOGRAPHY

Acheson, Dean. *Present at the Creation: My Years in the State Department*. New York: W. W. Norton, 1961.

Ambrose, Stephen E. *Eisenhower: The President*. New York: Simon & Schuster, 1984.

———. *Eisenhower: The Soldier and Candidate, 1890–1952*. New York: Simon & Schuster, 1983.

Beisner, Robert L. *Dean Acheson: A Life in the Cold War*. New York: Oxford University Press, 2006.

Beevor, Anthony. *The Fall of Berlin, 1945*. New York: Penguin Books, 2003.

Bird, Kai, and Martin J. Sherwin. *American Prometheus: The Triumph and Tragedy of J. Robert Oppenheimer*. New York: Alfred A. Knopf, 2005.

Bix, Herbert. *Hirohito and the Making of Modern Japan*. New York: HarperCollins, 2000.

Bohlen, Charles E. *Witness to History, 1929–1969*. New York: W. W. Norton, 1973.

Boyer, Paul. *By the Bomb's Early Light: American Thought and Culture at the Dawn of the Atomic Age*. New York: Pantheon Books, 1985.

Brent, Jonathan, and Vladimir P. Naumov. *Stalin's Last Crime: The Plot Against the Jewish Doctors, 1948–1953*. New York: HarperCollins, 2004.

Buchanan, A. Russell. *The United States and World War II*. 2 vols. New York: Harper & Row, 1964.

Bullock, Alan. *Hitler and Stalin: Parallel Lives*. New York: Vintage Books, 1993.

Burns, James MacGregor. *Roosevelt: Soldier of Freedom*. New York: Harcourt Brace Jovanovich, 1970.

Butler, Susan. *My Dear Mr. Stalin*. New Haven, Conn.: Yale University Press, 2005.

Chace, James. *Acheson: The Secretary of State Who Created the American World*. New York: Simon & Schuster, 1998.

Chen, Jian. *Mao's China and the Cold War*. Chapel Hill: University of North Carolina Press, 2001.

Christian, David. *Imperial and Soviet Russia: Power, Privilege and the Challenge of Modernity*. London: Macmillan, 1997.

Churchill, Winston S. *The Second World War: The Gathering Storm*. New York: Bantam Books, 1961.

———. *The Second World War: The Grand Alliance*. New York: Bantam Books, 1962.

———. *The Second World War: Their Finest Hour*. New York: Bantam Books, 1962.

————. *The Second World War: Triumph and Tragedy*. New York: Bantam Books, 1953.

Clifford, Clark. *Counsel to the President: A Memoir*. New York: Anchor Books, 1991.

Coffey, Thomas M. *Iron Eagle: The Turbulent Life of Curtis LeMay*. New York: Crown, 1986.

Cray, Ed. *General of the Army: George C. Marshall, Soldier and Statesman*. New York: W. W. Norton, 1990.

Cumings, Bruce. *The Origins of the Korean War*. Vol. 1, *Liberation and the Emergence of Separate Regimes, 1945–1947*. Princeton, N.J.: Princeton University Press, 1981.

————. *The Origins of the Korean War*. Vol. 2, *The Roaring of the Cataract, 1947–1950*. Princeton, N.J.: Princeton University Press, 1990.

Dallek, Robert. *The American Style of Foreign Policy: Cultural Politics and Foreign Affairs*. New York: Alfred A. Knopf, 1983.

————. *Flawed Giant: Lyndon Johnson and His Times, 1961–1973*. New York: Oxford University Press, 1998.

————. *Franklin D. Roosevelt and American Foreign Policy, 1932–1945*. New York: Oxford University Press, 1995.

————. *Harry S. Truman*. New York: Times Books, 2008.

————. *Lone Star Rising: Lyndon Johnson and His Times, 1908–1960*. New York: Oxford University Press, 1991.

————. *Nixon and Kissinger: Partners in Power*. New York: HarperCollins, 2007.

————. *An Unfinished Life: John F. Kennedy, 1917–1963*. New York: Little, Brown, 2003.

Dawidowicz, Lucy S. *The War against the Jews, 1933–1945*. New York: Holt, Rinehart and Winston, 1975.

Dear, I. C. B. *The Oxford Companion to the Second World War*. New York: Oxford University Press, 1995.

de Gaulle, Charles. *The Complete War Memoirs of Charles de Gaulle*. New York: Simon & Schuster, 1972.

Deutscher, Isaac. *Stalin: A Political Biography*. New York: Oxford University Press, 1966.

Divine, Robert. *Second Chance: The Triumph of Internationalism in America during World War II*. New York: Atheneum, 1971.

Djilas, Milovan. *Conversations with Stalin*. New York: Harcourt, Brace, 1962.

Donovan, Robert J. *Conflict and Crisis: The Presidency of Harry S. Truman, 1945–1948*. New York: W. W. Norton, 1977.

————. *Tumultuous Years: The Presidency of Harry S. Truman, 1949–1953*. New York: W. W. Norton, 1982.

Dower, John W. *Embracing Defeat: Japan in the Wake of World War II*. New York: W. W. Norton, 1999.

————. *War without Mercy: Race and Power in the Pacific War*. New York: Pantheon Books, 1986.

Dronin, N. M., and E. G. Bellinger. *Climate Dependence and Food Problems in Russia, 1900–1990*. Budapest: Central European University Press, 2005.

Eden, Anthony. *The Memoirs of Anthony Eden, Earl of Avon: The Reckoning*. Boston: Houghton Mifflin, 1965.

Fairbank, John K. *The United States and China.* New York: Viking Press, 1958.

Freidel, Frank. *Franklin D. Roosevelt: A Rendezvous with Destiny.* Boston: Little, Brown, 1990.

Friedlander, Saul. *Nazi Germany and the Jews: The Years of Persecution, 1933–1939.* New York: HarperCollins, 1997.

———. *Nazi Germany and the Jews: The Years of Extermination, 1939–1945.* New York: HarperCollins, 2007.

Gaddis, John L. *The United States and the Origins of the Cold War, 1941–1947.* New York: Columbia University Press, 1972.

Gallup, George H. *The Gallup Poll: Public Opinion, 1935–1948.* New York: Random House, 1972.

———. *The Gallup Poll: Public Opinion, 1949–1958.* New York: Random House, 1972.

Gardner, Lloyd C. *Approaching Vietnam: From World War II through Dienbienphu.* New York: W. W. Norton, 1988.

Gilbert, Martin. *Winston S. Churchill: Never Despair, 1945–1965.* Boston: Houghton Mifflin, 1988.

———. *Winston S. Churchill: The Road to Victory, 1941–1945.* Boston: Houghton Mifflin, 1986.

Goldhagen, Daniel Jonah. *Hitler's Willing Executioners.* New York: Vintage Books, 1997.

Goldman, Eric F. *The Crucial Decade—and After: America, 1945–1960.* New York: Vintage Books, 1960.

Goldstein, Gordon M. *Lessons in Disaster: McGeorge Bundy and the Path to War in Vietnam.* New York: Times Books, 2008.

Hamby, Alonzo. *Man of the People: A Life of Harry Truman.* New York: Oxford University Press, 1995.

Harriman, W. Averell, and Elie Abel. *Special Envoy to Churchill and Stalin, 1941–1946.* New York: Random House, 1975.

Herring, George C. *America's Longest War: The United States and Vietnam, 1950–1975.* New York: Alfred A. Knopf, 1986.

Jay, Anthony, ed. *The Oxford Dictionary of Political Quotations.* New York: Oxford University Press, 1996.

Jenkins, Roy. *Churchill: A Biography.* New York: Farrar, Straus and Giroux, 2001.

Kahin, George McTurnan, and John W. Lewis. *The United States in Vietnam.* New York: Dell, 1969.

Kennan, George F. *Memoirs, 1925–1950.* Boston: Little, Brown, 1967.

———. *The Nuclear Delusion: Soviet-American Relations in the Nuclear Age.* New York: Pantheon, 1983.

———. *Russia and the West: Under Lenin and Stalin.* New York: New American Library, 1962.

Kennedy, David M. *Freedom from Fear: The American People in Depression and War, 1929–1945.* New York: Oxford University Press, 1999.

Kershaw, Ian. *Hitler, 1889–1936: Hubris.* New York: W. W. Norton, 2000.

———. *Hitler, 1936–1945: Nemesis.* New York: W. W. Norton, 2000.

Keyes, Ralph, ed. *The Wit and Wisdom of Harry Truman.* New York: Gramercy Books, 1995.

Khrushchev, Nikita. *Khrushchev Remembers: The Last Testament.* Translated and edited by Strobe Talbot. Boston: Little, Brown, 1971.

Kimball, Warren F. *Churchill and Roosevelt: Their Complete Correspondence.* 3 vols. Princeton, N.J.: Princeton University Press, 1984.

Kissinger, Henry A. *White House Years.* Boston: Little, Brown, 1979.

Knight, Amy. *Beria: Stalin's First Lieutenant.* Princeton, N.J.: Princeton University Press, 1993.

Lankov, Andrei. *From Stalin to Kim Il Sung: The Formation of North Korea, 1945–1960.* New Brunswick, N.J.: Rutgers University Press, 2002.

Leffler, Melvyn P. *A Preponderance of Power: National Security, the Truman Administration, and the Cold War.* Stanford, Calif.: Stanford University Press, 1992.

Leuchtenburg, William E. *Franklin D. Roosevelt and the New Deal, 1932–1940.* New York: Harper & Row, 1963.

Levine, Lawrence W. *The Unpredictable Past: Explorations in American Cultural History.* New York: Oxford University Press, 1993.

Lilienthal, David E. *The Journals of David Lilienthal, 1945–1950: The Atomic Energy Years.* New York: Harper & Row, 1964.

Lippmann, Walter. *The Cold War: A Study in U.S. Foreign Policy.* New York: Harper and Brothers, 1947.

Lipstadt, Deborah E. *Denying the Holocaust: The Growing Assault on Truth and Memory.* London: Penguin Books, 1993.

———. *History on Trial: My Day in Court with a Holocaust Denier.* New York: Harper Perennial, 2005.

MacFarquhar, Roderick, and Michael Schoenhals. *Mao's Last Revolution.* Cambridge, Mass.: Harvard University Press, 2006.

Manchester, William. *American Caesar: Douglas MacArthur, 1880–1964.* Boston: Little, Brown, 1978.

———. *The Glory and the Dream: A Narrative History of America, 1932–1972.* Boston: Little, Brown, 1973.

McCullough, David. *Truman.* New York: Simon & Schuster, 1992.

Messer, Robert L. *The End of an Alliance: James F. Byrnes, Roosevelt, Truman, and the Origins of the Cold War.* Chapel Hill: University of North Carolina Press, 1982.

Miller, Merle. *Plain Speaking: An Oral Biography of Harry S. Truman.* New York: Berkeley Medallion Books, 1973.

Montefiore, Simon S. *Stalin: The Court of the Red Tsar.* New York: Vintage Books, 2005.

Mosse, George. *Fallen Soldiers: Reshaping the Memory of the World Wars.* New York: Oxford University Press, 1990.

Oberdorfer, Don. *The Two Koreas: A Contemporary History.* Reading, Mass.: Addison-Wesley, 1997.

Offner, Arnold A. *Another Such Victory: President Truman and the Cold War, 1945–1953.* Stanford, Calif.: Stanford University Press, 2002.

Paige, Glenn D. *The Korean Decision, June 24–June 30, 1950*. New York: Free Press, 1968.

Platt, Suzy, ed. *Respectfully Quoted: A Dictionary of Quotations from the Library of Congress*. Washington, D.C.: Congressional Quarterly, 1992.

Plokhy, S. M. *Yalta: The Price of Peace*. New York: Viking, 2010.

Pogue, Forest C. *George C. Marshall: Statesman, 1945–1959*. New York: Penguin Books, 1987.

Powers, Richard Gid. *Secrecy and Power: The Life of J. Edgar Hoover*. New York: Free Press, 1987.

Radzinsky, Edward. *Stalin*. New York: Anchor Books, 1997.

Reinharz, Jehuda. *Chaim Weizmann*. 2 vols. New York: Oxford University Press, 1985, 1993.

Rogow, Arnold A. *James Forrestal: Study of Personality, Politics and Policy*. New York: Macmillan, 1963.

Rovere, Richard. *Senator Joe McCarthy*. New York: Meridian Books, 1960.

Rubinstein, Joshua, and Vladimir P. Naumov, eds. *Stalin's Secret Pogrom: The Postwar Inquisition of the Jewish Anti-Fascist Committee*. New Haven, Conn.: Yale University Press, 2001.

Schaller, Michael. *Douglas MacArthur: The Far Eastern General*. New York: Oxford University Press, 1989.

———. *The United States and China in the Twentieth Century*. New York: Oxford University Press, 1979.

Schlesinger, Arthur M. Jr. *The Age of Roosevelt: The Coming of the New Deal*. Boston: Houghton Mifflin, 1959.

———. *The Imperial Presidency*. Boston: Houghton Mifflin, 1973.

———. *War and the American Presidency*. New York: W. W. Norton, 2004.

Schlesinger, Arthur M. Jr., and Fred L. Israel. *The State of the Union Messages of the Presidents, 1905–1966*. New York: Chelsea House, 1966.

Schlesinger, Stephen C. *Act of Creation: The Founding of the United Nations*. New York: Westview, 2003.

Schulzinger, Robert D. *A Time for War: The United States and Vietnam, 1941–1975*. New York: Oxford University Press, 1997.

Sheehan, James J. *Where Have All the Soldiers Gone? The Transformation of Modern Europe*. Boston: Houghton Mifflin, 2008.

Sherwin, Martin J. *A World Destroyed: Hiroshima and Its Legacies*. 3d ed. New York: Stanford, Calif.: Stanford University Press, 2003.

Smith, Jean Edward. *FDR*. New York: Random House, 2007.

Smith, Walter Bedell. *Moscow Mission, 1946–1949*. London: Heinemann, 1950.

Spanier, John W. *The Truman-MacArthur Controversy and the Korean War*. New York: W. W. Norton, 1965.

Steel, Ronald. *Walter Lippmann and the American Century*. Boston: Little, Brown, 1980.

Stevenson, William. *A Man Called Intrepid*. New York: Lyons Press, 2000.

Stueck, William. *The Korean War: An International History*. Princeton, N.J.: Princeton University Press, 1995.

Suh, Dae-Sook. *Kim Il Sung: The North Korean Leader.* New York: Columbia University Press, 1998.

Tanaka, Yuki, and Marilyn Young, eds. *Bombing Civilians: A Twentieth-Century History.* New York: New Press, 2009.

Taylor, A. J. P., Robert Rhodes James, and J. H. Plumb. *Churchill: Four Faces and the Man.* Middlesex, England: Penguin Books, 1968.

Taubman, William. *Stalin's American Policy: From Entente to Détente to Cold War.* New York: W. W. Norton, 1982.

Thompson, Nicholas. *The Hawk and the Dove: Paul Nitze, George Kennan, and the History of the Cold War.* New York: Henry Holt, 2009.

Tocqueville, Alexis de. *Democracy in America.* 2 vols. New York: Alfred A. Knopf, 1945.

Toland, John. *The Rising Sun: The Decline and Fall of the Japanese Empire.* New York: Random House, 1970.

Truman, Harry S. *Memoirs.* Vol. 1, *Year of Decisions.* Garden City, N.Y.: Doubleday, 1955.

———. *Memoirs.* Vol. 2, *Years of Trial and Hope.* Garden City, N.Y.: Doubleday, 1956.

Tuchman, Barbara W. *Stilwell and the American Experience in China, 1911–1945.* New York: Macmillan, 1971.

Ulam, Adam B. *Expansion and Coexistence: The History of Soviet Foreign Policy, 1917–1967.* New York: Frederick A. Praeger, 1968.

———. *The Rivals: America and Russia since World War II.* New York: Viking, 1971.

U.S. Department of State. *The China White Paper: August 1949.* 2 vols. Stanford, Calif.: Stanford University Press, 1967.

———. *Foreign Relations of the United States: The Conferences at Malta and Yalta, 1945.* Washington, D.C.: Government Printing Office, 1955.

———. *Foreign Relations of the United States, 1946: Eastern Europe.* Washington, D.C.: Government Printing Office, 1969.

Werth, Alexander. *Russia at War, 1941–1945.* New York: Avon Books, 1964.

Williams, William Appleman, Thomas McCormick, Lloyd Gardner, and Walter LaFeber, eds. *America in Vietnam: A Documentary History.* Garden City, N.Y.: Doubleday, 1985.

Wolpert, Stanley. *Jinnah of Pakistan.* New York: Oxford University Press, 1984.

———. *Roots of Confrontation in South Asia: Afghanistan, Pakistan, India & the Superpowers.* New York: Oxford University Press, 1982.

Wright, Gordon. *The Ordeal of Total War, 1939–1945.* New York: Harper & Row, 1968.

Yergin, Daniel. *Shattered Peace: The Origins of the Cold War and the National Security State.* Boston: Houghton, Mifflin, 1977.

Zubok, Vladislav M. *A Failed Empire: The Soviet Union from Stalin to Gorbachev.* Chapel Hill: University of North Carolina Press, 2007.

Zubok, Vladislav M., and Constantine Pleshakov. *Inside the Kremlin's Cold War: From Stalin to Khrushchev.* Cambridge, Mass.: Harvard University Press, 1996.

INDEX

Acheson, Dean, 185, 231, 249, 272–75, 281, 299, 346; appointed secretary of state, 272, 274–75; background of, 272; China and, 163, 284–88; Greek Communist uprising and, 231; H-bomb development and, 294–95, 296; Hiss affair and, 274, 290, 292; international control of atomic weapons and, 198–200, 201; Korean War and, 310, 312, 313–14, 317, 322, 330, 332, 354; McCarthyism and, 290–92; on national security concerns in Asia, 303–4, 309, 310; Roosevelt's conflict with, 272–73; Truman's relationship with, 273–74

Afghanistan, 365

African Americans, 219, 266–67

Air Force, U.S., 176, 252, 257, 344–45

Air Force Department, U.S., 248

Albania, 232

Algeria, 275, 365

Allende, Salvador, 365

Allied Control Council for Japan, 135, 158

Amerasia investigation, 224–25

American Society of Newspaper Editors, 42, 292, 351

anticommunism, 106, 163, 221–27, 236–37, 282–83; Acheson's confirmation hearings and, 274–75; of Churchill, 16, 18–19, 21, 26; Churchill's 1946 speeches on Soviet threat and, 203–8, 211–13, 218; congressional elections of 1946 and, 221–23, 224, 226; European defensive alliances and, 192–93, 255, 258, 259, 260, 275–77 (*see also* North Atlantic Treaty Organization); fear of Communist penetration of government and, 163, 233–34, 290–93, 348; of Hitler, 66, 74, 76,

79, 80; McCarthy and, 290–93, 300, 347–48; of Nixon, 221–22, 346, 368; Red scare of 1919–20 and, 26; Stalin's concern about postwar resurgence of, 66; Truman's apocalyptic rhetoric and, 231–35, 251–52, 255–56; Truman's standing as president and, 219–20, 224, 225–26; U.S. opinion surveys and, 218, 316–17

anti-Semitism: of Hitler, 5, 72–73, 74, 80; of Stalin, 215, 356–57. *See also* Holocaust

appeasement: Byrnes accused of, 134, 155–57; "lessons" of, applied to postwar circumstances, 125, 131, 258–59, 299–300, 312; Munich Pact and, 19, 75, 297, 312

Arab League, 270

Arabs, 233; Palestine issue and, 172–78, 270. *See also* Palestine

Ardennes offensive (1944), 79

Argentina, 103

Armenia, 158

Army Department, U.S., 148, 248

Arnold, Matthew, 179

Atomic Energy Commission (AEC), 198–202, 294; Acheson-Lilienthal committee and, 198–200; Baruch's plan for, 201–2

atomic weapons, 62, 101, 119–33, 134, 149, 184, 193–202, 216, 226, 241, 258, 259–60, 267, 283, 293–98, 336, 345, 354, 365, 368–69; alert of 1973 and, 196; atomic scientists' concerns about, 130, 194, 197–98; beginning of Cold War and, 122–24; Byrnes's information-sharing proposal and, 155–57; Churchill's readiness to fight Soviet Union with, 212; Cuban